# SALMOND
## Against The Odds

## David Torrance

BIRLINN

This edition first published in 2015 by
Birlinn Limited
West Newington House
10 Newington Road
Edinburgh
EH9 1QS

www.birlinn.co.uk

First published in hardback in 2010
First paperback edition published in 2011

ISBN: 978 1 78027 297 9

British Library Cataloguing-in-Publication Data
A catalogue record for this book is available from the British Library

Typeset by Iolaire Typesetting, Newtonmore
Printed and bound by Bell & Bain Ltd, Glasgow

# CONTENTS

# LIST OF ILLUSTRATIONS

# PREFACE TO THE THIRD EDITION

This biography was first published in the autumn of 2010, when Alex Salmond looked as if he might lose the 2011 Holyrood election, and last updated a year later, when a referendum on independence had yet to be agreed. Obviously a lot has happened in the almost four years since, indeed the first two editions neatly illustrated the difficulties of writing a biography of a serving politician, for by the time the author's observations are published, their career (and a reader's perspective) will inevitably have moved on.

Initially, I believed Salmond's resignation as SNP leader and First Minister in the wake of the independence referendum would finally give this biography a definitive ending, a chance to stand back and assess his eventful political career. Then came the SNP 'surge', a remarkable upswing in the party's Westminster support that carried Salmond and 55 other MPs into the House of Commons at the general election on 7 May, 2015. It was, as a former adviser put it to me, 'the fastest comeback in Scottish political history', and thus a good reason for retaining this book's original title: *Salmond – Against the Odds*.

The second edition ended up being overlong – more than 200,000 words – so this edition has not only been heavily edited but also extended to cover Salmond's second term as First Minister and, obviously, the referendum. Chapters 13-15 comprise almost completely fresh material; while a new conclusion – an attempt to assess his 'legacy' – replaces the previous chapter entitled 'Will the real Alex Salmond please stand up?' It should also be said that the remaining chapters contain some new material, mainly gleaned from interviews, profiles and books published since 2011. Some of the material has already appeared in my 2013 book, *The Battle for Britain: Scotland and the Independence Referendum* (Biteback), and in a series of biographical essays for the *Scottish Daily Mail* in the autumn of 2014. I have also corrected several errors – major and minor – present in the last two editions.

It would be remiss, meanwhile, not to mention a widely circulated letter penned by my subject a few days after his resignation as First Minister. In this (published in the *Herald* on 23 September 2014) Alex Salmond referred to me as his 'self-appointed biographer' (which was true enough), followed this up with a cheap jibe about having deprived me of 'a lucrative income stream' (he clearly has not kept up with industry rates) and concluded with 'two observations': 'First, I hardly know David Torrance. And secondly – and much more problematically for a biographer – he doesn't know me at all.'

It was a typically Salmond response, playing the man rather than the ball, a journalist rather than his arguments. Laying aside the obvious inconsistency (I'm not sure how he could know me better than I know him), what Salmond might have meant is, as the historian Owen Dudley Edwards shrewdly pointed out, is that I do not *know* him intimately, which is of course true. But then I have never claimed to, although I do 'know' him very well as a politician and this, after all, is a political biography. Besides, if knowing one's subject is to be a prerequisite for a biographer, then it presents obvious problems for those hoping to cast some light on long-departed historical figures.

The late Sir Bernard Crick put it well when he said a biographer had 'a duty to show how he reaches his conclusions, not to pretend to omnisci-ence', while sharing 'things that are moot, problematic and uncertain with the reader',[1] qualities I have attempted to bring to all three editions of this book. Another fine biographer, John Campbell, also said 'prob-ably the ideal relationship between a biographer and a living subject'[2] was that between myself and Salmond, i.e. no direct co-operation but, at the same time, no attempt made to hinder my research (apart from an eleventh-hour phone call prior to publication of the first edition) nor prevent me speaking to friends and colleagues.

This edition is certainly a lot more critical in tone than those published in 2010 and 2011, not least because it is now much easier to assess his legacy as First Minister given more than eight years have passed since the 2007 Holyrood election. Still, as ever, I have endeavoured to be fair, showing where at all possible – in line with Sir Bernard Crick's rule – how I have reached my conclusions.

Biographies are never possible without the help of papers, places and people, and the former archives at the superb National Library of Scotland proved invaluable, particularly its collection of modern political manuscripts. Regarding places, research trips to Linlithgow, St Andrews and Glasgow helped put my subject in context, while people provided the most insightful source of information and analysis. The following, in alphabetical order, either spoke to me about Salmond, provided me with source material or offered feedback on sections of this biography: Geoff Aberdein, Malcolm Anderson, Peter Bainbridge, Grant and Glynne Baird, the late Professor Geoffrey Barrow, Ian O. Bayne, Colin Bell, Lucy Hunter Blackburn, Ian Blackford MP, Peter Brunskill, the late David Cairns, Antoni Chawluk, Pam Chesters, Peter Clarke, David Cobham, Andy Collier, Michael Crick, Rod Cross, Gordon Currie, Jim and Margaret Cuthbert, Tam Dalyell, Julie Davidson, Dr Jason Davies, Jennifer Dempsie, Christina Dykes, Jim Eadie MSP, Lord Elis-Thomas, Jim Fairlie, Kenny Farquharson, Colin Faulkner, John Fellowes, Lord Foulkes, Alan Frith, Professor Tom Gallagher, Duncan Hamilton, Margaret Henderson, Alistair Hicks, Claire Howell, Aidan Kerr, Andrew Kerr, Malcolm Kerr, Iain Lawson, Isobel Lindsay, Liz Lloyd, Colin McAllister, Lord McConnell, the late Margo MacDonald, Colin Mackay, Tim McKay, Chris McLean, Henry McLeish, John MacLeod, the late Stephen Maxwell, Professor James Mitchell, Jonathan Mitchell QC, Iain More, Peter Murrell, Stephen Noon, Quintin Oliver, Douglas Pattullo, Kevin Pringle, Colin Pyle, Harry Reid, Jim Sillars, Martin Sime, Dave Smith, Nigel Smith, Lord Steel, Stewart Stevenson MSP, Jamie Stone, Ian Swanson, Desmond Swayne MP, Michael Torrance, Lord Wallace of Tankerness, Andrew Wilson, Brian Wilson, Gordon Wilson, Charlie Woods, and many others who wished, for several reasons, to remain anonymous.

Finally, a big thank you to Hugh Andrew and his team at Birlinn for first agreeing to publish this biography six years ago and, subsequently, two new editions. Who knows, this might not even be the last.

David Torrance
London, June 2015
@davidtorrance

Chapter 1

# 'A REAL BLACK BITCH'

Alexander Elliot Anderson Salmond was born on Hogmanay, 1954, in the midst of a particularly cold and snowy winter. Forty years later, Salmond reflected on the moment through the eyes of his grandfather, Alexander (known as Sandy) Salmond. 'It was hardly the preparation for Hogmanay that Sandy had expected,' he wrote.

With pipes frozen all over town times were busy even for a semi-retired plumber and besides his new grandchild was due. Indeed overdue. And here he was on the hill trudging through the snow to a lonely farmhouse. Still the weather would mean that the wean would more than likely be born in the royal burgh, for there was no safe route to Edinburgh on a day such as this. And just think if it were a boy, a namesake, and a real Black Bitch, born within the sound of St Michael's bells.

Salmond then linked his birth with the final hours of a recluse called Bob Jamieson, whom Sandy was visiting at his farmhouse that night. A young doctor called McKay arrived just as Jamieson slipped away. 'Well, that's a blessing,' he said to Sandy. 'One going and one coming, because you'll have a grandchild before this day's over.'[1]

This story not only drew upon Alex Salmond's obviously fond memories of his grandfather, but also suggested a heightened sense of his Linlithgow roots, and perhaps his place in the wider sweep of Scottish history. He did, after all, share a birthday with Bonnie Prince Charlie. The Scotland of 1954/55, however, was then at the height of its political Unionism, and Winston Churchill was approaching the end of his second premiership. 'My mum thought Churchill was the greatest man who ever lived,' Salmond later recalled, 'and my dad wanted to hang him because of what he did to the miners.'[2] Doubtless Mrs Salmond contributed to the victory at the 1955 general election of the Scottish Unionist Party (as the Conservatives were then known north of the border), which won a majority of both seats and the popular vote.

The SNP, by contrast, barely registered in electoral terms. The party contested just two seats, Stirling and Falkirk Burghs and Perth and East Perthshire, only retaining its deposit in the latter. The SNP's share of the national vote was a pitiful 0.5 per cent. The glory days of a decade earlier, when Robert D. McIntyre had triumphed in Motherwell as the first Nationalist Member of Parliament, were but a distant memory. The SNP was still perceived as a romantic movement, a collection of cranks who meant well but achieved little.

It was another two years before Harold Macmillan would famously declare that 'most of our people have never had it so good', and Linlithgow, which occupied a prime location along the southern shore of an epony-mous Loch in a broad agricultural valley, would not have escaped this relative prosperity. The town boasted an illustrious past, its much-favoured royal palace (the birthplace of Mary, Queen of Scots) ensuring the town's historical prominence. But the Linlithgow Salmond would have been familiar with in the 1950s and '60s was no longer charmingly rural, its road and rail links having transformed it into a busy residential settlement.

There was also ongoing redevelopment. Two large tracts of the northern side of the High Street – where Salmond's grandfather had been born – were demolished in the 1960s and replaced by flats and public buildings in a contemporary style. In 1964 came a controversial addition to the townscape, a modernist aluminium spire – representing Christ's crown of thorns – which was added to St Michael's.[3]

The young Salmond obviously took a keen interest in the history of his home town and even decades later a friend conducted round Linlithgow's magnificent ruins was surprised by the eloquence and feeling of 'Alex's guided tour'.[4] In the early 1970s he devoured Angus Macdonald's 1932 book, *Linlithgow in Pictures*, and used it as the basis of a knowledgably articulate letter to the local newspaper when he was just 17. It concerned a street in the town called 'Beinn-Castle Brae', of which he enclosed a print:

> The 'Beinn' in Beinn-Castle comes not as 'Incomer' seemingly suggests from 'Bean', the leguminous plant but from the Scots' 'Beinn' meaning 'rich' or 'well to do'. The term probably has most truth when applied to the West Port House . . . which was completed by one of the Hamiltons [in] about 1600. It possessed extensive grounds, and is, not to become too involved, the largest and oldest inhabited property in town. The three mid-17th-century

houses in the foreground were demolished by the Town Council, showing a surprising, if somewhat familiar, lack of vision, in 1930, and made way for the incongruous, though no doubt necessary, public conveniences.[5]

The letter is signed, formally, 'Alexander Salmond'. Prominent characteristics are already present: a love of history, confidence and a straightforward – if youthfully clumsy – writing style with a humourous turn of phrase. 'Politicians gain by cultivating the local'[6] observed Christopher Harvie, and indeed Salmond would assiduously cultivate Linlithgow, just as David Lloyd George did Criccieth, Nye Bevan Ebbw Vale and Gordon Brown Kirkcaldy. A university friend remembers Salmond making a point of going back home for a traditional ceremony known as the 'walking of the marches', 'which was very important to him. He wasn't a romantic at all but felt that where he came from was very important.'[7]

There had been people by the name of Salmond – a 'Crusader' name of Hebrew origins – in Linlithgow since the 16th century, and members of Alex's family since at least the 18th century, before which they had been cattle dealers in Stirlingshire, one of whom, Peter, was the last Salmond to be born in an independent Scotland, in 1704. By 1841 Alex Salmond's great-great-great grandfather John, a ploughman and a labourer, had moved his family to the West Lothian village of Torphichen, while by 1871 the next generation had ended up in Linlithgow.

At around that time another Alex Salmond – the nephew of the future SNP leader's great-great-great grandfather – sailed to New York with his wife Jane, teenage son Peter, and nephew Robert, with records showing he 'was wearing his kilt when he stepped off board and onto the new land' 11 days later. His family flourished and Peter later moved to Canada where he built two houses and a farm in the new province of Saskatchewan. In her book, *Alex Salmond: Cattle Dealer*, Myrla Salmond (a fifth cousin of the other Alex Salmond) wrote that the 'Salmond pioneers had the courage to flout adversity'.[8]

Back in Scotland, Alex's great-great-great grandfather, John Salmond, shows up as a ploughman in the old parish records held at the National Archives of Scotland, while the forename Alexander, or Alex, appears to have become a family favourite when John's son was christened in 1816. The Scottish Salmonds were modest citizens, mainly working as ferrymen or flour millers, while Alex's grandfather, the aforementioned Sandy, became a plumber.

Sandy's son (and the future First Minister's father), Robert Dobbie

Salmond,[9] was born on 21 August 1921 in an area of Linlithgow known as Low Port. Robert was by instinct a Labour voter, and indeed during his stint in the Royal Navy had been nicknamed 'Uncle Joe' because of his Stalinist leanings. During the Second World War Robert was an electrician on the aircraft carrier *Indomitable*, which was torpedoed (but not sunk) in the Mediterranean. Later he moved to the Civil Service, working as an executive officer at the Ministry of Pensions and National Insurance where, in 1961, a young Margaret Thatcher was appointed a junior minister.

In September 1950 Robert married Mary Stewart Milne, who also worked at the local National Insurance office as a 'clerical officer' but came from a more middle-class background. Her father, William Milne, had been a headmaster and her mother, Margaret Hamilton, a school-teacher. Robert and Mary eventually had four children, the second of which was Alex, a baby-boomer born at 4.30 p.m. on 31 December 1954 at 101 Preston Road, the Salmonds' family home.

Following a local church tradition Alex's two middle names came from the minister who christened him, G. (Gilbert) Elliot Anderson. 'I have tried to bear that name with pride,' Salmond told the General Assembly of the Church of Scotland in 2009,[10] and indeed the Rev Elliot Anderson appears to have made quite an impression on the young Alex, who later gave serious thought to becoming a minister himself.[11] As Salmond recalled in 2008, Elliot Anderson had 'a great liking for what Professor [William] Barclay[12] used to do and looked at the exact meaning of words in Latin [and] Greek. He used to do sermons about what was meant by . . . the apostles or what did it mean when Jesus said such and such to this group of folk. I used to think it was fantastic. I used to demand to listen to sermons rather than go to Sunday school. I would be sitting in rapt attention listening to the full thing. He was not a great preacher in the Barclay spellbinding nature but he was a good minister and wholly good.'[13]

Salmond attended church almost every Sunday until he was 18, but later fell out of the habit. Like many politicians seeking to broaden their appeal, he would later talk up his Kirk background. 'I do have a strong faith and always have had,' he said in 2009. 'I have a Presbyterian nature in that I like its ideas of individual responsibility and democracy.'[14]

Those trying to pin down the formative influences on the young Salmond need look no further than his grandfather, Sandy. 'I was . . . instructed in the Scottish oral tradition,' he reflected in 2002, 'literally from my grandfather's knee, and I have little doubt that this was the strongest influence in my life in determining my attitude to nationality and identity.'[15]

Alexander Salmond liked to impart Scottish historical tales and, as his grandson later recalled, 'the way my granddad told it gave it incredible local colour'.[16] 'If he was telling a story about the wars of independence,' Salmond elaborated, 'he didn't tell it like a history book. For example, Bruce's men captured Linlithgow Castle. They did it by using a hay-cart and stopping the drawbridge and charging in. But what my grandfather used to say was, there were a couple of Davidsons . . . an Anderson [and] the Oliphants were involved. The Oliphants were the local bakers, so at four years old I had this image of the local bakers, covered in flour, dusting themselves off and charging in. It was personal, colourful, vital. It would have won more Oscars than Braveheart.'

In retrospect, Salmond realised his grandfather had embellished these stories. 'He showed me, for example, the ground where he said Edward I had camped before the Battle of Falkirk,' he recalled, 'he showed me the window from where the Regent Moray was shot dead in the High Street.' It was because this oral history was 'unofficial, almost subversive' that made it so 'irresistible' to Salmond. He was detached enough to realise that while his grandfather 'did get the sweep of things about right', his 'Braveheart version of Scots history may have been vulnerable in the occasional point of detail'.[17]

Nevertheless, Salmond's grandfather did at least sow the seeds of Alex's Nationalism: 'Of course, a pro-Scottish inclination goes a lot deeper than economics. Robert Burns put it best when he wrote that the story of Wallace kindled a fire in his veins "which will boil along there till the floodgates of life shut in eternal rest". Burns got his inspiration from Blind Harry's epic poem, Wallace. I got mine, literally, from my paternal grandfather's knee.'[18]

'The fire that he lit still burns,'[19] Salmond concluded. 'Each of us is the product of all our experiences and I do believe there is a link between these early memories and the support I developed in later years for the Scottish cause.'[20]

This latent Nationalism was not, however, cultural. Salmond wore a kilt for the first time when he attended a family wedding at Harrogate in 1959; an experience that meant the garment was not part of his wardrobe until nearly 50 years later. It seems he found the 'shortbread tin' and 'white heather club'[21] image of the kilt in 1950s Scotland disagreeable.

Salmond's first school was Linlithgow Primary, where he was once belted for making farmyard noises. 'I kept clucking in class, which I thought was very amusing, but my teacher thought it was less so,'

Salmond recalled nearly 40 years later.[22] A happier memory was his first foray into populist politics, standing for the SNP in mock elections. 'It was the only party left,' he explained later. 'I had a landslide victory because I advocated half-day school and the replacement of free school milk with ice cream.'[23]

Given his allergy to almost every form of protein, however, the young Alex was not allowed to drink cow's milk, though he could take that from a goat. In fact, health problems had plagued him since birth. As a baby, he had required 'constant slathering in sulphurous jelly' due to severe eczema, and when, aged three, that abated, it was replaced by severe asthma, a condition that has affected Salmond ever since. As the journalist Alex Perry later recounted:

> Mumps and measles made the asthma worse. When Salmond was chosen for an experimental asthma treatment, he had an allergic reaction to the drug, ephedrine. Mary refused to give her son any reason to think he was different. 'I'd be wheezing and she'd just fling me out to school, and over the day, the attack would wear off,' he says . . . Mary also took him swimming twice a week, an exercise especially hard for her boy since his nose was always blocked. But Salmond remembers the trips to Falkirk pool as a treat: afterwards his mother would buy him fish and chips, one of the rare meals to which he was not allergic. 'She gave the appearance of total normality,' he says. 'She told me not long before she died it was the most difficult thing she had ever done.'[24]

But despite Mary Salmond's efforts, Alex later estimated he had missed half his schooling up to the age of 12. Whenever he suffered an asthma attack he was moved from his small room at the back of the house to his parents' bedroom at the front. 'It had a fantastic view over the swing park,' he recalled. 'I used to lie there, read and ponder.' He essentially became an autodidact, teaching himself about the world from books. 'My dad bought an encyclopaedia in 1960, when I was five,' Salmond remembered. 'There were 12 volumes, and I read them from cover to cover. I knew something about everything.'[25]

'I wouldn't wish my illnesses on anyone,' reflected Salmond following his resignation in 2014, the first time he had spoken of his ailments in such detail. 'But there is no question that kids who overcome illness or disability, it makes them much stronger.'[26] Indeed, thereafter contemporaries would notice a sort of inner calm, a resilience and self-sufficiency about the young Alex that he retained as a politician several decades later.

Rarely prone to self-reflection or worry, Salmond would always make the most of whatever situation he found himself in, however bad.

Salmond has often spoken about his paternal grandfather, Alexander Salmond, but says little about his mother's father, William Milne. This is understandable, for Milne died nearly 14 years before Alex was born, although he was also an impressive figure from whom one might have expected the future First Minister to derive some inspiration.

Milne moved to Linlithgow in 1929 to become Rector of the town's academy, the same school his grandson would later attend. He hailed from a comfortable background in Kirriemuir (his father had been an insurance agent) and moved from Webster's Seminary, where he was dux medalist in 1906, to St Andrews University – again like Salmond – from which he graduated with honours in 1910. 'This considerable "lad o'pairts",'[27] as one newspaper described him, then worked as classics master at Bo'ness Academy for 19 years, interrupted only by a commission in the 10th Royal Scots during the First World War. Milne was drafted to France as a captain, and taken prisoner in the spring of 1918, spending the remainder of the war in a German camp.

Milne took over as Rector at Linlithgow Academy as the school became an 'omnibus' institution, or prototype comprehensive. The abolition of the primary fee-paying department provoked a storm of criticism but, as another newspaper later noted, 'Mr Milne was a man who always said that difficulties and obstacles could be overcome'.[28] In 1935 – in addition to his duties with the local Educational Institute of Scotland, the Freemasons[29], local Boy Scouts and the church – Milne was elected to Linlithgow Town Council as a Unionist (or Conservative). 'One cannot live long in an old "city" like Linlithgow without falling in love with it,' he said upon his election. 'I have no experience at municipal work, but will do my best to serve the town.'[30]

In 1937 Milne was appointed treasurer and successfully decreased local rates during a four-year tenure. A talented orator, he was also president of the West Lothian Discussion Club. At one notable meeting in February 1939 he presided over speeches by Sir William Y. Darling, the National government's prospective candidate for Linlithgow (and great-uncle of Alistair), and Lieutenant-Colonel Dalyell of The Binns (father of Tam). Decades later, Milne's grandson would spar with different generations of the same families. Too old to serve in the Second World War, Milne instead became commander of Linlithgow's Home Guard.

Then on 31 March 1941, quite out of the blue, the *West Lothian*

*Courier* carried the following story: 'On going to the school before the usual hour of nine o'clock, a cleaner found the dead body of Mr Milne lying on the floor of his room in a pool of blood with wounds in the head and body, and a firearm lying nearby.'[31] As a mark of respect Linlithgow Academy was closed for the day and, in keeping with contemporary editorial etiquette, no speculation as to what lay behind Milne's apparent suicide was offered. His death certificate noted that he had last been seen alive at 11 p.m. the previous evening, adding simply 'Gunshot wounds (suicide)' under cause of death.

Tributes were glowing. 'There never could have been a more considerate or understanding headmaster,' observed the *Linlithgowshire Journal and Gazette*. 'Indeed, it was not too much to say that he was universally beloved by staff and pupils. A man of clear vision, he was, from his long experience, well fitted to advise parents in the directions best suited to the bent and ability of the pupil.'[32] Milne had been, noted several reports, one of the best-known men in West Lothian.

Why, then, no public reference from Salmond? The primary reason must have been the stigma associated then, as now, with suicide. Any reference to the death of her father must also have been acutely distressing for Salmond's mother Mary, only 19 at the time. Indeed, when asked to comment on the story in 2008 (although it never appeared in print), Salmond told the journalist Tom Gordon that the death had never been discussed at home. 'I found out about about it because my dad told me when I was growing up,' he said. 'I'm not callous or uncaring about it, but he died more than ten years before I was born so I never knew him.'

Salmond also believed the tragedy had helped shape what Gordon called his mother's 'compassionate but pragmatic approach to life . . . she became a tireless volunteer who tried to instill a can-do attitude in her son'.[33] Salmond also revealed a little more to a university friend. 'Alex spoke of him as a man of honour,' he recalled. 'The story he told was that as treasurer of Linlithgow Town Council his grandfather had become aware of a discrepancy in the finances which he had rectified immediately; however he felt bound to report the error although at the time it had not been discovered. As a man of honour he then took his own life.'[34] In 2010, asked to comment following publication of the first edition of this biography, all Salmond would add was that he had 'never speculated' on the reasons for his grandfather's death.[35]

Salmond's childhood appears, by all accounts, to have been a happy one. His parents were loving, encouraging and delighted not just in Alex's

progress, but also that of his brother and two sisters. 'Effectively my
parents had two sets of family,' Salmond later reflected. 'Margaret and me
three years apart and then, 10 years later, Gail and Bob.' Indeed, Margaret
Salmond had been born in 1951, followed by Alex in 1954, Gail in 1963
and, finally, Robert in 1967.[36]

The two Salmond families inhabited 101 Preston Road, what Alex
later called 'the best kind of council scheme in Scotland'. 'The houses
were nicely spaced out with a decent bit of garden,' he explained. 'My
parents started their married life in that house. They had the downstairs
and my aunt and uncle had the upstairs. A lot of folk lived like that back
then.'[37] The journalist Ian Jack noted that had Salmond been an English
politician, he might have made more of the fact that he had been 'born
in a council house . . . to stress his knowledge of another social reality,
but in Scotland it goes unremarked. Most of his Scottish generation grew
up in council houses.'[38] 'We weren't poor,' Salmond stressed in 1990,
'but money was tight. Education was important to my family and they
managed to send all four of us to university. It can't have been easy.'[39]

'He was a very happy child,' recalled Mary Salmond in 2001, 'We
never had any worries with him.'[40] Salmond himself recalled that as 'a
boy growing up in Linlithgow, I was hugely fortunate in having an
incredibly secure family background. If there were any problems during
my childhood – at school, with friends, etc – I had a loving family of
both parents and three siblings, and grandparents within 200 yards, to go
greetin' to. The extended family was very close – indeed, Linlithgow was
a sort of extended family in itself.'[41]

When not playing with friends, Salmond was a devotee of the original
*Star Trek* series then showing on British television, while an early enthusiasm for sports predated that for politics. Despite his asthma, Alex usually
played golf every Saturday evening, and 'Gentleman John' Panton was
a childhood hero. Three generations of Salmonds were also enthusiastic
supporters of the Edinburgh-based team Heart of Midlothian, or Hearts.
'I watched Hearts home and away all season, every season,' Salmond
recalled in 1993.[42]

Blessed with a good memory, Salmond took a train-spotter's delight
in memorising footballing facts and figures, while following the team also
took him south of the border for the first time in 1971, for the second
leg of the Texaco Cup final. Cricket, which Robert Salmond followed
avidly, was less attractive to the young Alex, although he began indulging
in 'the sport of kings' aged just nine. He watched in 'grainy black and
white' as Arkle won the 1964 Gold Cup, on which he had placed a

bet on his uncle's advice. 'My half-a-crown became seven-and-six,' he recalled in 2003, 'and I suddenly started to become interested in horse racing.'[43]

Betting also gave rise to an early moral dilemma when, having placed a bet on behalf of his grandfather (Sandy), a betting shop employee misread his initials as 'FPP', or 'first past the post', and erroneously paid out on a horse that had actually been disqualified. Perhaps revealingly, Salmond 'solved the dilemma' by telling himself that Sandy 'wouldn't know the horse had been disqualified . . . so when I got home I told him they'd all come in'.[44] Interviewed in 1999 Salmond revealed that his grandfather had taken 'to the bottle in his old age'[45] and Alexander Salmond died, aged 83, in September 1975.

Although current affairs were discussed at home, a neighbour once told Mary Salmond that she could 'see him in Parliament one day'.[46] The neighbour was Nan Borthwick, 'who figured very large in Alex's life', recalled a university friend, 'she was almost a surrogate grandparent.'[47] One of Salmond's favourite lines about post-independence relations with England – 'England will lose a surly lodger and gain a good neighbour' – might also have come from Borthwick.[48]

Robert Salmond was still voting Labour at the 1964 general election, although when – most likely at the 1966 election – a Labour canvasser came to the Salmonds' door, he shifted allegiance. His father joked that the party would have his vote, but that his wife's was lost to the Conservatives. 'That's OK,' said the canvasser, or so Alex recalled. 'Just as long as she's not voting for the Scottish Nose Pickers.'[49] It so happened that Robert's golfing partner was a miner and staunch Nationalist. Reacting badly to the indirect slight on his friend, he told the Labour activist he would never vote for the party again. 'Like so many Scots who love their country and its traditions,' Salmond said of his parents in 1990, 'they were nationalist with a small 'n'.'[50]

Robert instead backed the SNP in West Lothian, whose candidate, Billy Wolfe, would later take Alex under his wing, although his son was impressed by the then Labour Party leader and Prime Minister Harold Wilson, a skillful media operator, orator and tactician. 'What tends to get lost in the fog of his dubious behaviour in office is the inspiration Wilson provided as Opposition leader,' Salmond reflected in 1994. 'For example Wilson went into the 1964 election campaigning against Polaris.'[51] Wolfe, meanwhile, was the closest the SNP had to a household name at that time, arguing that the party's future 'lay in developing coherent policies, addressing the socio-economic conditions of ordinary Scots and explaining how self-government would deliver economic growth and social justice',[52] an analysis consistent with Salmond's as a future SNP activist, MP and party leader.

Even as a teenager, Salmond formed a lasting impression. 'He was confident, didn't go with the pack,' remembered a contemporary. 'He wasn't a loner but certainly stood out as an individual, he also wasn't afraid of standing up to teachers. In fifth and sixth year we all used to play cards in the common room and Alex played a big part in that.' Salmond had clearly added another gambling hobby to his growing interest in the sport of kings, while another fellow pupil recalled Salmond – known as 'Wee Fish' – once bringing a loaded roulette wheel into the sixth year common room. There was, however, 'no interest in girls at school', while a popular rumour was that Salmond had 'sub-contracted his paper round',[53] being a 'junior agent' for the *Edinburgh Evening News* on Saturdays. This love of gambling together with an aptitude for delegation clearly pointed to a career in politics.

Back in his first year, however, Salmond astonished his parents by revealing himself a talented boy soprano. Mary remembered arriving late at the school for a 'little concert' and being struck by a moving performance of the traditional Irish folk song, 'The Lark in the Clear Air'. 'I thought it was the most beautiful thing I'd ever heard,' she recalled. He sang a lot at home and on the way to school, and it seems that when the organist at St Michael's Church decided to start a boys' choir, a teacher at the Academy 'pointed Alex out'. 'He took us completely by surprise,'[54] added Mary. 'It was a strange thing,' Salmond recalled in 2009, 'on the one hand you kind of kept it quiet because some of my pals would have made a bit of a fool of me; on the other hand once you did it and everybody clapped and said that's terrific and you felt good about that.'[55]

Salmond's vocal talent reached a wider audience when an Edinburgh organist called Dr E. F. Thomas, who also taught at Callendar Park College of Education (a teacher training college), sought out a boy soprano for what would be the only Scottish touring production of Gian Carlo Menotti's *Amahl and the Night Visitors*, an hour-long one-act opera which was then a popular Christmas classic. Alex did two performances in the lead role at Callendar Park and St Michael's Church over the Christmas of 1967/68 and was, according to his mother, 'absolutely marvellous'.[56]

Covering the first performance at the end of 1967, the *Linlithgowshire Journal and Gazette* noted that Salmond was co-starring with 20 girls (Menotti had stipulated that Amahl must be played by a boy) but 'did not seem overawed in the slightest by his female company', an indication of his self-confidence even at a young age. Jean Graham of the *Falkirk Herald* also observed that 'Alex is a fine wee singer. He has a very pleasant voice and carried the part very well indeed.'[57] An alternative career might have beckoned, but Salmond's voice inevitably broke. 'I used to be able to sing lots of octaves and I ended up being able to sing about four notes, so I wasn't good at it anymore,' Salmond recalled. 'But the one thing it left me with was being able to be in front of audiences.'[58]

Otherwise Salmond's school reports were 'satisfactory without being brilliant'. In his second year he got the prize for history, no doubt aided by his grandfather's early tutorials, while for Sixth Year Studies English Salmond was urged by his English teacher to study the poetry of R. S. Thomas, a cleric who had become a committed Welsh Nationalist. His poetry largely concerned his twin passions, the Welsh landscape and the Welsh people, with graphic descriptions of the harsh working conditions many of them had to endure.

Evidence of how his prose and poetry shaped Salmond's thinking can be found in Thomas's essay, 'Some Contemporary Scottish Writing', which first appeared in 1946, and part of which reads: 'And so we come full circle back to the crude reality, the necessity for politics, distasteful as they may appear. For it is England, the home of the industrial revolution, and the consequent twentieth-century rationalism, that have been the winter on our native pastures, and we must break their grip, and the grip of all the quislings and yes-men before we can strike that authentic note.' Salmond quoted from this in one of his *Herald* columns in the 1990s and later reflected that it had been 'corroboration from the outside', an 'empowering' indication to his teenage self that Scotland had produced literature of some importance.

In his dissertation, 'R. S. Thomas: Poet of Mid-Wales', Salmond dwelled on the poet's 'middle period', finding himself 'particularly interested in the commentary behind the work – the political commentary, the nationalist commentary, the language commentary – and some of those attitudes, towards deforestation, industrialisation, ways of life being challenged'. Politically, he believed Thomas's poetry had 'consolidated' and 'articulated' thoughts he already possessed, although his favourite poem, 'Song for Gwydion', was not actually political. He also recalled reading another called 'The Musician' to his singing teacher, Old Beezer Brown, which reduced him to tears.

Salmond even wrote to Thomas seeking input for his dissertation and was 'gobsmacked' when he replied. Independently he also read the poet's early work concerning a Welsh hill farmer called Iago Prytherch, later telling a close university friend he identified with him, someone who remained an 'Enigma' to his creator: 'What is he thinking about? What's going on inside his skull?' The same question would later be asked about the equally enigmatic Alex Salmond. 'Thomas's work has had a powerful influence,' he reflected again in 2011. 'It's been incredibly utilitarian: it's been practical. It's not been some namby-pamby theory, it's been something that's really useful and has added, I hope, to the strength of human understanding.'[59]

His other Sixth Year Studies topic was history, with Salmond opting to study the American Revolution. 'It was my first year [1971] teaching at Linlithgow Academy and Alex chose the topic himself,' recalled Gordon Currie, Salmond's history teacher. 'When I spoke to him he knew more about it than I did.' They also discussed current affairs. 'When we spoke about politics it was obvious he wasn't a novice,' said Currie, 'he was very keen on it. I told him that in politics you've really got to capture the imagination of the people you're trying to get on board.'[60]

By then Salmond's political hero, Harold Wilson, had been replaced by the Conservative Edward Heath following the 1970 general election, at which an SNP surge beginning with Winnie Ewing's 1967 by-election victory in Hamilton fizzled out, returning just one MP in the Western Isles. In 1971, Salmond later recalled being 'fully behind'[61] the Upper Clyde Shipbuilders work-in, while a contemporary at Linlithgow Academy (though three years younger than Alex) was his future on-off political confidante Kenny MacAskill.

In the summer of 1972 Salmond left Linlithgow Academy having been encouraged by certain teachers to study at St Andrews University. His next year, however, was spent at the Edinburgh College of Commerce (later known as Napier College), an Edinburgh Corporation institution established in 1966 to provide the city and its surrounding area with vocational education. Salmond studied for a Higher National Certificate in industry at the College's Sighthill campus. Curiously, this year of Salmond's life has seldom been mentioned since, frequent accounts of his education giving the impression that he moved seamlessly from one medieval town to another. There was, however, a racing anecdote:

Back in 1973 I put the whole of Sighthill College HNC Business Studies course onto Crisp, who was the best chaser I had seen since Arkle and the most imposing horse I had ever seen . . . Crisp powered past fence after fence only to falter just after the very last. Crisp didn't so much hit the wall as almost hit the elbow on the famous finishing straight and in the shadow of the post was caught by the young Red Rum, to whom the gallant Australian horse was conceding 24lbs in weight. I thought that my fellow students would be suitably grateful that they had had such a memorable run for their money not to mention their each-way profit. Not a bit of it – they were all cheesed off that my tip had got beaten![62]

For the next four years, Salmond backed Red Rum every time; although the HNC does not seem to have engaged him and he considered switching to advertising or journalism instead. Above all, however, Salmond had left school with – as a 1997 profile put it – 'a burning desire to be a somebody'.[63] The first stage in his determination to fulfil that ambition would take him to the University of St Andrews.

Chapter 2

# 'ACT OF REBELLION'

St Andrews, wrote the Nationalist Douglas Young in a 1969 history, is a 'town at the centre of three great facets of Scottish life – learning, religion and golf'. These were three facets that, to varying degrees, interested the 18-year-old Alex Salmond when he arrived at the town's university, particularly the golf. Appropriately enough, as Young also noted, St Andrews had also been the 'Headquarters of Militant Nationalism'. The 3,000 students studying at St Andrews in 1973, however, were more likely to preach Conservatism than independence, and it remained 'a relatively small and intimate university'.[1]

'I just absolutely loved it,' Salmond recalled in 2009, 'and if it hadn't been for the money and the lack of it, I'd still be there.' There had been an element of chippiness in his choice, as he later admitted. 'St Andrews is a very Anglicised University, a very socially select university and so I went as a kind of Scottish punter because I wanted to demonstrate something.'[2] Having toyed with studying astronomy, instead he opted for both Medieval History, an obvious choice given his grandfather's influence, and Economics, perhaps chosen with an eye on a future career.

But neither Peter Brunskill, who became perhaps Salmond's closest friend during this period, nor Pam Chesters (née Beveridge), another student contemporary, could recall Salmond doing much work, rather he would sit 'in the SRC office reading the *Racing Post* rather more diligently then any economics notes'.[3] 'My most embarrassing moment', admitted Salmond in 2006, 'was when I attended a senior modern economics class and the entire class got up and applauded because it was the first time I'd been there.'[4] As a result, his degree took five years (rather than the standard four) to complete.

The pleasures of the turf provided an obvious distraction, and Salmond had an account with his local bookies, which was just off Lade Braes. 'There was a bookie there [in St Andrews] who used to give a

quarter the odds place-only,' he recalled in 2000. 'That was extreme
value – it certainly helped finance my studies.'[5] Quintin Oliver, an exact
contemporary of Salmond's (and later a political opponent), remembers
approaching him on their first day in David Russell Halls. 'I put out my
hand to say hello and was warmly greeted with an expansive description
of how Scotland was so suitable a place for a Northern Irish student to
study,' he recalled. 'We later that day attended together a freshers' event
on gay rights, commenting that the concept of "cottaging" summoned
up images of the rural idyll.'[6]

Studying economics, meanwhile, consolidated Salmond's pre-existing
interest in Nationalism, as fashioned by his grandfather's tales and R. S.
Thomas's poetry. 'I had a natural sympathy with the idea,' he later told
the journalist Ian Jack, 'but it was the economic arguments that convinced
me.' He added: 'I'd grown up with an assumption that Scotland was a
poor, wee deprived place that had never had a fair kick o' the ball and
could certainly never stand on its own two feet. I started to question that
assumption. And then I read a lot and thought a lot and decided that
assumption was based on hee-haw apart from an ingrained indoctrination
and pessimism.'[7]

'The [economics] department was a bit moribund,' recalled Peter Jones,
who did first- and second-year economics at around the same time as
Salmond, 'and very Keynesian.'[8] Charlie Woods, who studied economics
with Salmond, recalled that 'both leaned towards the Keynesian
viewpoint'.[9]

History, however, was probably Salmond's main preoccupation as a
student, and it was the Nationalist-inclined Geoffrey Barrow, Professor
of Scottish History at St Andrews 1974-79, who taught him about the
Wars of Independence. His book, *Robert Bruce and the Community of the
Realm of Scotland*, was highly valued by Salmond, and Barrow later told
the SNP's Paul Henderson Scott that Alex had been his 'star student';
someone it was obvious 'was going places'.[10]

St Andrews, however, was not an obvious context in which Salmond
could go places politically, unlike Michael Forsyth, Michael Fallon,
Robert Jones and Desmond Swayne, James Younger (son of George),
Eamonn Butler and Madsen Pirie, all of whom would later become MPs,
peers or policy advisers associated with the Conservatives, the party that
dominated campus politics. Jones, Butler and Fallon were members of
the Students Representative Council (SRC) when Salmond arrived at
St Andrews in the autumn of 1973, others including two future *Scotsman*

journalists, Joyce McMillan (who was treasurer) and Peter Jones. Those on the left included the future Labour MP Mark Lazarowicz, Martin Sime, later head of the Scottish Council for Voluntary Organisations and Kevin Dunion, who later became Scotland's freedom of information commissioner, while the student newspaper, *Aien*, was edited by both the future Green MSP Chris Ballance, and Brian Taylor, who rose through the ranks at BBC Scotland to become its political editor.

Taylor remembered Salmond as

> a lean and energetic individual who wore what I was later to lampoon as a Maoist cap while he rushed about the old town pursuing the cause of Scottish Nationalism ... Clearly on the Left, he could easily have been an influential figure within the university Labour Club. Indeed, he confessed to me that he had once voted Labour at St Andrews in a contest where there was no SNP candidate. He neutralized this, however, by also registering to vote in his home town of Linlithgow – where there was an SNP candidate to gain his support. Such options were available to wandering students.[11]

Salmond, however, appears to have remained aloof from SRC and journalistic activity for at least his first year at St Andrews, and his name does not appear in *Aien* until 1976, lampooning Liberals who believed 'in a federal Scotland, in a federal Britain, in a federal Europe, no doubt in a federal world'.[12]

But by Salmond's own account he wasted little time in joining the SNP, the result of an argument with an English girlfriend, Debbie Horton from Hackney,[13] who was secretary of the St Andrews Labour club. She apparently said: 'If you feel like that, go and join the bloody SNP.'[14] Salmond later took up the story: 'The next day, that is precisely what I did, trekking to Dundee from St Andrews ... Arriving [there] at the local SNP office in 1973, a companion and I were promptly given an address in St Andrews – and hitch-hiked back again, finally to sign on the dotted line. It may not have been the most auspicious and organised beginning to a political career but I like to think that at least it did display a degree of enthusiasm and fortitude.'[15]

That same evening, according to Salmond, he and his 'companion', Tony Lawson, turned up at a sparsely attended AGM of the St Andrews branch of the Federation of Student Nationalists (FSN). As the only two paid-up members, they were duly elected president and treasurer. But

Peter Brunskill, Salmond's best friend at St Andrews, remembered Alex assuming control about a year later. He recalled:

> I was sitting in my room one evening when there was a knock on the door and it was Alex. He sat there and talked to me for about two-and-a-half hours and a lot of it went way over my head, because this was a guy with a highly developed political philosophy even at the age of 19. He spoke about his influences, all left-wing radicals, then he spoke about the St Andrews FSN, which he said had been controlled by a right-wing group, so he and some mates had got some people elected and staged a coup. Thereafter a bunch of us followed the Salmond whip, but we were happy to do so. He was the best sort of evangelist; he made you feel happy to be helping out.[16]

The political backdrop of the times must also have influenced Salmond. The SNP's high-profile 'It's Scotland's Oil' campaign had begun the year before, and when Salmond arrived on campus for the first time, the local SNP association and university FSN were actively promoting the oil campaign. Then, in October 1973, the Royal Commission on the Constitution recommended a directly-elected Scottish Assembly, and on 8 November Margo MacDonald won the Govan by-election. It was, in short, an exciting time to be a Nationalist student at St Andrews.

So what sort of student was Salmond? Like other contemporaries, Christina Dykes remembered him 'as very thin – almost wiry – with long greasy thin hair, wearing a denim jacket with lots of political badges and frankly rather unkempt',[17] while like most undergraduates he also drank, enjoyed himself and probably spent too little time actually studying history and economics. One indulgence was a board game called 'Diplomacy', also a favourite of Henry Kissinger and John F. Kennedy, which he 'sometimes stayed up all night playing'.[18]

Another obsession was pinball, which Salmond would also play throughout the night at David Russell Hall. 'Alex had something called the "Salmond bum-up",' recalled Peter Brunskill, 'in which his first ball would knock down everything, producing the biggest score possible. At that point, just when he had everything, he would want that little bit more; tilt the machine and then lose the game. I mention that because that's Alex all over. He just had this idea that there was no limit to what he could do. I was the same as him, brought up in a council house and from a modest background, but while I reckoned I'd done pretty well to get into St Andrews; while the rest of us were pleased with position "A", Alex was already thinking about position "C". It wasn't just ambition, he had this feeling that the whole world was out there and that he could do what he wanted. This was really inspiring stuff and that's how he persuaded people to follow him.'[19]

Christina Dykes, who shared a medieval history tutorial with Julia Barrow (Professor Barrow's daughter) and Salmond, had a similar recollection. 'There was a breeziness about him which came from an inner confidence,' she said, 'while the rest of us were struggling with self-doubt and hesitation . . . he had the confidence from knowing what he wanted.'[20]

It was at this stage that Salmond's parents back in Linlithgow must have become aware that their son had caught the political bug. In the long summer holidays Salmond would base his political activities at 101 Preston Road, and Brunskill remembers him being 'massively devoted to his family'.[21] 'I used to sit here and they [Alex and his friends] would traipse through out to this old car,' recalled Salmond's father Robert, 'there was hardly room for them because of SNP banners.' He also remembered his son going 'about with Billy Wolfe a bit, being in Linlithgow'.[22]

Indeed, Wolfe's brand of Nationalist social democracy, as well as his emphasis on professional organisation, must have had a strong influence on the young Salmond. He later remembered advice Wolfe had given him 'as a young lad in West Lothian': 'always remember that the SNP stands for two things – independence for Scotland and home rule for Bo'ness!'[23] Salmond's first major political campaigning experiences were the general elections of February and October 1974, at which Wolfe was once again the SNP candidate for West Lothian. Quintin Oliver recalled having lengthy 'psephological conversations' with Salmond as to how the SNP would advance on its result in the latter election, at which it won 30 per cent of the vote and 11 MPs. 'An excited Alex drew a graph in the air with his finger,' he recalled, 'indicating the trajectory for victory next time round; his target was 50 per cent of Scottish seats, thereby, he argued eagerly, securing a mandate for independence.'[24]

The following year Salmond was also active in the referendum on the UK's continuing membership of the European Economic Community (EEC). Although the SNP formally campaigned for a 'no' vote, its opposition hinged upon being compelled to join as part of the UK rather than on Scotland's own terms. His speeches from this period reveal him to have been vehemently opposed to continued EEC membership.

'Scotland's bright economic future will be jeopardised by the remote and centralised policies of the Common Market,' he declared at one gathering.

> With no Scottish representation on the Council of ministers, oil will be next when the Scottish interests of controlled, planned development conflict with the exploitative, 'boom-and-bust' proposal of the EEC Common Energy Policy. The Common Market will drain jobs and investment away from Scotland to the 'Golden Triangle' of London, Paris, and the German Ruhr. Scotland knows from bitter experience what treatment is in store for a powerless region of a common market.
>
> Our economic future does not lie with that small segment of Europe called the Common Market,' Salmond continued. 'It lies with the wider world and it is there that the best trading prospects are to be found. If we in Scotland are to take full advantage of our tremendous economic potential, we must break the Brussels stranglehold.[25]

Salmond was also prepared to work with other parties to ensure this. In May 1975 he joined Mark Lazarowicz, chairman of the university's Labour club and later a Scottish Labour MP, to form the 'Students Against the Common Market' committee. Indeed, Lazarowicz recalled campaigning closely with Salmond. 'The only time when Alex Salmond put up a Labour poster and I put up an SNP poster,' he recalled, 'was when he had his SNP "vote no" posters and vice versa, so we'd take it in turns holding the ladders and so on.'[26] The party political dimension of the Europe debate would of course change over time. Gordon Brown, for example, was secretary of the East Fife 'Get Britain Out' campaign.

The dominant political issue of the mid-1970s, however, was that of devolution for Scotland. At this stage all four of Scotland's main political parties were committed to some degree of autonomy in the form of a Scottish Assembly, although the SNP obviously wanted to go much further. In November 1975 the Labour government finally responded to the Kilbrandon Commission by publishing a white paper, *Our Changing Democracy*, which promised directly-elected Assemblies in Scotland and Wales.

Tam Dalyell, Salmond's MP back in West Lothian, was already emerging as his own party's principal devolution rebel, and while staying with his parents in the summer of 1976, Salmond wrote to the local newspaper to criticise Dalyell's 'extreme Unionist standpoint'.[27] The wider Labour movement had also experienced a split in January 1976, when Jim Sillars quit the party to establish the ostentatiously pro-devo-lution 'Scottish Labour Party'. It is possible that Salmond met Sillars as early as December 1975, when he visited St Andrews to speak about the devolution white paper, just weeks before he resigned the Labour whip.

Even at this point, meanwhile, there was no overtly cultural dimen-sion to Salmond's Nationalism. 'Alex wasn't a cultural Nationalist at all,' recalled Brunskill. 'I learned to play the bagpipes when I was at university but he hated the sound of them, and especially the sound I made. He also abhorred tartan of any sort.'[28] When the historian Owen Dudley Edwards offered Salmond the opportunity to visit the poet Hugh MacDiarmid, for example, he 'passed it up for a football match'.[29] Otherwise he saw John McGrath's influential play, *The Cheviot, the Stag and the Black, Black Oil*, during its 1973 tour, enjoyed a BBC adaptation of Douglas Hurd's thriller *Scotch on the Rocks* (concerning tartan terrorism) and listened to the music of Paul Robeson, a big left-wing icon whose LPs could be purchased via the SNP. 'He was big on Paul Robeson and would quote him,' remembered Brunskill. 'It wasn't just the music and the voice, he admired the dignity of the man.'[30] 'Paul Robeson is a hero of mine,' Salmond later admitted, 'both musically and politically.'[31]

It is important to remember that Salmond's political consciousness developed, or coincided with, two big growths in Nationalism, between 1967 and 1968 when he was still at school, and between 1973 and 1977 when he was at university. During most of Salmond's university career the SNP were not a fringe concern, they were Scotland's second-biggest party and seemingly on the cusp of a great breakthrough. So although he was in a minority on the St Andrews campus, Salmond was not alone, particularly among young people. Indeed, Keith Webb observed that 'the party has for some years been disproportionately gaining the allegiance of new and young voters . . . nearly half of these voters between the ages of eighteen and thirty-four declare for the SNP, compared with around 20 per cent for Labour and Conservative'.[32]Most contemporaries from this period remember being impressed by perhaps the brightest of this youthful crop of Nationalists. To Mark Lazarowicz, Salmond 'had quite a coherent political philosophy',[33] while Michael Forsyth remembered always having 'the greatest respect for Alex' because 'he has always had the courage of his convictions'.[34] Indeed, Forsyth and Salmond make for a fascinating comparison. Both arrived at St Andrews from modest backgrounds (Forsyth's father owned a garage), and both were initially socialist by inclination; but while St Andrews transformed Forsyth into an evangelical Thatcherite, it consolidated Salmond's nascent Nationalism.

'Michael only became a Thatcherite,' said a dismissive Salmond in 1990, 'when he saw that was the way forward in the party . . . it was more ambition than ideology.'[35]

Throughout the next 30 years – as both became MPs and rose through their parties' respective ranks – Salmond's distaste for Forsyth did not diminish. Rather sharp barbs about Forsyth litter Salmond's Hansard entries; in 1997, for example, he described Forsyth as 'the Mekon, a malign influence in Scottish politics'.[36] Only occasionally did he admit to grudging admiration for Forsyth, reflecting in 1995 that 'then and now his real talent has been for ferocious backroom organisation . . . a determination to pick an opponent's weakness and then devote all resources to pursuing ruthlessly the point to destruction'.[37] Salmond regarded Forsyth as beyond the pale, someone from a modest background who had betrayed his class by aligning himself with the elitist and 'anti-Scottish' Conservative Party.

Snide references to 'Mike' Forsyth also litter the pages of the *Free Student Press* (FSP), the publication of which marked Salmond's first significant foray into front-line student activism. Peter Brunskill remembers

> getting visions of this student paper from Alex, which he wanted to give a free copy of to every student at a halls of residence in Scotland, which he calculated to be 20,000. He had no money, no support from the party, no journalists, no advertising, nothing. I think he needed to raise £2,000 to publish each edition. Undeterred, Alex called in favours from various people for advertising, for instance the Lea Rig Bar in Bo'ness was one of his locals and they agreed to place an advert, as did various party people. Then we distributed 20,000 newspapers on our own, using my beat up old car.[38]

The first edition duly appeared on university campuses across Scotland in October 1975, and its 'political position' was avowedly Nationalist. Salmond wrote many of its articles himself, including the mischievous 'McSlickley' diary column. He was a natural writer, if a little rough round the edges, and enjoyed the business of gathering quotes. Decades later Brunskill could still picture Salmond buttonholing Margaret Thatcher during a visit to St Andrews in 1976, although his attempt to photograph the unlikely duo did not work out. Another snap taken later that day shows a rather coy Alex, sans 'scruffy cap' but with shoulder-length hair and sporting his trademark beige jacket adorned with FSP and SNP stickers.

A regular target for the FSP was the National Union of Students (Scotland), then dominated by what was known as the 'Broad Left', a coalition of Labour, non-aligned and Communist students, and Salmond used the newspaper to promote St Andrews' disaffiliation from NUS Scotland and its memberhip of the new Scottish Union of Students, of which Salmond was one of the principal architects.[39]

Editing the FSP also brought Salmond into contact with Stewart Stevenson, who would become a lifelong friend (and ministerial colleague) despite being eight years older. 'He'd heard that I could take and develop photographs so he got in touch,' recalled Stevenson. 'It was typical of the way he approached things, he was able to draw people in, that was his absolutely key skill.'[40] The FSP's inaugural edition, meanwhile, captured the lively Scottish student scene in which Salmond was now a player, prominent figures including Gordon Brown (Edinburgh), John Reid (Stirling) and Alistair Darling (Aberdeen).

Salmond, in common with many other student activists at this time, appears to have fallen a little under the spell of Brown. Contrasting the performance of 'celebrity rectors' at Scotland's four ancient universities with that of 'student rectors' in an FSP editorial, Salmond praised the latter as 'models of diligence and effective representation'.[41] Salmond could only have been writing about Brown's tenure at Edinburgh University, where in 1975 he had edited *The Red Paper on Scotland*, a widely read tract that included contributions from the Scottish Labour Party MP Jim Sillars and Vince Cable, the future Liberal Democrat MP who was then a Labour member of Glasgow Corporation.

Partly in response, the SNP produced *The Radical Approach: Papers on an Independent Scotland*, which was prominently advertised in the summer 1976 edition of the FSP and described (probably by Salmond) as a work that 'promises to become a standard text'.[42] Edited by Gavin Kennedy and including contributions by left-wingers such as Margo MacDonald, Stephen Maxwell (a contributor to the FSP), Andrew Currie, Owen Dudley Edwards and Isobel Lindsay, *The Radical Approach* was an important early influence on Salmond. Indeed, in February 1977 he helped organise a conference entitled 'Scotland at the Crossroads' with seminars focusing on the SNP's 'radical approach' to political and social questions.

Salmond was also fully involved with the SNP beyond the St Andrews campus. He acted as press officer for the SNP's East Fife association, while in September 1977 he organised walkabouts by four leading SNP 'personalities', Stephen Maxwell, Margo MacDonald, George Reid and

Winnie Ewing. The last of these was a great success, and a beaming (and very thin) Salmond was pictured alongside Ewing in the 8 October edition of the *St Andrews Citizen*. The wider goal of the SNP's autumn campaign was, Salmond told the newspaper, 'to show how wealthy a country is in actuality and how, properly used by a Scottish Government, this wealth can eradicate unemployment'. By 'wealth' he did not simply mean oil. 'We also mean our wealth of energy,' added Salmond in a remarkably prescient outline of one of his favourite themes as First Minister 30 years later.

> How many countries have the potential choice of Hydro-electric, wave, solar and wind power to heat their homes and supply their industries with reliable sources of non-pollutant electricity? But above all, by wealth, we mean the people of Scotland . . . All the Scots need is the self-confidence that knowledge of their country's wealth can give them – and the Scottish Government to make the wealth work for them. Our slogan "Get the strength of Scotland's wealth around you" may sound terribly un-British to the comfortable mandarins of Whitehall. To almost two hundred thousand unemployed in Scotland it is a message of hope.[43]

After two years at the helm, Salmond resigned as editor of the FSP in June 1977. 'I have decided to make way for a younger man,' he joked.[44] Launching and editing a Scotland-wide student newspaper had been an ambitious undertaking for Salmond, but amply demonstrated – even in his early twenties – his self-assurance, campaigning flair, journalistic talent and capacity for hard work. He was, as Brunskill recalled, 'a phenomenal multi-tasker'.[45]

Another of those tasks was as a member of the St Andrews University SRC. It is not exactly clear how much time Salmond actually spent on the SRC (he failed to win a place, for example, in elections on 24 February 1976, despite polling 179 votes), but he was certainly one of a small band of SNP members who spent five years trying to outwit a dominant Conservative contingent (membership of the FSN in 1976–77 was 72 compared with 509 in the Tory club).

In debate Salmond was formidable but, according to Jamie Stone, later a Liberal Democrat MSP, 'had no lightness of touch. If you scored a lighthearted point he would come back with all guns blazing. He was fully in command of the facts during a debate, indeed he was feared, if not the most feared speaker. He would always enter debates late on and come in quickly and make the killer points. He was savage; spoke without notes. During a short pause you could see his mind whizzing and that was the moment he would formulate the attack.'[46]

Likewise, student contemporary Alistair Hicks recalled that 'he was always jumping up to intervene, often on a point of order. He could usually be relied on to make it difficult for the ruling clique. His rhetoric was not as well-honed as it now, and he had a hectoring, repetitive tone that made some of his audience doze off, as they thought they had heard it all before.'[47]

However Tim McKay, later a Liberal Democrat councillor in Edinburgh, remembers Salmond's rhetoric being polished and apparently spontaneous. 'I remember asking him what he was going to say and he replied: "I never know what I'm going to say until I stand up", then it just sort of came to him.' 'He was a serious politician even then,' added McKay, 'and it was obvious that's what he wanted to pursue. I remember debating Proportional Representation with him and Alex saying "PR's not a policy, it's just a procedural issue." '[48]

The budding Nationalist politician also aired his rhetoric beyond the confines of the SRC. One contemporary remembered accompanying him to an SNP meeting in 1977: 'He was in his early twenties but he was already a leader. The meeting felt like a gathering of a revolutionary cell in St Petersburg before the Russian Revolution. It was full of wild ideas and unrealistic people. Alex stood out because he was realistic and he could speak. People twice his age loved him for what they thought he could do. He was capable of sounding like a firebrand, hell bent on immediate independence and nothing less, but his mind was already in control of his emotions.'[49]

The St Andrews SRC was also a very social body, although the consensus is that Salmond remained aloof from that side of student life. Tim McKay remembered that he 'wasn't a social animal; he wouldn't go out drinking a lot although he liked to drink'. The fiercely private side of Salmond's personality was already evident. 'He kept himself to himself,' added McKay, 'In some ways he didn't open up a lot to people so I couldn't say what it was that motivated him.'[50] This did not mean that Salmond was unpopular. As fellow student Dave Smith put it, 'he wasn't the life and soul of the party but he was a good guy'.[51]

Des Swayne, later a Conservative MP, recalls a more convivial impression of Salmond:

He was a really nice guy. We were poles apart politically but we could not have been better friends. I recall cycling from Edinburgh to St Andrews having missed the last train to Leuchars one night and he passed me on the way back from some crucial by-election in 1978 on some windswept moor and he and Margo MacDonald insisted on cramming me and my bike into their little car. He was very left wing and a unilateralist but an excellent fellow to have a pint with.[52]

There were, of course, also girlfriends. One was Marion Macdonald, the daughter of a local SNP activist called Dennis Macdonald (whom Salmond and Brunskill tried very hard to get elected to North East Fife District Council at a May 1976 by-election). Described invariably as 'a complete doll' and 'absolutely gorgeous', Brunskill remembers staying with the couple at Salmond's parents' house 'and them both leaning out of the window to smoke – he smoked a lot – and it wafting into the flat'.[53] Likewise, Tim McKay remembers Marion being 'very pretty'. 'I remember thinking "you've done very well there Alex". The thing was he didn't see much of his girlfriend because he was always away at political things, and for about two years he didn't have a girlfriend at all.'[54] It seems the Macdonald residence became something of a 'home from home' for Salmond, and he 'organised and planned many of his political activities' there.[55]

As already mentioned, Salmond's closest friend throughout his student days was Peter Brunskill, who was the only other Nationalist member of the SRC. Both considered running for president in February 1977, but decided to pull out at the last minute, Salmond claiming that 'due to pressure of work he would be unable to give enough time to the campaign'. *Aien* had a bit of fun spoofing this joint withdrawal as the 'Society wedding of the year'. 'After a courtship of five years, Alex Salmond and Peter Brunskill finally took the plunge and bluffed their way to the altar,' the article spoofed. 'Both bride and bridegroom withdrew their nomination forms shortly before the five o'clock deadline as their respective campaigns would have "interfered with their honeymoon." '[56]

Instead, Salmond decided instead to stand for the education vice-presidency, probably with the intention of using it as a launch pad for the SRC presidency the following year. He won, and even 30 years later recalled the 'huge fights' he had with St Andrews over failure rates among first-year students in the science faculty, and it was a battle with Nationalist overtones: Salmond believed that the students 'weren't failing because they weren't clever. They were failing because the course structure in the 70s at St Andrews was oriented towards [English] A Levels, despite the fact that it was a Scottish University'.

Early the following year Salmond drafted a paper for the SRC urging action. 'It was a huge scandal,' he reflected in 2009.[57] These negotiations also brought Salmond into close contact with the university establishment. 'Even in his dealings with the university he had a certain authority,' recalled Tim McKay. 'He dealt with a chap who was master, Stuart McDowall, a well-known economist and establishment figure, and you could see that he was dealing with Alex as an equal.'[58] In December 1977, meanwhile, Salmond was nominated, along with two other members of the SRC, to join St Andrews Community Council, his first taste of non-university office.

Another contemporary political event that impinged upon St Andrews was the bitter Grunwick dispute, a long-running battle for trade union recognition among employees of the Grunwick Film Processing Laboratories in Willesden, North London. In early 1978 the campus Conservative Association invited George Ward, who ran the plant, to make his first public speech since the dispute began. Salmond responded by tabling a motion at a meeting of the SRC that condemned Ward's visit 'since it was likely to lead to violent demonstrations'. Des Swayne, however, introduced another amendment welcoming Ward that was eventually passed.

Salmond, however, sought to extract maximum political capital from the meeting, accusing the Tory Steve Masty of using Ward's visit as 'a crudely engineered publicity stunt depending on a violent demonstration for its success'. The accusation of publicity seeking was a little ironic considering Salmond's own flair for self-promotion, and his exploitation of the Grunwick affair has to be considered in the context of his bid for the SRC presidency, which was then well under way.

Indeed, Salmond's manifesto appeared in the same edition of *Aien* that covered Ward's speech. 'The job of SRC President is basically one of an advocate,' he wrote. 'Two things are crucial if the job is to be done well. First, realising that priority should be given to things the SRC can change rather than to things which are outside its control and second having a good idea of what your priorities are.' Salmond's priorities included weekend library opening, 24-hour visiting in halls of residence, financial help for self-funding students and keeping up the pressure on failure rates among science students. 'These things can be done this year and will be done if the arguments are put clearly and forcibly,' concluded Salmond, 'which is the way to get a positive response from the University.'[59]

Salmond's campaign flyer (entitled 'Are YOU sitting on the Fence?') took a more humorous approach:

Dear Student,

In this leaflet I have tried to steer clear of the usual ridiculous drivel found in SRC leaflets, what a nice guy I am etc. What is surely more relevant is what my record is and what my policies are.

One final point. The basic division in student politics is not between left and right but between students and their own representatives. The one way that gap can be closed is for the SRC to be seen to be achieving results. That is what I pledge myself to ensure.

Yours aye,

Alex Salmond.[60]

He continued by reminding students that he had implemented the manifesto upon which he had stood as education vice-president the previous year. Although Salmond was well known on campus as chairman of the FSN, he stood for the SRC presidency on a 'Broad Left' platform.

At this point there was only one other candidate, a post-graduate divinity student called Bill Hogg who was also the SRC's publicity officer. He was, in Salmond's retrospective opinion, the best candidate, although it was the Conservative candidate, Peter Bainbridge, who posed a much bigger threat to his chances of success. The final result in what *Aien* described as 'the closest ever fought presidential election'[61] was nail-bitingly tense. Although Salmond pulled into an early lead of more than 100 votes, a new voting system meant Hogg's votes were reallocated according to his supporters' second preferences.

Initial reallocations were fairly even but after three hours of counting it became clear that Bainbridge was ahead, and he won by only 54 votes out of a poll of 1,311. On the face of it, however, Salmond had performed extremely well considering the relative strength of Nationalists and Tories on campus. Anticipating this, Salmond had enlisted virtually all the foreign students at St Andrews, who voted as a block, but it still had not been enough. Salmond came to refer to it as the only election he ever lost. 'It serves me right because I called him Braindamage throughout the campaign,' he reflected in 2008. 'Last I heard of him he was an executive with BP, doing very well.'[62]

Bainbridge, in fact, went on to work at RMIT University in Vietnam. He remembers Salmond being sharp ('not an intellectual but savvy and hard working') and possessing a 'caustic sense of humour and a clear determination'.[63] He also had 'faint memories of Alex storming out of the count quite vociferously'[64] following the declaration, something later denied by Salmond. 'Peter . . . acted like St Andrews Tories in those days in thinking they had a divine right to win every election,' he recalled in 2011. 'I had no hard feelings at all.'[65] Peter Brunskill also remembers Salmond's temperament in this sort of situation. 'I said to Alex once that he wasn't a good loser,' he recalled. 'He quoted Jackie Stewart: "Show me a gracious loser, and I'll show you a loser." He really felt it because he'd thrown everything into it. It was personal to him; he didn't think there was any need for graciousness in defeat.'[66]

It must have been all the more galling that Bainbridge, by his own confession, was a political 'amateur with no real interest in a political career', although he 'enjoyed the cut and thrust of political debate'.[67] Bainbridge did, however, contest the Clydesdale constituency for the Conservatives at the 1983 general election, abandoning active politics thereafter. Salmond later pinned a photocopy of the front page of *Aien*, which announced the result, to the wall of his office at Westminster, as a reminder of his early political failure.

Salmond's defeat coincided with the beginning of a steep decline in the SNP's electoral fortunes. This was clear from its performance in the May 1978 local government elections, as well as in three Parliamentary by-elections throughout the year. For Salmond, however, the experience was invaluable in both personal and political terms, and also betokened a growing inclination to take advantage of political circumstances.

One such opportunity presented itself at around the time of the SRC elections, when the Young Liberal magazine *Liberator* alleged that the Scottish wing of the Federation of Conservative Students had agreed to draw up blacklists of left-wing students for employers concerned about giving jobs to known trouble makers. 'Even Alex Salmond, not noted for his right-wing affinities,' reported *Aien*, 'conceded that no legitimate organisation unless it was ridiculously naïve would associate itself with such politically suicidal underhand activities.'[68]

Salmond had colluded with Brian Taylor, *Aien*'s editor, to get the story on the campus newspaper's front page, which was then picked up by the *Dundee Courier & Advertiser*. 'It concerned, of course, the outrage of Scotland's oldest university keeping tabs on potentially disruptive students,' Salmond joked in August 2008. 'There was a modicum of vested interest for Brian and I in exposing this story, it should be said . . . in retrospect I can find and see that it was an entirely sensible precaution. But the university's authorities were dressed up by Brian to look like a major sinister conspiracy.'[69]

The months leading up to Salmond's graduation were busy politically as well as journalistically. The sitting MP was Sir John Gilmour, whom Salmond defeated in a debate (assisted by the Nationalists Willie MacRae and Hamish Watt) on the Union in February 1978, while the prospective Liberal candidate was Menzies Campbell, and the Labour hopeful Henry McLeish. At an FSN day school Salmond (still its vice-president) launched a bitter attack on the economic policies of successive Tory and Labour governments. 'The Scottish economy has reached the point of no return,' he said. 'A generation of Westminster bungling and indifference has reduced Scotland, a country with immense economic potential, to the status of an underdeveloped region. The message coming from Westminster is quite clear – Labour government works, 200,000 Scots don't. The message we should send back is that only a Scottish Parliament with economic muscle and full control over Scotland's resources can pull Scotland out of the Westminster cycle of unemployment and emigration.'[70]

The similarity of Salmond's language to that used decades later is quite striking. There were also regional council elections that May, at which Dennis Macdonald and Salmond's friend David Hunt stood for divisions in St Andrews, and the Hamilton by-election on 31 May, at which Salmond once again campaigned for Margo MacDonald. More prosaically, that year saw him earning some extra cash by 'ball spotting' for the Royal and Ancient golf club.

Salmond collected his MA honours degree in Economics and Medieval History on 6 July 1978, having been awarded a second-class degree. Almost 30 years later, and just a few months after becoming First Minister of Scotland, Salmond took to the same stage in the Younger Hall to deliver the graduation address in November 2007. St Andrews University, he told them, had been a 'massive success story in Scotland'.[71]

# Chapter 3

# 'WEST LOTHIAN LEFT'

Alex Salmond left St Andrews University with the basic political beliefs and tactical instincts that would remain with him for the rest of his career. As the journalist Brian Taylor put it, 'he was almost a fully-formed politician even at that stage'.[1] Yet he also graduated during a difficult period in his early life: losing the SRC election had been a disappointment, while he also struggled, at least initially, to find work.

After graduating, Salmond moved back to his parents' house in Linlithgow – as is clear from a steady stream of letters to his local newspaper – and immersed himself in West Lothian politics, chairing the SNP's Linlithgow branch while applying for jobs. 'Alex wanted to be a journalist,' remembered Peter Brunskill, and indeed he was 'devastated' not to get a graduate position at BBC Scotland.

His failure might have been partly down to a slight speech impediment; a lispy delivery that meant Salmond's 'ths' came out as 'fs', something that had not been rectified by childhood elocution lessons organised by his mother. 'He was quite self-conscious about it,' recalled Brunskill, 'and it initially limited his opportunities to speak in public.'[2] Even so, it is also possible Salmond, despite his youth, contemplated attempting to become an SNP candidate for Scottish Assembly elections expected to take place in 1979.

By November, nearly six months after graduating, Salmond was still without a job. When a couple of English readers accused him of calling Scots émigrés 'unpatriotic' in a letter to the *Linlithgowshire Journal and Gazette*, Salmond replied that such a charge was 'ridiculous' given that 'the vast majority of the million Scots who have emigrated since the War have been forced to through lack of employment opportunities', and particularly so because he 'too will shortly, in all likelihood, be joining this sorry procession'.[3]

It appears Salmond found work at the Scottish Office – Whitehall's northern outpost – just as he was preparing to join that 'sorry procession' south of the border. The language is telling. While many of Alex's university contemporaries were perfectly content to head to England for employment (Michael Forsyth, for example, worked in PR before becoming a councillor in Westminster), Salmond certainly was not.

Having sat and passed the Civil Service entrance exam, Salmond ended up at the Department of Agriculture and Fisheries for Scotland (DoAFfS), which had a large Economic and Statistics Unit (ESU). He clearly found the work tedious and longed for something more stimulating. To make matters worse he was based at Chesser House, a grim government building on the outskirts of Edinburgh. Although Salmond's title, assistant agricultural economist, sounded reasonably grand, he was in his own description 'the lowest form of life in the Governmental economic service', carrying 'little pay and precious few privileges'.[4]

However pedestrian, the Civil Service also provided useful experience for an ambitious young economist. Salmond contributed to 'an estimable and serious journal entitled *Scottish Agricultural Economics*', while his ESU duties also took him to London, representing the Scottish Office at quarterly forecasting meetings in Whitehall. 'The first thing that struck us was that he was scruffy,' recalled David Dalgetty, a colleague with whom Salmond would lunch almost daily for about a year and a half. 'He had on an open-necked shirt and jeans. None of us looking at him at that time could have imagined he would become an under-secretary, let alone First Minister.'

Another regular luncheon companion was Tony Cameron, whose political outlook was closer to Salmond's. Together the trio usually discussed politics, and indeed there was plenty to talk about: the economic situation was bleak, the notorious 'winter of discontent' was imminent, and the age of Thatcher was less than a year away.

'I remember Alex being derisory about the socialism of the Labour government,' recalled Dalgetty, 'he was more socialist than they were; they weren't socialist enough.' He added: 'There was something in the soul of the man [Salmond] that burned with a sense of injustice to the Scots – everything was the result of exploitation or neglect of Scotland by governments in London. But when you went through all the arguments you were left with the impression that he didn't know if Scotland would be better or worse off as an independent country, all that mattered was that Scots should rule themselves.'[5]

Salmond, meanwhile, did not last long enough for anyone to ascertain how far he might progress, soon leaving to work at the Royal Bank of

Scotland. But before departing he had met an 'executive officer' called Moira French McGlashan, a motor engineer's daughter from Peebles, and on 6 May 1981 she became Mrs Alex Salmond following a service at St Cuthbert's Parish Church in Colinton, Edinburgh. Conspicuously, the *Linlithgowshire Gazette* carried no photograph of the happy couple, simply reporting that Alex was now 'settling down to married life'.[6]

The newlyweds soon moved to a new home at Rivaldsgreen House on Linlithgow's Friars Brae, Salmond having finally moved out of his parents' house at 101 Preston Road. Everyone who knew either Alex or Moira at this time recalls them being a perfect match, while their 17-year age gap was barely perceptible. Although not the political animal her husband was, Moira had significant political influence. She was among those unfailingly credited in pamphlets edited by her husband, taught him to drive shortly after their marriage and happily fed grateful firebrand Nationalists visting Alex in Linlithgow.

Some contemporaries, however, regarded Salmond's marriage to Moira with 'bemusement'. 'It was so out of character, so out of style with Alex generally,' recalled one, 'this young radical working-class person marrying someone not only 17 years older than him but, by her own admission, of a more Conservative-leaning background and so much more proper than he was.'[7] It certainly must have been a big decision for Salmond to make: by marrying a woman in her early 40s he was more or less deciding that children would not be part of his life. But while these considerations would intrigue journalists and, indeed, biographers, it is difficult to reach any conclusion other than that Salmond was deeply in love with Moira and wanted to spend the rest of his life with her.

When Salmond first met Moira Scottish politics was about to enter one of its most turbulent periods. Not only was the Labour government of Jim Callaghan in its death throes, it and every other party north of the border was preparing for a referendum on Scottish devolution, to be held on 1 March 1979, as well as an imminent general election.

The prospects for the SNP, and particularly its eleven Members of Parliament, did not look good. Opinion polls showed the Nationalist tide had turned, while there were also internal tensions between the party's Westminster representatives and its Edinburgh-based leadership. One such flash point concerned how the party ought to approach the 1978 Queen's Speech.

Salmond weighed in to the debate in a lengthy, and typically well-written, article for the *Scots Independent*, a monthly journal read by many

Nationalists although independent of the party. Salmond criticised a recent article by Douglas Henderson, the MP for East Aberdeenshire, as representing 'attitudes that can only bequeath the SNP missed opportunities in the present and serious problems for the future'. Instead he urged a more 'fruitful strategy':

> I'm not talking here about pacts or agreements, formal or informal. That idea would be rejected out of hand by all responsible nationalists. But what I am talking about is the difference between positive and negative policies. The difference between passively reacting to what the Labour Government decides to offer in 24 hours in November (which is what the Parliamentary Group appear to be doing) and positively seizing the political initiative by stating and restating what the SNP believe should be in the Government's programme (which is what I believe the Parliamentary Group should be doing).

He suggested an oil fund for the Assembly, an early date for the devolution referendum and safeguards against nuclear dumping.

> Then when the big day dawns, if the Queen's Speech has met a substantial part of the SNP programme our MPs could keep the Government in power safe in the knowledge that they had provided the Scottish public with devastating proof of our claim to be 'Good for Scotland'. If, on the other hand, the Government refused to meet the SNP priorities our MPs could bring them down safe in the knowledge that they had clarified the issues on which the election in Scotland could be fought and won.

Salmond was also concerned about the party's 'split leadership' which, if left unsettled, could produce a 'farcical' situation 'where there will be four separate branches of SNP leadership – one for Westminster, one for the EEC Parliament, one for the Assembly and one for the rest of us'. He took care to acknowledge the 'enormous problems' SNP MPs faced 'operating in a hostile Parliament reported by a hostile press' but urged immediate discussion 'if present and future Westminster balance of power positions are to be made to work for us rather than allowed to work against us'.[8]

The article demonstrated a strong tactical brain at work, with Salmond seeking to maximise the SNP's strength in a challenging political context. The pages of the *Linlithgowshire Gazette* also provided him with ample opportunities to defend and promote the aims of the SNP. In October 1978 he evangelised that

> Nationalists . . . want Scotland to achieve the same degree of economic success and social progress of every independent European nation. To that end the SNP have developed and published the most comprehensive and detailed policy programme ever offered to the people of Scotland . . . a programme based on radical democratic reform and social justice, designed to propel Scotland out of its present provincial backwater and back into the mainstream of world affairs as a free and prosperous country.[9]

In another letter Salmond put his economic expertise to good use:

> In the modern economy around 70 per cent of industry is 'footloose', i.e. it can locate virtually anywhere for similar costs. Far from being disadvantaged in a geographical sense Scotland is in an excellent strategic position for world trade in the American and European markets with unrivalled deep-water facilities . . . Scotland's fundamental economic problem is not distance from markets but distance from Government and the lack of the social and economic infrastructure that it is the duty of governments to provide.[10]

Unsurprisingly, Salmond saw the solution to Scotland's economic woes primarily in constitutional terms. In a letter to the *Guardian* written in September 1978, he railed against 'the complete failure of the English "quality" press to seriously analyse the political revolution that has occurred in Scotland over the past 10 years'. 'How many of your readership,' asked Salmond, 'have been informed of the motivation and philosophy of the party?'

The 40 per cent rule, under which 40 per cent of the Scottish electorate were required to vote yes in order for a Scottish Assembly to be established, was a particular bugbear for Salmond, and indeed for any serious supporter of devolution. 'I suggest that if democracy was being so abused in a UK referendum,' Salmond added in his *Guardian* letter, 'then you would be screaming criticism from every leader.'[11] Elsewhere, Salmond called this 'the most disgraceful distortion of democracy', and that ballot-rigging 'by which everybody who doesn't vote be they dead, on holiday or at home in the bath is counted as being against Devolution' was 'something which the Scottish people are unlikely to forgive or forget'.[12]

In January 1979 Salmond was appointed press officer for the West Lothian 'Yes for Scotland' campaign and, in advance of a public meeting at Linlithgow Burgh Halls, he demonstrated his willingness to work with political opponents. 'Anyone who cares about Scotland's future is welcome in this campaign,' he said. 'We intend to win this fight on the strength of the overwhelming arguments in favour of Devolution.'[13]

On constitutional strategy, Salmond was instinctively a 'gradualist', viewing devolution as a staging post on the road to full sovereignty, a belief he would hold for the remainder of his career. The *Scotsman* journalist Neal Ascherson later recalled watching as Salmond's campaign team 'deftly' slid 'its message into local papers and radio stations'. 'This group was a coalition of SNP, Tories, Liberals, Communists, the National Union of Mineworkers and some of the brightest survivors of the "Sillarsite" SLP,' added Ascherson. 'They took turns haranguing the shoppers in the Steelyard at Bathgate, who took pains not to be impressed.'[14]

An inactive local Labour campaign (on account of Tam Dalyell's opposition) also led to some covert activity which would no doubt have infuriated some local Nationalists. 'The Labour Party nationally were campaigning yes, but in West Lothian they were not campaigning,' recalled Stewart Stevenson, by then chairman of the West Lothian SNP. 'So Alex and I arranged to collect the leaflets and posters for the Labour Party and we ran a virtual Labour Party campaign on their behalf.'[15]

On 1 March 1979 both the Lothian and Central regions of Scotland voted 'yes', but only just. The result nationwide was similarly close and, having failed to secure a 'yes' vote from 40 per cent of the Scottish electorate, the Scotland Act – and with it the Scottish Assembly – was effectively dead in the water. To make matters worse, he had not been able to cast his vote. Salmond later explained to his local newspaper that his 'name had been entered by mistake on the absent voters' list'. Beyond a mad dash to his old student digs in St Andrews, there was not much he could do.

Following cursory attempts to salvage the Scotland Act through cross-party talks, the Labour government lost a motion of no confidence on 31 March by a single vote and, in a decision that was to haunt them for decades, the SNP's 11 MPs joined the Conservatives in the 'no' lobby. This, claimed the West Lothian Labour Party, meant the SNP had voted *against* devolution, something swiftly rebutted by Salmond: 'However much the SNP and the Liberals might like to accept the responsibility of bringing down a Government which has doubled unemployment and prices (and which is now engaged in strike-breaking against public sector unions) the fact is that Jim Callaghan was brought down by his own back-bench MPs. For Mr Dalyell and his fellow anti-devolutionists made it quite clear that they would rather see the Government fall than vote for the Devolution Act.'

Salmond concluded with a standard pop at the local MP. 'Mr Dalyell is not a bad MP for West Lothian because he is an aristocrat,' he wrote. 'He is a bad Labour MP for West Lothian because on issues like Devolution and the EEC he has ignored the democratic decisions of the Labour Party and the majority wish of his constituents.'[16]

The use of the word 'aristocrat' indicates Salmond's Marxist leanings during this period. Even the fact that Dalyell was a Black Bitch ('Alex and I are males of the species,'[17] he later remarked) did not absolve him, leading Salmond to conclude that on the issues of devolution and Europe 'he will be defeated at the coming election'.[18]

This proved to be wishful thinking. At the general election held on 5 May 1979 Billy Wolfe was again the SNP candidate, but was again defeated by Dalyell, this time by a decisive 36,713 votes to 16,631. In the rest of Scotland just two SNP MPs survived the electoral cull, and a few weeks later Salmond admitted the SNP had taken 'a real hammering', adding that 'the lesson that Scots should take from the results is that you cannot thwart a Tory majority in England by voting Labour in Scotland'.[19]

Completing an electoral hat trick were the first direct elections to the European Parliament in June 1979, at which the SNP polled a respectable 19.38 per cent of the vote, enough to elect Winnie Ewing in the Highlands and Islands. 'During that period I think Alex and I were surviving on about three hours' sleep a night,' recalled Stewart Stevenson. 'I lost a lot of weight and so did Alex, although he was already skinny, and it probably didn't do his health an awful lot of good.' He continued:

At the end of the campaigning day we'd go back to my house in Linlithgow and we'd work on the next day's press release, which I'd type up with several carbon copies. That would take us up to 1 a.m. and the next day I'd drive through to Edinburgh and distribute them to the media. Alex had a flair for organisation. He had a very clear idea that campaigning was a business activity with measurable inputs and measurable outputs and that it could and should be done in a professional way, that nothing you did was without a purpose. Yes you had to create the political environment that enabled people to vote for you but at the same time you had to identify the people likely to vote for you on the day and make sure that they did.[20]

Salmond, therefore, found the referendum and general election results profoundly depressing, later referring to 1979 as 'that *annus horribilis* in British politics'.[21]

Indeed, the referendum experience had a deep impact on the SNP as a whole. The 'experience of 1979 when the SNP had campaigned full tilt for an inadequate Labour scheme, while Labour campaigned half-heartedly,' reflected Salmond in 2000, 'had soured many in the party to the idea of being "entrapped" in the devolution process.'[22] It also convinced many Nationalists that no UK government could be trusted with consultations on Scotland's constitutional future, a suspicion that would cause Salmond problems as leader of the SNP more than a decade later. 'With the drumbeat of self-determination silenced,' he later observed bleakly, 'Scotland lapsed into a dark political decade of acrimony and recrimination.'[23]

Salmond, meanwhile, did not pursue a conventional political route within the SNP. While others pounded the streets, kept their heads down and drafted dull but worthy resolutions for the party's National Council, he took a much riskier option. It was the Australian-raised Scot Roseanna Cunningham who, together with her brother Chris, first floated the idea for what became the '79 Group' during the February referendum campaign. On the Saturday following the referendum 'defeat', Margo MacDonald, the party's deputy leader, also made an influential speech at a meeting of the party's National Council.

MacDonald's analysis was simple: while working-class Scots had voted 'yes' in the referendum, Scotland's middle classes had voted 'no'. The SNP, therefore, had to look to the former in order to build future support. Although this interpretation of the referendum result was flawed, eight Nationalists sympathetic to MacDonald's viewpoint met in Edinburgh on 10 March, and between 30 and 35 attended a second meeting at the city's Belford Hotel on 31 May. There, the clumsily named 'Interim Committee for Political Discussion' became the 79 Group with three spokesmen, Margo MacDonald, Andrew Currie and Alex Salmond.

Although not the group's leader as such, the former Lothian Regional councillor Stephen Maxwell quickly became an influential figure, while on the fringes was Billy Wolfe, whom Salmond had known for nearly a decade via West Lothian politics. Though no longer SNP leader following the 1979 general election, he became a sort of father figure to the 79 Group (or 'their stooge',[24] according to Arthur Donaldson, another former party leader). 'Not only did the West Lothian members enjoy the prestige of West Lothian SNP's long and vigorous challenge to the Labour Party in an industrial constituency,' observed Maxwell in 1985, 'but they were well organised and led by two of the "discoveries" of the Group: Alex Salmond . . . and Ken MacAskill.'

The latter was a radical young lawyer whom Salmond had persuaded to join the SNP following years of intermittent activism. Maxwell called this contingent the 'West Lothian Left', which also included Stewart and Sandra Stevenson, who hailed, like MacAskill, from Linlithgow. 'Their influence within the Group,' added Maxwell, 'helped to confirm a model of Scottish society in which the industrial working class figured as the only potential challenger to the British state.'[25]

In an early paper for the 79 Group, meanwhile, Salmond penned a critique of the SNP's performance in the late Parliament. 'There is a distinction to be drawn between policies and philosophy,' he observed. 'I would suspect that the Parliamentary Group of Oct 1974-May 1979 would come out rather well if an examination were made of the number of specific SNP policies they voted against . . . And yet I would say that, by in large [sic], SNP elected representatives have not presented an image consistent with Party feeling.'[26]

Later, in 1982, Salmond would reflect that 'the "all things to all men" approach, further muddied by the voting habits . . . of our Parliamentary Group, drove us to complete defeat in the class-dominated election of 1979',[27] another example of his then tendency to adopt a Marxist analysis.

The 79 Group's three guiding principles were Nationalism, socialism and republicanism, although as the academic James Mitchell recalled of a conversation with Salmond, 'he agreed with certainly one of the three objectives of the 79 Group – independence; [had] some sympathy with the second – socialism; but not a lot of sympathy with the third – republicanism'.[28] Rob Gibson, another contemporary, recalled that Salmond and MacAskill 'were more pragmatic and had a difference of emphasis; they didn't see the monarchy as the highest priority'.[29] Indeed, Salmond later told the journalist Arnold Kemp that he reckoned the group's biggest mistake had been its espousal of republicanism.

In Salmond's eyes the SNP's recent problems had not only been tactical, but also structural, and he was especially critical of the 'haphazard process' by which elections for party office were held. 'The result is to favour seniority and notoriety regardless of politics and, one suspects,

merit.' A 'remarkable feature' of the party, he added, had been 'that
it has been more of an apolitical party than a political one', so that
'political uniformity has not brought unity and conflicts have emerged
on a personal level rather than a political one. It may be unfair, but it is
certainly revealing, to point out that the most passionate speech at the
last National Council, climaxed by a Party Vice-President "gesticulating"
at the audience, was not over some philosophical divide but because
someone had suggested he was "heartless" '.[30]

Salmond, meanwhile, remained active in his local party. In April 1980
he was unanimously re-elected chairman of the Linlithgow branch while
it geared up for district council elections in which the SNP hoped to
secure a second term. Instead, Labour regained control of the council
and, demonstrating an emerging talent for presenting defeat in the best
possible light, Salmond said the Labour Party were 'now on a hook of
their own devising'. 'We shall see if the Labour promises made in this
campaign will stand in the political winds which will blow over the next
few years.'[31]

Salmond warmed to this theme at the Rothesay SNP conference in
June 1980. 'The Labour Party are political eunuchs who have neither
the will nor the means to stop Mrs Thatcher,' he told delegates. 'Despite
having a clear mandate from the people of Scotland, they have failed to
prevent the worst excesses of Thatcherism.'[32] Scotland, therefore, was
'totally helpless against a Government we did not elect but was forced
upon us by the Tory voters of the south-east of England'.[33]

This critique was to remain virtually unchanged over the next decade,
that of a 'feeble' block of Scottish Labour MPs unable to deliver a tangible
response to, or protection from, Thatcherism, although Salmond was
always careful not to rubbish the spirit of the Labour movement. 'While
many of us, as socialists, are attracted to the original aims of the Labour
Party,' he said in late 1979, 'we cannot stomach the sort of hypocrisy at
national level, incompetence at local level, and corruption at both, which
has disgraced Labour administrations over the past 25 years.'[34]

The aims of the 79 Group, meanwhile, were outlined in a series of 'papers'.
These varied in quality but two, *The Case for Left-Wing Nationalism* (No 6)
and *The Scottish Industrial Resistance* (No 7), came closest to putting flesh
on the bones of the group's thinking. The former, written by Stephen
Maxwell in 1981, proclaimed that 'the SNP must look to the urban
working class to . . . establish itself as the radical Scottish alternative to the
Labour Party'.[35] *The Scottish Industrial Resistance*, meanwhile, attempted to

explain how. This included an account of the Plessey dispute – during which more than 200 workers had 'occupied' the Bathgate electronics plant in protest at its planned closure – by Kenny MacAskill, who had given the workers creative, and ultimately successful, legal advice. This, according to an introduction by Salmond, was a key event in his party's development. The SNP's track record on industrial politics, he lamented, had not 'been a distinguished one' with no attempt to preach 'nationalism on the shop floor as well as on the doorstep'. As a result of 79 Group agitation, Salmond argued, the 1981 SNP conference had recognised 'that a real Scottish resistance and defence of jobs demands direct action up to and including political strikes and civil disobedience on a mass scale'.

It is clear Salmond took this strategy seriously. Writing to the *Glasgow Herald* in January 1982, he took issue with the 'argument that factory occupations damage the economy . . . Are you seriously saying that there would be production now at Lee Jeans and Robb Caledon if their respective workforces had not fought for their jobs. The mythology that militancy is a problem in Scottish industry conceals the reality that apathy has been the real weakness. And, given the impotence of their present political representatives, working people are starting to mount their own "Scottish Resistance" '.[36]

Salmond concluded *The Scottish Industrial Resistance* with a characteristic historical flourish: 'In 1812 Marshall Kutuzov startled his Czar by arguing that Napoleon's occupation of Moscow was irrelevant because "Russia is the army". In 1982 with our economy and political life still in tatters Scotland is our factories. For it is there that a real Scottish resistance has begun.'[37]

The driving force behind the 'Scottish Resistance' and 'civil disobedience' campaigns was Jim Sillars, who joined the SNP (and the 79 Group) just days before the 1980 SNP conference. Formerly the Labour MP for South Ayrshire and a hard-line Unionist, Sillars came to the party via his own breakaway grouping, the pro-devolution 'Scottish Labour Party'. Highly personable, his oratory blended humour, personal testimony, passionate advocacy and anger in the best tub-thumping Ayrshire tradition.

At this stage, the relationship between Sillars and Salmond was, according to the SNP activist Isobel Lindsay, akin to that of 'mentor and protégé'.[38] 'He is without question one of the most eloquent figures in Scottish politics and will prove an immense asset to the SNP,' Salmond told his local paper shortly after Sillars joined the SNP. 'His decision to

join the SNP now reflects the fact that the issue of Scottish self-government will not go away as the Tory and Labour leadership fondly hope.
Jim Sillars represents someone of intelligence and courage who has been
convinced of the necessity for independence by the force of argument. I
believe that many others will follow him into the SNP.'[39]

'He had a tremendous messianic speaking style,' Salmond recalled of
Sillars in 2001. 'They say . . . a diplomat's someone who can tell you to
go to hell and leave you looking forward to the trip; if you listen[ed] to
a Jim Sillars speech you could come to believe just about anything.'[40]
As the 79 Group's orator-in-chief, Sillars frequently worked his magic
at meetings in West Lothian, at Salmond's invitation, and around the
country.

Salmond, meanwhile, had spoken in support of the civil disobedience
policy at the 1981 SNP conference, the 'justification' being that 'we face
a Tory Government with less than a third of Scottish MPs; less than a
quarter of the Scottish electorate behind them at the last election . . . It's
a government of occupation that we face in Scotland, just as surely as if
they had an army at their backs, and when you think about it, perhaps
they have.'[41]

This was the firebrand Salmond, willing to use militaristic imagery
to convince Nationalists of his argument. But although endorsed by
conference, the twin campaigns enjoyed but a fleeting ascendancy. They
ran for only a few months, by Salmond's own admission, 'before being
overtaken by public opposition in the Party leadership'.[42] Nevertheless,
he pointed to a brief push above 20 per cent in the polls in November
1981 as proof the strategy had enjoyed public support, however transient.

Although Gordon Wilson, SNP leader since 1979, thought civil
disobedience was 'likely to backfire . . . particularly if some of the fringe
elements get to work'[43] and shrewdly made Jim Sillars responsible for the
policy, it was Salmond who drafted the proposals to put the conference
resolution into practice. This, observed Arnold Kemp, 'showed a subtle
mind at work'. 'The campaign was within the law and it was aimed at the
Labour grass-roots,' observed Kemp, 'bypassing the leadership.'

Salmond had also drawn inspiration from the nascent Solidarity movement in Poland, where the Polish flag had played a prominent symbolic
role. 'From the shipyards of Gdansk to the coalfields of Silesia,' he
said, 'the flag is hoisted to show solidarity with the struggle against an
unwanted regime. We in the SNP call upon the people of Scotland to
show something of the resistance displayed by the Poles, and raise the
Saltire on Sunday [St Andrew's Day] in protest against the unwanted

government, foisted upon our nation by the pampered south-east of England.'[44]

At the 1981 Aberdeen conference, the 79 Group appeared to be on a roll, with Andrew Currie elected vice-chairman for organisation and Sillars vice-chairman for policy. These were influential positions, while the group and its allies came within one vote of having a majority on the party's governing National Executive Committee (NEC), including a place for Salmond, at the age of only 26. He attended his first NEC meeting on 21 June 1981, during which he was elected to the SNP's Demonstrations Committee, along with Jim Sillars, and also its Election Committee, beating Winnie Ewing on a tie. This prompted an angry response from Margaret Bain, the former MP for East Dunbartonshire, which betrays how many in the party perceived Salmond at this time. She told Gordon Wilson she regarded Salmond 'as a lackey to the anti-MP faction within the party' and, therefore, 'devolutionists' and 'extreme lefties concerned (so they say) with the West of Scotland' would 'give no real cutting edge to the Scottish dimension'.[45] Such were the ideological and tactical divides within the SNP at that time.

Salmond, meanwhile, told his local paper he was 'highly pleased' with his election. 'The SNP have returned to the youthful exciting image which brought us success in the mid-1970s,' he added modestly. 'We have also come clean with the Scottish people and owned up to our distinct left of centre position on the political spectrum.' The aim, therefore, was for the SNP to 'build up the coalition of stable electoral support from the urban working class, the rural working class and the progressive section of the middle class which will win Scotland its independence'.[46]

During his year on the NEC, Salmond was a positive and reforming member to some, and a nuisance to others. One ally was Iain More, who liked that 'Alex was a supporter of change'.[47] They got along well despite both having applied for the post of SNP research officer in mid-1980. Although Salmond was deemed to be of 'high quality',[48] given the sensitivity surrounding HQ staff (many of whom had helped form the 79 Group), it is likely his political allegiances counted against him. When More resigned from the party two years later, Salmond said it was 'one of the tragedies of the Scottish National Party . . . that they don't make it easy for extremely competent achievers to have their head and get on with the job of building up the party.'[49] The 79 Group's hubris following the Aberdeen conference, meanwhile, was understandable, yet misplaced. The issue of Europe, for example, divided even 79 Group members, with

Sillars as strongly pro as Stephen Maxwell was anti (Salmond was by then supportive). There were other tensions. At a meeting in February 1980 Roseanna Cunningham proposed 'that the 79 Group opposes the [John] Corrie Abortion Bill in all its provisions as detrimental to women's rights in society'. That this was backed by a majority vote did not prevent Salmond querying 'the political relevance to the Group of this issue'.[50]

Beyond tactical considerations, Salmond had little time for abstract discussions about political ideology. He had 'no interest in the theories of nationalism,' recalled Stephen Maxwell. 'His eyes used to glaze over when we started discussing Gramsci, and I remember him once confessing [that] he'd never heard of him.'[51]

Direct action was anything but theoretical. On 16 October 1981 Jim Sillars and five other members of the 79 Group broke into Edinburgh's old Royal High School building. As an act of 'civil disobedience' the symbolism was obvious, but tactically disastrous. Salmond was not among them but did attend a demonstration to commend the act, telling the crowd that the 'SNP is committed to ensure that those who are prepared to undergo personal sacrifice in the pursuit of our policy of non-violent civil disobedience will not suffer any financial sacrifice'.[52]

The damage was only compounded, the same autumn, by the suggestion of formal links between Provisional Sinn Fein (PSF) and the 79 Group. The SNP's National Council had passed a motion of non-co-operation with Sinn Fein in 1980 but the 79 Group had discussed a request from the PSF to send a speaker to its annual conference. The 79 Group's executive, however, scented trouble. 'In response to the PSF letter, Alex Salmond, seconded by Chris McLean moved that we do not grant the PSF request,'[53] recorded minutes from a meeting in August 1981. Unfortunately for the 79 Group, a record of this meeting was then leaked to the *Glasgow Herald* via William Houston, vice-chairman of the SNP's Craigton branch, who was in the midst of a vigorous one-man campaign against the 79 Group.

There was obvious tension when the leak was discussed at the next meeting of the SNP's NEC. While Salmond 'said the minutes had not been ratified and contained several inaccuracies', Winnie Ewing claimed she 'had been contacted by Mr [Chris] McLean, Chairman of the 79 Group and he was satisfied that these minutes were substantially correct'.[54] Whatever the case the 79 Group was sufficiently concerned to make Salmond, Sillars and Maxwell available to answer questions about the incident over a 'pie-and-pint' lunch at the SNP's National Council. At the height of the Troubles in Northern Ireland, and with controversy surrounding the republican agenda of the 79 Group, this was hardly helpful coverage for its members.

Indeed, when the Campaign for Nationalism in Scotland (CNS) launched itself at the June 1982 SNP conference in Ayr, it pointed to the PSF incident and the Royal High School break-in as irrefutable proof that the 79 Group was a menace to the party. 'I am now fighting back for the survival of my party,' cried Winnie Ewing at a CNS fringe meeting. 'For the triumph of evil, it just takes good men to do nothing.'

The 'civil disobedience' policy, meanwhile, was being laid to rest. Salmond warned delegates that the SNP would be adopting 'a defeatist and cringing mentality'[55] if it foreswore the use of civil disobedience on matters of principle, citing the Plessey dispute to support his argument. 'Hostility to the policy was abated when the conference heard of Salmond's successful campaign aimed directly at the workforce,' observed Arnold Kemp, 'and this reduced the size of the majority by which the policy was abandoned.'[56]

Later, writing in *The Scottish Industrial Resistance*, Salmond called the conference decision 'perverse'. 'The Scottish character flaw that enables us to face difficult or even hopeless challenges bravely but proceed then to fluff the short putts in an agony of self doubt is a major psychological phenomenon,' he mused. 'Nothing is more terrifying than the prospect of success.'[57]

Then, on 4 June, long-running internal tensions came to a head. Despite the absence of any formal motion to proscribe the 79 Group on the conference agenda, in the midst of his keynote speech, Gordon Wilson said he was 'now convinced that the party will not recover its unity until all organised groups are banned'. 'Those of us who put Scotland and the party above narrow personal or political obsession,' he added, 'cannot and will not tolerate behaviour which is divisive and harmful.'[58]

With that, dozens of delegates rose to their feet to clap and cheer, while a few dozen members of the 79 Group marched out of Ayr's Dam Park Pavilion in protest, although Salmond was not among them. Significantly, the walkout overshadowed the main thrust of Wilson's speech, what the *79 Group News* described as 'an innovative strategy for a Scottish Elected Convention to draw up proposals for self-government'[59]. So personalities, more than policies, had brought the 79 Group to its knees. 'I don't think anybody going into the conference . . . thought that [it] would end with the party effectively in two armed camps,' reflected Salmond in 2001, 'of which it would have to be said that the armed camp against the 79 Group was bigger than the armed camp for it.'[60]

Wilson, however, had deliberately polarised the debate and in doing so, cleverly outmanoeuvred the 79 Group. He not only forced delegates to vote for or against the 79 Group, but by implication also for or against his leadership of the party, a bold move that generated some rare positive headlines. The majority for proscription – 308 votes to 188 – was decisive without being overwhelming, although the mood was strong enough to sweep Salmond, Rob Gibson, Kenny MacAskill, Roseanna Cunningham and Owen Dudley Edwards from the NEC on 19 June.

For the next few months the SNP's internal battles were played out in the correspondence columns of the *Scotsman*. In a long letter published on 24 June, Salmond accused certain SNP members of 'running away from political reality'. Instead, he argued, the 'reality of Scottish politics in 1982' amounted to the prospect 'of a Labour Scottish majority permanently isolated from power in Westminster'. Salmond pointed to two trends, 'the nationalist one in Labour and the Leftist one in the SNP', arguing that they were 'not mutually exclusive and indeed could be of substantial benefit to each other and to Scotland'. Finally he turned on Gordon Wilson's leadership. Although the Dundee East MP had 'correctly defined the SNP policy position' as 'moderate Left of Centre', 'most people in Scotland remain unaware of it and he seems hardly in any position now to strengthen the party's radical image'.[61]

Nor, however, was the 79 Group. When more than 100 members of the group met in Edinburgh's North British Hotel on 28 August 1982, a motion was passed disbanding the group as of 30 August. Crucially, that meeting also took the decision to simultaneously re-form under the same name, but with a wider membership drawn from other political parties. Wilson warned that members of this new organisation (subsequently called the Scottish Socialist Society, or SSS) were 'following a high-risk policy which could place in jeopardy their continuing membership of the SNP'.[62]

Indeed, a few weeks later Salmond received the following letter by first-class recorded delivery:

Dear Alex

Annual Conference 1982 – Resolution regarding organised political groups

I refer to your letter of 18 September 1982 in response to my letter of 13 September conveying to you the decision of the National Executive Committee in regard to organised political groups within the Party. As you have not indicated your resignation from the Interim Committee of the 79 Group Socialist Society, I have to inform you that you are expelled from membership of the Scottish National Party with effect from the date of this letter.

In terms of Clause 67 of the Constitution and Rules you are entitled to exercise a right of appeal against this decision.

Yours sincerely

Neil R MacCallum
National Secretary[63]

Six others, including Stephen Maxwell, Chris Cunningham and Kenny MacAskill, all received identical missives. 'The Scottish National Party,' stormed Owen Dudley Edwards in the *Scotsman*, a tad hyperbolically, 'by expelling Mr Stephen Maxwell, Mr Alex Salmond and their five associates, have committed intellectual suicide.'[64]

For the next few decades Salmond made light of his involvement with the 79 Group, in 2008 dismissing his expulsion as the result of being a 'brash young man'.[65] At the time, however, he found it deeply traumatic, while his already cool relationship with Wilson never recovered. Having been added to the SNP's list of approved candidates in June 1982, meanwhile, Salmond now had little chance of being selected to fight a seat at the forthcoming general election.

Idealist, impractical and ultimately quite damaging, the 79 Group proved an endeavour more worthy than wise. Always small in number – there were never more than 100 active members – it was tactically naïve, most notably over civil disobedience, while the assumption that every vote for Labour in 1979 was explicitly 'socialist' proved simplistic. Even had Salmond *et al* succeeded in convincing the SNP to declare itself 'socialist' in an attempt to displace Labour as Scotland's main political party, there was little evidence that it would have worked. In Wales, for example, Plaid Cymru had done precisely that in 1981, and achieved little electoral benefit.

In a 1990 interview, Kenny MacAskill acknowledged that 'lots of folk active in the 79 Group weren't socialists'. 'It was really an opposition group, a counterweight to the ruling party establishment, which tried to put forward fresh ideas on policy and strategy,' he explained. 'It was oppositionist; it didn't have firm views on ideological issues.'[66]

Even so, Salmond regarded the group's central aim as essentially correct. 'I regarded the issue of political identity and of arguing that case,' he later reflected, 'and also intervening in political issues, as the most important thing and I thought the work that the 79 Group, and the 79 Group members, [did] in supporting workers' occupations, in Bathgate for example, was absolutely fundamental.'[67] Later, he would also acknowledge a degree of youthful hubris: 'It was a bunch of Young Turks basically . . . absolutely certain that they knew everything there was to know about politics and we couldn't understand for a second why our elders in the SNP didn't see things our way.'[68]

Nevertheless, Salmond's involvement with the 79 Group also helped hone his media, propaganda and tactical skills, while consolidating some long-lasting alliances, most notably with Stewart Stevenson, Kenny MacAskill and Roseanna Cunningham. All became ministers when, under Salmond's renewed leadership, the SNP finally attained power. The experience also marked him out as a pragmatist. 'Some in the Group felt you had to polarise the debate in order to edge forward,' recalled Stephen Maxwell, 'others took a more pragmatic approach, of which Alex was one.' He continued: 'At no point was he simply a careerist just looking for personal advancement. He's not particularly profound – he's never written very much for example – but he was always quite keen on persuading people that they needed to think and analyse where Scottish politics was at, rather than indulging in reflexive nationalism.'[69]

Despite Salmond's best efforts, however, the 'reflexive' attitude of the SNP had resulted in his expulsion from the party of which he had been a member for less than a decade. But the future First Minister was nothing if not a great political survivor, and for this 'brash young man' his time in the wilderness would not last long.

## Chapter 4

# 'THE PRAGMATIC LEFT'

'I mean I get emotional about some things but I'm not a hyper emotional person,' reflected Alex Salmond in 2001, 'and therefore I was surprised at myself to the extent that even after a few years in the SNP I'd become extremely loyal and passionate about the party, and was extremely disconcerted not to be in it.'[1] Salmond later told the journalist Andrew Marr that the whole experience 'was traumatic enough to give him a strong desire to expel no one from the modern SNP'.[2]

'After the 79 Group expulsion he was much more willing than the rest of us to build bridges,' recalled Stephen Maxwell, 'he was the one keenest to remain in touch with the mainstream party.'[3] Several contemporaries observed that the whole affair, however, had noticeably hardened Salmond's character, fostering a determination never to appear vulnerable or weak.

His expulsion was effective from 20 September 1982, by which date Salmond and his allies had failed, as directed, to repudiate the Scottish Socialist Society (SSS) in writing. Salmond chaired its inaugural meeting in Glasgow on 30 October 1982. Writing in *Radical Scotland* a few months later, he declared that the SSS could 'play an increasingly important role in Scottish politics', drawing together 'Scotland's Left majority' in order to combat 'rampant Thatcherism' in its second term.[4]

Indeed, at this time there was much talk of 'realignment' on the Scottish left, the grand yet elusive design of socialists since the 1920s. There were even tentative gatherings at the New Town home of the political scientist Malcolm Anderson, attended by Salmond, Stephen Maxwell and Isobel Lindsay from the SNP, and figures like George Foulkes and Robin Cook from Labour. Nothing, however, came of them, although Salmond continued to tease Foulkes about them years later.

Jim Sillars, meanwhile, tried to persuade the SNP's ruling National Executive Committee to rescind the expulsions, while Salmond and Stewart Stevenson embarked upon a tour of selected SNP branches, screening a self-produced video of events at the Ayr conference. 'It was just a response to what had happened,' recalled Stevenson. 'It was Alex's idea – he persuaded me to find a video camera, which I did and we filmed some links. I put it together using three Betamax machines, although we were careful to put both sides of the argument.'[5]

The NEC and the party, however, were in no mood to forgive and forget, particularly when Wilson and others learned about Salmond's video roadshow. The expulsions were confirmed at a National Council meeting in Glasgow on 5 December, an act that struck many present as short-sighted. 'I remember sitting in the Moir Hall in Glasgow in late 1982 when the national council voted to expel the '79 Group, one of them being Alex Salmond,' recalled John Swinney 18 years later, 'and sitting there with my head in my hands thinking: "What on earth have we done? What are we doing to ourselves? We've lost the plot here, we've totally lost the plot." '[6]

Those expelled decided to appeal and Salmond asked Jonathan Mitchell, a young advocate and fellow 79 Grouper, to represent them. The Appeals Committee then met for seven Sundays between December 1982 and March 1983, taking some 40 hours to consider their case. Kenny MacAskill likened it to a 'Star Chamber' in the *Glasgow Herald*, while Jonathan Mitchell called it a 'quick little kangaroo court'.[7]

The 15-strong committee comprised a mixture of friend and foe. Stewart Stevenson, whose minority report ultimately secured the return of Salmond and others to the party, was an ally, although others such as Kenneth Fee and Bill Houston were sworn enemies of the 79 Group. Billy Wolfe, meanwhile, intervened on behalf of his West Lothian protégés. 'These two young men . . . whom I met for the first time 21 years ago next month,' he told Gordon Wilson, 'have been great nationalist workers.' Chris McLean, the SNP's press officer, also wrote to Wilson calling the Appeals Committee's report 'a travesty' and urging him to be conciliatory.[8]

The Appeals Committee, however, upheld the expulsions by nine votes to two, presenting its decision to the Larbert National Council on 30 April 1983. It concurred, by 157 votes to 138. 'The debate was reasonably restrained, but tense' recalled Gordon Wilson, 'and Alex Salmond, speaking for the appellants with a complete absence of nerves, made a notable contribution.'[9] He later recalled having been 'incredibly impressed by Alex's confidence, his articulacy. He spoke very smoothly and strongly and made mincemeat of the convener of the committee. That's when for the first time I took the view that he was a person who could play a leading part in the development of the party in future – if he behaved himself.'[10]

Following what Salmond later called 'the speech of my life',[11] the respected Nationalist Neil MacCormick put forward a creative compromise, commuting outright expulsion to temporary suspension (from 21 September 1982 until 25 May 1983) with the proviso that each suspended member wrote to the party's National Secretary accepting the National Council's position and requesting their suspension be lifted. Any appellant refusing to do so would remain expelled. 'This was accepted by an overwhelming majority and a sense of relief by delegates,' remembered Wilson. Although not all of the 'seven' agreed with these terms Salmond did, and was thus readmitted to the party. With that, four years of ruinous infighting finally ended. 'The 79 Group then disappeared,' wrote Peter Lynch in his history of the SNP, 'though it had a considerable legacy in terms of personalities and the ideological outlook.'[12]

Salmond duly returned to the SNP fold at the end of April, but that did not mean he abandoned the Scottish Socialist Society, which still aimed 'to marshall Scottish opinion for a counter-offensive against Thatcherism'.[13] The Society then began to produce a steady stream of literature devoted to articulating its 'socialist alternative', with Salmond contributing his editorial and journalistic skills to a newsletter, while a series of conferences attempted to put tactical flesh on rhetorical bones.

Salmond's professional and political careers, meanwhile, began to overlap. Not long after narrowly missing out on the job of SNP research officer in 1980, he had secured a position as an assistant economist at the Royal Bank of Scotland, where he would remain until entering Parliament seven years later. This, rather than the humdrum world of the Civil Service, was much more to Salmond's liking. He rose steadily through the ranks, becoming an oil, or energy, economist in 1982; and, from 1984, combining those duties with that of Royal Bank economist.

The Royal Bank of the early 1980s was not the global player it later became. Indeed, early in Salmond's tenure the Hong Kong and Shanghai Banking Corporation, or HSBC, moved to absorb the Royal Bank, followed by an outright takeover bid from Standard Chartered. 'Both bids were referred to the Monopolies and Mergers Commission' (MMC), recalled Salmond, 'and I found myself as a very young junior economist fetching and carrying for the bank team who were attempting to argue the impossible, ie one takeover was bad and should be disallowed while the other was good and should be given the OK.'

To everyone's surprise, however, the MMC actually 'alighted on the Scottish interest' and favoured retaining the bank's HQ in Edinburgh.

'After it recovered from the shock of being saved from itself,' noted Salmond with some satisfaction, 'the Royal Bank marched from strength to strength through the 1980s.'[14] This experience consolidated Salmond's economic and political thinking, chiefly a belief in government intervention, particularly that with a Nationalist undercurrent.

Working at the Royal Bank also planted a neo-liberal seed in Salmond's mind. 'I remember as a young economist working in the financial sector,' he recalled in 2010, 'how new financial instruments and innovative techniques had earlier been developed to exploit North Sea oil and gas.'[15] Not only would the wealth of the North Sea convince Scots to support independence, Salmond's argument ran, but the exploitation thereof could lead to even greater riches via the wizardry of the financial services sector.

Until the ignominious near-collapse of RBS in 2008, this portion of Salmond's CV was an invaluable political tool with which to counter political criticism of the economic case for independence. Salmond not only talked the language of economics but also had practised it professionally, and although the Royal Bank was not a big financial player between 1980 and 1987, it was respected. Salmond had also been part of the Royal Bank's public face, broadcasting and writing extensively on oil and gas economics for the Fraser of Allander Economic Commentary, *Petroleum Review*, *Opec Bulletin* and the *Three Banks Review*.

One of Salmond's projects also allowed him to indulge his historical interests. In 1983 he researched and compiled *The Royal Bank in Glasgow 1783-1983*, a pamphlet commemorating the Bank's bi-centenary in that city. Salmond revealed himself to be talented historian with an eye for a good quotation, and an engaging writing style that betrayed obvious affection for the Royal Bank, its history and character. He was particularly taken with Robert W. Service, a Scots-born poet and former Royal Bank employee who had 'found fame and some fortune' in Canada,[16] and in whom he obviously saw something of himself, slightly in awe of wealthy individuals and institutions. Even in the early 1980s, there existed political tension between two different Alex Salmonds: one a self-professed socialist, the other a liberal-minded financier.

Even though Salmond's activities at the Royal Bank were far removed from the less genteel world of Scottish politics, he consciously acquired deeper economic knowledge while working there, pouring over oil and energy statistics in the Bank's library, doubtless realising it would prove useful should he eventually become an MP. 'It was Alex's job to write, on yellowing paper, a weekly report on oil prices for those who were interested,' recalled the journalist and historian Michael Fry. 'That was his job, other than standing in the Abbotsford [an Edinburgh bar] with Grant Baird.'

Baird, a chain-smoking St Andrews graduate and former Bank of England economist, was not only Salmond's immediate boss as chief economist, but also a political ally. 'The fact that he was a Nationalist was Alex's essential qualification as far as Grant was concerned,' judged Fry. 'Bright young men leaving university, who were also Nationalists, were pretty thin on the ground in those days.'[17]

Baird was clearly very fond of his discovery, later praising Salmond's 'cool head' and 'ability to play a long game'.[18] The admiration was mutual, with Salmond following his boss's lead on viewing the European Community as an opportunity rather than a menace. The office Salmond shared with Baird was decorated with a poster from the magazine *Radical Scotland*, featuring Tom Nairn's dictum that 'Scotland will be reborn the day the last minister is strangled with the last copy of the *Sunday Post*'.[19] (A few years later, when Tories in Banff and Buchan tried to use this against their new MP, a rather oversensitive Salmond instigated legal action.)

Fry, as well as BBC Scotland's economics correspondent Peter Clarke, were frequent visitors. 'I would just turn up at their office and argue about economics,' remembered Fry. 'I was a monetarist and Alex was a Keynesian. He wasn't much of an economist but was obviously a talented student who could absorb information and argue about it.'[20] Similarly, Clarke remembered lunching with them 'most weeks'. 'They were a good duet, him and Grant Baird,' he said, 'if you needed a quote they gave you one; and unlike most men in suits they didn't dribble on in corporate prose. Alex pulled rank a wee bit because he loved being on radio and television, but he was what you might call a natural.'[21]

It was Clarke who came up with the idea that the Royal Bank ought to compile a monthly 'oil index', a statistical commentary on the latest trends in the North Sea. Salmond launched it in January 1983, later recalling that when Clarke told 'us another Scottish bank had already tried and failed, it presented a challenge we could not refuse. After a few months of preparation we secured the co-operation of all the oil companies and were ready to go public in January of last year'.[22]

Indeed, Baird remembered that 'we went all over Aberdeen and saw all the big oil companies. All of them signed up except BP, so Alex said to them, "well we've got Esso, Shell and so on; if you won't agree we'll publish it anyway and say you wouldn't co-operate". So he actually persuaded them. One of the great things about him was a very good tactical sense, a very good tactical brain.'[23]

The index acted as a month-by-month guide to the level of oil production, while the commentary placed a value on output and forecast the effects of oil on government revenues and the Balance of Payments. 'We look to appeal not just to the specialist but also to the general public,' explained Salmond on its first anniversary. 'For example we don't just talk about Government oil revenues being worth £9,500 million in the current fiscal year, but point out that this figure represents over £1m every hour of every day through the year.'

The index's high point came when it successfully predicted that the government was underestimating oil revenues (in 1984) by £1,000m. 'The Treasury seemed quite pleased that we had found the money for them,' commented Baird. 'Unfortunately they didn't offer us the usual finder's fee of ten per cent.'[24] This quote helps explain why Baird got on so well with his young protégé; Salmond liked people who were sharp and amusing, and Baird was both.

But however much Salmond enjoyed his work at the Royal Bank, politics remained his primary focus. 'It was his life', remembered Grant Baird's wife, Glynne, 'that was his driving force.'[25] Similarly, Peter Brunskill remembers visiting Alex and Moira in Linlithgow in around 1983. 'They were great together,' he said. 'I remember Alex showing me videos of all his political activities over the previous few years, and Moira was as interested in all the stuff Alex was showing me as I was.'[26] By then, Salmond had an impressive collection of political footage stretching back to the late 1970s, preserved for posterity using a Philips Video 2000 recorder.[27]

Although the Royal Bank allowed its staff to engage in political activity, his activities in this arena must occasionally have led to furrowed brows in the boardroom. Perhaps conscious of this, Salmond billed himself as an 'economist', or an 'economist working in the financial sector', when writing for *Radical Scotland* or the *Scottish Government Yearbook*. For both, Salmond made a special study of British Leyland's management at Bathgate, while making use of his Royal Bank expertise in talks to branches of the Federation of Student Nationalists. Occasionally he could kill two birds with one stone. In 1985, Salmond co-wrote *The Oil Price Collapse* with Dr Jim Walker of the Fraser of Allander Institute, who would succeed Salmond as Royal Bank economist in 1987.

From 1983 the SNP began to rebuild under the steady if unflashy leadership of Gordon Wilson. Determined to maintain a broad church, Wilson stressed that the party had 'always had a radical, left of centre bias',[28] although this had clearly become a little too inflexible for his liking. Three policy positions were within Wilson's sights: the SNP's anti-NATO policy, its antipathy to membership of the European Community and finally its fundamentalist constitutional stance of 'Independence – nothing less'.

The results of the 1983 general election demonstrated what a monumental task Wilson faced. The SNP lost 54 deposits and slipped from 17.3 to 11.8 per cent of the vote, squeezed by the SDP/Liberal Alliance and a surprisingly resilient Tory vote. Of the nine SNP MPs defeated four years before, seven contested seats in 1983 but not one was returned. This ensured that not only did Gordon Wilson remain leader, but that figures such as Salmond and Kenny MacAskill were able to rise within the SNP without much competition from the party's Old Guard.

In order to unite a still fractious party, Wilson established a Commission of Inquiry to examine the SNP's organisational structure, which remained largely unchanged since reforms initiated by Billy Wolfe in the 1960s, and invited Salmond to join Alasdair Morgan and John Swinney ('all of whom were rising in the Party'[29]) as representatives of the SNP's National Council on the Commission. Salmond looked at the party's branches and constituency associations, concluding that the latter should receive more resources and greater representation at the annual conference, while district and regional associations ought to be abolished. Salmond also reflected that the SNP's 'lack of organisation in workplaces may be one reason why our strength in the country has not been reflected in the trade union movement'.[30]

The previous year's SNP conference at Rothesay, meanwhile, had proved central to Wilson's strategy of nudging the party back into political reality. A resolution easing opposition to the European Community was moved by Salmond, supported by Winnie Ewing, shored up with effective speeches from the Jims Fairlie and Sillars, and endorsed overwhelmingly. But Wilson's proposal for an elected 'Scottish Convention' to determine Scotland's constitutional future was defeated, despite the backing of Salmond and Sillars. Nevertheless, on reflection Wilson thought 'the 1983 Conference was one that altered the course of the Party radically and in my view for the better. The gamble had paid off. The separatist, isolationist image had been shattered.'[31]

From 1984 most prominent Nationalists agreed on broad strategy, even if there were varying personal emphases. 'The most notable political figure to emerge during this period was Alex Salmond,' judged the academic James Mitchell a few years later. 'His view that the SNP required to project a clear position on socio-economic matters did not lead to the party changing its policies so much as presenting them more coherently. The "moderate left of centre" label, pro-European position and advocacy of a constitutional convention were widely accepted.'[32]

The constitutional convention, usefully, could conclude in favour of either full independence or devolution, neatly reconciling so-called 'gradualists' and 'fundamentalists' within the party. Tentatively, meanwhile, the SNP began to engage with the Campaign for a Scottish Assembly (CSA), a cross-party group it had hitherto shunned. Salmond thought this attitude reflected his party's lack of self-confidence. 'It is my opinion that when the SNP is about to make a leap forward and grow it takes a relaxed attitude to self-government,' he observed in 1984, 'but when it is on the defensive it adopts a tight, narrow attitude.'

Salmond was one of the delegates chosen by the NEC (which he had rejoined in late 1983) to meet the CSA's executive. 'They are not earth shattering in importance but do provide a useful method of focussing debate,' he later reported. 'Not to go would confer a political penalty, which, of course, is why the Labour Party have started to attend albeit in a semi-official capacity.' The NEC agreed, and for the next two years Salmond acted as the SNP's main liaison with the CSA.

The party's 'pragmatic left', as the academic Roger Levy called it, was in the ascendancy. Their aim was to target the Labour vote on a number of specific social and economic issues while gradually softening the party's position on constitutional reform. Salmond urged 'sustained discussion of the political options facing the Party' at the NEC level. 'Knowing what you are doing and why is not a sufficient condition for electoral success,' he reasoned, 'but, in the medium term, it is a necessary one.' He believed that the 1983 general election had revealed the 'fulcrum' of Scottish politics to be on the left, and therefore the SNP ought to put Labour on the defensive with a series of cross-party anti-Tory campaigns. But when a strategy paper to this effect was considered by the NEC it simply 'noted the paper and thanked Salmond for leading the discussion'.[33]

Responding to an opinion poll suggesting that a third of Labour voters supported independence, Salmond expanded on his strategy via the *Scotsman*'s letters page, observing that

> the fact that people who support independence vote for the Labour Party confirms the pre-eminence for most people of social and economic issues over constitutional ones. This may be irritating to many in the SNP but it is unlikely to change. One solution . . . [is] for the SNP to present a stronger political profile, not, I repeat not, by adopting "extreme Left"

policies but rather by being prepared to accept a Left of Centre label on the radical policies the SNP already largely possesses. This should both help voters to identify the SNP more clearly as a *political* party and also assist the SNP's leadership in making judgments on the day-to-day issues on which there can be no detailed policy.

In other words, the SNP should 'win over the independence voters currently supporting Labour'.[34] But Salmond's analysis was simplistic. Not only did it rest too heavily on one opinion poll; it implied a degree of engagement with independence from a section of Labour voters that arguably did not exist. 'Our economic policies are radical but our social policies are conservative, because that's the way Scotland is,' was how Jim Sillars characterised the SNP's 'pragmatic left' grouping to the *Toronto Star* in August 1986. 'That's why we wear suits. The striped-jersey style of British, leftist, polytechnic lecturers doesn't go over here.'[35] Both Salmond and Kenny MacAskill did indeed wear suits; usually grey ones with red ties, perhaps in an effort to resemble Labour apparatchiks of the time.

Central to the Salmond/Sillars analysis was that Scotland and England were different. As the 1980s progressed, they reasoned, England was becoming an inescapably Conservative country, whereas Scotland was, if anything, becoming more socialist. Sillars identified the consequence as 'an active and progressive nationalism, not ugly, not born of a desire to do down anyone else, with a wish to free the energies and attributes of the Scottish people so that they can engage not only on the reconstruction of our own society but on the problems that keep the vast mass of humanity in a miserable existence'.[36]

In early 1985, meanwhile, the SNP's Commission of Inquiry finally published its recommendations. National Secretary Neil MacCallum said the party had become 'too bureaucratic, too introspective and too conservative'[37] and recommended abolishing the National Assembly and strengthening the party's central leadership by appointing a general convener and general secretary while streamlining the NEC. Covering the report, the *Glasgow Herald* depicted Salmond and Kenny MacAskill as the comeback kids, 'highly articulate and full of talent',[38] determined to seize executive control of their party.

Almost every proposal in the 42-page report, however, was thrown out by a special conference in Stirling on 23 February. After almost two years' work and hundreds of hours devoted to gathering evidence, Salmond felt understandably resentful, particularly towards Gordon Wilson, whom he believed should have utilised more fully the fruits of his labours. In a surprising volte-face, Wilson explained that he had established the Commission in a panic following the 1983 general election, and now that the party had stabilised the need for radical organisational reform had passed.

Salmond, however, remained active on the party's unreformed NEC, developing an already keen, and occasionally devious, tactical style. 'I remember him asking me to push this line for him at an NEC meeting he couldn't attend,' recalled Isobel Lindsay, 'and he said "if it looks as if you won't get the votes try and leave it to the next meeting". Now I didn't feel particularly strongly about it but I got it postponed to the next meeting. Alex then came in the following month and says "I see, looking at the minutes, that at the last meeting Isobel and someone else took rather extreme positions so let me try to find a compromise!" '[39]

Salmond had long coveted Lindsay's old post of vice-convener for publicity, first standing against her in 1982 (he had lost by 373 votes to 161), and then against the journalist Colin Bell in 1983, when he lost by 251 votes to 177. The party, however, seemed conscious that Salmond's abilities were not being put to good use. In May 1984 Gordon Wilson asked him to act as campaign research director for that year's autumn 'Save Scotland Campaign', while in August 1984 Bell included Salmond's name on a list of potential party broadcasters.

At the 1985 SNP conference Salmond was finally elected to the publicity post, his victory being further evidence of his restored standing within the party hierarchy. Just two years ago he had not even been a member, and had only rejoined the NEC 18 months before. Gordon Wilson was not yet disturbed by Salmond's rise, noting in his memoirs that he 'was already an experienced and skillful politician'.[40]

The position played well to Salmond's strengths as a talented SNP propagandist. He wanted to concentrate more on direct-mailing techniques, as well as an SNP letter-writing club to circulate supportive comments to the press. Salmond also had 'reservations' about the 'exact style' of the new logo developed in 1984 (this was a more casual version of the traditional thistle motif, looking as if it had just been painted on a wall), although he accepted 'the underlying idea of updating our symbol'.[41]

Salmond wasted little time on assuming office. On 9 March he told the NEC that he would breakfast every Friday with Chris McLean, SNP press officer, and Alan McKinney, the National Organiser, to plan and co-ordinate short-term activity such as press releases. Meanwhile, Salmond asked Jim Sillars, John Swinney and, interestingly, Isobel Lindsay to assist him as members of the party's Publicity Committee, which he now chaired. 'This post – probably the most important of the Party's five Vice-Chairs – also includes Campaigns and PPBs,' observed an approving *Radical Scotland*, 'which effectively makes Salmond's 8-person sub-committee into the SNP's Saatchi & Saatchi.'[42]

Following his first spring campaign in charge of publicity, Salmond was full of confidence, telling conference that the 'SNP's campaigning strength has been renewed. We are once more a credible political force – and self-government is once again on the Scottish political agenda.'[43] He subsequently unveiled 'The New Scotland Campaign' and addressed 'the SNP's perennial problem of having little or no social and economic profile'. Salmond wanted to campaign on a 'limited number' of issues to combat this, including Scotland in Europe ('We should move on to the offensive with our new EEC policy'); a renewed oil campaign ('Hardly a new issue but it can be revamped'); the Scottish Convention policy ('Important to indicate SNP are examining the mechanics of transferring power from Westminster to Scotland'); and 'One Social Issue' ('Probably housing is the issue which provides the most scope for developing in a variety of ways'). 'It is important to define our objective in these attacks', he concluded, 'apart from our understandable desire to be nasty to our opponents.'[44] The *Free Student Press*, created by Salmond in 1975, was to be relaunched, while he urged longer annual conferences in order to maximise party publicity.

Though there remained a 'fundamentalist' and 'gradualist' divide in the SNP, the 'pragmatic left' held the advantage. 'From this period on,' observed Gordon Wilson, 'there was relative unity within the party as it entered a series of political campaigns over the steel industry, coal and education.'[45] These demonstrated that the SNP, with Salmond in charge of publicity, had returned to its (and the 79 Group's) industrial strategy of the early 1980s. To this end Salmond met with Campbell Christie, the new general secretary of the Scottish Trades Union Congress and an articulate devolutionist. He also persuaded the NEC to back a new publication, *SNP News*, partly to compete with the *Scots Independent*. By January 1986 this was self-financing, with circulation having risen from an initial run of 30,000 to 45,000.

By March 1986 Salmond was busy preparing campaigns on the future of Dounreay, British Steel at Gartcosh and the controversy surrounding the government's cold climate allowance and its application in Scotland.

It was, arguably, during the period 1985-86 that the Conservative government lost the political initiative north of the border, with it appearing hostile to the very concept of 'Scottishness'. Most elements of the Salmond strategy were in place by the regional local government elections of April 1986, at which the SNP's principal slogan was 'Play the Scottish Card'.

It appeared to pay off, with the SNP polling 18.2 per cent of the vote, up nearly 5 per cent compared with 1982. By now a great believer in sustaining political momentum, Salmond's sights were now set on an autumn campaign ('designed to build on that success'), that would also serve as a launch pad for the general election expected in 1987. 'Our job is to produce the Scottish dimension to that debate,' he urged, 'but at all costs we must avoid being pushed to the fringes of what are perceived to be the "real issues" of the campaign.'

Even at this stage, however, Salmond was not without his critics. In September 1986 one vice-convener 'expressed concern about the method of preparation of Autumn Campaign material',[46] while he also clashed with John Swinney, then the SNP's acting National Secretary, over who would lead a press conference launching that year's conference agenda. Although Swinney was supposed to fill this role, it seems that Salmond decided he would do a better job. 'I spoke with the Executive Vice Chairman who indicated that although unwilling to "pull rank", he had every intention of doing so,' complained Swinney to Gordon Wilson. 'He said it was necessary to have an elected Office Bearer leading the Press Conference as I held office only in an appointed capacity. He refused to acknowledge any merit in the argument that as Convener of the Standing Orders and Agenda Committee I was entitled to lead the Press Conference. He also made no comment on the fact that I executed all functions of the National Secretary's position without question or quibble yet was being denied this opportunity to fulfil the post.'[47]

It was typical of Salmond to spot a weakness in another's position – in this case Swinney's lack of party mandate – and exploit it to ruthless effect. This spat also illustrated Salmond's fondness for getting his face on television, although his use of non-party members to assist in preparing campaigns and television broadcasts also got him into trouble. Technical assistance for the autumn campaign had come from two leading lights in Jim Sillars' defunct Scottish Labour Party, Bob Brown and Alex Neil, the latter a future MSP and minister. The *Glasgow Herald* quoted a 'leading right-winger' complaining about Salmond's decision to 'consult such eminent Left-wingers', but the publicity vice-convener argued that

Brown and Neil were both 'sympathetic to the SNP', adding that he asked 'advice from a wide range of people, many outwith the party, for professional reasons'. 'That is the way I work and will continue to work,' was Salmond's uncompromising conclusion. 'I would consider anyone's skills if it benefited the party.'[48]

Nevertheless, after 18 months in control of the party's publicity machine, Salmond believed he had made considerable progress. 'I remain relaxed about Party morale and unity and the mood at Annual Conference vindicates this viewpoint,' he reflected. 'Relative to the other parties our internal mood is excellent and a complete transformation from the position at the last election.'[49] The SNP, with considerable help from Salmond, now geared up to fight a general election.

From the outset Salmond thought a third Conservative victory was the most likely outcome of the election, although this did not preclude the possibility of the SNP performing well in Scotland. Publicly, however, Salmond promoted the 'hung Parliament' strategy, under which the SNP could extract concessions for Scotland should neither the Conservatives nor Labour gain overall control in the House of Commons, a strategy he would deploy at almost every general election thereafter. 'We will demonstrate', he explained, 'that a vote for the SNP is the one sure way to guarantee real progress for Scotland in the next parliament.'[50]

The hung Parliament strategy, however, had its critics, including Gordon Wilson. Undeterred, and having commissioned a £20,000 study of Scottish electoral attitudes, Salmond predicted the SNP were 'set to oust seven Tory MPs at the coming Election – one third of their total representation in Scotland – and our most spectacular gains will come between the Tay and the Moray Firth'.[51] The survey also revealed that 45 per cent of the electorate might vote SNP under certain circumstances, prompting Salmond to highlight 'the tantalising prospect that a bridgehead breakthrough might be possible in Central Scotland before the election if the Labour Party is brought under pressure during the Campaign'.[52]

It was during this election campaign that Salmond first pursued the SNP's soon familiar 'anti-Scottish Tory Party' theme. 'Anti-Scottish is the phrase which, better than any other, sums up how the vast majority of Scots view Mrs Thatcher's English Tory regime,' he explained. 'Just a few of the Tories' policies make it crystal clear that they are a Government of the South of England, elected by the South of England, for the South of England.'[53] In May 1987, meanwhile, Salmond stormed 'not since the

Spanish stole the Inca gold has there been a case of robbery on such a grand and international scale',[54] a reference, of course, to revenue from North Sea oil.

Privately, party planning was geared towards winning between 8–10 seats, while in public Salmond predicted at least seven gains (in addition to the two seats it already held) and a possible total of 12 MPs. One of the SNP's top target seats was the rural constituency of Banff and Buchan, for which Salmond had been selected two years before. The impetus had been his speech supporting Gordon Wilson's policy of an elected Scottish Convention at the 1984 party conference. 'The chairman of the Banff and Buchan constituency at the time, Alex Sim, saw the speech,' recalled Salmond in 2001, 'and thought this is the kind of guy we should be including in our panel of candidates and approached me at the conference.'[55]

Banff and Buchan had one of the smallest majorities in Scotland, the former SNP MP Douglas Henderson having come within 938 votes of defeating the Tory incumbent Albert McQuarrie in 1983. That Salmond was headhunted to stand in the SNP's most winnable seat seems remarkable. He had no local connections and just three years before had been expelled from the party.

In January 1985 his name had been added to a short list of four (another of whom was councillor Mike Weir, later an SNP MP) drawn up by the Banff and Buchan constituency association. This led to charges of 'discrimination' against local candidates from councillor Jim Ingram, who told the *Press and Journal* that his name ought to have been in the final four.[56] Douglas Henderson, meanwhile, lobbied against Salmond, deepening Alex's already negative attitude towards the former MP.

When Salmond was selected a few weeks later by a single vote, Ingram decided not to renew his SNP membership, while his fellow councillors Sam Coull and Ian MacKinnon also quit the party citing 'growing left-wing influence'.[57] By that, the trio presumably meant Salmond, which goes to show how long the wounds caused by the 79 Group took to heal in some quarters of the party. 'I feel it is only Tory by default and that being Left is not only compatible but necessary in that seat,' Salmond told the *Glasgow Herald*. 'It was only held by 900 votes last time and if we unite the anti-Tory vote in a constituency with a high working-class population, then it will come back to us.'[58]

Later, Salmond remembered 'some understandable internal resistance to the idea of a left-winger, not long restored to membership after expulsion, standing for a key target seat in the North-east'. 'I wasn't too pleased at the time but, in retrospect, it was the best thing that could have happened,' he added. 'In particular, the constituency was united in the belief that the way to win Banff and Buchan was to offer a radical alternative to the Tory incumbent, not some sort of substitute.'

Salmond must have been delighted. 'No one of my generation in the SNP seriously expected to pursue politics as a full-time career as opposed to a passion or a hobby,' he later reflected. 'Lots of people were willing to travel hopefully. Few expected to arrive.'[59] And now he was on course for the House of Commons, Salmond wasted no time in transforming himself from an urban socialist into a champion of rural Scotland. He suddenly discovered an interest in the fishing industry and even trans-ferred his footballing 'allegiance from Tynecastle to Pittodrie, for obvious reasons'.[60]

The Royal Bank, however, had 'difficulty in adjusting to the fact that one of its economists wanted to be an MP'. Grant Baird and chief executive Charles Winter, however, turned out to be Salmond's 'friends and protectors', not least when the Scottish Conservatives 'organised a letter-writing campaign threatening to withdraw their accounts if the Royal allowed an employee to stand as a Scot Nat'. Winter ('a lovely man') even showed Salmond a bundle of 'sack him' letters in the bottom of a drawer when it was all over. 'After first finding it hard to accept that I really wanted to do it,' he recalled of Winter, 'he stoically refused to believe that I had any chance of winning.'[61]

Salmond's principal opponent was the Tory incumbent Albert McQuarrie, who revelled in his 'Buchan Bulldog' epithet. SNP support was mainly concentrated in the seat's coastal areas but Salmond was confident it would change hands 'on a puff of political wind'. He targeted 4,000 first-time voters with direct mail and the slogan 'Only 938 more to win',[62] a reference to McQuarrie's modest majority, while calling upon Stewart Stevenson, who had developed an early computer system to catalogue every constituent and their voting intentions, and his brother Robert, who took time out from his studies at Aberdeen University to support his older sibling's bid to become an MP. Moira Salmond even ironed his SNP rosette for him every day, sending him out, as the *Scotsman* noted, 'in the neatest political shape'.[63]

The journalist John MacLeod, then a young SNP activist, recalls encountering Salmond at campaign HQ in Edinburgh at around this time.

He was the only who sat down with us, stuffed a few envelopes alongside us . . . and seemed not only to appreciate our efforts but genuinely be interested in us. He was hard to place. There was an extraordinary calm about him – a self-possession, a security, a centredness that was at once real, sincere, cool, and calculating. A cynic might suggest he already had serious internal ambitions and already aspired to climb higher, and climb soon, and was smart enough to know that fanatical envelope-stuffers might, even that very autumn, be Annual National Conference delegates.[64]

And climb the cool, calm and collected Salmond did. The election also boosted his profile nationally, with appearances on Radio 4's *Any Questions* and the BBC's *Question Time* alongside Ken Clarke, Alan Beith and Denis Healey. Salmond, judged the *Glasgow Herald*'s Julie Davidson, 'is one of our most able young politicians'. 'Relaxed and unintimidated by the heavyweights from Westminster,' she wrote, 'he brought grace and humour to his contribution, as well as fluent intelligence.' 'He will go far,' concluded Davidson wryly, 'but probably not with the SNP.'[65]

That was surely a joke, for Salmond won Banff and Buchan decisively, with a majority of 2,441 on a 3.9 per cent Tory-to-SNP swing on a 71 per cent turnout. Salmond's father Robert called his son's eve-of-poll speech 'one of the highlights of my life', while his mother Mary recalled being 'over the moon'.[66] Albert McQuarrie, the defeated Tory candidate, was singularly ungracious, refusing to shake Salmond's hand at the count, and announcing for all to hear that he would not 'shake hands with scum'. Not only that, but Salmond believed he had won by a much bigger margin than the official result, a suspicion fuelled when the returning officer refused to let him inspect certain bundles of ballot papers. When, a few days later, Salmond called on Charles Winter at the Royal Bank to say his farewells, 'he promptly offered me my job back after the next election'.[67]

Alexander Elliot Anderson Salmond, aged just 32, was now a Member of a Parliament that he did not acknowledge as having any legitimacy to govern Scotland. A discussion paper written by Salmond and Isobel Lindsay hinted at how he was likely to respond once he reached the green benches. 'SNP M.P.s could use Parliamentary procedures to delay legislation,' it had suggested, 'certainly the Scottish Grand Committee and the Scottish Standing Committees will need to be exposed as sham institutions or turned into effective ones.'[68] After his declaration, meanwhile, Salmond had promised 'to break the power of English Toryism over the Scottish people'.[69] The stage was set for an eventful two years in the life of the new Member for Banff and Buchan.

Chapter 5

# 'THE INFANT ROBESPIERRE'

There was the usual convivial atmosphere as Members filled the House of Commons on Budget day, 15 March 1988. While Nigel Lawson, Chancellor of the Exchequer since 1983, settled onto the government benches, the SNP's three MPs – Margaret Ewing, Alex Salmond and Andrew Welsh, all elected the year before – took their usual places opposite.

By long-standing tradition the Budget statement was heard in respectful silence by Members on all sides of the House, as it was as Lawson worked towards a section – widely trailed in the media – announcing a cut in the basic rate of income tax. 'Lawson was a tease,' remembered Salmond. 'Time and time again it looked like he was coming to the key passage only for him to announce some other gimmick.'[1] Hansard recorded what happened next:

Mr Nigel Lawson: The basic rate of income tax for 1988–89 will be 25 pence in the pound. The small companies' rate of corporation tax will similarly be reduced to 25 per cent. This means that the basic rate of income tax and the corporation tax rate for small companies will both be at their lowest level since the war.

Mr Alex Salmond: This is an obscenity. The Chancellor cannot do this. [Interruption]

Mr Deputy Speaker: Order.[2]

Salmond's intervention had been barely audible above the ensuing uproar, although the *Glasgow Herald*'s lobby correspondent reported hearing him shout 'Tax cuts for the rich, the poll tax for the poor' before adding 'a protest about the lack of any extra cash for the NHS'.[3] 'Lawson sensibly ignored me,' recalled Salmond in 2000. 'However, the Tory benches started to roar and the Commons authorities turned my microphone off. Pandemonium broke out. Lawson turned to Thatcher and I could read his lips saying: "This is terrible." '

Salmond also remembered the withering look he was shot by the Prime Minister herself. 'I reckon that . . . was a good reason to keep going,'[4] he later joked. 'It was at that moment I decided not to sit down,' he added. 'If it was terrible for Lawson it would probably be good for us.'

> After a few quick instructions for me to sit down he [the Deputy Speaker] rapidly raced through the disciplinary procedure from naming me to suspension. However, I was ready for that. To suspend someone from the Commons requires a vote, and a vote takes the best part of 20 minutes. This was before parliament was televised, so in television and radio studios, not to mention stockbrokers' offices, round the country there was confusion as they tried to grasp the significance of why this young Scottish Nationalist was interrupting this sacred Westminster event.

Despite Salmond's later claim that his intervention was spontaneous, it had been planned well in advance as part of the SNP's programme of Parliamentary disruption, as prepared by Salmond and Isobel Lindsay prior to the 1987 general election; they had simply been waiting for an appropriate moment. In an autobiographical piece written 12 years later, Salmond explained the background:

> One of the first things I had done at Westminster was to digest the parliamentary bible Erskine May and Standing Orders to look for opportunities to make an impression. For a party of three MPs out of a parliament of 650 this was not easy. At any rate, I determined that if Lawson went ahead with a tax cut for the rich while the Tories were imposing the poll tax on Scotland then I would intervene. It had never been done, but there was nothing in Erskine May to say the Budget speech had to be listened to in silence. My experienced colleagues Margaret Ewing and Andrew Welsh were at first taken aback by my idea, but then supportive. The only question remaining was whether I had the guts to do it.[5]

Never lacking in self-confidence, Salmond did, although it seems likely that actually pushing his protest to the point of suspension had not been part of the plan. The *Scotsman* reported that 'Margaret Ewing tugged at Salmond's jacket in an attempt to get him to sit down', while the

*Glasgow Herald* observed that both Ewing and Dafydd Wigley, a Plaid Cymru MP, 'told him he had made his point'.[6] 'You can't imagine the psychological pressure when even your colleagues are tugging at your jacket to get you to sit,' Salmond recalled in 1998, giving the impression that he could have been persuaded to desist. 'It was terrifying.'[7]

When the leader of the House, John Wakeham, proposed Salmond's expulsion, there was a great roar of support from both sides of the Chamber. The motion was then put that he be suspended 'from the service of the House' for five days. This was then voted on, with the Labour front bench and the government supporting the Deputy Speaker Harold Walker ('he had been anxious to get me for several months,' said Salmond, 'he didn't like me'). A handful of the Labour left (including Scottish MPs Dennis Canavan and David Lambie) joined the Scottish and Welsh Nationalists in the 'no' lobby, where the final figures – 354 to 19 – revealed that most Labour Members had abstained.

As Salmond, Ewing and Welsh left the Commons they were hissed and jeered from both sides of the Chamber. 'A nice policeman suggested it was cold outside and I might want to go back to my office to fetch my coat,' remembered Salmond. 'I have never seen so many cameras as was awaiting me by the time I left.'[8] That, he added in another account, 'gave me my opportunity to explain to a wider audience why the poll tax was a dreadful thing and that they would be hearing much, much more from the SNP'.[9] Reflecting on the incident in his own memoirs, Nigel Lawson said he 'could not help wondering what kind of democracy the Nationalists would establish in Scotland if ever they had the opportunity'.

Salmond's intervention was, however, 'no more than a curtain-raiser'[10] compared to what happened when Lawson announced that the upper rate of income tax was to fall from 60 to 40 per cent. Then all hell broke loose with Militant-aligned Labour MPs creating such disorder (crying 'shame' repeatedly) that the sitting had to be suspended for ten minutes. Indeed, the *Glasgow Herald* speculated that Salmond might have got wind of plans by Labour MPs to interrupt the Chancellor's speech when he reached the well-trailed announcement about the 40 per cent rate, thus seeking to rob them of their moment in the spotlight. 'If that is correct, it would explain the timing of his intervention,' commented the newspaper, 'which looked as if he had jumped the gun slightly.'

Neil Kinnock, the leader of the opposition, then prompted a walkout by one of his own MPs, Dennis Canavan, when he condemned Salmond's actions. 'In this, as in everything else in this democracy,' said Kinnock, 'argument is always superior to the form of action we have seen

in the course of this afternoon.' Other Labour MPs were equally critical.
Donald Dewar, the Shadow Scottish Secretary, dismissed it as 'a sad little
incident' and 'a charade'; John Reid said: 'The man's a twit. It was a
calculated and premeditated attempt to grab publicity'; Sam Galbraith
called it 'a classic gimmick. They have been stung by the criticism that
they are not doing much here'; while Brian Wilson, Salmond's nemesis
since the 1979 referendum, said simply: 'A rehearsed stunt; cretinous.'[11]

These responses, however, betrayed more than a hint of irritation that
an SNP MP had stolen their oppositionist thunder, while conveniently
ignoring the fact that Tam Dalyell had been expelled twice from the
Chamber for similarly disruptive antics. Indeed, Salmond enjoyed rubbing
salt into their wounds by pointing out afterwards that had Labour's 50
Scottish MPs backed his protest it would have had even more impact.
'This is what Labour's feeble opposition should have been doing for the
last nine years,' he told the *Scotsman*. 'The SNP is prepared to lead the
fight against this Government and the poll tax, as Labour have shown
themselves totally incapable of so doing.'[12]

With that, Salmond, Ewing and Welsh held a celebratory dinner
at Vitello D'Oro, a nearby Italian restaurant where the trio most
likely chewed over the political consequences. As the SNP's finance
spokesman, Salmond's suspension meant he could no longer take part in
the Budget debate, which lasted until Monday (his suspension continued
until Tuesday), so the following day he flew to his constituency to catch
up with mail and to speak to the Portsoy ladies' circle. The topic, aptly
enough, was Parliamentary procedure. Meanwhile, television viewers in
the south of England witnessed, for the first time, 'a short, neat young
man, soberly suited beyond his years, a little sleek about the jowls,
wearing a smile suggestive of some secret and superior knowledge'.[13]

Ewen MacAskill also profiled Salmond at length in the *Scotsman*: 'Mr
Salmond is smart, single-minded and combative. He is seen by some
Labour MPs and by some SNP members as arrogant, abrasive and
cold. Anti-social is an adjective he frequently attracts. Not for him the
bonhomie of Westminster's Annie's bar, the drab haunt of some journalists and MPs. Even when he does put in an appearance, he is more likely
to be drinking orange juice than alcohol.'

But his Budget intervention, noted MacAskill, 'will have done him
no harm in nationalist circles, and increased his already strong chances of
leading the SNP'. Indeed, SNP HQ reported a steady number of phone
calls. 'I have had only one call against, and about 30 for his action,'
reported Peter Murrell, then working in Salmond's Peterhead office but

a future chief executive of the party. 'They have been not just from around here, but from all over Scotland.'[14] Even the *Scots Independent* wrote approvingly that he had 'defied the rules of cricket', while the paper's columnist Jim Fairlie, again no fan of Salmond's, said his action 'should be applauded by every Nationalist'.[15]

Indeed, a subsequent opinion poll showed SNP support rising to 20 per cent, which gave the party an invaluable boost ahead of May's district council elections, the SNP's plans for a Poll Tax non-payment campaign and, within a few months, the battle to win the Glasgow Govan by-election. Salmond's belief in creating and maintaining political momentum was again at play. 'We are giving fair warning that we will indulge in these tactics again if the circumstances arise,' he told the *Scotsman*. 'We are totally united in our willingness and preparedness to strike hard, but we do not wish to telegraph our intentions.'[16] Later Salmond would reflect that it had been apparent to him 'that if the SNP was to make progress, any sort of progress, then the first thing [it] had to do was get noticed'.[17]

The disruption of Nigel Lawson's Budget speech was clearly a defining moment in Salmond's political career, and he certainly thought so, later telling the journalist Bernard Ponsonby it had been 'pretty important on a personal level in terms of reputation'.[18] Although ironic in that Salmond would later support precisely the sort of low-tax business-friendly economics Lawson had outlined, at the time it neatly encompassed all of Salmond's thinking on politics, tactics and publicity. 'His tax cut was daft economically as subsequent events were to show,' was Salmond's rather disingenuous explanation in 2000, 'but it wasn't the economics I was waiting to protest against, just the morality.' With one Parliamentary act, the SNP's deputy leader also became 'known' across the United Kingdom. 'It was a simple demonstration,' he added modestly, 'but one that fitted the times. The mood in Scotland and certainly in the SNP was that someone had finally done something.'[19]

'The House of Commons is a place where new MPs arrive, fresh from real life, knowing almost everything about something,' Salmond wrote in 1994. 'Over time, at best, they end up knowing a little about everything. At worst they know nothing about anything.'[20] He had arrived at Westminster in the summer of 1987 intending not to fall into that trap. The 1987–92 Parliament, as James Mitchell has observed, offered the SNP significant opportunities. Labour was reeling after a third successive defeat; the Tories in Scotland had been reduced to a rump of ten MPs;

and although the election had returned just a trio of SNP MPs, within
18 months the party would appear to be on the cusp of an electoral
breakthrough. The new Member for Banff and Buchan appeared to
many to embody this new political reality. 'A younger generation of
SNP activists,' wrote Mitchell, 'much tougher and more sophisticated,
was emerging around Alex Salmond.'[21]

His maiden speech indicated that Salmond was more than ready to
take up the challenge. Assured, articulate and clear-minded, he laid
his predecessor, Albert McQuarrie, to rest by 'wishing him a long and
happy retirement', waxed lyrical about Banff and Buchan (whose 'robust
characters . . . work with their hands and get their faces dirty') and asked
if, 'when there is a dramatic political divergence between Scotland
and England . . . would it really hurt them [Conservatives] so much to
concede a little justice to the Scottish nation?'[22]

Salmond had been given special responsibility for maintaining the
pressure on Labour at the first meeting of the SNP Parliamentary group
on 14 June. His colleagues were just two: Margaret Ewing (née Bain),
daughter-in-law of Winnie, who was elected Parliamentary leader, and
Andrew Welsh, another of the 1974 intake who had returned for Angus
East. One SNP staffer at Westminster, however, found the transition
from working with Gordon Wilson and Donald Stewart to this new trio
difficult. 'I am getting on all right with the new "team",' a short note
informed Wilson in July 1987. 'However, I must admit that I find Alex
very difficult. He is very patronising when he speaks to me and that
approach does not bring out the best side of my character. I think he is
just overwhelmed by the House. I hope he settles down quickly and can
perhaps make an attempt to treat me like an equal.'[23]

If Salmond was 'overwhelmed' by the House of Commons, then he
disguised it well. Of the three new MPs, however, he undoubtedly had
the most ambition and the least Parliamentary experience. Ewing too had
her eye on the top job and, as Wilson was effectively a lame-duck leader
having been defeated in his Dundee constituency, it was only a matter of
time before the pair would battle it out for the succession.

The value of a Commons seat in boosting Salmond's profile was
immeasurable, leading to newspaper profiles and even an appearance on
Terry Wogan's popular television chat show. Indeed, so important did he
consider the media that at the end of each day he would pick up the first
editions of the following day's newspapers at London's Victoria Station,
thus enabling him to tout his services to the BBC's early-morning
broadcasters.

And as the SNP's spokesman on energy (he joined the Energy Select Committee in November 1987), finance, fisheries, trade and industry, meanwhile, Salmond also had a wide-ranging remit which allowed him to comment on major aspects of government policy. In that context his continuing role as the SNP's publicity vice-convener seemed almost superfluous. By October, his ally Mike Russell had taken over, a useful position from which to mastermind Salmond's leadership campaign, which effectively began the moment he became an MP.

A profile of Salmond in the *Glasgow Herald* ('Rising star of SNP faces his toughest test'), written soon after his election, neatly captures the new MP for Banff and Buchan as he prepared to climb the greasy pole:

> He is already fleshing out around the jowls, and his dapper, neatly-suited appearance suggests someone who is conservative and hypercautious rather than radical. For someone still in his early 30s, he can seem almost too mature; his style is cool and contained and he is always totally in control . . . he can exude just a touch of self-satisfaction [but] his political assets are formidable. He is highly intelligent . . . He can, and does, work extremely hard. He is not a fiery orator, but he is a good concise public speaker, and he can throw in the odd populist phrase to stir things up.

Harry Reid's profile also quoted Stephen Maxwell on Salmond's political journey: 'It's hard to produce evidence that he's changed, but in the 79 group he argued that it should be a left-wing party with a socialist policy; now I gather it's to be a moderate left-centre consensus party. I am marginally sceptical about the seriousness of his commitment to a left-wing programme. I suspect he's going to be very pragmatic. But he is organised, relaxed and very capable.'[24]

But while Maxwell grumbled that Salmond was not left-wing enough, others in the SNP believed he was insufficiently centrist. In the *Scotsman*, for example, the former SNP councillor Sam Coull (who had resigned when Salmond got the Banff and Buchan nomination in 1985) warned that in his 'Right-of-Centre constituency' he would 'have a continuous struggle between his political ambition and the impact and cost in lost votes of his Left-wing principles'.[25]

At the 1987 SNP conference in Dundee, meanwhile, the divisions were tactical rather than ideological, with Salmond forced to defend the party's election strategy against criticism from Jim Fairlie. And when he learned that Gordon Wilson was considering resignation, Salmond invited him 'to lunch and offered his support'. As Wilson recalled: 'This was strange. Alex and I had not been close . . .' Nevertheless, since he had just been elected MP for Banff/Buchan, he had the 'platform to be a future leader. If it came to the crunch, his mentor, Jim Sillars was ahead of him in the queue on the Left. Of course, either would have been up against Margaret Ewing who would almost certainly have been elected at that time.'[26]

Concerned lest Margaret Ewing or Jim Sillars beat him to the leadership, Salmond obviously considered that keeping Wilson in place, at least for the time being, was his best option. The race for deputy leader, meanwhile, continued between Fairlie, George Leslie (vice-convener for policy) and Salmond. By way of a manifesto, Salmond warned at a fringe meeting that 'It's not enough to argue for independence and nothing else. The constitutional case must not be presented in isolation but as the route to social and economic change in Scotland. The priority is to win the economic argument for independence, but we must also present Scots with a challenging, outward-looking vision of Scotland's potential as an independent state.' [27]

Salmond won easily, while Fairlie barely survived as an ordinary member of the party's National Executive Committee. Wilson's subsequent appeal to his party to be realistic and not to try competing with Labour 'on the far left of the political spectrum'[28] was interpreted as a warning shot to his new deputy.

Indeed, Salmond would enjoy, at best, a workmanlike relationship with Wilson over the next few years. There is little evidence of direct correspondence between leader and deputy among Wilson's papers, while Mike Russell remembered the relationship being 'very poor'. Whatever the case, for the next three years Wilson was occupied with running the party from Scotland, while Salmond was equally busy at Westminster. A committee of senior office bearers (known as SOBs) ran the party at that time, and while ordinarily that would have been chaired by the senior vice-convener (Salmond), Wilson took the chair himself for obvious reasons. Many contemporaries certainly got the impression that as soon as he became deputy leader Salmond was campaigning to succeed Wilson, while Mike Russell later admitted that it was an 'open secret'.[29]

The 1987 conference, meanwhile, backed Salmond's autumn campaign theme, 'The Real Choice – Independence or Thatcher', which was framed partly as a response to Labour's Scottish Assembly Bill, soon to be tabled in the House of Commons. Salmond likened it to the 'Scotland Free or a Desert' slogan of the 1820 radical uprising. 'Both crystallise the stark choice for Scots,'[30] he said, reasoning that Labour's Bill would inevitably 'go down to defeat'. 'That is one bit on which we will be hanging our campaign,' argued Salmond, 'that devolution is no longer an option, having been rejected by Westminster.'[31] Sure enough, when MPs voted on the Bill on 27 January 1988, the SNP's three MPs backed it while gleefully taking advantage of its subsequent defeat.

The SNP had, throughout the mid to late 1980s, finessed its position in relation to the European Economic Community (EEC) or European Community. Indeed, James Mitchell reckoned the party's decision to commit itself 'to independence in Europe as its fundamental political goal . . . was one of the most significant changes in SNP policy in the 1980s'.[32] A vehement opponent of the EEC as a student, Salmond had changed his view of Brussels since the early 1980s, as had his former mentor Jim Sillars.

It had been Sillars who articulated the main tactical point in favour of 'independence in Europe', that with 'an independent Scotland within the Community, the charge of separatism disappears'.[33] The slogan was adopted at a senior office bearers meeting in early 1988, while on 11 July 1988 the SNP's three MPs marched into the 'aye' lobby with Mrs Thatcher's Conservative government (for only the second time in that Parliament) to support the Single European Act, which compelled the EEC to establish a single market by the end of 1992.

The debate preceding that division found Salmond on eloquent form:

I want to look at Scotland's real choice – whether we want to play a bit part on the British stage or whether we want to find a new role for our nation within the European Community. I find the British state funda-mentally unattractive. It is unattractive in the attitude displayed towards foreigners and unattractive in terms of the breakdown of social cohesion. It is a depressing vision for the Scottish people to have to continue to play a subsidiary role within a declining and out-of-date Britain. Steinbeck once wrote that Scotland was not a "lost cause" but a "cause unwon". The Scottish National party gives notice to the House of Commons that it intends to win that cause.[34]

It is clear Salmond saw the policy primarily in terms of positioning, although he warned in the journal *Radical Scotland* that 'conversion to the European cause must be more than a mere tactic for the SNP'. 'To win real converts the SNP and the Scottish left in general,' he added, 'will require to be convinced that Europe post 1992 will not be an economic straightjacket with all major economic decisions predetermined and increasingly remote from those who take the consequences.'

Salmond acknowledged that membership of the European Community 'involves a degree of sacrifice of sovereignty', but, he said, 'in Scotland's case it is very much an academic loss since we are starting from a position of no control'. Although the Single European Act was 'not without its challenges', the case, concluded Salmond, 'depends on realpolitik'.[35] Importantly, Salmond failed to outline exactly how far this 'freedom' to develop economic policy would actually extend, a vagueness that would cause him difficulties – particularly in the context of the single currency – later on in his career.

The Inverness conference endorsed Salmond's stance with a large majority, although an important caveat dictated that, as in 1975, Scots would decide whether or not to remain a member of the European Community via a referendum after independence. The first test of the 'independence in Europe' policy, meanwhile, came at the June 1989 elections to the European Parliament. Salmond played an active role, not least in pursuing his enduring interest in energy policy, now given an added edge by the emergence of 'green' politics. A clean environment, he said, was 'not just a desirable aim from a Scottish perspective – it is also a vital economic necessity'. The SNP's policy was 'to phase out nuclear power as fast as possible',[36] instead utilising Scotland's wind, tide and hydro power to generate electricity.

This positive vision, as well as the party's new slogan, appeared to work, for on polling day the SNP secured 25.6 per cent of the vote, beating the Conservatives into third place and helping make Scotland, at least on the European map, a Tory-free zone. It was the party's best result in a Scotland-wide election since October 1974. Salmond, however, came to resent the identification of Jim Sillars with the 'independence in Europe' policy, claiming figures like Winnie Ewing, George Reid and Neil McCormick had in fact laid the groundwork in the mid-1970s (whatever his personal views at that time).

The Nationalists achieved another breakthrough, albeit more modest, at May 1988's district council elections, increasing their share of the vote from 1984's abysmal 11.7 per cent to 21.3 per cent, and nearly doubling its number of councillors from 59 to 113. The SNP, however, still only controlled one district council, while its performance in Labour's heartland was good but patchy. But given that the SNP's aim, as calculated by Salmond, had been 'obtaining a mandate at the District Elections to lead a mass campaign of non-payment against the Poll Tax',[37] then the outcome was not exactly a triumph.

Also backing non-payment were the Scottish Trades Union Congress, the National Union of Students (Scotland) and a range of other Labour-affiliated organisations, although they focused on frustrating the registration process in order to make the tax administratively unworkable. Brian Wilson, meanwhile, orchestrated Labour's 'Stop It' campaign, which ironically stopped short of advocating non-payment. 'No less than 71 per cent of Labour voters agree with the SNP on the need for a mass campaign of non-payment to defeat the poll tax,' was Salmond's response. 'The real division over the poll tax is not between the SNP and the STUC but between the Labour leadership and their own supporters.'[38]

Nevertheless, at the end of April the SNP withdrew from the STUC's cross-party Poll Tax initiative. Campbell Christie, its general secretary, claimed the Nationalists had demanded the other parties agree to lead an illegal non-payment drive, while Salmond said they had simply requested a 'modest commitment to preparation'.[39] Salmond then led efforts to recruit 100,000 wealthy non-payers to declare 'Can pay, won't pay', a policy endorsed by the SNP's June National Council. At that autumn's annual conference, meanwhile, he highlighted the inequities of the Poll Tax by contrasting what the Queen would pay for her 'holiday home' at Balmoral, £400, and the £750 a 'postie' in his constituency would be forced to shell out.

The Poll Tax policy was, Salmond later reflected, 'a significant registration of the SNP on the political landscape of Scotland',[40] although it was not necessarily an electorally successful one. Despite being the major issue at the 1990 regional council elections – held when the Poll Tax was a reality rather than a prospect at the 1988 district poll – there was 'little evidence . . . that its campaign or policy of . . . non-payment . . . brought significant dividends in support'.[41] The Conservative vote, meanwhile, actually went up, while the SNP managed only a modest increase from 18.2 to 21.8 per cent of the vote and 42 seats, far short of the 30 per cent Salmond had predicted back in 1987.

At the 1988 SNP conference Salmond was also re-elected, unopposed, as deputy leader. He had by then consolidated his position within the SNP, and was popular with all but a vocal minority on the fundamentalist fringes. A sign of how effective Salmond was at this time can be gauged by the strength of opposition attacks, not only from Labour but the Conservative government. During a lengthy debate in the Commons on 6 July 1988 Malcolm Rifkind, the mercurial Scottish Secretary (or

'the Walter Mitty of Scottish politics',[42] as Salmond had dubbed him),
launched a particularly scathing attack on the Member for Banff and
Buchan, whom Rifkind likened to 'the infant Robespierre' and someone
who, since having 'been allowed to return to the fold of the SNP' had
'been less noticeable for his propositions of Socialist policy than he was
some years ago'. 'Perhaps', added Rifkind saracastically, 'that has something to do with representing Banff and Buchan.'[43]

Just weeks later Bruce Millan, formerly Secretary of State for Scotland
in the late 1970s, resigned his Glasgow Govan constituency to become one
of the UK's European Commissioners in Brussels. Salmond immediately
took an active role in the resulting by-election campaign, emphasising
that given the 'media importance of this by-election . . . the candidate
has to be a politician experienced at national level'.[44] He realised the
benefits of a victory, not least in terms of momentum and in the context
of the ongoing the anti-Poll Tax campaign.

Salmond personally took charge as convener of the SNP's Govan
By-election Campaign Committee, preparing a leaflet on the Poll Tax
and accelerating membership growth in the SNP's Govan constituency
association. Jim Sillars, who emerged as the candidate, was the campaign's
biggest asset, certainly when face to face with a particularly weak Labour
candidate called Bob Gillespie. On 10 November 1988, Sillars emerged
triumphant with 14,677 votes and a swing of more than 33 per cent from
Labour to the SNP. That same night, the SNP also came from third place
to win a by-election to West Lothian District Council. 'It is an indication
that something is happening right across the board,' remarked Salmond
a little melodramatically, 'that there is outright rejection of Thatcher in
Scotland.'[45]

Although many Nationalists hoped, like Salmond, that the Govan
result indicated a sea change in support for the SNP, it in fact represented
little more than a protest vote against the Poll Tax rather than a genuine
realignment. Salmond, therefore, was not complacent, and urged the
SNP to review its campaign structure the following month. The ever-
confident Jim Sillars, meanwhile, had arrived at the House of Commons
denouncing Mrs Thatcher as 'malicious, wicked and quite evil in respect
of the policies being pursued in her counter-revolution for the welfare
state'.[46]

It did not take journalists long to speculate what form the Sillars/
Salmond dynamic would take. 'Some Westminster-watchers say both are
on the Left of the party and that they are buddies,' observed the *Scotsman*.
'Others feel Sillars is such an overpowering personality that tension is

inevitable.' Salmond was at least able to joke about it. As Sillars prepared to address a rally of supporters outside Parliament, he was spotted in a supporting role, carrying half a dozen precariously balanced glasses and a jug of water. 'See what I've been reduced to?' quipped Salmond.[47] But he was probably only half joking.

Sillars probably looked upon Salmond as an indispensable ally – although certainly not an equal – but within just two months of Sillars' remarkable victory, he began to shift ground, not least in taking soundings about standing for the leadership (something he later denied), which would inevitably have come to the attention of Salmond. There was also the problem of proximity. Although the pair had long worked together, most closely within the 79 Group, they did not know each other intimately, while the rigours of Parliamentary life – of which Sillars had considerably more experience than Salmond – would have produced tensions of its own.

Most striking, however, was Sillars' change of tack politically. During the Govan campaign he had attacked the STUC and co-operation with Labour on Scotland's constitutional future; immediately after his victory he talked about reaching 'out the hand of friendship to like-minded people in the Labour Party in Scotland'; but within weeks of that he had launched a strong personal attack on leading Labour figures, even likening Donald Dewar to 'Uncle Tom' during a speech in Castlemilk.[48]

The final break, however, occurred when the SNP decided to withdraw from ongoing cross-party talks concerning a 'Scottish Constitutional Convention' tasked with coming up with a blueprint for a devolved Scottish Parliament. Initial negotiations, led by Gordon Wilson, Margaret Ewing and Sillars, had gone well, but gradually the mood changed. In late January 1989, Wilson began to consult senior office bearers by telephone, all of whom expressed opposition.

Crucially, however, Salmond – as senior vice-convener – was not among those contacted. What exactly happened is unclear but it seems likely that Wilson delegated consultation with Salmond to Sillars, not surprising given that the leader and his deputy were hardly close. Sillars did call him (Salmond was in Peterhead), but failed to mention the impending decision, even though many journalists had already been briefed to that effect. That same evening, Gordon Wilson used a Burns Supper at the Edinburgh SNP Club to denounce the composition of the Convention as 'a travesty of reality'.[49]

Isobel Lindsay, who was contacted, later told the journalist Arnold Kemp that Salmond, despite subsequent claims to the contrary, 'wasn't unavailable' on the weekend in question. 'They assumed Alex,' she explained to Kemp, 'would want to participate.'[50] This was broadly correct; although neither Lindsay nor Salmond was starry-eyed when it came to the Convention, having argued in a February 1987 paper that it seemed unlikely that 'a glorified public meeting' could provide the basis for 'a constitutional challenge to Tory rule in Scotland'.[51] Kemp summarised Salmond's position thus:

> Salmond took a different tactical view though there was no strategic disagreement. He felt the SNP should go along with the convention to the point that it could be shown that it would not discuss independence as a serious issue or allow it to be presented to the people of Scotland. He also thought the SNP should argue within the convention for a multi-choice referendum (independence, devolution, the status quo). On these tactics Salmond thought he had the agreement of Sillars.[52]

Almost a decade later Salmond gave the broadcaster Brian Taylor a similar account, describing it as 'the right decision at the wrong time', not least because it would not have 'been possible for the SNP to run into the 1992 election on the same platform, effectively, as the Labour and Liberal parties'.[53] However, on Sunday, 29 January 1989, the SNP issued a press release – drafted by Sillars – that condemned what it called 'a rigged Convention which can neither reflect nor deliver Scottish demands'.[54]

The press response the following day was universally negative. Although Wilson *et al* protested that they had not withdrawn from the Convention, they had merely refused to join it, the impression generated was one of deliberate, and small-minded, sabotage on the part of the SNP. 'I couldn't believe it at first,' reflected Salmond several years later. 'That was the first time that I think our relationship of trust broke down,' he added of Sillars' handling of the move, 'and it broke down not because we disagreed about the issue, which we did, it broke down because I'd had that conversation and he'd pointedly not told me what was going on.'[55] Isobel Lindsay concurred. 'That was the first time I had seen hostility openly expressed between Alex and Jim,' she later recalled. 'Before that Alex would never criticise Jim.'[56]

It is easy to sympathise with Salmond on this point. Sillars was, he believed, a close colleague, yet he had deliberately kept him in the dark as the party, of which Salmond was deputy leader, made a key tactical decision. Their relationship, however, had already cooled by the beginning of 1989, Sillars' behaviour being a manifestation of that rather than the cause. But in spite of his reservations, Salmond swiftly fell into line, telling reporters that the 'problem with the convention is that it isn't going to get anywhere anyway'.[57]

There is nothing like the zeal of a convert. At a National Council meeting in Port Glasgow five weeks later, Salmond even turned on those, such as Isobel Lindsay, who continued to argue that the party had made a mistake. According to the *Glasgow Herald* he launched a 'stern attack . . . accusing her of being more of a Unionist than the Secretary of State for Scotland and "more of a Unionist and a Conservative" on the referendum issue than Mr Charles Gray, leader of Strathclyde region.'[58]

As the journalist Iain Macwhirter observed, 'Comparing an SNP executive member to the Labour leader of Strathclyde Region is the most outrageous abuse in the SNP lexicon, and Mr Salmond was taken to task by other speakers'.[59] Contrition came a lot later on. 'If I had my time again I'd take back that speech,' reflected Salmond in 2001. 'I think Isobel probably had the rights over that argument.'[60] Recalling the Port Glasgow meeting more than 20 years later, Lindsay was philosophical, speculating that it was possible that 'Alex felt he had to prove his credentials with his own supporters or with the wider party'.[61] That those 'credentials' were relatively new hardly mattered, although the incident also demonstrated how aggressive the once even-tempered Salmond could now be.

The strength of Lindsay's argument, however, did not stop the resolution being crushed by 198 votes to 48. There were a number of factors at play, which went some way to explaining Salmond's behaviour as well as that of the wider party. The devolution debacle of the 1970s still hung over the party, not least the internal strife that followed. Party unity was certainly at the forefront of Salmond's mind. 'There is a time in politics for holding your nerve and not being stampeded,' he argued during the National Council debate. 'If we buckle under Press pressure now what will we be like when we are approaching independence?'[62]

Privately, however, Salmond believed the political momentum of the Govan by-election had been squandered, a view supported by the SNP's subsequent decline in opinion polls. He attempted to regain the initiative by disrupting meetings of the House of Commons' Education Committee (which included English Conservative MPs considering Scotland-only Bills), while Sillars attempted to do a Salmond during the 1989 Budget statement. 'There are opportunities on the floor of the House to pursue our case,' warned Salmond, 'which will heavily inconvenience both the Government and the Leader of the Opposition.'[63]

The *Scotsman* speculated that Charles Stewart Parnell, leader of the

Irish Parliamentary Party in the 19th century, had been the model for the renewed guerilla action. Such tactics, however, had already outlived their usefulness. The novelty, at least from a media perspective, had passed, and although the 1989 SNP conference unanimously congratulated the party's four MPs for 'selective parliamentary disruption which is providing genuine Scottish opposition to English Tory legislation',[64] there were few serious attempts to disrupt Parliament between then and the next general election.

The Glasgow Central by-election, held on 15 June 1989, also added to the altered political mood. Alex Neil, a former Labour member and close friend of Sillars from his short-lived Scottish Labour Party, had been selected as the SNP candidate, but Labour held the seat convincingly (although there was a 20 per cent increase in the SNP's vote share). Salmond responded by promising that the SNP would not hesitate to resort to 'street fighting' in future contests. 'The future for Scottish politics,' he declared, 'will be eyeball to eyeball confrontation.'[65]

Perhaps Alex Salmond's most significant contribution during the 1987-92 Parliament, and certainly in the longer term, was his development of what became known as the 'economic case for independence'. In late 1987, he had established the Scottish Centre for Economic and Social Research (SCESR), taking care to stress that it 'would not interfere in the normal Policy making processes of the Party' but would 'provide valuable information which should be of great aid to the Party in the future'.[66] Peter Murrell acted as secretary, while several Salmond associates (including Grant Baird and Stephen Maxwell) became members, although non-SNPers like the journalist Alf Young and economist David Bell also contributed papers.

To Salmond, fleshing out its economic policy was a key component of the SNP's strategy following the 1987 general election. In the autumn of that year he had circulated a paper in which 'The Economic Case for Independence' (Phase Three), flowed naturally from attacking 'Labour's Feeble Fifty' (Phase One) and presenting the real choice between 'Independence or Thatcher' (Phase Two). 'We will make a serious and sustained attempt to take the initiative in the economic arguments about Independence,' he explained, 'by the presentation of quality material designed to inspire the confidence first of our own activists, then key opinion formers and through them the people.' 'Credibility,' concluded Salmond, 'is still the single most important missing ingredient for so much of what we wish to do.'[67]

The following year, the SNP also issued its first 'Scottish budget', based on (it claimed) available government statistics and independent analysis. This, said Salmond, 'demolished completely the myth of a subsidised Scotland'.[68] His own proposals were published a few months later. 'This is no Marxist budget,' he protested, preferring a 'social democratic' label under which commercial success would be encouraged in order to fund anti-poverty and employment programmes, a sort of nascent Third Way later embraced by New Labour. Although the Fraser of Allander Institute gave the proposals qualified support, another economist dismissed it as 'garbage for garbage'. 'You feed hypothetical figures into a model,' he said, 'they'll tell you anything.'[69]

Salmond, meanwhile, fleshed out his critique of Labour's economic policies in a review of Gordon Brown's recent publication, *Where There is Greed*. His 'economic indictment of the Thatcher years,' judged Salmond, 'although comprehensive, is pedestrian,' adding that 'it seems a poor ideological base from which to confront Thatcherism . . . [reflecting] the now-accepted Labour wisdom that the trouble with the lady is that she is ideological and dogmatic as opposed to having the wrong ideology and the wrong dogma. When Brown writes (effectively) of the beneficiaries of Thatcher largesse he still leaves the distinct impression that it is only the top 1 per cent who need fear any Labour redistribution of income.'[70]

Salmond was not exactly an ostentatious redistributionist himself. Indeed, another emerging economic refrain was his growing attraction to the 'Irish model'. At the 1989 SNP conference, for example, both Salmond and Alex Neil pointed to the Republic of Ireland as an economic example for an independent Scotland, particularly its lower interest rates having joined the European Monetary System (EMS). Inflation, said Salmond, was also down to just two per cent, something he claimed would be 'possible in an independent Scotland, too'.[71]

Salmond's reputation within the SNP certainly grew as a result of his articulate espousal of the economic case for independence, and in 1989 he and almost every other party office bearer were returned unopposed. A rumoured leadership challenge by Jim Sillars, meanwhile, failed to transpire, leading one insider to refer sardonically to the 'most serious outbreak of harmony for many years'.[72] It was not to last.

On 24 January 1990 Salmond told a meeting in Dollar that whatever devolution blueprint was drawn up by the Scottish Constitutional Convention should, together with 'independence in Europe' and the status quo, 'be put to the test in a referendum of the Scottish people'.

Westminster opposition to such a poll, he argued, could 'be overcome by the Scottish local authorities organising a simultaneous postal ballot of all electors in their areas'. 'After a year of fundamental transformation in Eastern Europe,' he added, 'it would allow the Scottish nation our own opportunity at people power.'[73]

The idea of a multi-option referendum was not new, but this speech demonstrated that Salmond was growing in confidence as a politician, making a deliberately ecumenical constitutional pitch. To opponents, however, it sounded like rapprochement to Labour, and fuelled suspicion of Salmond's motives. Not only was the referendum plan defeated at the next meeting of the SNP's NEC but it opened up a 'major fissure' between Salmond's camp and a 'group of neo-fundamentalists' often referred to as 'central belt activists', code, as the academic Peter Lynch later wrote, 'for neo-fundamentalist left-wingers who opposed Salmond and his gradualist strategy'.[74]

The scene was set, therefore, for an acrimonious fight over the future course of the Nationalist movement and, more to the point, the SNP leadership. 'The end game approached,' recorded Gordon Wilson in his memoirs. In early May 1990 Sillars went to see Wilson in Dundee and told him

Alex Salmond was likely to make a bid for the leadership and proposed that we stand together on a joint ticket. During the previous two years, he and Alex had drifted apart and relationships between them and their respective teams were, to put it mildly, not cordial. I was non-committal and promised to think things over and let him know. The news was half expected and there would have been no surprise if I had received a courtesy call from Alex to tell me of his intentions.[75]

Sillars, however, disputes Wilson's version of events, suggesting that Salmond had been minded to make his bid for the leadership the previous year: 'Alex was going to challenge in 1989 but I said no [to supporting him] and that was the beginning of the breach. You're either for him or against him. Margaret Ewing also wanted to stand and I knew she wouldn't win against Alex, and I couldn't stand because I would have split the party from top to bottom. Gordon Wilson wanted me or Margaret.'[76]

Given that Wilson had wanted to resign as leader since 1987, if Salmond had challenged him in 1989 he would, as one senior Nationalist put it, have 'been pushing at an open door'.[77] It is possible, however, that Salmond was genuinely stung by the refusal of Sillars to support a leadership bid in 1989. 'The first year he went for the leadership, there was a heavy-handed refusal from the older and wiser ones like Jim and me,' recalled Margo MacDonald, 'we just thought he wasn't ready yet. Jim had a conversation with him saying "we both think you'll be leader but not yet". I didn't realise just how much he had resented that.'[78] Age was certainly an issue. Seventeen years Salmond's senior, Sillars perhaps felt his chance of leading the SNP was slipping away. So by 1990 it seems that both Salmond and Sillars had resolved to stand, although Salmond later claimed, unconvincingly, that had Sillars 'stood for party leader in 1990 . . . I might well have supported him'.[79] And, having been alerted to Salmond's intentions by Sillars, Wilson decided to announce his resignation sooner rather than later. 'I saw no merit in being involved in what would be a bitter election,' he recalled in his memoirs. 'The Party needed fresh leadership.'[80]

'Fresh', however, did not mean Salmond, and he and Mike Russell were virtually the last to be informed of Wilson's intentions. Most of those on the NEC also did not want Salmond to run, considering him talented but fractious. Knowledge of this opposition, however, simply made Salmond more determined to stand:

> The argument was put to me last May [1990] that the SNP should not have a leadership election. Far better, it was said, to have an agreed leader, ie Margaret Ewing, emerge from the collective leadership and then possibly a contest after the general election. I thought it was a threadbare argument then. I still think so now. The SNP claims to be the voice of Scottish democracy in the 1990s would look silly if we adopted the same system of selecting a leader as the Tory Party discarded in the 1960s.[81]

Although Salmond's stock was rising in the party – regional council candidates in his constituency had performed particularly well at the May 1990 elections – and he 'had just about persuaded many on the Right to forget his involvement in the 79 Group crisis and the claims that he is not a "real" Nationalist',[82] he was believed to be unprepared for a summer contest. Nevertheless Salmond declared his candidacy at a constituency meeting on 27 May.

Asked about the gamble he was taking in challenging Margaret Ewing, Salmond wielded some of his favourite lines of poetry by James Graham, the 1st Marquess of Montrose:

> He either fears his fate too much,
> Or his deserts are small,
> That puts it not unto the touch,
> To win or to lose it all.

'What happened to Montrose?' asked one former SNP MP rhetorically. 'He was hanged for his trouble.'[83] He was torn limb from limb in the Grassmarket after falling foul of his supporters, and Salmond's opponents expected the same fate to befall him, although not literally.

Ewing's campaign, however, quickly ran into difficulties. As SNP historian Peter Lynch put it:

> First, she had no real vision for the SNP in terms of policy, organisation or identity. Salmond, by contrast, had a range of issues and initiatives he was keen to advance as party leader, and was more keenly aware of what needed to be done within the party to improve its position. He was also impatient with the condition of the party under Wilson's leadership in terms of organisation, finance and campaigning. Second, in terms of the leadership campaign, the Ewing candidacy was ill-organised and rather complacent compared to Salmond's.[84]

As well as being ill-organised it soon became clear that Ewing had two parallel campaigns, one run by her husband Fergus and the other by Jim Sillars. When the latter invited around 50 SNP activists to a 'Left caucus' meeting in Paisley, accompanied by Kenny MacAskill and Alex Neil, he revealed his hand by urging those present to support Ewing. But the meeting, which lasted five hours, also gave rise to some less than gentlemanly remarks about Salmond, indicating to one journalist with 'shocking clarity just how much of a threat Salmond appears to have become to some of his long-standing comrades'.[85] Salmond later recalled 'a succession of phone calls from people highly embarrassed to have been invited to a "left caucus" meeting in Glasgow where my motives for seeking the leadership were denounced. Trotsky apparently had got off light[ly] in comparison.'[86]

Although the disagreements, both personal and political, between Sillars and Salmond dated back to late 1988, they had not previously spilled over into the public domain. The repeated implication from the Sillars camp was that Alex was 'soft' on Labour, and from Sillars himself that, at 35, Salmond was simply too young for the leadership. Both Sillars and Kenny MacAskill (running as deputy leader) depicted Salmond as superficially talented, good on television but lacking substance.

Interviewed by John MacLeod for the *Scotsman*, MacAskill damned Salmond with feint praise. 'No-one is putting down Alex's abilities, indeed the opposite. His integrity's self-evident and he's vital to our success,' he said. 'But who's doing the writing, the thinking, producing pamphlets? It's Jim Sillars. He's the one with vision, Margaret could unite the party.' The implication was that Salmond was an intellectual light-weight seeking to impose his media-friendly personality upon the party.[87]

Salmond's restraint was admirable during the campaign, although one supporter told the *Guardian* that he had been 'alarmed' by Sillars' stridency.[88] Of the attacks, Salmond reckoned party activists were 'well able to separate legitimate campaigning from some of the desperate nonsense which has appeared in print over the last week . . . no supporter of ours should allow themselves to be sucked into any exchanges with our colleagues in the opposition'.[89] Ewing, thought Salmond, was 'suffering from having so many influential backers – they were in danger of eclipsing her own personality'.[90] His campaign, meanwhile, had 'sewn up vast areas of the country before the contest had even started',[91] aided by a small band of committed supporters he had been nurturing since entering Parliament in 1987. From these he selected the party's publicity vice-convener, Mike Russell, who – although dismissed as a lightweight by the Sillars camp – guided Salmond closely throughout the next few months.

He and team Salmond (consisting of ten key individuals[92]) had taken early soundings within the party membership and actively campaigned for the votes of delegates, who would choose Gordon Wilson's successor at the September conference. Always keen on modern campaigning techniques, Salmond and Russell set up a special telephone line where members could listen to a two-minute recorded message about his leadership ambitions, while their slickly produced literature was quickly dispatched around the country. The party's youth wing, the Young Scottish Nationalists (whose leading lights included a Glasgow University student called Nicola Sturgeon), backed Salmond, as did the SNP's trade union group. By the end of July his team reckoned that, 'at worst', they were level with Ewing.

In terms of ideology an outside observer might have found it hard to put a voting slip between Ewing and Salmond. Ewing's campaigners claimed it was the difference between 'bedding down with Labour' (Salmond) and remaining true to the SNP's tradition of being 'the only political vehicle that can set Scotland free' (Ewing).[93] Ewing herself struggled to articulate the difference, telling one interviewer that it was said 'Alex would like to pull back a little on the poll tax non-payment campaign, whereas I think it's vital at this stage to keep up the pressure',[94] although in July Salmond declared that he had 'never made any secret' of his being 'a socialist within the Scottish National Party'.[95] To one observer, meanwhile, Ewing exuded the 'fatal' impression 'of not appearing to know exactly why she was running in the first place'.[96]

Salmond, on the other hand, focused on leadership and, most importantly, his ability to deliver it. 'It is the economic case for independence which will be the key for transforming the latent sympathy for our policies into hard votes,'[97] he told a press conference in Glasgow towards the end of the campaign. In Dick Douglas, who had quit the Labour whip in protest at his party's refusal to advocate non-payment of the Poll Tax, Salmond found the perfect case study for another aspect of his campaign. 'If I am elected next month, the SNP will make an explicit appeal to rank-and-file Labour supporters who agree with us on the poll tax, on nuclear weapons and on fighting for the Scottish economy,' he said, having paraded Douglas as his 'guest of honour' at an SNP barbeque in Aberdeenshire. 'The SNP must never forget that our enemy is not the Labour rank-and-file but its grey Scottish leadership, who wish only to keep Scotland quiet and safe for their own private interests.'[98]

In the summer edition of *Radical Scotland*, meanwhile, both leadership candidates set out their stalls. 'The party must present a moderate left-of-centre policy profile,' said Ewing, 'we must never be subsumed in an amalgam of British and Scottish hoodwinking as a Mark II Labour Party or as prisoners of a mock convention.' This was clearly an attack on Salmond, whose 'arrogance' and 'domineering personality' were also referenced. Both charges were true, to an extent, yet hardly killer blows. He, in turn, quoted polls showing 40 per cent support for independence but only 20 per cent for the SNP. This, argued Salmond, was 'the faultline in Scottish politics' which gave the party something to aim for.

In an adjoining article Alasdair Morgan, Salmond's running mate for the deputy leadership, proclaimed him 'a nationalist for the 1990s'. 'Alex has also proved over the last few years that he can present all our policies tenaciously and with confidence,' he added. 'In an era when television creates the cockpit for electoral success or failure these skills are essential.'[99] So far from being a drawback, Morgan viewed Salmond's media prowess as his principal strength in a new political era. Ewing, by contrast, repeatedly stressed her political experience, prompting one of her supporters to quip: 'Maggie offered a CV. Alex offered a manifesto.'[100]

During August it became clear that Salmond was attracting

greater-than-anticipated support. Panic, therefore, probably motivated Kenny MacAskill and Alex Neil to stage a press conference, of which Ewing was unaware, during which they savaged Salmond, the former referring to him as a 'smooth talker', and the latter likening him to a 'latter-day First World War general'.[101] Ewing appeared confused when asked why her supporters were attacking her opponent, and during the subsequent media row declined interview requests while Salmond accepted every opportunity to state his case. The campaign reached its final phase as Salmond returned 'well refreshed' from a holiday on Colonsay at the beginning of September. Encouraged by the response of North of Scotland delegations to what he modestly called 'one of the best impromptu speeches of my life', Salmond's confidence grew and by the time of his last campaign meeting on 14 September, 'our information put the margin at 3-1 with the undecided's [sic] breaking in my favour'. 'The large rural constituencies where we thought initially our campaign might be badly mauled,' he added, 'were enthusiastically supporting us.'[102] A *Scotsman* poll, however, put Margaret Ewing ahead among the general public.

The oratorical showdown came on Thursday, 20 September, at the SNP's annual conference in Perth's City Hall. Ewing took a hard line against the Scottish Constitutional Convention and the Labour Party, receiving ecstatic applause despite her nervous delivery. Salmond, by contrast, used a three-minute slot in a separate debate to deliver what the journalist Peter Jones described as 'a punchy, polished speech larded with statistics designed to show his knowledge of economic affairs'.[103] Both candidates had cause for concern. The signs were that Ewing had not fully swayed uncommitted delegates, while the mood still seemed to be against Salmond's referendum strategy. Thursday's newspapers, however, still gave Ewing the edge. 'The actual voting delegate doesn't seem to have been consulted by the press,' responded Mike Russell in a campaign diary for the *Scotsman*. 'They are clearly sticking by Alex.'

Salmond was nevertheless 'moody'. 'The pressure he and Moira have been under has been tremendous,' wrote Russell. 'Old allegiances based not just on politics but on friendship have been broken by the campaign – although they can and will be reformed.' Indeed, when asked about reports that he had barely been on speaking terms with Kenny MacAskill over the past six months, a diplomatic Salmond replied: 'Since I brought Kenny MacAskill into the SNP, I have always recognised his substantial talents. He is going to be a major figure in the SNP for a long time to come.'[104]

In his farewell address as national convener, Gordon Wilson praised both Ewing and Salmond as good people, although there was a subtle subtext. 'The convenership is more like being a team captain than a striker, or even team manager,' he said. 'Under our constitution, the convener has plenty of influence and initiative but little power.'[105] Despite assurances to the contrary, there remained a lingering suspicion that Salmond would not be a good team player, that he would be presidential, centralising power and sidelining opponents. Indeed, a 'well informed Nationalist' told the Liberal Democrat Charles Kennedy, that 'all of those who had known and worked with Alex the longest – well, they were all voting for Ewing'.

There were, therefore, gasps of surprise when the result was announced on Saturday, 22 September. Salmond had won, but instead of the 60:40 margin he had privately hoped for, he had managed 70:30, matching almost exactly Mike Russell's prediction from that morning. Although the NEC had backed Ewing 9-3, the 30-strong National Council had supported Salmond 18-12, and he had secured an overwhelming majority among conference delegates. It represented a crushing blow for Ewing, although she was gracious in defeat. 'If there is going to be a change in the party it must be decisive. Alex clearly has the endorsement of the party,' she said. 'The SNP's ultimate goal of independence is much more important than my slightly dented ego.'

In his victory speech – watched by Moira, who had slipped quietly into the back of the hall before the result was announced – Salmond declared that Labour's days of dominating Scottish politics were numbered. 'Labour may win the yuppie votes in the south of England, we are going to win the battle for the hearts and minds of the Scottish people,' he said. 'The SNP is not interested in running a good second. We are not running for a medal, we are going for gold.'[106] Salmond also took care to remind delegates that he considered himself a 'socialist' while sounding an inclusive note: 'The SNP needs to campaign for all Scotland, and all Scotland needs the talents of all the SNP.'[107]

Salmond's victory showed him to be an inspired strategist, securing his base in the constituencies before managing an efficient campaign that completely outflanked the combined might of the Sillars-led left, party traditionalists loyal to Margaret Ewing and, not least, the wishes of the outgoing convener, Gordon Wilson. Charles Kennedy also saw parallels with Paddy Ashdown: 'Both started as outsiders and, in remarkably short periods, gained the top job.'[108]

Perhaps, like Winston Churchill (who had also been nominated to lead a party that had once spurned him), Salmond had always felt a sense of destiny. 'At last I had the authority to give directions over the whole scene,' read Churchill's famously self-confident account of his becoming Prime Minister. 'I felt as if I were walking with destiny, and that all my past life had been but a preparation for this hour . . . I was sure I should not fail.'[109]

## Chapter 6

# 'FREE BY '93'

'Within minutes of winning the SNP leadership in Perth in 1990,' observed the academic James Mitchell, 'Alex Salmond's opponents were talking to the media about his overthrow. His demise was predicted and hoped for by some of his erstwhile associates from the '79 Group days.'[1] Indeed, and as Charles Kennedy observed, 'leadership contests do have an uncanny and an unhappy knack of bringing out the daggers'.[2]

Indeed, it would take Salmond a few years to consolidate his position as leader of the SNP although he was, by his own admission, 'a resilient character'.[3] The Jim Sillars camp remained strong while Margaret Ewing – popular and respected despite her defeat – was still in place as Parliamentary leader at Westminster. Nevertheless, it is possible that Salmond underestimated his own strength. Of the SNP's nine senior office bearers – its 'inner cabinet' – seven were Salmond supporters, an outcome almost as surprising as his margin of victory. 'In short,' wrote the journalist Peter Jones, 'Mr Salmond asked the party grass-roots to give him a team to back him up rather than one which would cramp his style, and he got it.'[4]

Beyond elected office holders, Salmond also did his best to heal the wounds of the campaign. 'After he was elected he invited me for a meeting and said he knew what my views were but that it didn't matter,' recalled Chris McLean, then the SNP's press officer and a Ewing supporter.[5] Salmond also sought to placate John Swinney, their relationship having turned sour back in 1986. 'Alex knew that John was a very effective operator,' recalled a senior Nationalist. 'Alex, however, had to take the initiative, something John would never have done.'[6] Indeed, as presiding officer in the leadership election, Swinney had been in 'a difficult position'. 'Alex and I had up to that time not been terribly close politically,' he later admitted, 'but that afternoon Alex made a point of saying his would be an inclusive leadership.'[7]

Salmond's victory, meanwhile, had created a feel-good factor, helped by the new leader's adoption of a more high-profile approach than his predecessor. 'Members believe he can, and want him to, lead them to victory,' assessed the *Scotsman*.[8] Also enthusiastic was the academic Tom Gallagher, later a critic of Salmond as First Minister: 'Salmond's energy, media skills, and the sharpness of his thinking means that the identity of the SNP is likely to be far less blurred in future. To a grassroots member-ship cheated of sustained electoral success, the prospect of dynamic leadership boosting the appeal of the party was enough to silence doubts about a responsibility so grave falling to one so young and, at times, impetuous.' 'If a leader like Alex Salmond fails to lift the party from the trough it has found itself in since 1979,' added Gallagher cautiously, 'then it is hard to see how it can emerge as a serious contender for power in Scotland.'[9]

Salmond's first test came with by-elections in Paisley North and South. The selection of the SNP candidate for the former caused the first row of his leadership, when Salmond was accused of trying to block the former Tory activist Iain Lawson from putting his name forward, something he strenuously denied. Roger Mullin (the SNP's vice-convener for organisation) was chosen, achieving a 16.5 per cent swing and a credit-able second place for his party. Lawson instead stood in Paisley South, managing a 13.5 per swing and, again, a good second place.

The two by-elections were perhaps more memorable for providing an electoral backdrop to the protracted demise of Margaret Thatcher. 'She is fatally wounded,' Salmond told reporters following the first Tory leader-ship ballot, 'and must go as soon as possible.'[10] Although Salmond had once dismissed Mrs Thatcher as 'this formidable but limited and, in some ways, rather absurd Prime Minister',[11] there was a private respect for her steely resolve and clarity of purpose that perhaps mirrored his own.

Salmond's elevation to the top SNP job had, of course, an impact on another important woman in his life – Moira. Already commuting between their constituency home in Strichen, their Linlithgow house (still at Friars Brae) and a Westminster flat, the inevitable demands of leading a party were about to make married life even more complicated. Although Moira had not been completely invisible since her husband's election in 1987, working for a while in his Peterhead office, she remained better known to the party faithful rather than the general public. 'She is invariably cheerful, optimistic, welcome and friendly, but determined to stay in the background,' wrote the veteran Nationalist Paul Henderson

Scott in his memoirs. 'She never speaks to the press or appears on a political platform but it is apparent to everyone who has met her that Alex could not have a more sustaining ally.'[12]

That was certainly true, although Moira was – at least initially – not as reluctant to shun the limelight as has often been stated. For example, in February 1991, she accompanied Salmond to a celebration of his victory in Linlithgow, which was photographed and reported in the local paper, while the previous year she even gave an interview (jointly with Alex) to, of all things, the *Sunday Post*. In the absence of many, if any, competing accounts, this is worth quoting from at some length, not least for its insights into the Salmonds 'at home'.

'I'm no Glenys Kinnock,' Moira told a reporter. 'I married Alex, not politics. That's his life and I am happy to be in the background.' Rather she saw the role of an MP's wife, and that of herself, in the more traditional Tory mould, helping with constituency work, opening flower shows and supervising their three homes, not least their 'tiny' Strichen cottage 'with its open log fire, beams and stripped pine floors', where this interview took place. 'Sometimes I go to make a cheese and tomato toastie in Linlithgow,' said Moira, 'absolutely sure I've got a pound of cheese in the fridge, and then I remember it's in the kitchen in Strichen!' It seems colleagues later teased Salmond about this particular revelation.

There was little expansion, however, upon Moira's political views. 'I share his convictions,' she said firmly, 'but one politician in the family is *quite* enough!' Salmond's new duties, however, meant less time with his wife. 'I do get lonely when he's away all week in Westminster,' she said thoughtfully, 'so our time alone together is very precious. We drive up to Strichen on a Friday and like to potter around the cottage, having meals by the fire and a long leisurely fry-up on a Sunday morning.' The couple also liked playing Scrabble and cards, although it invariably caused rows due to Alex's revealing tendency to change the rules as he went along. 'He gets mad because I invariably win Scrabble,' said Moira. 'The thing is, he can't spell.'

Salmond, it seems, was not really a man for the Nineties, at least in his private sphere. 'He can't cook, is reluctant to do housework and still hasn't put up the new pole for her curtains,' noted the *Sunday Post*, 'even though she's had it for six months!' 'Let's just say I'm not inspired by doing household jobs,' admitted Salmond. 'Moira gets on to me for spending a lot of time on other people's problems and never having time for our own.' Then, slipping into uncomfortably Freudian analysis, Moira declared: 'His mum did everything for him and I've just fallen into the same pattern.'

Alex did, however, remember anniversaries, although sometimes dinners had to be delayed due to other commitments. Moira also admitted doing all Alex's packing and always making sure he had enough shirts to last a week. 'Sometimes I switch on the six o'clock news and I'm horrified by what he's wearing,' she said with a shudder. 'He hasn't a clue about the colours of ties, shirts and socks. He just puts on the nearest thing to hand.' Alex then broke into another grin: 'She phones me up to give me a telling off!'[13] Indeed, as he waited to be grilled by Brian Walden in the run-up to the 1992 general election, Salmond took care to pull up his socks with his wife in mind. 'I was on Panorama a few weeks ago and I got gip from Moira,' he explained to a bemused Walden, 'I came home and said "how did I do?" and she said, "I could see your legs." '[14]

Moira's hobbies, meanwhile, included collecting antiques, gardening and floral art. 'She's a homemaker with a sure touch for making a room look calm, restful and pretty,' reported the Sunday Post in typically home-spun – and it has to be said sexist – style. 'Her feminine influence can be seen around the house, in places like the alcove she made herself, filled with books, old china and flowers. She also enjoys the painstaking job of stripping down doors, waxing and restoring them.' Above all, Moira desired privacy. 'I regard myself as public property,' explained Salmond, 'but I like to protect Moira as much as I can from the limelight. We are not a political couple and I find it refreshing to come home and let off steam to someone who isn't in the thick of it.'

Moira and Alex evidently complimented each other well. 'It has to be said that Alex Salmond is such a good talker,' observed the Sunday Post, 'a man with a flow of words and arguments which he delivers with confidence and conviction, that it was a wise move to choose a wife with a gift for listening.'[15] The journalist Kenny Farquharson remembered having lunch with both Mr and Mrs Salmond in the early 1990s, an encounter that captured a more playful aspect of their marriage. 'Alex was obviously playing up to Moira, putting on a show, telling anecdotes and providing mischievous commentary on the events and political personalities of the day,' he recalled. 'Moira had her elbows on the table, leaning forward and lapping it all up, occasionally shooting me an "Oh! Isn't he awful!" look, as if she was an aunt with a naughty favourite nephew.'[16] Such meetings, however, were rare, and it seems that having seen the result of Moira's one and only interview in the Sunday Post, Salmond decided there would be no more.

Salmond's honeymoon as leader, meanwhile, was marked by sunny optimism. 'Labour is very vulnerable now in Scotland and that's why

I'm convinced the time has come for our party to make a major break-through,' he told a reporter towards the end of the year. 'I couldn't have become leader at a more challenging time. There may be a General Election next year and I believe the sky's the limit.'[17]

On the constitutional question, Salmond's stance was already well known: no longer would he pretend that the Scottish Constitutional Convention did not exist (it had published its interim report a week after his election), instead arguing – as he had at the beginning of the year – that its recommendations ought to be put to Scots in a three-pronged referendum. This time, however, Salmond won the backing of the NEC, as well as that of Charles Gray (the same Charles Gray with whom he had earlier compared, unfavourably, Isobel Lindsay), the Labour leader of Strathclyde Regional Council. 'By asking for a referendum,' declared Salmond, 'we are throwing down the gauntlet.'[18]

At the SNP's National Assembly in Perth, meanwhile, Salmond continued his journey away from socialism by telling delegates that independence in Europe would 'slash' interest rates, giving Scots a direct say on a single currency and escaping the overheated economy of the south-east of England. 'In terms of economic affairs,' Salmond explained to the journalist Peter Jones, 'I think that as a country on the periphery of the European Community, Scots recognise that the economy has got to be productive and competitive.' He also denied that an independent Scotland would be interventionist and subsidy-dependent. 'I have never believed in anything other than a mixed economy,' he said. 'I am not uncomfortable at all about the market place and about the economy being competitive and productive.' 'I am quite happy to proclaim my socialism in that context,' he declared paradoxically, 'but that doesn't make the SNP a socialist party.'[19]

Constitutionally, Salmond also attempted to square circles, acknowl-edging (unlike later in his career) that there were strict limits to the degree of independence available within the European Community, while when it came to devolution, he maintained the SNP's job was to convince people that only full independence was the most viable option. 'Now that is an entirely different thing from saying, do I think that a devolved parliament would be better than the status quo? I happen to think it would be,' he explained. 'Would the SNP in Parliament vote for or against a devolution scheme? Well, I think the SNP would vote for it, as being better than the status quo. But we won't argue for that case.'

This position was, at best, contrived, although Salmond was convinced that it gave the SNP a more credible, and potentially electorally successful, stance, while he tried to nudge his party towards a more pragmatic position. Many Nationalists remained suspicious. In October 1990 the NEC had again considered a multi-option referendum but was regarded – probably correctly – as an attempt to bounce the party into a discussion about devolution. As Gordon Wilson later wrote, there were reservations about Salmond's 'dallying with devolution front bodies such as Scotland United (which had Labour activist involvement) as gradualism carried too far'.[20]

Interviewing Salmond in February 1991, Peter Jones noted that he was 'much given to talking about undercurrents of opinion, underlying tensions, both here and abroad, and then relating them to scenarios and strategies. Such talk gives him a wily, perhaps cunning, image, not necessarily the image which makes him as trusted by his party . . . but qualities which make him a politician to be reckoned with'.

Above all, what made Salmond a politician to be reckoned with was his tactical nous. 'When the opportunity presents itself, before and after the election,' he told Jones, 'you know where you are going, and you seize it with both hands.'[21]

At a special SNP conference in late March 1991, Salmond put his party on an election footing while laying to rest the three-year-old 'Can Pay, Won't Pay' Poll Tax campaign. 'The battle now transfers to the ballot box,' said Salmond, following a debate in which only his speech and a 'final oratorical flood'[22] by Jim Sillars had turned the tide in their favour. Having been pressured into not speaking in the debate, the party's Poll Tax spokesman (and architect of the non-payment campaign), Kenny MacAskill, was then demoted to defence spokesman. Although MacAskill and Salmond had long since drifted apart, this incident did little to improve relations between the two Linlithgow Academy boys who had once dreamed of a Scottish socialist republic.

There was further bad news for Salmond in April, when a MORI poll put SNP support at just 15 per cent and Salmond's personal rating at its lowest level since becoming leader. Later that month, Salmond also lost a key ally when Mike Russell, the SNP's publicity vice-convener since 1987, stood down due to external work commitments.

The first year of Salmond's leadership had, according to some, 'produced doubts about his facility for working with other people',[23] just as Sillars, Wilson, et al, had feared back in September 1990. By the summer of 1991 several Parliamentary candidates were also complaining about inactivity and lack of leadership, not to mention the drift in the polls. 'We don't know what we are campaigning for,' complained one, 'there is no energy about the party . . . it's not the strategy that is wrong, but that it is just not being implemented.'

Although Gil Paterson, a Ewing supporter who was by then in charge of party organisation, thought Salmond was 'a hard taskmaster' ('If he thinks you are not putting the work in, he will tell you'),[24] otherwise he had no complaints, while others began to get all nostalgic for the days of Gordon Wilson's unflashy yet capable leadership. Wilson was even pressed to stand for re-election to the NEC, while Margaret Ewing received calls urging her to challenge Salmond at the 1991 conference.

Some of these complaints were not of Salmond's making – favourable news coverage of his election had quickly been overtaken by the Gulf War and Mrs Thatcher's demise – although others were. His handling of the non-payment policy had offended talented campaigners like MacAskill, for example, while depriving activists of an emotive issue with which to convince voters that the SNP cared about social as well as constitutional matters.

What Salmond called the 'Big Idea' of independence in Europe also suffered from presentational problems. Rather than pitching this as Scotland securing its proper place in the world it emerged as a techno-cratic idea involving the European Central Bank (which Salmond argued ought to be located in Edinburgh) and incomprehensible monetary mechanisms. And while accusations of 'inactivity' were unfair (Salmond was, if anything else, prodigiously hard-working), he attracted criticism for travelling abroad with the Commons Energy Select Committee instead of attending party rallies. The failure to have an election strategy in place as late as May despite the prospect of a June election also appeared complacent, something Salmond conceded when he told the US consul-general that a June 1991 general election would be 'disastrous'[25] for the SNP.

If all this was not enough for Salmond to contend with, it then emerged towards the end of July that Jim Sillars was planning to chal-lenge Alasdair Morgan for the deputy leadership. 'The Salmond guile, plus the Sillars bombast, makes for an intriguing mixture,' wrote one journalist, 'potentially exciting, but potentially also divisive.'[26] Salmond said he was perfectly relaxed at the prospect of working again with Sillars, although privately he would have preferred there to be no contest. As if anticipating controversy, meanwhile, he warned in a message to SNP members that one requirement of electoral success was 'self-discipline throughout the party and particularly among our prominent members'.[27]

'He [Salmond] is still perversely mistrusted by many members for his cool confidence, intellectual certainty and apparent lack of passion,' observed the journalist Julie Davidson in a 1992 newspaper profile. 'And in a party where sociability is important he remains aloof from the fun and games, drinking sparingly and avoiding all choruses of Flower of Scotland. What's more, Jim Sillars wants his job.'[28]

But whatever his internal and external problems, Salmond soon demonstrated his aptitude for seemingly spontaneous political rejuvenation. On the Monday prior to the 1991 conference the Edinburgh-born actor Sean Connery – whom Salmond had met at the actor's Freedom of Edinburgh ceremony earlier that year – appeared in a party political broadcast urging Scots to support the SNP. It was a notable publicity coup for the media-savvy Salmond, and his reward was a revived opinion poll showing in which the party edged towards the psychologically important level of 20 per cent.

'The way I see the conference is re-positioning the SNP in peoples' minds,' said Salmond, 'getting away from the idea of the SNP as a vehicle for protest towards a view of the SNP as a party which is bidding for government.'[29] Despite his campaigning past, Salmond now believed the SNP could not sustain itself by moving from one isolated campaign to the other, and that the secret of electoral success lay in remoulding it as a 'social democrat' party of government. 'We are evolving a party programme which would be recognisable to any of the great Social Democratic parties in Europe,' he told delegates in his first conference speech as leader, 'not to the right-wing aberration which has fizzled out in the UK – but to European Social Democrats.'

This was a significant departure, not only from the party's ideological past, but also from Salmond's. For more than a decade he had argued that the SNP could only attract disaffected Labour voters from the left, now he was saying it ought to be done from the political centre ground. But this did not mean old left-wing shibboleths had been ditched. On the contrary, Salmond vowed never to 'desert the cause of unilateral nuclear disarmament', while he paraded steel workers on the conference platform, alongside middle-class professionals, in order to emphasise the party's broad, but still essentially left-wing, appeal. Salmond also took several smaller gambles, announcing that the party's principal spokesmen, MPs and other supporters would form a 'Scottish cabinet – a government-in-waiting of people with the ability to take Scotland forward',[30] a structural innovation with the added benefit of giving Salmond tighter control over party policy.

Also important, particularly in the longer term, was the SNP's decision at that conference to participate in elections for a Scottish parliament, should one be set up following the next general election. 'I advanced this position,' Salmond later explained, 'for I believed the establishment of the parliament would be a defining moment in the process of independence.'[31] Many Nationalists, however, continued to suspect that at heart their new leader was little more than a devolutionist.

Salmond's first conference speech, at least in presentational terms, had been a success, although it was overshadowed by a damaging row over the SNP's target date for independence. At a press conference on 18 September Alex Neil, the party's new publicity vice-convener, told reporters the SNP had set a target 'to reach independence by 1 January, 1993'. When senior Nationalists expressed surprise, fearing such a date would be seen as unrealistic, Neil insisted it had been agreed in advance, arguing that his wording was simply a logical extension of Salmond's own statement that the SNP would be 'ready to form the government of an independent Scotland after the coming general election'.[32]

Although this incident quickly blew over, the slogan would return to haunt Salmond during and after the 1992 general election. Critics, however, believe Salmond grew wise after the event. ' "Free by '93" was agreed by the [National] Executive under the leadership of Alex Salmond,' protested Iain Lawson, 'and this again is the rewriting of history to suit political objectives.' 'I thought to myself,' Salmond later recalled of the press conference, 'I didn't realise that was in the script . . . Iain's recollections of SNP documents must be larger than mine. I don't recall Executive meetings sitting around saying "Free by 93" shall be our election slogan.'[33] Writing in 2000, Salmond also allocated some of the blame to Jim Sillars. 'The words were not his but the off-stage direction was pure Sillars,' he said. 'It was never an official SNP slogan, nor an election theme. It was just a silly boast to reporters before the conference even began.'[34] At least that silly boast had one great virtue, as Donald Dewar memorably quipped: it could be recycled every ten years.

Significantly, rather than dump the phrase as he had the non-payment campaign, Salmond decided to go along with it. 'I think that raises one serious question about Alex Salmond's leadership,' pondered James Mitchell, 'which I think has recurred occasionally and that is his unwillingness to take on his opponents.' Mitchell had a point. 'I don't think it was my most glorious moment of leadership,' concurred Salmond. 'I should have caught on to what was happening quicker and perhaps re-orientated the strategy before it got too strong a hold.'[35] Instead of controlling what he called a 'trite phrase', however, Salmond 'tried to manage the position and set about giving the claim some degree of credibility'.[36]

Also unveiled at the 'Free by '93' press conference was a more angular version of the SNP's traditional thistle-shaped logo, ostensibly to highlight the party's new, crisper political message. Commentary instead focused on its resemblance to an early version of the Nazi swastika, while upside down it was virtually identical to that of a German neo-Nazi organisation active in the 1950s and '60s. The press had a field day, particularly as delegates debated the rise of fascist, neo-Nazi movements throughout Europe. 'The logo is clearly recognisable as a revamped and updated version of the long-established SNP symbol,' said an irritated Salmond, 'based on the St Andrew's cross – the Saltire.'[37] Moira Salmond, meanwhile, confessed that she was 'not sure about the logo . . . because it is so sharp; it tends to jab you if worn as jewellery'.[38]

Ironically, another conference fixture – the election of a deputy leader – actually passed off rather smoothly despite widely anticipated trouble. Jim Sillars won by 279 votes to Alasdair Morgan's 184, and although this was interpreted as him putting down a leadership marker following Salmond's difficult summer, the two would actually complement each other well. Sillars was good on detailed policy, carefully addressing lots of hypothetical positions about, for example, Scottish membership of the EEC, while Salmond concentrated on political positioning. 'The SNP put on a skilful, good week,' judged Charles Kennedy in his *Scotsman* column. 'The Cain and Abel phase comes later.'[39] That biblical analogy would prove eerily prophetic.

Fifteen months after becoming SNP leader, and having successfully recovered from a summer of discontent, Salmond now bristled with confidence. 'Alex and I didn't always see eye to eye,' admitted Gordon Wilson, 'but he seems to be growing into the job.'[40] While Isobel Lindsay declared him to be 'far and away the best leader the SNP could have at the moment'.[41] Other critics grudgingly admired his obvious ability ('a cool, professional television performer, the master of the six-second soundbite, who gives no quarter') while pointing out that he could still come across as 'a bit of a smart Alex, a smirker, maybe just a bit too clever'. 'The problem is that Alex is not a natural team player,' said one former senior official. 'He's very bright, a first-class soloist, but it's important for a party to have a good conductor.'

From the Christmas of 1991 up until the general election of May 1992, that 'first-class soloist' was in fine voice. Continuing his determination to attract support in unlikely quarters, Salmond began to speak 'the language of Edinburgh's alternative business establishment, dispensing oil revenue statistics or trading surpluses to justify Scotland's potential self-sufficiency'.[42] 'We need constitutional change to allow Scotland to move on to a higher economic plane,' he had informed an economics seminar a few months before. 'My message to the business and financial community is a straight one. It should wake from its true blue slumber and start to consider the future. Business should join in the search for the best constitutional future for Scotland and our people.'[43]

Edinburgh's Usher Hall also provided the former boy soprano with the perfect acoustics for a memorable multi-party debate on 19 January 1992. Just two days after British Steel announced it was to close the totemic Ravenscraig, 2,500 people filed into the venue, another 6,500 having been turned away. Opening the debate, Salmond appeared uncharacteristically nervous but settled quickly to deliver the most commanding performance of the night. 'Scotland isn't being governed we're being misgoverned,' he declared. 'We're not represented in Europe but misrepresented in Europe.' Salmond was also buoyed by a vociferous and, frankly, partisan audience. He was also effective during a question-and-answer session, scoring points when he asked Donald Dewar to name a single Scottish industry saved by Labour. 'Labour offers us a plasticine parliament. The form but not the substance of power,' said Salmond, although he admitted he would probably back a Labour devolution bill in the House of Commons and also stand in 'plasticine' elections. Dewar, meanwhile, freely conceded 'that if the clapometer measured anything then no doubt Alex Salmond would win that European Song Contest tonight', while boiling his political argument down to basics: 'He can't win; we can.'

Interestingly, Salmond was much weaker when challenged about the nature of the country he aspired to govern. When the Scottish Democrat leader Malcolm Bruce asked 'what kind of Scotland' an independent Scotland would be, he dodged the question, while later, when asked what law he would pass first in an independent Scotland, Salmond's response was less than inspiring: 'A law abolishing direct mailings, which come cascading through your letterbox.'

Overall, however, Salmond exuded reason and authority:

The case for national independence is at heart a simple one and rests on three basic propositions. Firstly, no one, but no one, will make a better job of running Scotland than the people that live here. Government by remote control is, has and would continue to be a failure. Secondly, we have got a distinct contribution to make to the international community; we have a voice well worth hearing and we've a responsibility to make it heard. Thirdly, in the new Europe which is now developing, it offers Scotland an unrivalled opportunity right now to achieve both domestic self government and a defined international role.[44]

Although Salmond was naturally a good performer, he had clearly rehearsed at length for this much-anticipated debate. 'Close as I was to the preparations, the Great Debate was still an eye-opener,' reflected Mike Russell. '[Alex's] Meticulous attention to detail, the covering of all the bases, prodigious hard work and then a sparkling performance.'[45]

The so-called 'Great Debate' at the Usher Hall and a later head-to-head with Labour's Shadow Scottish Secretary George Robertson did much to shore up Salmond's position, not least within the SNP. Indeed, the resulting media coverage was virtually unanimous in proclaiming Salmond the winner. 'The debate went well for me and pretty badly for Dewar,' recalled Salmond. 'It was an extraordinary occasion, a throwback to pre-television politics.'[46]

But if this was to be Salmond's first pre-election fillip, there were more to come. On 23 January 1992 the Scottish edition of the *Sun* newspaper, previously a Conservative-supporting tabloid owned by Rupert Murdoch, declared support for the SNP, its front page urging Scots to 'Rise now and be a nation again'.[47] This political conversion, in which Salmond had been influential, clearly had a lot to do with challenging the dominant (and Labour supporting) *Daily Record*, but still constituted an invaluable boost for a party hitherto starved of such positive coverage.

The icing on the electoral cake came just under a week later when an ICM poll for the *Scotsman* and ITN put support for independence at a staggering, and unprecedented, 50 per cent. 'When nations across Europe are achieving their independence, Scotland will not be left behind,' responded Salmond. 'All it takes is for those Scots who already believe in independence to vote for the only party that can deliver it – the Scottish National Party – and we can make this Scotland's Independence Election.'[48] 'I surfed this political tide for all it was worth,' admitted Salmond in 2000. 'At one point in the campaign, when we touched 30% in an opinion poll, it seemed that Scots might just "rise and be a nation again", but we had next to no money and a poor organisation in many seats.'[49]

There was an assumption (supported by some opinion polls) that the election would produce a hung Parliament or a Labour victory. Initially, however, Salmond was cautious when it came to forecasting the SNP's performance, predicting that three or four Tory marginals might fall to Nationalist candidates. In one previous Tory marginal, meanwhile, two full-time party workers (Peter Murrell and Richard Lochhead) continued to nurse the constituency that their candidate was about to defend for the first time. 'People hear stories about Alex being a rabid socialist', commented Murrell, 'but when they meet him it's no contest.'[50]

Salmond kicked off the national campaign at Macduff harbour on a sleet-sodden March day. His transportation was the so-called 'Natmobile', a converted mini-bus driven by Stewart Stevenson, while at a summit meeting of the SNP Scottish cabinet and NEC in Edinburgh, the party's campaign plans were finalised. 'With a third of Labour voters thinking of switching to the SNP,' said Salmond, 'we can push our vote up to 40 per cent and win a majority and a mandate to negotiate Scottish independence.'[51] Inflated rhetoric, therefore, was not the sole preserve of Messrs Sillars and Neil.

A feature of the campaign was a dramatic increase in television coverage for the SNP, both in Scotland and across the rest of the country, although Salmond was deprived of a UK-wide platform when three ITV companies – Granada, Central and Yorkshire – decided not to screen a set-piece election interview by Brian Walden, arguing that it was of no relevance to their viewers. Walden vigorously pursued Salmond over an independent Scotland's position within the EEC, which he referred to as a 'beguiling prospect'.[52] By the end of their 50-minute joust Walden clearly had the edge, although Salmond had held his own, gaining valuable coverage during a campaign in which Jim Sillars and Alex Neil had featured more prominently.An opinion poll released a week before polling day put the SNP just seven points behind Labour, prompting Salmond to claim that his party was now 'surging' to victory.[53] The campaign, however, was not all plain sailing. Labour launched a damaging attack on Salmond's financial case for independence, branding his analysis 'Toytown economics', while the senior Nationalist Roseanna Cunningham remembered thinking about half way through that 'this is not working, we're not doing this, we're not connecting, we're not getting anywhere'.[54]

Unexpectedly, meanwhile, John Major also fronted surprisingly effective Scottish and UK campaigns centred on a robust defence of the Union. 'If I could summon up all the authority of this office, I would put it into this single warning – the United Kingdom is in danger,' he said at one rally. 'Wake up, my fellow countrymen! Wake up now before it is too late!'[55]

Surprisingly, it appeared to work. 'In the SNP headquarters, the day after the 1992 election, a mute tableau summed it all up,' the historian Christopher Harvie later wrote. 'On a table stood an untouched bottle of champagne and an empty bottle of whisky.'[56] Indeed, despite expectations of a breakthrough, the SNP had won, or rather held, just three seats, the 1987 contingent of Salmond (his majority increased to 4,108), Andrew Welsh and Margaret Ewing.

Beyond the Nationalist north-east, an impressive increase in vote-share from 14 to 21.5 per cent was scant consolation for the failure to hold two seats, Dunfermline West (an SNP constituency by virtue of Dick Douglas's defection) and perhaps more damagingly, Jim Sillars in Glasgow Govan (gained at a by-election in 1988). Although little remarked upon at the time, even more humiliating was the fact that the apparently unelectable Scottish Conservative Party had modestly increased its number of votes and MPs.

'The 1992 election was an object lesson in how to turn a campaign triumph into a perceived defeat,' reflected Salmond, before blaming Sillars: 'In the run-up to 1992 . . . Sillars was obsessed with securing "the mandate" – a majority of 36 seats that would precipitate immediate independence.' This was unfair, given that Salmond himself had spoken of winning an outright majority. 'In addition, as the UK election progressed,' he added, 'we got caught in a political vice. Labour supporters deserted [their party] to keep out the Tories; Tories turned out to keep out the SNP. On polling day, instead of "Free By '93" it was "three MPs in 1993".'[57]

# Chapter 7

# THE FUTURE OF NATIONALISM

'The campaign wasn't a failure – our vote soared,' reflected Salmond eight years after the 1992 general election, 'but the perception was disastrous.'[1] Predictably, he received much of the blame, although supporters argued there had been too little time between Salmond's election in September 1990 and the election to sort out a party that was 'underfunded, badly organised and unmodernised as a political organisation'.[2]

There were, however, upsides. Salmond was widely acknowledged, even by opponents, to have performed well during the campaign, thus strengthening his leadership, something also aided by the departure of Jim Sillars from the Commons. Salmond later claimed to be genuinely saddened at his fortmer mentor's defeat in Govan, claiming to have 'patched up a decent working relationship' over the past couple of years. This, however, was destroyed when Sillars bitterly described Scots as '90-minute patriots' in a post-election interview 'before jetting off to his villa in Portugal'. 'Fielding the substantial fallout,' recalled Salmond. 'I determined that Jim and I had had our last political conversation.'[3]

Nevertheless it gave Salmond space to think about the next, more substantive phase of his leadership. 'I think Alex had a number of problems in the early years of his leadership,' reflected Mike Russell.

> He didn't have a programme he wanted to put in place . . . I think he had a generalised programme but the nuts and bolts took longer, he had difficulties in knowing exactly where he wanted to go to, and also had problems with other people who had a different view of where they wanted the party to go . . . Alex is a very pragmatic politician, he reacts to circumstances as they exist. You have to push Alex a little to make him plan, and make him plan systematically.[4]

Planning was essential when it came to the SNP's constitutional stance. Although a devolved parliament or assembly had long been seen as a 'stepping stone' to full independence, the party's dramatic exit from the Scottish Constitutional Convention in 1989 had left, as Salmond put it, 'a misleading but enduring public impression of a purist SNP unwilling to engage with the political process in Scotland'.

So after the 1992 election, Salmond and others 'worked to change the SNP's stance as it seemed obvious . . . that independence was more likely as a process building from devolution than some sort of instantaneous political "big bang".'[5] And just a week after polling day he sought to persuade a disappointed and divided SNP to back a revived multi-option constitutional referendum while also seeking cross-party co-operation.

Salmond was nothing if not energetic in doing so, even attempting to frame May's district council elections as a second chance to decide Scotland's constitutional future. Gordon Wilson, however, branded the referendum a 'dead duck' at the SNP's Stirling National Council, while Iain Lawson said it was the party's 'job to remove the strength from Labour', which he did not think likely to happen 'by joining up with them'.[6] Salmond responded by cleverly presenting the referendum as a campaigning device that would expose divisions within the Labour Party. 'The idea of a Scottish-built referendum goes down one of the deepest fault lines in Scottish politics,' he told activists. 'One of our major Unionist opponents is disintegrating before our very eyes. Let's get the lever in and prise them apart.'[7]

With the overwhelming support of his party, Salmond now had the authority to meet with Scotland United and Common Cause, two umbrella groups devoted to Scottish devolution, saying he would be 'extremely friendly' in his approach.[8] But when the Labour MP George Galloway (a 'crypto-nationalist' according to Salmond) and the STUC's Campbell Christie led a Scotland United delegation to meet Salmond at the SNP's North Charlotte Street headquarters, Labour's Donald Dewar accused some of his colleagues of 'collaborating' with the SNP and thus 'the idea' of an ecumenical devolution campaign was, as the journalist Iain Macwhirter judged it to be, 'all but dead'.[9]

Speaking at the 1992 SNP conference Gordon Wilson and Margaret Ewing heaped scorn on the idea of co-operating with Labour politicians in pursuit of devolution, with many delegates still smarting from the election result. Salmond unveiled a new medium-term strategy highlighting the economic disadvantages of the Union, condemning Labour's refusal to fight for constitutional change, and reviewing the party's organisation, finances and campaigning ability, but this was rebuffed. The previous conference's proposal for a 'Scottish cabinet', meanwhile, was finally passed, although not by a margin sufficient for inclusion in the party's constitution.

In a combative keynote speech, Salmond reasserted himself, signalling his determination to press on with cross-party co-operation, culminating in a demonstration at the European Summit in Edinburgh later that year. That, at least, went well, with some 25,000 people listening to speeches, including one from Salmond, at a dignified, if ultimately fruitless, gathering.

Then, early the following year, an otherwise non-contentious Commons division over the Maastricht Treaty plunged Salmond's still-fragile leadership into crisis. It all began when the Conservative government reached a deal with 21 Liberal Democrat MPs, four Plaid Cymru Members and the SNP's three to pass an amendment it feared losing because of rebellious Tory backbenchers. Although the SNP (which was pro-Maastricht) argued for a second-question referendum on Scottish independence in return for its support, when John Major told Margaret Ewing (who was leading the talks) that everything was non-negotiable except representation on the Committee of the Regions (CotR), a pan-European body for local and regional authorities to be created post-Maastricht, discussions inevitably focused on that.

Instead of Scottish members of the CotR being chosen by the UK government, Ian Lang, the Scottish Secretary, offered to let Scotland's four political parties nominate their own representatives from among members of local authorities. Labour, however, refused to co-operate and the SNP – its approach agreed by Ewing, Salmond and Andrew Welsh – looked forward to a tactical triumph in which they could point to a major government concession while thwarting Labour plans to hog all Scotland's CotR seats. The division, however, did not go to plan. The government lost and, having spotted Salmond *et al* in the 'wrong' lobby, Labour MPs quickly rounded on the Nationalist trio, jeering and pointing. Wrong-footed, the SNP MPs left the Chamber, Ewing to prepare for a difficult press conference, and Salmond to sign a declaration with Scottish Liberal Democrat leader Jim Wallace calling for the old Scottish parliament to be recalled.

This took place in a meeting room just off Westminster Hall, where Campbell Christie and Bill Spiers of the STUC were also present. Embarrassingly for Salmond, television cameras caught the moment when the Labour MP Henry McLeish looked in and told Christie privately that the cross-party talks were off as a result of the vote. Labour MPs, meanwhile, signed a motion condemning the SNP and calling on

Salmond to resign. 'In the morning Salmond called on all Scotland to unite against the Tories,' McLeish quipped during one radio debate. 'In the evening, he united with the Tories against Scotland.' The Labour-supporting *Daily Record* even ran front-page pictures of Salmond *et al* under the headline: 'The Three Stooges.'

There was an immediate backlash from ordinary SNP members, many of whom had watched events unfold on Channel 4 News. At a specially convened meeting of the NEC, Alex Neil and Kenny MacAskill submitted a motion condemning the MPs' actions, while Rob Gibson, ordinarily a Salmond supporter, submitted another sympathising with the MPs but regretting their action. (Neil and MacAskill eventually dropped their motion and endorsed Gibson's.) Winnie Ewing and Gordon Wilson, meanwhile, supported Salmond's motion (signed by all three SNP MPs), arguing that being an MP required taking quick decisions.

The first half of the NEC meeting – during which Salmond apologised – had been relatively civil, but during a break it was alleged Salmond had leaned on two youth representatives (Shirley Anne Somerville, a future MSP, and Stewart Hosie, a future MP), who looked set to vote against him. In the second half of the meeting, according to reports, Salmond hit back at his opponents in deeply personal terms. Alex Neil was blamed for bouncing the party into 'Free by '93'; Iain Lawson was criticised for his candidacy in the Paisley by-election, while Roger Mullin was accused of leaking a fax critical of Salmond to the BBC.

In the event, Salmond's motion passed by 13 votes to 11, with the two youth representatives abstaining. Neil, MacAskill and Mullin, however, all felt Salmond's assault on them meant they no longer enjoyed his confidence and they promptly resigned from his 'Scottish cabinet'. Some SNP branches called upon Salmond to resign, although six of the 11 NEC members who had voted against the MPs – including Gibson, Roseanna Cunningham, Fiona Hyslop and Nicola Sturgeon – asked for the NEC's decision to be accepted in a letter to the *Scotsman*. 'There was an over-reaction within the party because some feared it was a repeat of 1979,' recalled one of those present at the meeting, 'and ironically that over-reaction probably prevented it from becoming so. For the first time the SNP did what Labour had done all the time, allowed its left wing to let off steam while also managing to keep its head.'[10]

Salmond penned a lengthy defence of his actions for that weekend's edition of *Scotland on Sunday*, arguing that having a 'genuine cross-section of the Scottish population' on the Committee of the Regions would have represented 'a modest but important gain for Scotland'. Conceding that it was 'certainly rare for the SNP to be in the Tory lobby', he remained defiant. 'The SNP must be pro-Scottish, not only anti-Tory,' he wrote. 'If that means holding my nose as I go through the division lobbies then I will do it.'[11]

Although this incident had been damaging, at no point was there the prospect of a serious challenge to Salmond's leadership. 'If it told you anything about Alex then it was him as a team player,' observed the future MSP Jim Eadie, who worked for the SNP group at Westminster at that time. 'He didn't attempt to distance himself from the decision or hang Margaret out to dry, as he could have done. Retrospectively he thought it had been the wrong decision, but stood by it in public and took the flak.'[12]

The flak was considerable. Activist Brendan O'Hara, later a colleague of Salmond's in the 2015-20 UK Parliament, wrote to the *Herald* that his leader failed 'to recognise the deep hurt and dismay of the ordinary party activist', observing 'a sense of betrayal in the party which was compounded by the refusal to atone for their actions'.[13] But by the Perth National Council of 5 June, the heat had gone out of the issue and a motion critical of the leadership was defeated by 147 votes to 81. 'We have put introspection behind us,' declared Alex, 'and [have] decided to attack our opponents instead of navel gazing.'[14] Salmond – leader of the SNP for only two-and-a-half years – had lived to fight another day.

The row over Maastricht lasted nearly three months and effectively killed off any hope of cross-party co-operation on constitutional reform, although Salmond continued to reposition his party in order to take a more constructive approach to devolution. Meanwhile, he spent the two months leading up to the SNP's 1993 conference delivering a sextet of speeches at locations around Scotland, an attempt to flesh out his political philosophy.

This amounted to a Third Way between Thatcherite and left-wing orthodoxies, something Salmond chose to call 'social democracy', although he took care to pre-empt accusations that this meant selling out on core principles. 'I think the SNP's cutting edge and radicalism will remain, on issues like nuclear weapons, on a whole range of social policy,' he said. 'But I don't think we can allow *sentiment* to interfere with the absolute requirement for an economically successful Scottish economy.'[15]

What the party and Scotland has to realise is that our social programme is predicated on economic success which requires the economic strategy we are outlining. You can't have a hazy belief that it will be OK if we intervene here, nationalise this. If we don't like that sector we'll take it into public ownership. That's silly and stupid. The government's job is to provide the springboard from which our industry can compete successfully.[16]

It was, as ever, a delicate balancing act. As Salmond removed traditional socialist tenets from the SNP's economic policy, he injected a counter-balancing radicalism into its social agenda.

In the sixth and final speech, Salmond also spelled out how Scotland would achieve its freedom:

> The first thing a victorious SNP will do, after winning a mandate for Independence through a majority of Scottish seats at a General Election, is to invite all other Scottish MPs to join us in an interim Scottish Parliament. We shall then open negotiations with both London and Brussels on the exact terms of Scottish Independence. The next step will be to submit these terms and our detailed proposals for the constitution of an independent Scotland to the people for their approval in a referendum. Once the constitution is agreed, we shall then as quickly as possible hold the first democratic elections to a Scottish Parliament.[17]

All six speeches were issued in pamphlet form at the 1993 SNP conference, let down by a less than inspiring title, *Horizons Without Bars*, which rather than advocating a drink-free Scotland was a quote from an essay by William McIlvanney. As political manifestos go it was more tactical than philosophical, but it served a valuable purpose, not least in shoring up Salmond's intellectual credentials among the ever-important media.

'I think in [those speeches] you began to see ... the beginnings and the development of a very clear political philosophy,' reflected Mike Russell in 2001. '[They began] to map out the socially democratic vision for the party [that was] seeking to engage and bring in the widest possible constituency.'[18] The speeches codified existing thinking rather than generating new ideas, but however socially democratic, Tony Crosland's *The Future of Socialism* it was not, although the subtitle was 'The Future of Scotland'. Perhaps Salmond could have called it 'The Future of Nationalism'.

'He [Salmond] is, pretty much, a pragmatist,' judged the *Scotsman* as delegates gathered for the SNP's Dunoon conference, 'but is suspected by fundamentalists of all persuasions of closet gradualism. That is why he does not yet command unstinting rank-and-file support.'[19] Salmond was, therefore, clearly under pressure, one office-bearer observing 'a degree of irritation with him that wasn't there last year'.[20]

Salmond was also frustrated, as he later reflected, that 'occasional outbreaks of ideological purity' were often 'a comfortable substitute for progress'.[21] Nevertheless the tension focused his mind, and his constitutional refrain of the previous three years – a multi-option referendum – was abandoned in favour of a strong solo tune. Until 1994's regional council and European Parliament elections, announced Salmond, it was the SNP's 'job to attack our political opponents. The Tory Party for what they have done to Scotland and Labour for what they have not done for Scotland. But our most important task is to present our inspiring vision for Scotland's future.'[22]

Conscious of criticism that his oratory lacked the fire of Sillars or Alex Neil, Salmond brought delegates to their feet with some stirring passages. 'SNP success will send our Unionist opponents into a spiral of fear, fear not of the present but fear of the future,' he declared. 'Neither wants to lose Scotland. The Tories fear the loss of Scottish resources, Labour the loss of Scottish votes.' To roars of applause he also pushed the right nuclear and energy buttons, demanding that 'rotting nuclear hulks' be removed from Scotland while branding the piping of North Sea gas to England as the 'Great Gas Robbery'.

Salmond also took on his critics, slapping down Jim Sillars '90-minute patriots' jibe by declaring that if Scots had failed to vote for change then 'that's my fault for not explaining the case clearly enough, your fault for not winning on the doorsteps, our fault collectively for a lack of resolution'.[23] Salmond's speech earned him a standing ovation, supporters talking it up as a personal triumph while even critics acknowledged that it was just the sort of 'fire in the belly' speech needed to rouse the party following a difficult year. 'Finally,' declared a *Scotsman* editorial, 'Alex Salmond has taken command of the Scottish National Party'.[24]

The final day of conference, however, demonstrated that that command was not yet total. For the second year running Alex Neil topped the poll for the NEC, while two other Salmond critics, Kenny MacAskill and Iain Lawson, were also easily elected. Shrewdly, Salmond hinted that Neil and MacAskill would be brought back into the fold with Scottish cabinet posts. 'As I have said before,' he told reporters, 'there is no such thing as a lost soul.' The party, Salmond added, was in 'fine fettle', while 'this excellent, united and purposeful conference' would act as a 'launchpad for the electoral contests ahead'.[25]

The year 1994 was indeed the year of elections. First up were May's regional council elections, the last before the Conservative government planned to abolish Labour strongholds like Strathclyde Region to make way for 32 unitary authorities. Although the SNP had long supported this reform, Salmond chose a meeting of the standing committee considering the Local Government (Scotland) Bill for his first bout of Parliamentary guerilla warfare since 1989, chiefly to highlight Scottish Secretary Ian Lang's need to 'parachute' five English Tory MPs onto the committee in order to let the Bill proceed.

On 1 February Salmond forced the abandonment of its first session 'by merely turning up, sitting down and (loyally) reading a copy of The Herald newspaper'.[26] As in 1989, he was not a member of the committee, and not only did his action wreck detailed consideration of the Bill, it forced the government to pass a resolution preventing Salmond or anyone else taking part. Unlike in 1988-89, however, Labour joined with the SNP in objecting to the presence of English MPs, although Salmond's tactics were, it seemed, subject to law of diminishing political returns. It 'all comes dressed up in fine points of argumentation, a sophisticated gloss implying a long-term strategic analysis and approach,' sneered the Scotsman, although it had a point. 'Of course it is nothing of the kind. It is about headlines, pictures and soundbites.'[27]

Whatever it was, the disruption meant the Local Government (Scotland) Bill was still working its way through Parliament as Scots voted in the last regional council elections in early May 1994. The SNP secured 70 seats and 26.8 per cent of the vote, up from 43 and 21.8 per cent in 1990, its second-best result in the two-decade history of regional authorities. The party also captured the Airdrie South ward in the Monklands East constituency. 'Maybe not free by '93, but we have opened the door by 94,' quipped Salmond. 'Labour can feel the ground shift from under their feet in Scotland.'[28] The ground continued to shift as Scotland's political parties geared up for June's European Parliament elections. With 32.6 per cent of the vote and nearly half a million votes, the outcome was the SNP's best-ever performance in a national election and firmly established it as Scotland's second party.

The regional and European elections of 1994 were central to Salmond's bid to restore electoral credibility after the humiliation of the 1992 general election. In that context, the Monklands East by-election of July 1994 – held in the wake of Labour leader John Smith's premature death – was both a setback and an epiphany. 'Nationalism is in the air again in Scotland,' remarked a Labour MP on the eve of the by-election, 'you can smell it.'[29] Unfortunately for the campaign that preceded it, there was also a distinct whiff of sectarianism.

This hinged upon allegations of sectarian bias on the Labour-controlled Monklands District Council, which included the Monklands East constituency. It was alleged that the authority favoured spending in the predominantly Catholic Coatbridge, and had therefore neglected the largely Protestant Airdrie. The by-election itself was essentially a straight fight between the SNP's Kay Ullrich (later an MSP) and the former general secretary of the Scottish Labour Party, Helen Liddell, most recently an aide to the media tycoon Robert Maxwell.

Relishing the prospect of an SNP win in an urban Labour heartland, Salmond was fully involved with the campaign, so much so that he even cancelled 'plans to attend his niece's baptism in Aberdeen'.[30] Two years earlier Salmond had also missed his mother's 70th birthday celebrations in order to attend a CND rally in Glasgow. Usually very much a family man, these absences illustrated Salmond's overriding commitment to politics.

Salmond later claimed to have noticed problems with sectarianism while campaigning in Monklands during the regional council elections in May. In the by-election itself, his own 'observations' turned up 'many occasions late in the campaign on which SNP voters – who happened to be Catholic – were told in the clearest terms by Labour canvassers that the SNP would discriminate against them. These voters were told that we would close Catholic schools and – when that argument failed to stick because it was a lie – that we would "create a Northern Ireland".'[31]

On the other hand, Labour later claimed that the SNP had indulged in similar tactics. Charge and counter-charge were par for the course, heightening even the usual tensions of a particularly febrile by-election campaign. At the count on 30 June this tension finally burst out into the open. Liddell won, but with a much reduced majority of only 1,640, while Kay Ullrich came second with an impressive swing of more than 19 per cent. In what Salmond later described as 'the most graceless acceptance speech I have ever heard', Liddell accused the Tory and SNP candidates of having 'played the Orange card' during the campaign, something Salmond dismissed as 'absolute rubbish'.

But it was an ill-judged editorial in the following day's *Herald* that really riled Salmond. Headlined 'Tawdry SNP campaign', the newspaper singled out the Nationalists as having 'sought to revive the "Billy and Dan" factor in Scottish politics from which we have fought so hard to escape'.[32] Although the next edition of the *Herald* admitted 'the official

SNP campaign [had] strenuously avoided this question', the damage was done. In the same edition Salmond launched a blistering defence of the SNP and its conduct.

> Most of the recent leadership of the party – and many of its members – have their origins in the central belt, Margo MacDonald from Lanarkshire, Jim Sillars from Ayrshire, Winnie Ewing from Glasgow, Andrew Welsh from Govan – and myself from West Lothian – the list goes on, but all of those on it are united in this common purpose. We were all forged in the same fire, a fire that sometimes flickered evilly with the tittle-tattle of bigotry and the actual experience of political gerrymandering for religious ends . . . Membership of the SNP was for us, and for many like us, a declaration that rejected utterly such wrongs.[33]

Telling by its absence from this roll call of leading Nationalists was Billy Wolfe, the former SNP leader whom Salmond knew well from West Lothian politics. This was not surprising, for in advance of Pope John Paul II's visit to Scotland back in 1982, Wolfe had voiced opposition in the pages of the Church of Scotland magazine *Life & Work*. The row that followed ended Wolfe's career within the party and did much wider damage to the SNP. Monklands was, therefore, Salmond's epiphany. 'I was very affected by that by-election,' he reflected in 2009. 'The nature of the whole campaign just made you feel dirty.'[34]

But, as Salmond said in a 1995 speech, the Monklands experience also 'made the SNP look very closely at the whole issue of discrimination'.[35] Within weeks of the by-election both Salmond and Liddell met with Thomas Winning, the Roman Catholic Archbishop of Glasgow, who would be appointed Cardinal later that year. According to a biography of Winning, he told an 'unimpressed' Liddell that the Labour Party had problems with bigotry, which she denied, but immediately warmed to Salmond, marking the 'beginning of a close political friendship that would bloom over the next seven years'. As Salmond later put it: 'I liked Tom Winning, and I think he liked me.' Winning also reminded him that the Catholic Church in Scotland had always been distinct, a point Salmond absorbed and made many times over the next two decades.

'His goal when asking for a meeting with Winning was to convince him of the changed face of Scottish Nationalism,' wrote Winning's biographer Stephen McGinty, 'but when he arrived the door was already ajar.' Privately, it seems, Winning had 'developed into a Nationalist' despite confessing to Salmond that he had voted against a Scottish Assembly in 1979. Salmond's calculation in meeting Winning was also tactical, viewing Scotland's large Catholic population (representing around 800,000, mostly Labour, voters) as an 'untapped resource'. He duly informed Winning (over spaghetti) of 'his ambition to remove all trace of anti-Catholicism from the party [the SNP] and to provide a natural alternative to the Labour Party'.[36] In response, according to Salmond, Winning said simply: 'By your deeds are you known.'[37]

Salmond's deeds, articulated in a series of speeches over the next year, further repositioned the SNP in just the sort of long-term strategising at which he excelled, and was if anything more successful than his various attempts to rebrand the party ideologically. Not only did Salmond's personal interest in Catholicism deepen, but that, together with political contacts in Ireland, also fed into his economic strategy. 'The SNP is engaged in the process of reinforcing our identity as a civic national party appealing to all of the people of Scotland regardless of origin,' he wrote in his *Herald* column towards the end of 1994. 'We will be judged on how consistently and successfully we pursue that task.'[38]

Having been run ragged during the council, European and by-election campaigns, Salmond was laid low with pneumonia at the end of 1994 and found it hard to shake off the after-effects for several months. For what limited rest and relaxation he and Moira enjoyed, two weeks each August were still spent in Colonsay, one of the quietest and least accessible Hebridean islands, where Alex could indulge his love of golf and the West Highland scenery.

His marriage, meanwhile, remained strong, despite the demands placed upon Salmond as leader. Moira, as Winnie Ewing had informed the 1993 SNP conference, was 'an absolute cracker'. Having campaigned with Mrs Salmond, added Ewing, she could vouch that she was 'dynamic, efficient, totally dedicated and Alex is a very lucky man to have her. And we have an extra weapon, we've Moira as a secret weapon.'[39]

Earlier in 1994 Salmond had helped celebrate the SNP's 60th anniversary by boldly claiming that the party had helped convert Scotland from a Unionist to a Nationalist frame of mind, while attending a dinner in Edinburgh 'at which all four of my extant predecessors spoke in spellbinding fashion'[40] about the party's great strides over the past six decades. That year also saw the publication of an updated version of Christopher Harvie's much-praised 1977 tome, *Scotland & Nationalism*, as well as a new work by the historian Richard Finlay on the origins of the SNP, *Independent and Free*. Despite his love of history, however, Salmond was slow to appreciate the contribution his predecessors had made to the National Movement.

Indeed, when the SNP had been constituted in April 1934 it had advocated a form of Imperial Federation, with Scotland taking its place as a self-governing Dominion within the British Empire. Sixty years on, and Salmond was still redefining the nature of independence long after Britain had lost that Empire and struggled to find a role. 'There is no pure independence in this world,' he reflected on the eve of the 1994 SNP conference, although he reckoned devolution within the UK was 'likely to be unstable'. 'The one thing about independence', added Salmond, 'is that it is highly unlikely to revert to un-independence, it is stable.'[41]

The *Herald* dubbed what followed in Inverness 'the most successful SNP conference in recent times', and indeed it was the least contentious gathering of Salmond's leadership to date. In his keynote speech he got stuck into George Robertson ('Scottish on the outside, British on the inside') and the new Labour leader Tony Blair ('floating along on hot air, sound bites and photo-opportunities').[42] There was also more constructive content, most notably lavish praise for the Catholic faith's contribution to Scotland intellectual life. 'The Catholic view of social justice informs our attitude to inequality in Scotland and internationally,' Salmond told delegates, contrasting the 'institutionalised religious discrimination'[43] of the UK Act of Settlement (which barred Catholics from acceding to the throne) with the status Catholics would enjoy under a written bill of rights in an independent Scotland.

Reflecting on Salmond's speech in his column the following day, the journalist John MacLeod remembered observing 'hundreds and hundreds of clapping hands, adoring eyes, mesmerised smiles, the great roar of the multitude and their intoxicating applause',[44] an indication that the SNP leader was finally winning his party round. Indeed, after four full years in charge, Gordon Wilson reckoned his 'star was rising within the Party', although there remained dissent on its left wing and also 'more traditional supporters of independence who were dubious about readopting devolution'.[45]

MacLeod also ruminated more broadly on Salmond's character, reflecting that 'politics and economics are all he knows and, seemingly, to him all that matters. He is not a man of books and perspective, and seems secular to the core.'[46] The same could not be said of Mike Russell, the ostentatiously cultured Episcopalian who returned to SNP HQ at the end of 1994 in the newly created position of chief executive. Not only had Russell been a valued ally since the mid-1980s, but the television

producer also imbued his new boss with that hitherto absent hinterland.
When Salmond had to provide his cultural influences for a March
1995 edition of the *New Statesman*, for example, there are unmistak-
able elements of both men. Asked which books and authors had had
the greatest effect on his political beliefs, Salmond listed 'John Steinbeck
for *The Grapes of Wrath* and *Cannery Row*, and William McIlvanney
for his range of works', while also offering *Our Scots Noble Families* by
Tom Johnston ('a former secretary of state for Scotland's tirade against
Scotland's aristocracy') and John Buchan's *Montrose* ('which shows that
there were one or two saving graces'). As for his favourite poem and
song, Salmond predictably nominated 'A Man's a Man for a' That' by
Robert Burns. Intriguingly, when asked who was 'the greatest prime
minister we never had and why?' Salmond offered Jim Sillars 'as the most
talented politician of his generation',[47] a charitable reference given his
former mentor's regular tabloid attacks.

Russell, like Salmond, also possessed a natural journalistic flair, and
occasionally ghosted the SNP leader's weekly *Herald* column, as did
Kevin Pringle, another key aide who had joined the SNP as research
officer in 1989. Although more often than not a rather bland reflection
on the week's political events, not to mention regular attacks on the
'spivs' who ran privatised utilities, a few were not only well written, but
also provoked bulging mailbags in response. One in May 1993 on the
golfer John Panton, for example, went down particularly well while,
more broadly, the very presence of the column in a serious newspaper
like the *Herald* was invaluable for a party still building its profile and
respectability.[48]

As the Conservative government of John Major faltered, Salmond spent
the next two and a half years attacking the Tories and lamenting Tony
Blair's New Labour. And as talk of a cross-party approach to devolution
diminished Salmond also sought, this time more decisively, to toughen
up the SNP's stance on devolution. To that end, an NEC meeting
in early 1995 backed a new dual-path strategy entitled 'Highway to
Independence', under which a majority of SNP MPs at Westminster
or in a devolved parliament would constitute a legitimate mandate for
beginning independence negotiations.

Salmond also used an interview with *Scotland on Sunday* to test his
party's mood, telling Kenny Farquharson there was no 'holy grail' in
terms of how independence was achieved and that the party 'must not
get itself hung up on the route'. 'I would only have difficulty in the party

on this matter if I stopped arguing for independence and started arguing for devolution,' he said, clearly trying to pre-empt fundamentalist attacks. 'That isn't going to happen.' Unhelpfully, however, the banner head-line accompanying the interview was the provocative 'Salmond backs devolution'.[49]

There were predictable attacks from the usual suspects, including Jim Sillars, still 'fighting for independence' according to his byline in the ostensibly pro-independence *Scottish Sun*. Salmond likened Sillars to 'an old volcano – each eruption is less significant than the last',[50] although at the next meeting of the SNP's NEC Salmond survived what was in effect a vote of confidence by 17 votes to 6, which he described as a 'fairly resounding endorsement'. 'In a sometimes heated meeting,' reported *Scotland on Sunday*, 'one executive member even produced a thesaurus to challenge the interpretation of some comments.'[51]

Normally reluctant to pick a fight with his party, Salmond had calcu-lated in this instance that it was necessary to shift its line on devolution, however subtly, although on other matters, such as the SNP's hostility towards NATO, he remained reluctant to instigate reform. 'If he thinks the time isn't right to do anything you cannot make him do anything,' reflected Mike Russell in 2001. 'I have a feeling at some points that his touch on the party was too light . . . he was curiously reluctant at times to have a heavier touch on the party itself which I think is a very interesting aspect of his character.'[52]

In this instance, however, Salmond's heavier touch not only got him off Labour's constitutional hook during a head-to-head debate at Edinburgh's Old Royal High School with the Shadow Scottish Secretary George Robertson, but it handed him an unexpected political gift. It began with a brilliantly simple question from a lady in the audience by the name of Lorraine Mann. 'We all know what the first choice of you gentlemen is, between independence, devolution and the status quo,' she said. 'But what's your second choice?' 'A small, cruel smile appeared on Salmond's face,' observed Neal Ascherson. 'The question, naturally, gave him no problems: his second choice was devolution, as a stepping-stone towards independence. Then he turned to enjoy the spectacle of George Robertson under torture.'[53]

This, according to Gordon Wilson, allowed Salmond to further direct the SNP down a more devolutionary path, going to National Council in March 1995 and subsequently to conference to obtain delegates' support for 'a more gradualist route to independence and permit the Party to give positive, instead of reluctant, support to devolution'.[54] Success in public debate also provided a useful backdrop for two more elections, to Scotland's new unitary local authorities and in the Perth and Kinross by-election due on 25 May. The SNP vote actually slipped in the first, to 26.2 per cent, while, paradoxically given the seat's history, it performed surprisingly well in the by-election caused by the death of the colourful Tory MP Sir Nicholas Fairbairn (whom Salmond liked and respected). Following a difficult selection contest involving tabloid revelations about Roseanna Cunningham, she was eventually chosen as the SNP candidate. Another contemporary of Salmond's from the 79 Group, Cunningham was, in the words of one newspaper, a 'left-wing republican feminist'. She was also articulate, striking and a talented campaigner. 'Our candidate has got grace,' said Salmond, as well 'true grit' and 'gumption'; she was not, he added, 'anybody's else's clone'.[55] The result was an 11.6 per cent swing and a 7,311 majority over Labour's Douglas Alexander.

Alexander was close to the Labour Party leader Tony Blair, whom Salmond initially praised as 'both an intelligent and engaging politician' who 'appears like a political general in full command of his forces'.[56] A little later, however, Salmond's attitude had hardened. 'Although I have always found him personally engaging and talented I have never had much time for Tony Blair's politics,' he wrote. 'For some considerable period before the awful truth dawned on sections of his own party, Blair struck me as someone who would be perfectly comfortable leading a post-Thatcher Conservative Party.'[57]

The two leaders had more in common than either would have cared to admit. Both had begun their political careers on the left of their respective parties before reaching the view that only by shedding left-wing shibboleths and modernising could they hope to expand their support. Although there was no real equivalent of Labour's 'Clause 4 moment' for SNP, many of Salmond's pre-1994 reforms anticipated Blair's own approach on becoming leader. There were also striking similarities between both leaders' handling of political presentation, party management and the use of media professionals to hone their respective messages. In short, both men wanted to turn their parties from election losers into election winners.

'Although political leaders have a right – perhaps even a responsibility – to shape the future of the party they lead,' reflected Salmond of Blair's battle to rid his party of its Clause 4, 'that right is not an arbitrary or exclusive one. It certainly does not give the leader a special purchase over a party's collective past.'[58] That, of course, was precisely what many of Salmond's opponents believed he was attempting to do with the SNP, although these remarks demonstrated an obvious belief that his reforms were firmly in keeping with the traditions of his party, as, no doubt, Blair also believed of his. The anti-Poll Tax activist Tommy Sheridan saw Salmond as in the Blairite mould, referring to him as a 'nationalist Neil Kinnock'[59] while Labour, the Liberals and SNP were like 'soap powder sellers, all promoting the same brand of free market capitalism wrapped in different packages'.[60]

Salmond's diligent courting of Scotland's business community certainly echoed Labour's so-called 'prawn cocktail offensive' in the City of London. In July 1995 he addressed Edinburgh's Chamber of Commerce, while his Oban speech the previous year had attempted to reassure businessmen that the SNP was not the tax-and-spend, public sector-orientated party of old. 'I am very, very influenced by Ireland,' admitted Salmond in 1997.[61] A *Herald* column in March 1996 had also extolled the many economic virtues of the Emerald Isle before concluding that Ireland had 'only one striking difference from Scotland: it is no longer ruled from London'. 'With the advantage of full independent membership of the European Union,' added Salmond, 'it has used that membership to attract resources and invest in the future.'

This was, of course, a simplification of recent Irish history. Salmond did not mention the economic and social stagnation that lasted from the creation of the Irish Free State in 1922 until the Irish Republic's membership of the European Community in the early 1970s. Instead Salmond emphasised the 'difference between the status quo, devolution, and independence'. 'Power is the difference – power that can create jobs and prosperity,' he wrote. 'We will be better off with independence – and Ireland proves it.'[62]

Holding Ireland up as a model also served another purpose, chiefly attracting working-class voters of Irish origin who had hitherto been hostile to the SNP, thus neatly dovetailing with Salmond's ongoing wooing of the Catholic vote. It also helped plug some of the gap left by the SNP's gradual neglect of the once-mighty 'independence in Europe' cry. 'Put simply,' judged the academic Peter Lynch in September 1995, 'the SNP has not given much thought to the European Union since Maastricht.'[63] This had created the European Union, but the electorate had also become increasingly Euro-sceptic and the SNP had been less willing to advance pro-European arguments as a result. What seemed positive and forward-looking in the late 1980s now appeared negative and regressive.

'Independence in Europe' had never been much more than a slogan, a tactic which shot the Labour fox, for Salmond, and slogans – however cleverly crafted – were difficult to adapt when political circumstances changed. Praising Ireland was much more straightforward, and it rewarded Salmond's interest with invitations to speak at seminars and summer schools (he visited Ireland six times in 1996–97). At Ballina, County Mayo, he concluded that Scotland was being stifled by 'the dead hand of Westminster'.[64] Such talk obviously went down well in a nation that had shaken off that 'dead hand' more than 75 years earlier.

Salmond also developed the economic case for independence in other areas. Michael Forsyth, Scottish Secretary since 1995, had recently published Government Expenditure and Revenue in Scotland, or GERS, statistics to demonstrate that high public spending north of the Border amounted to a direct subsidy from the Treasury. Salmond recruited a young economist called Andrew Wilson to scrutinise GERS more closely. He recalled:

> William Waldegrave was chief secretary to the Treasury and I'd asked [via the SNP MP Andrew Welsh] about the deficit going all the way back to 1978 and for some reason the Treasury had responded, effectively conceding that Scotland would have been in surplus had it been independent. The Herald splashed on this and Alex was delighted. Then Michael Forsyth came back with quite a clever retort questioning the methodology, but when I tabled some more questions, thinking I was being clever, Salmond at first gave me a bollocking ('never underestimate how clever your opponents are, these are serious people') until the responses, which actually strengthened our position, came chuntering out of the fax machine. He just looked at me and said 'you were lucky'.[65]

That Salmond took care to promote Wilson as the economic marksman behind the GERS ammunition, rather than himself, also demonstrated his generosity when it came to encouraging young political talent.

Even Treasury figures and bright young economists, however, did not appease all the SNP's critics. In the run up to the 1997 general election, for example, the Liberal Democrats published a pamphlet entitled Alex in Wonderland, which questioned the SNP's commitment to spending 'huge amounts of additional money', paid for 'by the revenues from an exogenous boost to the Scottish Economy arising from Independence'.[66]

In June 1996, meanwhile, the Leader of the Opposition also dropped a constitutional bombshell, announcing that before establishing a Scottish

Parliament a Labour government would hold a two-question referendum on devolution, a reversal of the party's existing policy that prompted the resignation of several front bench spokesmen. 'For years Labour have said that a referendum was totally unnecessary since the constitution would be centre stage in a general election, but they are now set to do a cynical U-turn under Tory pressure,' blasted Salmond. 'Tory pressure is dictating new Labour policy on the constitution.'[67]

In truth, however, the U-turn put Salmond in an awkward political position. 'How will you urge SNP supporters to vote in the referendum?' soon became a question he could not avoid. Initially, Salmond simply refused to answer, knowing how divisive the issue remained within his party, while preparing privately for the inevitable. The 1979 debacle still loomed large, yet the dynamic was palpably different. Not only was there greater public support for devolution in 1996 than there had been in 1979, but on offer was a more cohesive, powerful settlement.

Publicly, however, Salmond played it cool and simply repeated that until the general election the SNP would not state its view on what he described as a 'rigged referendum', exactly how he had always referred to the 1979 ballot. And with the party performing well in the polls, it was also clear he intended to avoid the mistakes of the 1992 campaign, focusing on around a dozen marginal seats instead of spreading resources thinly across the whole country. A combination of donations, bequests and celebrity donations (most notably from Sean Connery) also meant the SNP's election fund stood at £500,000, instead of £100,000 as in 1992.

'Since the 1992 election,' Salmond told the *Toronto Star*, 'we've concentrated not just on being a political party, but on shaping a move-ment.'[68] That civic Nationalist 'movement' now included Pensioners for Independence, Business for Independence and New Scots for Independence. Perhaps the most important of these was Scots Asians for Independence. 'It is the members of Scotland's Asian communities who are, in many ways, the most patriotic of all Scots,' wrote Salmond the following year. 'Many have direct family experience of self-deter-mination struggles, and they appreciate the dignity and promise which Independence brings.'[69]

Salmond's attempt to present Scottish Nationalism as a positive force was undermined when, at the 1996 Inverness conference, Alex Neil (still vice-convener for policy) compared George Robertson with the Nazi propagandist Lord Haw-Haw. Salmond demanded an apology and recovered the situation with another successful conference speech in which he implored all those who wanted change in Scotland to 'come and join us'.[70]

'What makes Alex Salmond tick?' asked *Scotland on Sunday* at the beginning of 1997, answering with a quote from a recent Salmond interview: 'Some people can look at a picture and recreate it, capture in their mind a flower or a mountain – I've always been able to capture a row of figures.'[71] The comment, judged the newspaper, summed up Salmond's greatest strength, his command of economic statistics, and also his biggest weakness, a perception that he was little more than a political number cruncher with no real vision or passion. While that was undoubtedly the view of some in the SNP, Salmond's relationship with his party had changed significantly over the past six years. 'Salmond is more relaxed now than ever he was,' observed the academic James Mitchell. 'When first elected leader, the party had respect for him. Now there's an affection as well . . . That has changed the relationship not only with the party but also with the audience outside.'

An internal Labour survey, meanwhile, revealed that most Scots 'accepted without question that he [Salmond] understands the Scottish psyche', while a *Scotsman*/ICM poll in February also ranked him as the 'toughest' of Scotland's four party leaders. There was, nevertheless, another public perception of Salmond as 'Smart Alex', an undoubtedly clever politician who was perhaps a little too aware of his own talents. This he had managed to control, particularly at the 1996 conference, although not his temper, 'which as any senior party official or activist will privately testify, is notoriously short'.[72]

With less than four months until an important election, however, Salmond had to keep his cool. 'Returning from a huge meeting in Crieff,' he wrote in early April. 'I catch sight of the Hale-Bopp comet, lighting the sky above the Wallace Monument. This, I decide, must be an omen for the campaign.'[73] The theme of that campaign was, anticipating Barack Obama in 2008, 'Yes We Can'. 'Our message to the Scottish people is: "Yes, we can win the best future for Scotland",' said Salmond at its launch. 'We are better organised, better financed and more solidly based than ever before and our freedom message will prosper between now and polling day.'[74] Launching the SNP's manifesto a few days later, Salmond wisely refused to predict how many seats the party would win, or when Scotland would achieve independence, unlike in 1992, while presenting the party's policy platform as a combination of prosperity and social justice, enterprise and compassion, head and heart. 'The SNP's vision is of an enterprise economy and a compassionate society,' he had said the previous month, 'both going hand in hand with the other.'[75]

The SNP's was a positive, upbeat campaign that appeared to be vindicated when a *Sunday Times* poll towards the end of April put the SNP at 28 per cent, rising to 38 per cent when people were asked how they would vote in elections for a Scottish parliament, its highest-ever opinion poll rating. Salmond placed a £500 charity bet that the SNP would win between 7 and 40 seats.

The sole gaffe of the campaign, oddly enough, concerned Salmond's mother Mary. 'People across the political spectrum in Scotland', he said at a press conference in London, 'including my mother who has voted Tory since 1945 – believe Cedric Brown [the head of British Gas] should be contributing a bit more', thus revealing for the first time that Mrs Salmond had been a lifelong Conservative. Seeking to manage the subsequent press interest, Salmond then issued a press release, purporting to be from his mother, which said she was concerned about 'fat cat salary awards and corporate greed at a time when vital services like health and education are being starved of funds'. 'Therefore,' added Mary, 'for the first time in my married life, I will be voting the same way as my husband.' That was, of course, SNP.

Not only was the language rather unconvincing, but when doorstepped by a reporter several hours later, it became clear that no one had informed Mary Salmond of her new voting intentions. 'I'll make up my own mind on the day when I cross the road to the polling station,' she said at her home in Linlithgow. There was, at least, an endorsement of sorts. 'If I was in Alex's constituency,' she added, 'I would definitely vote for him because I think he is a superb MP and I think he listens to people.'[76]

Always protective of his family, Salmond was genuinely annoyed that the *Daily Record* had involved his mother in the campaign, although his initial mention, and subsequently mishandling of the situation, had hardly helped. He remained close to his parents, first footing them each Hogmanay as he and Moira saw in the New Year at their home in Linlithgow. 'In the ensuing parties, faither is prevailed upon to sing the Red Flag,' Salmond had written as 1997 dawned. 'He knows every verse, and is word-perfect – more than can be said for Tony Blair.'[77]

The incident with Mary Salmond, however, was but a minor distraction from a broadly successful campaign, which must have made the result on 1 May even more disappointing: the SNP got just 22.1 per cent of the vote, representing only a modest improvement upon the 21.5 per cent of 1992; although this time it was masked by an increase in seats from three to six. Not only did Roseanna Cunningham achieve a Nationalist first by consolidating her 1995 by-election gain in Perth and Kinross, but the party also gained Tayside North (John Swinney) and Galloway & Upper Nithsdale (Alasdair Morgan), largely due to a collapse in the Conservative vote that left Scotland a Tory-free zone. Closer analysis, however, revealed that the SNP had lost ground in Scotland's four cities while holding their vote share in most other areas. Banff and Buchan, as ever, was the exception to the rule. There, Salmond's majority nearly trebled to 12,845.

The overall result encapsulated the paradox of the first phase of Salmond's leadership. Although the 1990s were to some extent the Salmond decade, in which the SNP's new young leader slowly transformed his party into a mainstream political force, electoral reward was patchy (the 1994 European elections representing the high watermark) and, if gauged between the 1992 and 1997 general elections, modest to the point of being non-existent. Salmond's personality, media performance and work ethic had propelled him and the SNP to a new level of political prominence, but frustratingly for both, there had been no corresponding change in voting patterns.

Like the first few years of Robert Bruce's kingdom, since 1990 Salmond's authority had constantly been challenged. Bravely, therefore, he had consistently pushed his party, nudging it into gradualist (but still pro-independence) positions it did not necessarily like, while rebranding its political ideology and transforming its organisational capacity. Most importantly, perceptions of the SNP had shifted substantially since 1992, and if that did not produce immediate electoral dividends then Salmond was not necessarily concerned. 'I am the eternal optimist,' he had remarked as the SNP celebrated its diamond jubilee in April 1994, 'always hopeful that trumps are about to be revealed, and just occasionally they are.'[78]

# Chapter 8

# 'THE SPIRIT OF '97'

With a landslide Labour victory, a devolved Scottish Parliament was by May 1997 an imminent reality rather than an esoteric dream. That realpolitik transformed the dynamic of Scottish politics, and therefore the Scottish National Party. As Alex Salmond later wrote, 'theory confronted practice and the SNP had to confront the reality of a devolution referendum'.[1] Ironically, the SNP's modest performance in the election ('a sobering lesson on how realistic objectives bring real political reward'[2]) actually strengthened Salmond's hand in working with the new government to make devolution a reality.

The weeks following polling day, however, did not show Salmond at his best. Beyond the usual talking up of a modest result ('The SNP have made advances in terms of seats and votes, making the 1997 general election one of the most successful ever'[3]), he ignored the outcome completely in his first *Herald* column after polling day, instead launching a rather silly attack on Brian Wilson, his arch-nemesis since 1979, whom he claimed intended to scupper devolution from his new ministerial berth at the Scottish Office.

That charge was self-evidently unfair, but Salmond's suspicion had been fuelled by recent statements from Wilson to the effect that any future move towards full independence would come via Westminster rather than through the Scottish Parliament. Salmond and Mike Russell, who began talks with Scottish Office ministers soon after the election, feared any such caveat in the devolution white paper would amount to a 'glass ceiling', thus making formal SNP support in a referendum campaign impossible.

Given the subtleties involved, the appointment of Donald Dewar as Secretary of State for Scotland, rather than the less sympathetic George Robertson, had been an important development. Brian Wilson's view was that there was no need to formally invite Salmond back inside the 'devolution tent' which, ironically, Wilson had reluctantly entered via the Scottish Constitutional Convention (SCC), from which the SNP had abstained. He recalled:

> Donald, and even more so, Gordon Brown, were terrified of losing the referendum – hence the rush to get the Bill through and hold it as quickly as possible off the back of Labour's election victory. Donald was persuaded that they needed the Nats' support in order to deliver a "yes" vote. I argued that they would get that support anyway because, when it came to the bit, SNP voters were not going to sit on their hands when it came to a referendum on a Scottish Parliament. What we should not do was welcome Salmond back like the prodigal son and allow him to pretend forever thereafter that he had not contributed nothing but abuse to the process leading to devolution via the Constitutional Convention.[4]

Wilson had a point – Salmond had, for obvious reasons, airbrushed the SCC from his political CV – but even so, Dewar's inclination towards an ecumenical approach prevailed. Tactically, for the SNP, it was also a no-brainer. Campaigning for a 'no-no' vote (there were to be two questions, the first on establishing a Scottish Parliament, a second on equipping it with tax-varying powers) was out of the question; campaigning 'yes-no' on the grounds that the fiscal powers were inadequate was untenable; while urging SNP supporters to write 'independence' on their ballot papers would have looked absurd (although that is precisely what SNP activist Christine Creech proposed to do). Therefore, concluded Salmond, 'The most important thing was to get the Secretary of State as saying quite unequivocally that if the people of Scotland wish to move to independence through their default Parliament then that's exactly what they could do'.[5]

Dewar did just that in the House of Commons on 21 May 1997:

> Even though the hon. Gentleman and I may have differences of interpretation, I hope that he will accept that I should be the last to challenge the sovereignty of the people or to deny them the right to opt for any solution to the constitutional question which they wished. For example, if they want to go for independence, I see no reason why they should not do so. In fact, if they want to, they should. I should be the first to accept that.[6]

There had been a degree of choreography in this pronouncement, which Dewar later reiterated, but it was enough to satisfy Salmond, who would reflect in 2014 that the strategic 'point' of his discussions with the Scottish

Secretary was to 'make sure that Parliament could have a Referendum when a majority was there'.[7] As ever, he was thinking long-term.

The tricky bit came in squaring short-term political realities with Nationalist aspirations. Salmond prepared the ground by holding five regional meetings with around 1,000 activists in the weeks following the election, successfully calming the fears of those who still harboured bitter memories of 1979. He later described this process as being 'like therapy',[8] and it worked. Just three days after the devolution white paper was published on 24 July, the SNP's National Executive Committee unanimously endorsed co-operation with 'Scotland Forward', an umbrella body charged with delivering a 'yes-yes' vote in the September referendum, and therefore an implicit endorsement of devolution. Putting his usual deft spin on the decision, Salmond said the white paper opened a 'door of opportunity'[9] for the Scottish people to move towards independence. The only dissenting voices were Gordon Wilson, still bearing the scars of 1979, and, less surprisingly, Jim Sillars, who warned of a Labour trap from his *Sun* column.

It was the vindication of a long-running campaign by Salmond, both before and during his leadership of the party and, for the first time, gave him absolute authority over the SNP. 'It is the time to put the baggage of the 1970s back in the cupboard,' he said presciently. 'This is an historic opportunity and we must seize it. Once Scots taste power, they will want the whole thing.'[10] As Salmond later reflected: 'We all seem to have become gradualists now.'[11] He judged the NEC vote to have been 'the single most important decision in my tenure of office'.[12]

The relationship between Salmond and Dewar was crucial to the referendum campaign that followed. Despite their political differences, Salmond believed that 'without question Dewar was a Scottish patriot and I like to think it was this desire to do the right thing by Scotland . . . which persuaded him to embrace the joint campaign with the SNP' in August and September 1997.

> He was well aware that the decision created party difficulties for me just as it created internal problems for him. We therefore worked out a position we could adhere to throughout the campaign and one which was based on principle as well as convenience. We both argued that what brought the devolutionist and independence positions into a joint campaign was our overriding belief in the right of the Scottish nation to determine our own constitutional future whatever it may be.

Salmond called this the 'spirit of 97',[13] and indeed the agreement by Labour, the SNP and the Liberal Democrats to put aside their differences and campaign for a 'yes–yes' vote represented a remarkable outbreak of unity given the usual tenor of Scottish politics over the last two decades. The referendum campaign would, contrary to what some critics claimed, prove that Salmond was capable of working with other people, and those from different parties at that.

On 30 August 1997, Diana, Princess of Wales, died following a car accident in Paris, temporarily putting the referendum campaign on hold, but after that Salmond spoke of 'the most intensive, active and participative 100 hours of political campaigning in Scottish political history'.[14] Even Sean Connery played a part, taking a boat trip across the Firth of Forth with Gordon Brown, later joining Donald Dewar, Salmond and Wallace at New Parliament House (the proposed location for the Scottish Assembly in 1979), where Connery recited passages from the Declaration of Arbroath. When he reached the passage 'it is not for glory or riches but for liberty alone' Salmond felt the hairs standing up on the back of his neck. 'It set the tone for the final few days of campaigning,' he recalled, 'where the Yes-Yes camp were totally dominant and the No-No rivals were blown away completely.'[15] When it later emerged that Dewar had personally blocked a knighthood for Connery, Salmond made it known that the affair had damaged his long-term opinion of Dewar.

Polling took place on 11 September 1997 and, as polls had predicted, more than 74 per cent of Scots backed the first question, that there should be a Scottish Parliament, while 63.5 per cent backed the second, that it should have tax-varying powers. Following the official declaration, Salmond and Jim Wallace emerged from the Edinburgh counting centre and punched the air with delight. Finally, after more than 18 years, the constitutional sins of 1979 had been absolved and Salmond's vigorous pursuit of gradualism vindicated.

Writing three years later, Mike Russell reflected that Salmond's role in the referendum campaign 'was his outstanding moment in a decade of many outstanding moments'.[16] Even Jim Sillars praised (with qualifications) Salmond's performance as 'brilliant'.[17] Salmond said he regarded the previous few months as some of the most 'fruitful and productive during my time as leader of the SNP'.[18]

His relationship with Dewar also endured long enough for Salmond and his wife to be invited to the Secretary of State's Christmas party later that year. At Bute House, while Salmond was talking to Muir Russell, then permanent secretary at the Scottish Office, he looked around but

could not see either Dewar or Moira. 'Muir said, "They've gone up
to the private apartments," ' recalled Salmond jokingly. After heading
upstairs he discovered them coming out of a cupboard. It was, of course,
perfectly innocent; Dewar had merely been showing Moira the Bute
House library. 'You want to be careful with Moira,' joked Salmond to
the future First Minister. 'You don't realise she's got a measuring tape in
her handbag for the curtains.'[19]

The referendum result also provided a perfect backdrop for the SNP's
autumn conference, and speaking to the *Scotsman* shortly before, Salmond
went out of his way to stress that the SNP would not seek to wreck the
new parliament. 'Everything has changed,' he said. 'We are now fighting
on a Scottish agenda. The key elections are no longer the elections for
the next Westminster parliament, the key elections are 1999 and the
elections for the Scottish parliament.' The centre of political gravity had
shifted from London to Edinburgh.

Despite Salmond's tactical triumph vis-à-vis devolution and the
referendum campaign, the 1997 conference demonstrated that his relationship with the SNP remained a curious one. A motion demanding
a referendum on the monarchy post-independence was imminent, and
Salmond was clearly irritated, his preferred position being that the Queen
remain head of state even after independence. The Perth MP Roseanna
Cunningham, however, had other ideas, arguing that not only should the
party campaign *for* an elected head of state, but that few activists would
openly support the status quo. 'There are gey few of you who would be
out there,' she told delegates to rousing applause. 'I know that, you know
that, the press know that and the public know that too and most of them
think we're already a Republican party and are not bothered about it.'

As usual, Salmond put on a brave face. 'When political leaders insist on
having every delegate agree with them on every iota of a party's policy,
as some do,' he said, 'that assumes the leader is the only one with any
intelligence and that the rest of the party is brain dead.'[20] He took some
solace, meanwhile, when an amendment calling for the SNP to campaign
openly *against* the monarchy fell following a 208-153 vote.

It is worth going local for a paragraph, to record more modest (yet
important) achievements often neglected by political biographies. On 1
October 1997 a fishing trawler called the *Sapphire* sank a few days after
sailing from Peterhead in Salmond's constituency, leaving skipper Victor
Robertson the only survivor. When the government refused to recover
the vessel, families of the victims set up the Sapphire Trust to raise the

money required to hire a giant floating crane to lift the boat from its resting place in 270 feet of water. Salmond was fully involved, drawing upon his formidable skills of networking, cajoling and organisation. The cash was raised in just four days and on 14 December Salmond was with the families as the trawler returned to her home port with the bodies of Bruce Cameron, Victor Podlesny, Adam Stephen and Robert Stephen.

Salmond had always been a gambling man, both personally and politically, and in early 1998 he took over from Robin Cook, the new Foreign Secretary, as the *Herald*'s racing tipster. 'Herald readers should know that I'm starting as the only newspaper tipster in the world with a 100% record,' he joked before his debut column.[21] Any profits from the 'Salmond Selections' were to go to Shelter in Scotland and the Scottish Catholic International Aid Foundation.

Away from the turf, the SNP's internal divisions came back with a vengeance. The catalyst was the party's failure to submit its accounts to the Neill inquiry into political party funding. It eventually had to disclose its level of donations, including those from Sean Connery, while the lapse was 'passed off as a glitch or an error of communication', the implication being that party treasurer Kenny MacAskill was to blame. Given the well-known differences between MacAskill and Salmond, the *Scotsman* (according to the SNP) ran 'an aggressive' front-page story 'designed to test the internal unity of the party'.

The next morning Mike Russell, the SNP's chief executive, faxed MacAskill's legal practice in Edinburgh suggesting that he make no comment, but the treasurer was having none of it, accusing Russell of 'spinning' the story to damage him. The situation then deteriorated to such an extent that Salmond 'instructed the staff members involved to make a written record of their conversations with the national treasurer'. MacAskill then spoke to the *Scotsman*, prompting the headline 'Civil war breaks out in SNP ranks'. The story included criticism of Russell and other senior party officials. Salmond also met with MacAskill, who apologised to a number of those named, but not Russell, forcing Salmond – according to his account – to take the matter to the National Council.

The result was the imposition of a strict disciplinary code to avoid further rows, chiefly collective responsibility among office-bearers, a ban on office-bearers impugning the integrity of staff or speaking to the press about party business without either Salmond's permission or that of the vice-convener for publicity. 'Over the course of the next year our party discipline will be tested as never before,' warned Salmond, 'and I have no intention of going into this year fighting front and back.'[22] The National Council backed the three-point code but, as the *Scotsman* observed, it made Salmond's frequent criticism of Tony Blair for not tolerating internal dissent look a bit rich. But as if to demonstrate his humility, Salmond also moved to abolish his 21-member 'Scottish cabinet', the source of so much discontent in the early 1990s, instead creating a smaller team in charge of seven 'superministries'.

Unusually, however, these internal tensions did not appear to affect the opinion polls. Throughout 1998 the SNP were riding high, with one System Three poll in March putting the party on 38 per cent, just one point behind Labour, a buoyant showing that lasted until July. It seemed that Salmond could do no wrong, an impression confirmed by other polls that showed him to be the preference of Scottish voters as the first First Minister of Scotland. 'We are not in a sprint, we are in a marathon,' Salmond told the *Daily Record*. 'We are not counting any chickens.'[23] Shortly after, he unveiled yet another new SNP logo – which closely resembled that of the early 1980s – and a new slogan, 'Scotland's Parliament needs Scotland's party'.

The new Labour government had not done itself any favours since the previous year's landslide election victory. Lone parent benefits had been cut, proposals for student tuition fees had proved controversial, while the Sean Connery knighthood affair had made Labour appear deceitful and petty. Salmond, therefore, sought to portray the first devolved election as a straight fight between the SNP and its traditional enemy, while doing his best to sound positive. 'We will articulate the practical policies we believe will make a difference to our country,' he wrote in the *Scotsman*. 'And we will promote the right of Scotland to grow in confidence, ability and standing so that we can move forward as a nation.'[24]

This was not hyperbole, for another opinion poll in July showed support for independence at 56 per cent. Obviously panicked, Labour upped the ante, and its attacks. When Tony Blair was interrupted by the ringing of a photographer's mobile phone during a visit to Scotland, he quipped: 'It's probably Mr Salmond calling to say he's discovered an SNP policy.'[25] Labour also accused the SNP of removing a host of costly policies from the relevant section of its website. 'No democratic western European political party has ever fought an election on its previous election's manifesto, said Salmond, laughing off the charge. 'Times and events change.'[26]

Times and events did indeed change, as did perceptions of Salmond himself. He had always possessed chameleon-like instincts, not least

during his transition from urban socialist to rural pragmatist following his
election in Banff and Buchan. There was also an ostentatious attempt to
become a sort of Scottish everyman. The journalist Alan Cochrane was
not alone in noticing his use of colloquialisms: 'We increasingly hear
him saying, among other things, "dinna", instead of "don't" and "mair"
instead of "more".'[27]

The journalist Peter MacMahon, meanwhile, commented that the
'slightly awkward mateyness, the mock punches on the arm for voters
in Fraserburgh, the hand on the knee of a wheelchair-bound woman in
Peterhead hospital, though genuine, appear to betray a rather reticent
man behind the public bravado'.[28] There was also increasing commentary upon a darker side to Salmond's character. 'Alex Salmond is quite
a nasty piece of work,' observed the *Guardian*'s Ian Aitken. 'This comes
across most clearly when he faces up to Labour's Secretary of State,
Donald Dewar. Poor Dewar, though brainy and decent, is no match for
Salmond's verbal cruelties.'[29] Often accused of having a short temper,
Salmond would only admit to 'an occasional exasperation'.[30]

Despite Salmond's disparaging references to Tony Blair, comparisons
between the SNP leader and Prime Minister were frequently made as the
decade drew to a close. 'He [Salmond] used to be an advocate of high
social spending, increased taxation on the rich and renationalization,'
wrote Iain Macwhirter. 'Now we understand that he is going to cut business taxes to the lowest in Europe; hold business rates down; and make
Scotland a haven for what he might once have called "multi-national
super-profits". Alex Salmond is a "modernizer", in the best Blairite
tradition,' added Macwhirter. 'He has transformed the Scottish National
Party from an introverted, fractious club for romantic nationalists into a
highly effective political opposition. His "project" now is preparing for
power.'[31]

Recent critical remarks from Mike Ross, the chairman of Scottish
Widows, and Iain McMillan of CBI Scotland had, therefore, caused
Salmond consternation. Just as Salmond had moved to neutralise suspicion of the SNP among Catholic voters, he now prepared to tackle a
perception among Scotland's business community that the economics of
independence did not quite add up. He established another pseudo-lobby
group, Business for Scotland, while pledging to reduce corporation tax in
an independent Scotland to as little as 12.5 per cent. The model, as ever,
was Ireland, with Salmond becoming a devotee of the 'Laffer Curve',
the phenomenon by which Ireland had actually increased its revenue by
cutting business taxation.

Although Salmond had first cast his eyes westward in the late 1980s, a key event had been a lecture at the 1997 SNP conference by John D. FitzGerald, an eminent Irish economist and son of the former Taoiseach Garret FitzGerald. Salmond chaired the lecture, at which FitzGerald's arguments immediately persuaded him, Andrew Wilson and others to be more pro-business and more pro-Ireland. The governor of Ireland's central bank, Maurice O'Connell, later took the contrary view, telling the *Scotsman* that emulating the Irish model could cause 'considerable disruption'[32] of an independent Scotland's financial system. Salmond, however, regularly wielded a letter from Professor Laffer himself, making positive noises about his plan, while Garret FitzGerald openly endorsed the notion of Scottish independence within the European Union in a short film the SNP leader fronted for STV.[33] Looking wider afield, Salmond brushed aside criticisms of his proposed admission of an independent Scotland to the European single currency (announced, to the surprise of many colleagues, in a speech to the European Movement), the details of which he believed to be 'trivial', or issues of 'management'. 'It's our policy to seek entry,' he stated simply, 'because we think it's in Scotland's economic interest to do so.'[34] But it remained a 'no' to control via the European Central Bank. 'We're very pro-EMU, and we'd probably make do with the European Monetary Institute in Frankfurt,' he told the *Independent* on the eve of the 1998 SNP conference. 'It would be to everybody's convenience to maintain parity with sterling until entry, although I wouldn't want to venture into EMU at the current rate of sterling.'[35]

Sensing a chink in the Nationalist armoury, Labour tried another attack. Gordon Brown, the Chancellor, accused Salmond of being 'economically illiterate', a calculated insult to a former professional economist, while Donald Dewar – as of August 1998 the *de facto* leader of the Scottish Labour Party – pointed to what he claimed was a £1.5 billion hole in the SNP's plans for taxation in an independent Scotland. Salmond dismissed this with ease, not least because surveys showed nearly half of Scottish voters believing the SNP to be 'the friend of business and enterprise'.[36] Dewar, he claimed, did not understand the demands of a modern economy.

The SNP's annual conference, meanwhile, got under way against a backdrop of familiar claims that Salmond had engineered a deliberately bland agenda. Indeed, notable by its absence was any debate on the monarchy, no doubt, suspected cynics, because a meeting with Prince Charles was now a more pressing concern. This, it has to be said, was a notable coup for Salmond. The date was set for 13 October and Buckingham Palace asked for secrecy, although Salmond took care to give Roseanna Cunningham, the SNP's most prominent republican, advance notice. Nevertheless, the story was broken by *Sunday Times* Court correspondent, Christopher Morgan, who by chance had been a university contemporary of Salmond's.

Describing the meeting a few years later, Salmond recalled forgetting to bow before indulging in the required small talk. 'I knew the Prince swore by chiropractors and thought a conversation about our common affliction might help get things moving,' he wrote.

> And so it proved. He gave me some incredibly useful advice on posture and some totally useless advice on not having an operation – I subsequently did and it proved a great success . . . Eventually, an hour after we first sat down, we got round to discussing the future of Scotland. He asked me if I was committed to independence. I said that I was. He then asked a tentative question about the prospects for the monarchy in that circumstance. He seemed comforted by my explanation of support, with the important proviso that the people of Scotland must so wish.

'My overall impression of the Prince was favourable,' judged Salmond. 'He has a genuine love of Scotland. The Scotland that he loves may not be real, and certainly not typical, but that doesn't make his affection for it any less sincere.'[37]

This marked the beginning of a new Salmond strategy, emphasising the positive aspects of change through independence, while also stressing continuity, in this case that which 'the monarchy brings. I'm interested in presenting the case for Scottish independence in a way that doesn't unnecessarily confront or upset people south of the Border. I don't think anybody would say if you are starting with a clean sheet of paper you would write in a royal family. I wouldn't do it. I don't think most sensible people would. But we're not starting with a clean sheet of paper.'[38] Retaining the monarch, Salmond argued, would 'secure a living link with our neighbours in the south, with whom we seek equality and social union'.[39]

An independent Scotland, claimed Salmond, would 'get rid of what is bad' while making better 'those things that have served us over the years'.[40] This constituted yet another ideological guise for the pragmatic Mr Salmond, this time as a Burkean conservative. Indeed, many of his political heroes were, curiously enough, centrist Tories, including John Biffen ('the purest voice of Englishness in the Commons') and Ted

Heath ('his dogged streak, his stamina'), although his own ideology remained vague and ill defined. 'I've always wanted to call it the Scottish Independence Party,' he confessed to an interviewer. 'It's a much better encapsulation of what we're about. Independence is our idea, and our politics are social democrat. I'm a post-nationalist.'

Opinion polls, meanwhile, continued to show support for independence hovering at around 50 per cent, while Salmond pointed to another finding that showed two thirds of Scots believing that Scotland would eventually become independent. 'When something becomes the currency of inevitability,' he said, 'you're well on the way.'

The leader of the SNP could be forgiven for being upbeat, particularly after such a good summer. 'He is an approachable, ebullient figure, chubby, with prominent dark brown eyes,' judged the *Independent*'s Stephen Fay. 'Words bubble up in him and pour out. Salmond is a compulsive talker – he admits that he sometimes talks too much. But he is generous with his time, and eager to please.' Fay also captured his rather shameless approach to the media:

> We are on the Aberdeen bypass [*sic*] when the public relations man at party headquarters in Edinburgh calls on the mobile to report that Gordon Brown has dropped plans for a new tax on North Sea oil. Salmond instructs the driver to divert to Grampian TV. Arriving unannounced, he offers an interview. Undeterred when Grampian's newsroom rebuffs him, Salmond directs the driver round the corner to the BBC's Aberdeen studios. There he is made welcome, recording an interview that will be broadcast the following morning. On the way out of town, he slips into an independent radio station for one last fix.

Nevertheless, concluded Fay, his 'energy, stamina and commitment are compelling'.[41] A September *Scotsman*/ICM poll, meanwhile, revealed that Salmond was the SNP's most recognisable figure, leading to his heavy promotion at that year's autumn SNP gathering. 'The SNP conference is about three things,' observed Peter MacMahon. 'Alex Salmond, Alex Salmond and Alex Salmond. Increasingly the SNP is Mr Salmond; policy is largely what he says it is. He dictated the terms of SNP involvement in the devolution referendum. His startling conversion to right-wing policies on taxation and the Laffer curve has been unopposed and largely unremarked. The "modernizing" policy review, which trims on issues such as rail nationalisation and student grants, is being conducted without a voice raised in protest.'

Although he had lost a few minor battles, Salmond now dominated his party to an extent unmatched by almost any other political leader. 'Not even the ultimate control freak, Tony Blair,' added MacMahon, 'with whom Mr Salmond is increasingly being compared, enjoys such unchallenged authority.'[42]

By the time Salmond rose to address delegates at the 1998 conference, however, there were already signs that discipline would not be enough. Another *Scotsman*/ICM poll showed Labour edging ahead of the SNP in both the constituency and party list votes, prompting Salmond to put what he called 'clear tartan water' between the two parties during his keynote speech. This he did in vague terms, appealing for the support of public sector workers while pledging to remove a government-created 'climate of fear'.[43] He also reiterated the three themes of the conference: enterprise, compassion and democracy. The only bum note was Kenny MacAskill's reference to the English football team as the 'Great Satan' in his valedictory speech as treasurer.

The SNP leader's stock, at least with the media, was still high. In November 1998, for example, the *Spectator* named Salmond its Parliamentary Tactician of the Year, which he accepted immodestly with a claim to be 'the real political heavyweight leader of the opposition in Parliament'.[44] Determined to put him in his place, Labour initiated a 'Nat-bashing' strategy, headed up by the pugilistic deputy Scottish Secretary Helen Liddell, but initiated by Tony Blair in a speech ('stronger together − weaker apart') at Strathclyde University. Salmond retorted that the gulf between Labour and the SNP was 'deeper than the issue of independence'. 'It is a contest of approach and ideology,' he said of the forthcoming Scottish Parliament election, 'and it is a contest that the SNP intends to win.'[45]

Salmond also did his best to tap into the zeitgeist of the 'new Scotland', typified by an upsurge in public engagement with the country's history, culture and politics, while he was also buoyed by victory in the North-East Scotland Euro by-election on 26 November 1998. On St Andrew's Day he said that the recent opening of Edinburgh's new Museum of Scotland by the Queen was 'another sign that our nation is rediscovering itself and, confident in its past, is preparing for its future'.[46]

The same could have been said of the SNP. Reflecting on his eight years as leader at the end of the year, Salmond wrote that on taking charge in 1990 he 'reckoned the SNP had plenty of idealism, plenty of enthusiasm, and plenty of commitment. But I thought it needed a bit more professionalism and a bit more economic and political rigour. I hope I have helped to bring that about. I look at old videos of the party conference. In 1990 they elected me so I can't really complain but I have to say the 1998 version is a lot stronger.'

As a result of that 'stronger' party, Salmond remained genuinely confident of victory in the first elections to the Scottish Parliament. 'I would say we have got a very big chance,' he told the *Mirror*. 'We're playing to win.' He conceded, however, that Labour was the 'bookies' favourite'. 'But one thing you learn as a racing tipster is that the favourites don't always win,' added Salmond mischievously. 'If you spent your life backing favourites you would lose a lot of money.'[47]

The New Year, meanwhile, brought unwelcome news. Fundamental-ists, most notably Margo MacDonald, began to do well in regional party hustings, while Labour – which had looked so tired and inept a year earlier – began to score notable successes, attacking Salmond's under-standing of economics and exploiting every inconsistency in SNP policy. Advising Donald Dewar ahead of his first televised debate with Salmond, Labour's spin doctor Alastair Campbell even tried to take advantage of a perception that the SNP leader was 'slippery'. 'I suggested to DD [Donald Dewar] he find an opportunity to say at one point "You are not being honest, Alex",' recorded Campbell in his diary, 'but DD, as ever with anything involving risk or conflict, was ultra-cautious and reluctant.'[48] Polls, however, indicated that Dewar's instincts had not prevented him emerging as most Scots' choice as First Minister, although Salmond's approval ratings remained relatively high and even Labour's focus groups revealed a perception 'Salmond would get more for Scotland'.[49]

Salmond's memorable triumphs in 1992 and 1995, however, were not matched by a *Scotsman*-sponsored debate in February 1999. Chaired by the journalist Andrew Neil, Salmond failed to tackle trickier questions with his usual aplomb, perhaps still suffering from flu-related symptoms that had recently laid him low. He also appeared less sure-footed when it came to policy pronouncements, about which he had always cautious to the point of inactivity. The weekend after his head-to-head with Dewar Salmond committed an SNP administration to meeting in full any public sector pay recommendations from various review bodies ('a huge, great blank cheque' said Labour), while refusing to say whether it would use the parliament's 3p variable rate in order to fund it. It was a difficult call, a choice between a straightforward pitch to left-wing voters happy with higher taxes, and younger swing voters who naturally approved of low taxation. There was also a characteristic lack of detail on other policies such as education.

A key plank of the SNP's 1999 manifesto, meanwhile, was the Scottish Public Service Trust (SPST), which Salmond launched as the 'first big idea'[50] of the election campaign. Devised as an alternative to the controversial PFI, it was roundly attacked by business leaders upon publication. 'PFI was the clear dividing line between us and Labour,' recalled someone involved in developing the policy, 'but it was impossible to sell to the electorate as it was too complicated.'[51] Prior to the 2007 Holyrood elections, the SPST would morph into the Scottish Futures Trust.

Labour, meanwhile, had successfully been rounding up – and promoting in the press – businessmen critical of the SNP and the likely effect of independence upon the Scottish economy. Salmond's damage limitation strategy in this respect, however, appeared not to be having the desired effect. He pushed champagne nationalism with great bonhomie (and wearing, for the first time, tartan, although trews rather than a kilt) at various swanky functions, while referring to the business vote, with a deliberate Star Trek reference, as the SNP's 'final frontier'. He popped in and out of Edinburgh boardrooms while Dennis MacLeod, a US-based mining engineer, promoted events under the auspices of Business for Scotland, and Brian Souter of Stagecoach hosted a private meeting with financiers at his Perthshire home.

The SNP leader's immediate circle did, at least, lend these efforts considerable credibility. John Swinney, the finance spokesman, had been a planner with Scottish Amicable, while Andrew Wilson, a Treasury spokesman, had been – like Salmond – an economist at the Royal Bank of Scotland. Some party activists, however, were less impressed, dismissing these business-friendly young Turks as 'Thatcher's children'.[52]

Salmond also continued to push his pro-England message, telling the London School of Economics that he wanted to see 'the next great adventure' of independence 'shared with those who live next door to us, and who will benefit from it too'.[53] Far from being damaged by independence, he argued, England could benefit from the 'new dynamism' that constitutional change had already released north of the border. This built upon Salmond's notion of a 'social', rather than a political, union between Scotland and England, an argument which would gain even greater prominence during the independence referendum campaign 15 years later.

This was a creative departure from voters' expectations of Scottish Nationalism, although subsequent remarks to BBC Radio Scotland's *People and Power* programme appeared to undermine it. Britishness, said Salmond, had been claimed by thugs and racists while Englishness was an 'aristocratic, almost medieval concept', adding: 'It is one of the great problems in English society.' This betrayed Salmond's rather dated notions of national identities beyond Scotland, and Donald Dewar, sensing an opportunity, accused the SNP leader of being 'offensive'.[54]

Then, as each of Scotland's parties geared up for their pre-election conferences, Salmond decided to take two calculated gambles. The first, the so-called 'Penny for Scotland', came in the wake of Gordon Brown's Budget decision to lower the basic rate of income tax by 1p. The orthodoxy until that moment had been that the SNP should not contemplate using the new parliament's 3p variable tax rate through fear of being depicted as a tax-raising party, although Mike Russell had consistently argued for a penny increase. Salmond's position on this had fluctuated, but within hours of Brown's Budget statement on 9 March, Russell, Salmond and John Swinney were engaged in a series of phone calls to discuss the options.

Accounts differ as to how Salmond handled what amounted to a major policy U-turn. 'There was this very dramatic day at HQ where he [Salmond] called in various senior people and told them what was now happening,' recalled one aide. 'There was obviously a case for the change, but doing it at the last minute and with so little thought was not the way to handle it, although typical of Alex.'[55] Andrew Wilson, however, recalls that Salmond 'didn't railroad it, he won it by the strength of his argument'. 'There was a meeting of the NEC on the tax policy and it was hanging in the balance. John Swinney and I arrived late and Alex reckoned that we would argue against it, but we backed it and it went through.'[56] Whatever happened, by 8 p.m. that evening, the Penny for Scotland had become SNP policy.

Salmond then set about swinging a pre-election conference behind the party's new position. Delegates overwhelmingly backed the decision, although it soon became clear that the speed with which the decision had been taken had left no time for fleshing out the detail. When asked what the additional revenue raised would be spent on, for example, Salmond did not have a ready response. 'It was too rushed,' recalled someone close to the events, 'so only the price to people was communicated and not the benefit to public services – that was our error.'[57]

The second gamble could not be said to run counter to Salmond's natural instincts. The Allied bombing of Serbia had recently got under way and he had been invited to make a five-minute broadcast in response to Tony Blair's televised address the previous week. It was the first time the SNP had been given such an opportunity and, going out on the

BBC just before the Six O'Clock News and later on ITV's three regional stations in Scotland, it was bound to reach a wide audience. Trailed in advance by the *Scotsman*, Salmond said simply that he would voice 'grave reservations' about a bombing campaign he thought was 'difficult to justify'.[58]

In the broadcast itself, Salmond's language was pungent. He accused Tony Blair and the UK's NATO allies of pursuing a 'misguided' policy of 'dubious legality and unpardonable folly', although he accepted that Milosevic was chiefly to blame for the situation in the Balkans. Salmond went on to argue that the bombing would neither help the Kosovars nor weaken Milosevic. 'In virtually every country which has been blitzed this century, the reaction has been to steel the resolve of the civilian population,' he said. 'This is what happened in London in the Second World War. It is also what happened in Clydebank. Why should we believe that there will not be the same reaction in Serbia?'[59]

Instead, Salmond called for an all-out humanitarian aid effort, a full-scale economic blockade of the Serbs and the involvement of United Nations, rather than NATO, forces. Watching the broadcast 11 years on it remains impressive – Salmond is composed, sober and authoritative. But the response, not least from the New Labour machine, was swift and brutal. 'Salmond made the mistake of comparing the air strikes – targeted at a dictatorship – with the Blitz of London or Clydebank,' wrote Alastair Campbell in his diary. 'Silly boy. Bad judgement and we went for him.'[60]

Went for him they certainly did. The Prime Minister branded Salmond's comments 'shameless', while Foreign Secretary Robin Cook, acting on a leaked text of the broadcast, said the remarks would make the SNP leader 'the toast of Belgrade'. There was also more measured criticism from less tribal political opponents. Scottish Liberal Democrat leader Jim Wallace, for example, accused Salmond of 'blatant opportunism' in using the broadcast to criticise military action when neither he nor any of his MPs had voiced such opinions before, despite numerous opportunities in and beyond Parliament.

Salmond was unapologetic. 'I am not retreating an inch from my views,' he said the next day. 'I am not going to by silenced by the New Labour spin machine.'[61] 'I had steeled myself for press criticism,' he later admitted, 'but the extent of the propaganda machine surprised even me.' Only the *Herald* offered qualified support, while retired generals and political heavyweights like Denis Healey and Lord Carrington shored up Salmond's position. Salmond also cited support from the independent MP and former war correspondent Martin Bell, as well as 'serving and retired service personnel' who had spoken to him or SNP colleagues 'in the last 24 hours'.[62]

It was a robust defence of a controversial broadcast, and indeed with the benefit of hindsight it seems clear that the opprobrium heaped upon Salmond owed more to his unfortunate phraseology rather than the central thrust of his critique. Brian Taylor later wrote that he should have 'made his intentions clear in measured, restrained vocabulary'. Instead, however, Salmond had used the phrase 'unpardonable folly' and there-fore chosen 'an absolutist tone in setting himself apart at that time from other political leaders in Britain and NATO'.[63] Indeed, later Salmond conceded that if he had his time again he 'might have changed a few of the phrases'.[64]

But to suggest, as some have, that the broadcast had been a terrible mistake, however, would be to do Salmond a disservice. Not only did the NATO action genuinely offend him, but he believed his statement would chime with a significant portion of public opinion, particularly among those on the left. As the *Herald* journalist Murray Ritchie put it in his account of the election campaign, Salmond had 'cunningly got himself national UK exposure' by 'breaking the British political consensus with his outspoken comments'.[65] Only some time later did Salmond admit the resulting media onslaught had 'dented' the SNP's election campaign. 'It took us,' he added, 'some weeks to recover.'[66]

Such was the backdrop to the SNP's manifesto launch on 6 April 1999. There had been much talk at around this time of 'triangulation', an American concept that described the art of presenting a party's ideology as being 'above' or 'between' the traditional 'left' or 'right' sides of the political spectrum, and indeed the SNP's policy agenda was a case in point. 'Alex regularly referred to triangulation,' recalled an aide, 'whereby we said the same as everyone else but with a unique rhetorical twist.' This, however, was not necessarily a good thing. 'The 1999 manifesto,' added the aide, 'never had the expressed desire or inclination to be original or a little bit daring.'[67] There was also controversy over a New Labour-style pledge card, not least because a proposed referendum on independence appeared bottom of the list.

But then by this point, as Gordon Wilson later wrote, Salmond had become 'the dominating figure within the SNP and only his decisions counted. I recall being at one of the planning meetings called for a Sunday to set the themes of the campaign. Alex was nearly an hour late. The meeting had reached agreement on most of the policy and campaign issues. When Alex arrived, these proposals were abandoned and he dictated what he thought should take place.'[68]

It also did not help that the SNP leader was clearly not on top form. The BBC journalist Brian Taylor, a university contemporary of Salmond's, later wrote that at the manifesto launch his 'opening presentation seemed low-key. He seemed unnecessarily irritated by some of the questions . . . The sharp leader – and Salmond is incontestably sharp – tackles and rebuts questions, the penetrating and the vacuous, the distinct and the repetitious. That particular day, he seemed to me to be wearying of the task.'

At a photo call held at the Edinburgh's old Royal High School after the launch, Taylor suggested to Salmond that he looked and sounded a little tired. 'I wondered whether a previous problem with back pain had resurfaced,' he later wrote, referring to an operation Salmond had recently undergone. 'Never, he insisted, had he felt better.'[69] Close associates, meanwhile, had mixed impressions. John Swinney thought his leader seemed fine, although Roseanna Cunningham disagreed: 'He was tired. It wasn't jaded or anything. I [just] thought he was exhausted.'[70]

Reflecting upon the election campaign a few years later, Taylor believed that as well as lack of resources and a punishing schedule, there had been an 'additional strain'. '[Salmond] was facing persistent pressure from gossip that was circulating privately among politicians and the media,' wrote Taylor.

> The smear circulating . . . was that he had indulged his interest [in gambling] overenthusiastically, that he had run into debt. The gossip was given added colour by claims that he owed a substantial sum to an Irish bookmaker. Salmond believes, privately, that the smear was spread by political rivals. The problem was that he had no opportunity to rebut the gossip. One newspaper after another investigated the claims and found no substance whatsoever to stand up the story. Not a word was printed and so no rebuttal could sensibly be issued.

Privately, Salmond insisted repeatedly that he had never placed a 'credit' bet in his life. Taylor also recorded 'one particularly febrile weekend – at the mid-point of the campaign – when the Sunday newspapers appeared convinced that one of their number was about to break the story'.

Salmond and party officials were besieged by phone calls from journalists. Eventually, Salmond broke from campaigning to phone the editor of the paper concerned. He was told that the claims had been investigated some time back, and completely dismissed. For Salmond, this was the worst dilemma possible. He was not facing an enemy he could challenge directly, a political or personal claim he could counter. He was facing an insubstantial rumour, wild gossip without foundation. Little wonder he was under strain.[71]

Eight years later, during the 2007 Holyrood elections, very similar gossip resurfaced. 'I have been perfectly open about my interest in horse racing, an interest shared by many, many people in Scotland,' responded Salmond. 'And, incidentally, I have never had a gambling debt in my life.'[72]

Back in 1999, there were also tabloid stories alleging a split between Salmond and Mike Russell over the former's Kosovo broadcast, an unlikely story given Russell's role in drafting it. On 9 April, a 'furious' Salmond telephoned the *Herald* journalist Murray Ritchie to ask if he planned to follow up the story. Ritchie said no; because he did not believe it, and they went on to discuss the SNP's tactics. 'He swears he is convinced he is winning with the Penny for Scotland policy and that his critical comments on Kosovo have not damaged his standing,' recorded Ritchie in an election diary. 'This is not what the opinion polls have been saying, he admits, but he insists he is more impressed by reaction on the streets where his remarks are playing positively.'[73] Salmond's personal approval ratings, meanwhile, were in decline.

Even the prospect of a coalition with the Liberal Democrats was problematic, Jim Wallace making it clear that such an arrangement would be conditional upon Salmond giving up his commitment to holding a referendum on independence. 'I believe if we emerge as the leading party there will be enough support in the parliament to enable us to hold a referendum within the four-year term,' responded Salmond. 'I accept we might have to negotiate on timing, and I think that is entirely reasonable.'[74] It was a sticking point between the two parties that would remain unresolved even at the third set of elections to the Scottish Parliament in 2007. Salmond was at least respectful towards Wallace, unlike the Labour Party (they 'can be such arseholes' he apparently told the *Sunday Mirror*) and Tony Blair ('He'd sell his own granny to a glue factory').

'You operate on pure adrenalin,' Salmond said of campaigning in general. 'The rush is unbelievable.'[75] Yet the usual Salmond rush appeared to be absent for much of the first two weeks of the campaign. When the

*Guardian*'s Peter Hetherington put it to him that he was not up to the pressure of Scotland's first 'general election', 'Balls,' was Salmond's blunt response. 'Absolute balls.' 'So what?' he added. 'Let them write what they like . . . "The mair they talk, the better I'm kent".' The SNP leader was, judged Hetherington, 'A private man, he can appear warm and generous on the street; yet critics insist he is cold, calculating, arrogant. But he presents the only credible face of the SNP. He is the party.'[76]

And therein lay the problem with the campaign. Often susceptible to charges of being a one-man band, that one-man band was clearly hitting the wrong notes. Perhaps the nadir of the campaign came on 22 April when a *Herald* poll gave Labour a 20-point lead over the SNP. The newspaper's front-page headline, 'SNP in Freefall', may have been an exaggeration, but it captured accurately what many Nationalists believed to be a loss of direction. 'The most awful prospect which must haunt Alex Salmond tonight is that perhaps the worst is not yet over,' wrote Murray Ritchie in his diary. 'As of this day his leadership ability is unlikely ever to go unquestioned again.' Asked about the *Herald* poll at a press conference, Salmond quoted the US naval hero John Paul Jones: 'I have not yet begun to fight.'[77]

Then Salmond demonstrated his remarkable capacity for turning things around. Boldly unveiling a two-week strategy he said would be 'vital, urgent and barnstorming', he cancelled daily press briefings in favour of a campaign that would take the fight for votes direct to the streets. 'As far as this campaign is concerned, the SNP have not yet begun to fight,' said Salmond. To pacify fundamentalist critics, meanwhile, he branded the SNP 'Scotland's independence party'.[78] In short, declared Salmond, there would be more political 'razzmatazz': 'We will be here, there and everywhere.'[79]

The first constituency to experience that razzmatazz was Glasgow Govan, where Nicola Sturgeon was hoping to repeat previous Nationalist successes in 1973 and 1988. 'It's not the press who are going to dictate the circumstances of this campaign,' he said at another constituency visit, 'it's the people of Scotland.'[80] *The Times*' sketch writer, Matthew Parris, captured what he called the 'mechanical ferocity' of the SNP leader's campaigning style: 'A Salmond walkabout moves at about eight miles per hour, chased by cameras and reporters and trampling the weak and unsuspecting underfoot as, eyes blazing, Scotland's best campaigner ricochets from handshake to photo opportunity. He spots a chip shop, dives in, buys a token portion, admires each chip – "Scottish chips" – signs a plastic Scottish flaglet, shakes a hand, and dives out.'[81]

'The SNP seemed to undergo something like a collective breakdown on Thursday, a loss of self-belief,' observed the journalist Iain Macwhirter. 'The Herald poll was only that – a poll. It shouldn't have led to such a drastic collapse of morale.' Problems had, of course, been building over the previous fortnight 'as SNP candidates were hammered, day after day, on the war and tax – first by the tabloids, then on the doorsteps. From seeming to do nothing wrong, somehow nothing was going right.'[82]

On Monday 26 April, the beginning of the last full week of the campaign, the SNP relaunched with Sean Connery at the helm. The suite at Edinburgh's International Conference Centre was packed and the atmosphere electric; for the first time during the campaign the SNP had matched Labour with an effective and slick operation. Connery arrived amid a sea of mini-Saltires and delivered a rousing speech, attacking Labour control freaks he claimed had destroyed the enthusiasm that had marked the referendum campaign.

Then came publication of a much-anticipated Economic Strategy for Independence, which Labour had been hounding Salmond about for several weeks. He tried to 'manage' the event by unveiling it at a gathering of favourable businessmen, but even a sympathetic journalist thought Salmond and John Swinney proceeded to 'make an inglorious hash of their press conference'.

Alex simply refuses to put a figure on the cost of – or benefit to – an independent Scotland from the year 2000. He is asked several times and tries to dodge the question, inviting other people to ask other questions (which they do not) and he tries to offload the questions on John. But eventually after much needless obfuscation he admits that an independent Scotland would be £1.5 billion in the red in its first year, but that it would quickly move into the black in subsequent years.[83]

It actually fell to Andrew Wilson to work out the figure, which was initially given as £1.7 billion, but later corrected to £1.5bn. 'Well you know', Salmond later admitted, 'I don't think that was the finest press conference we held in the history of my political career.'[84]

Again, Labour went to town, Gordon Brown condemning the document as lacking even a shred of credibility and Tony Blair lambasting it at a charity lunch in Glasgow. During Blair's speech Salmond – who was also sitting at the top table – smiled, reached into his pocket and pulled out a folded orange card. This, emblazoned with the word 'BLUFF' in large letters, was then held up for all to see, cleverly undermining

Blair's speech without actually making a coherent – or arguably very mature – point.

Opinion polls began to indicate the SNP was clawing back support, a trend the party tried to consolidate by launching its own four-page newspaper – 'Scotland's Voice' – later that week. Distributed by party activists in a quixotic attempt to bypass the mainstream media, the SNP claimed that circulation, which began at 50,000, peaked at 120,000 on the Monday before polling day. But it was clearly propaganda, and expensive propaganda at that. Even as polls continued to suggest Labour would comfortably emerge as the largest party, Salmond did not falter. 'Not for one moment,' observed his putative biographer Alan Taylor, who followed him in the last few days of the campaign, 'did he show a flicker of doubt that victory was within his grasp.' A headline in the *Scotsman* captured this well: 'Convinced of Victory Against The Odds.' 'Certainty and self belief are attributes which any leader must have to survive in the brutal, judgemental and egocentric world of politics,' wrote Peter McMahon. 'Salmond has all these attributes, in spades.'[85]

On polling day, Salmond embarked upon a hectic tour of his picturesque constituency. 'Throughout the day, the SNP leader was accompanied by his wife, Moira, a familiar face in these parts,' wrote Taylor. 'A veteran of several general election campaigns, she is his unsung strategist, a formidable force at local level.'

> Through a loud hailer, he proclaimed: "Good afternoon. Good afternoon. My name is Alex Salmond. Today is polling day; let's make it Scotland's day. Vote SNP – one, two and three." Eight seconds, he says is the optimum time he has to deliver his message, which he rattles off with machine gun consistency. Stephen Noon, who runs Mr Salmond's Westminster office, said: "Alex always judges his chances by how quickly and positively people are waving at him."[86]

He must have misinterpreted the waves, for shortly before 1.40 a.m. the morning after polling day, Noon picked his way through the crowd on the viewing balcony of Macduff Town Hall, tapped Salmond on the shoulder and whispered: 'We've lost Govan.' It was, Salmond later admitted, his worst moment of the election.[87] 'Dawn was breaking over Macduff harbour as Alex Salmond and his wife Moira emerged from the town hall,' observed Alan Taylor. 'But if anyone expected him to show disappointment they were mistaken. While all around exhibited signs of fatigue, Salmond insisted on returning to the Banff Springs Hotel and cracking open a bottle of the champagne he had won as The Scotsman's best performer in the grinding election battle.'[88] 'I said we would drink this – win, lose or draw,' he told a group of close aides and friends. 'I'll drink now to a win.'[89]

At the historic first elections to the new Scottish parliament the SNP had won 28.7 per cent of the constituency vote and 27.3 per cent on the regional list, giving the party a total of 35 seats, five short of the threshold critics had warned was required for Salmond to remain as leader. And although Labour's share of the vote declined by 6.8 per cent compared with the 1997 election result, it still managed to secure 56 seats. In short, with a vote increase of 6.6 per cent, it was a reasonable result for the SNP, just not good enough, while the weight of expectation obscured a significant swing and real progress in Scotland's cities. In Banff and Buchan, meanwhile, Salmond secured 16,695 votes and an impressive 11,232 majority.

It had been a curious campaign, dominated by events in a faraway country of which most Scots knew nothing, and one that saw neither Labour nor the SNP truly shine. Donald Dewar had been sidelined while the SNP had the opposite problem, depending too much on Salmond as its public face. The same dynamic, however, had not existed in terms of press coverage. The *Herald* aside, which had made much of its attempts to treat the SNP in a balanced way, the Scottish media had been uniformly hostile, displaying editorial viciousness that had caught the SNP unawares. Apocalyptic Labour broadcasts, meanwhile, depicted the UK breaking apart. The columnist Andrew Rawnsley rightly suspected that although Salmond had repeatedly complained of 'a London-controlled campaign, based on a deeply negative agenda', his 'real grievance was that it was working'.[90]

# Chapter 9

# 'DYNAMIC OPPOSITION'

A devolved Scottish Parliament was the leitmotif of a whole political generation, representing the hopes, aspirations and ambitions of those from several different parties and none. Alex Salmond was as much a part of that generation as Donald Dewar and Jim Wallace, having campaigned since his student days for a Scottish Assembly, albeit as one step on the long road to independence. Curiously, having waited so long for its creation, it was a forum in which neither Salmond nor his contemporaries would initially thrive.

There were 35 SNP MSPs out of 129, a greater number of elected representatives than at any point in the party's Parliamentary history. As Salmond put it: 'The SNP campaign reflected the nature of a PR election. We piled up votes around Scotland, and piled up seats on that basis. As the official opposition – a new status for Scotland's Party – the SNP will be a powerful force in the Scottish Parliament, introducing innovative policy ideas to make it work for the people of Scotland, including measures to abolish the scandal of tuition fees.'

And the SNP, he added, would seek a fresh mandate for independence 'at the first available opportunity'.[1] This was a characteristically upbeat assessment; a decade later Salmond would remember it as 'a fairly towsy election' in which expectations had been 'sky high and probably unrealistic'.[2]

Inevitably, there was post-election self-flagellation. Margaret Ewing blamed Salmond's Kosovo broadcast, Alex Neil Mike Russell's election strategy, and Margo MacDonald the party leader's neglect of the core independence message. The truth was probably a combination of the first two, not to forget remorselessly hostile press coverage, often in concert with a ruthless and efficient Labour operation that had co-opted the future Labour leader Ed Miliband and Gordon Brown's spin-doctor Charlie Whelan from London.

*Left.* Salmond's maternal grandfather, William Milne. 'Mr Milne was a man', noted a newspaper, 'who always said that difficulties and obstacles could be overcome.' Yet in 1941 he committed suicide. (*Courtesy of Lodge Ancient Brazen No. 17, Linlithgow*)

*Below.* Alex's parents, Mary and Robert Salmond, a 'Winston Churchill Conservative' and 'Uncle Joe', a Stalinist in his youth. (*Courtesy of STV*)

*Above.* A family snap of Salmond. 'He was a very happy child,' recalled his mother in 2001, although the young Alex was also afflicted by several ailments.

*Right.* The Reverend (Gilbert) Elliot Anderson, from whom Salmond took his two middle names. 'I have tried to bear that name with pride,' he told the General Assembly of the Church of Scotland in 2009.

# OPERA PART FOR ALEX (12)

A young Linlithgow lad took part this week in an operatic production . . . and co-starred among 20 girls.

The production was Callendar Park College of Education's Christmas Opera, "Amahl and the Night Visitors" and the lucky fellow was 12-year-old Alex Salmond.

Alex, of 101 Preston Road, is a boy soprano with St. Michael's Church Choir and he was picked for the part because the composer laid down that the part must be played by a boy.

The show was held in Callendar Park College Hall, on Monday and there was a fine turnout to see it.

Alex will appear with the girls in Linlithgow in January when they bring the show to St. Michael's Church.

Alex fairly enjoyed playing the part and Jean Graham, of the "Falkirk Herald," who saw the show said "Alex is a fine wee singer. He has a very pleasant voice and carried the part very well indeed. He did not seem overawed in the slightest by his female company."

Young Alex: Three early portraits of Salmond by his university friend Peter Brunskill. 'He just had this idea that there was no limit to what he could do,' recalled Brunskill. (*Courtesy of Peter Brunskill*)

Salmond as education vice-president of St Andrews University's SRC, with some of his contemporaries. Back row, left to right: Tim McKay, Pam Beveridge, Oliver Ash, Nigel Callaghan, Salmond, Mark Call; front row, right to left: Jamie Stone, Des Swayne, Peter Brunskill, Chris Roffey, unknown. (*Courtesy of Peter Adamson*)

Salmond hosting a walkabout with Winnie Ewing at St Andrews in September 1977.

# aIeN

**S.t. Andrews University Newspaper**

**Vol 17 No8**

**Wednesday March 1st**

**10p**

**Bainbridge 517**

**Salmond 506**

**Hogg 288**

# CLOSEST ELECTION EVER

Atmosphere was tense in the debating hall on Thursday as the votes were counted for the closest ever fought presidential election.

The final result gave Pete Bainbridge a lead of only 54 votes in a poll of 1311, but it was not until after three hours of counting that it became clear that he would win. Alex Salmond pulled into an early lead of over 100 votes and it was thought that this would be the general trend until the results for University Hall were counted and Pete recouped over 50 of the difference. Again in Chattan he collected 40 votes more than Alex and by the end of the first count he was winning by the narrow margin of 11, Alex having won more polling stations with a ratio of 11:6. Under the new voting system, started last year, Bill Hogg's votes were reallocated according to the second preference given on the ballot papers. Initial redistribution was fairly even until Hall clinched it again, giving Pete a gain of 24 votes, nearly half of his final majority.

**NIGHTLINE** ST. ANDREWS 5555

Attendance at the SRC hecklings last Wednesday night was, to say the least, disappointing. Heavy rain kept away all but 50 students who heard 13 candidates being heckled at School 3 in Quad. A pile of information hand-outs 3" thick, showing that a better turnout was expected, remained almost untouched. As a result the actual heckling tended to be one-sided, depending on whose side the speaker in question was on. Style and speed of delivery varied greatly, from the lively, fast-talking Dave Applebaum to the more measured tones of Dave Hunt.

The usual political banterings were exchanged by the Swayne/Masty/Blacklocks/Salmond sectors though most effort was wasted since there were probably only one or two dozen people in the theatre who had actually gone along to hear what all the candidates had to say.

There was a certain amount of light relief, with the meanderings of Nigel Callaghan as he tried to form actual questions, and the occasional wheeze of amazement from Des Swayne at what someone else had to say.

The presidential candidates within their time limits managed to cover most of the main election issues, which had already been discussed in their publicity handouts, plus their general attitude towards the presidency and what they would like to see done in the future. Alex Salmond got the best general reception. Pete Bainbridge was applauded mainly from one corner of the room, while Bill Hogg got off fairly lightly.

The final results in full are as follows:

| | | | |
|---|---|---|---|
| P. Bainbridge | 517 | 648 | (after redistribution) |
| A. Salmond | 506 | 594 | |
| B. Hogg | 288 | | |

| | | | |
|---|---|---|---|
| Services: | O.Ash | 689 | D. Hunt | 445 |
| Education: | D. Swayne | 433 | S.Blacklocks | 653 |
| Secretary: | D. Batchelor | 658 | D. Applebaum | 489 |
| Treasurer: | D. Graham | 662 | R. Corbett | 400 |

## CARS FOR THE BOYS ?

News that the SRC is to spend £500-1000 to buy a car to be used exclusively by members of the executive council caused a stir last week. A motion was passed at the last SRC meeting agreeing to such a purchase. A car is to be bought because it will be considerably cheaper than a minibus and because the Union has already just bought another minibus to hire out to students. It is to be used to transport SRC members to and from meetings outside the town, and also to move the large amount of printing materials handled by tghe SRC, as well as distributing and collecting ballot boxes around the town at election time.

SRC member Dave Hunt is to propose a motion at the next meeting that the car be made available for hire to other student bodies such as the societies, after strong views were expressed against the SRC having their own private transport.

However, Pam Beveridge has said that she would have no objections to the car being hired out once the problem of insurance and running costs had been settled.

Published fortnightly by AIEN at the Students' Union, St.Andrews.   Tel. 3080.

*Aien*'s coverage of Salmond's defeat in the SRC presidential election of 1978. It still rankled decades later. (*Courtesy of St Andrews University Library Special Collections*)

Salmond forged many long-lasting associations during the 1970s. 'He was able to draw people in,' recalled Stewart Stevenson. 'That was his absolutely key skill.' (*Courtesy of Stewart Stevenson MSP*)

Salmond with the 79 Group. Left to right: Billy Wolfe, Jim Sillars, unknown, Stephen Maxwell, Salmond and Ian Blackford. 'I thought the work that the 79 Group…[did] in supporting workers' occupations', Salmond later reflected, 'was absolutely fundamental.' (*Courtesy of Radical Scotland*)

Salmond shows Grant Baird his oil index at the Royal Bank of Scotland. 'If ever there was an old head on young shoulders,' Baird once said, 'then it's Alex Salmond's.' (*Courtesy of The Royal Bank of Scotland Group*)

Salmond with Jim Sillars in the mid-1980s. For many years their relationship was, according to Isobel Lindsay, akin to that of 'mentor and protégé', although it later turned sour.

As the SNP's publicity vice-convener with Andrew Welsh in 1986. *Radical Scotland* dubbed Salmond's publicity sub-committee 'the SNP's Saatchi & Saatchi'. (*Courtesy of The Scotsman Publications*)

Alex celebrates with Moira after winning Banff and Buchan at the 1987 election. Maureen Watt is second from the right, Dr James Mitchell is third from the left, and Eilidh Whiteford – who succeeded Salmond as MP in 2010 – is to his immediate right.

Salmond as a young MP outside the Houses of Parliament. Malcolm Rifkind likened him to 'the infant Robespierre'.

*Above.* Salmond celebrates after being elected SNP leader in September 1990. In his acceptance speech he pledged to 'win the battle for the hearts and minds of the Scottish people'. (*Courtesy of STV*)

*Left.* Alex and Moira Salmond in late 1990, photographed following their one and only joint interview. 'I married Alex, not politics,' Moira told the *Sunday Post*. 'That's his life and I am happy to be in the background.'

The 'Great Debate' at Edinburgh's Usher Hall in January 1992. 'It was an extraordinary occasion,' recalled Salmond, 'a throwback to pre-television politics.' (*Courtesy of The Scotsman Publications*)

Contrary to expectations, Sillars complemented Salmond well as his deputy in the run up to the 1992 general election. 'The Salmond guile, plus the Sillars bombast', assessed one journalist, 'makes for an intriguing mixture.' (*Courtesy of The Scotsman Publications*)

Toasting the 1997 devolution referendum result. Mike Russell reckoned that Salmond's role in the campaign 'was his outstanding moment in a decade of many outstanding moments'. (*Courtesy of The Scotsman Publications*)

Being sworn in as a Member of the new Scottish Parliament in 1999. He promised 'innovative and determined opposition', but his remaining year as SNP leader was neither. (*Courtesy of the Scottish Parliament*)

*Right.* Salmond embraces his adviser Kevin Pringle after announcing his resignation as SNP leader in 2000. He quoted Harold Wilson: 'It's better to go when they're asking why you're going rather than wait until they're asking why you're staying.' (*Courtesy of The Scotsman Publications*)

*Below.* Four years later and Salmond announces his comeback at the same Aberdeenshire hotel. He told journalists that he was 'not just launching a campaign to be SNP leader' but his 'candidacy to be First Minister of Scotland'. (*Courtesy of The Scotsman Publications*)

*Above.* Salmond becomes First Minister following a vote at Holyrood in May 2007. He later remembered it as 'a hell of a moment'. (*Adam Elder/Courtesy of the Scottish Parliament*)

*Left.* The First and Prime Ministers after signing the Edinburgh Agreement in October 2012, a personal triumph for Salmond that paved the way for an historic referendum on independence. (*Getty Images*)

A memorable image of Salmond on referendum night, apparently disappointed at the outcome. In fact he was looking at results on his iPad. (*Newsline Media Ltd*)

Back in the House of Commons after a five-year absence, Salmond was clearly in his element. He became a father figure to 'the 56', an unprecedented number of SNP MPs. (*Getty Images*)

Following nearly a week of negotiations, Labour and the Liberal Democrats had agreed a coalition deal with relative ease and the new Parliament met for the first time on 12 May 1999. Salmond prefaced his oath of allegiance by stressing that the SNP group's 'primary loyalty lies with the people of Scotland, in line with the Scottish constitutional tradition of the sovereignty of the people'. He then added, somewhat presumptuously: 'I know that all members of this Parliament will share that view.'[3]

The following day saw the formal election of the First Minister, during which Salmond singularly failed to rise to the occasion, simply observing that it was 'a Parliament of minorities'. When it came to the vote, every SNP MSP backed Salmond, although the Labour MSP Mike Watson later claimed that two told him they ought to have backed Donald Dewar, so inevitable was his victory and to demonstrate that the new Parliament was not like Westminster.[4] Indeed, at an SNP group meeting Duncan Hamilton and Andrew Wilson suggested they do so, but lost heavily when it was put to a vote.

With Dewar the Parliament's nominee as First Minister, Salmond struck a more constructive note, promising that when the new Executive 'proposes things that we think are in the interests of the Scottish people, we will not criticise for the sake of it'. The SNP, he added, would be an 'innovative and determined Opposition'.[5]

Salmond's year as leader of that opposition, however, turned out to be neither innovative nor, or so it seemed to observers, particularly determined. Although officially termed 'Shadow First Minister', Salmond rarely looked like a leader in waiting, while his Shadow Cabinet – unveiled towards the end of May 1999 – seldom appeared like the next Scottish Executive. Of Salmond's critics, only Kenny MacAskill made it to the first SNP front bench team as transport and environment spokesman. Alex Neil was given social security, an important portfolio albeit one not devolved to the Scottish Parliament, while Andrew Wilson – one of Salmond's bright young things – was given the crucial finance portfolio. 'The party is united,' declared Salmond. 'The constitutional debate within the SNP was whether devolution was a route to independence. Since the devolution Parliament is now a reality, that debate now ceases.'[6]

That particular debate did cease, more or less, although following elections to the European Parliament in June (in which the SNP won 27.2 per cent of the vote), internal debate instead focused – predominantly but not exclusively – upon Salmond's handling of the SNP's finances, both internal (donations) and external (its tax policies). The opening salvo between Ian Blackford, the party's national treasurer, and the party leader came in July when questions were raised about the fundraising activities of Business for Scotland (BfS), a pro-independence group of entrepreneurs that had been established the previous year.

It began when the founder of Stagecoach, Brian Souter, found himself at the centre of speculation that he had donated £200,000 to the SNP prior to the 1999 election. Suspicious that BfS was being used to channel donations from people who did not want publicity, Blackford (who had been elected treasurer – defeating Andrew Wilson – in order to 'bring higher standards of scrutiny' to SNP accounts) was only given access to its accounts after he threatened to resign. Salmond refused publicly, however, to say whether money raised for BfS included any contributions from anonymous donors, i.e. Souter. Furthermore, he maintained that he was under no obligation to reveal such donations if they had been made before 14 January 1999, at which point new rules on party funding had been agreed in accordance with Lord Neill's committee on public standards.

This Blackford/Salmond spat was to last nearly a year and only end upon Salmond's resignation as SNP leader. When the list of SNP conference motions was published that August, it emerged that the Edinburgh Newington branch (of which Blackford was a member) had tabled a motion calling for a rethink of the Penny for Scotland policy. Blackford insisted this was not intended critically, but when it emerged that Billy Wolfe – the party's former leader – was preparing to stand as treasurer, it seemed clear Salmond had interpreted it that way.

'We have not been happy with each other,' Blackford told the *Daily Express*. 'I would like to think I have got the support of the leadership. I expect to be re-elected.'[7] But Salmond had other ideas, particularly after details emerged of a report by Blackford that was to be presented to conference. Without naming either Salmond or Mike Russell, this clearly blamed the duo for a £200,000 budget overspend in the Scottish Parliament election campaign. The SNP's finances were indeed in a parlous state. Its overdraft was running at £400,000; it had just appealed to party members for interest-free loans until the end of 2000, and it was preparing to sell its Edinburgh New Town HQ in order to raise around £300,000.

Despite his opposition to higher income tax, Blackford had been, like Salmond, on the left of the SNP, and in the midst of the row was portrayed as an outlet for Margo McDonald and Jim Sillars' general dislike of Salmond. The Scottish media now sensed a 'crisis' and willingly lapped up dissent. MacDonald, since May an SNP Lothians list MSP, duly delivered, calling the Penny for Scotland 'confusing and muddled' and accused her leader of bouncing his party into it. 'Fundamentalists do not get sucked into the unionist system,' she added for good measure. 'Alex Salmond unfortunately lacks my clarity.'

'Total hot air,' retorted Salmond,[8] who fought back by launching the SNP's strategy for the first year of the new Parliament – building support for independence by demonstrating that devolution could be a success – and described the SNP's MSP group as 'very cohesive'. 'I don't think that Margo has changed her opinion of me greatly over the last few years,' he joked. 'A group has to be big enough to tolerate dissent and the SNP has always put a premium on self-discipline.'[9] Privately, however, Salmond found his colleagues' lack of Parliamentary experience frustrating.[10]

There were also murmurings about his future as SNP leader after nearly a decade at the helm. Alex Bell, who had worked for Salmond in the run-up to the 1999 election, wrote that if he did not return from a summer break 'the feisty, bonny fechter of Scottish politics . . . then people will begin to say, well if he doesn't have his aggressive qualities, is he the right man to be leading this party now? He's done it for ten years and the clock is certainly ticking on his leadership.'[11] Others privately held the same view that the time had come for a change.

Speculation over Salmond's future – the first since 1993 – hung over the SNP's annual conference in Inverness. Mike Russell, spoken of as a possible successor, felt compelled to tell reporters that Salmond was the 'best leader the SNP has ever had. He is the leader who will take us to independence', while Salmond echoed Harold Wilson's message to his plot-ridden party: 'I know what's going on – I'm going on.' He also claimed to be 'enjoying this parliament enormously'. 'I have spent a lot of time in the last ten years running round looking like a crowd,' he quipped. 'Now we are a crowd. We are now 35. We are many. And it's important that the many get the opportunity to show what they can do.'

In other words, the SNP was no longer a one-man band. Salmond, for example, heaped praise on Andrew Wilson, who had recently claimed a sense of 'Britishness' could survive Scottish independence. 'Nobody in Scotland must feel excluded from voting for independence,' responded Salmond. Did he not feel at all British himself? 'No I don't,' he replied, although this would change later on. 'I feel Scottish and European. I am entitled to my identity . . . The question you want to ask is can you feel British and still vote for the SNP and the answer is "yes, of course you can".'

Conference would have been more difficult (Ian Blackford criticised Salmond's independence strategy and Andrew Wilson caused a stir by describing the Union flag as an 'offensive symbol'[12] of colonialism) had it not been for a surprisingly good result in the Hamilton South Westminster by-election, which took place – with deliberate timing by Labour – during the conference. Labour held the seat, but the SNP's Annabelle Ewing reduced its majority to just 556. Salmond's troubles quickly evaporated while his party celebrated near victory in an unlikely constituency. Politics, much like gambling, relies upon a mixture of skill and good fortune; at Inverness in September 1999 Salmond had been dealt a lucky hand.

Perhaps emboldened by the result, Salmond even predicted that the Union would 'not see its 300th anniversary' in 2007, a risk given the humiliation of the earlier 'Free by '93' but also prescient in that the SNP would achieve an important breakthrough at that point. Kenny MacAskill, meanwhile, gave Salmond a personal and political fillip by declaring an end to hostilities. 'Alex,' he said, was 'running a very good and tight ship at present.'[13] With those words, MacAskill was welcomed back into the Salmond camp after a lengthy absence.

At this point Salmond began to gaze across the Atlantic. In November 1999 he finally undertook a long-planned visit to the United States with a view to replicating the lobbying power of Irish-Americans, following the recent inauguration of 'Tartan Day' by the US Senate. He had developed a strong rapport with Alison Duncan, a Scots-born corporate lawyer based in Washington DC who would become his key fixer in the US.

It is easy to see why Salmond appeared smitten. Not only did he see fund-raising potential in the US, but he enjoyed giving lectures at Harvard and Princeton and being taken seriously by movers and shakers on Capitol Hill. Yet at the same time he stood apart from other UK politicians in having no obvious interest in the world beyond Scotland. There is no record of Salmond having travelled as a student, or even in his 20s, his only holiday each year being two weeks in Colonsay. Even as an MP he does not appear to have taken much advantage of the usual perks. Only after a few years as SNP leader did he begin to engage, at first with Ireland, then with the US. Despite, or perhaps because of, his intervention over Kosovo, he was not as sure-footed when confronted with questions about international affairs, dodging questions (during his US tour) about a possible Scottish withdrawal from NATO and relying instead upon charm. Why would Salmond want an independent Scotland, asked one American reporter, because if it 'isn't broken, why fix it?' 'I think,' replied Salmond, 'that's what George III said, too.'[14]

Back on home turf, where internal criticism had (for the moment) subsided, Salmond appeared equally confident. Asked for an analysis of the situation he would chuckle and offer some folksy Scots wisdom to characterise his opponents' difficulties, yet there were, as ever, challenges. The first related to his own performance as 'Shadow First Minister'. Although SNP MSPs appeared content with his weekly jousts against Donald Dewar, the opinion in the press gallery was that he was yet to land a blow on the First Minister. During one exchange Salmond attacked Dewar on the basis of quotes in a six-day-old newspaper article, prompting the First Minister to accuse the SNP leader of 'boring him'. 'I am not sure that I was emotional or tired last night,' was another memorable Dewar retort when confronted with a snippet of information gleaned from a pre-internet news service, 'but I certainly was not sitting at 1 am looking at Ceefax.'[15]

To be fair, as First Minister Dewar had more back-office support than the leader of the opposition, yet even then there was criticism that preparation work by Noel Dolan, a former television producer and effectively Salmond's chief of staff, was inadequate. Although Dewar, as a result, found Salmond easy to deal with, he also found his aggressive style difficult to stomach. 'Donald Dewar respected Alex Salmond but did not like the sharp invective to which he was subjected,' reflected Henry McLeish. 'Salmond's style is cocky, divisive and very adversarial, the kind of person and politician Donald just did not like.'[16]

The nadir came in May 2000 when Salmond faced not Dewar, who was recovering from heart surgery, but acting First Minister Jim Wallace, the Scottish Liberal Democrat leader. Although Wallace came under heavy fire from MSPs in general, when Salmond attempted to divide the Executive parties over the issue of British membership of the Euro, Wallace successfully turned the tables on the SNP leader having been accused of 'shilly-shallying'. 'I think if anyone shilly-shallies it's the man who postures but never gives us any answers himself,' replied Wallace. 'We hear more about the euro from Mr Salmond than independence, but on both issues he's vague about how it's going to work in practice.'[17]

In total Wallace filled in for Dewar nine times at First Minister's Questions and came out on top against Salmond on almost every occasion. The Labour MSP Mike Watson was not alone in being 'genuinely surprised that Alex Salmond, with more than a decade's experience in the House of Commons, did not make a better job of it'.[18] Always regarded as an excellent Westminster performer, with a firm grasp of procedure and ready one-liners, Salmond was clearly having difficulty making the transition from guerilla leader to battalion chief.

There was also a growing sense that however well equipped and resourced, that battalion lacked discipline and direction. Reports suggested that Salmond had adopted an Army-style exercise regime in an effort to lose some of the weight he had acquired over the past few years, fitting in sit-ups and rounds of golf meeting engagements, but the old killer instinct – once so feared by Labour – appeared to have deserted him. In short, Salmond appeared to lack any genuine interest in the Scottish Parliament for which he had long campaigned. 'It is perhaps a pity that Alex Salmond became leader a decade ago, because in today's terms that is about the limit any political leader can survive,' commented Margo MacDonald, albeit with an obvious agenda. 'Look how tired and worn out [Bill] Clinton is after eight years and it's getting close to Alex's limit.'[19]

Salmond, as usual, affected nonchalance. 'Every political leader will get this occasionally,' he said. 'Donald Dewar gets it every day. I think you ignore it.' Dismissing reports that he was preparing to quit politics for a highly-paid oil industry job, he joked that things could be worse: 'I could be Donald Dewar, Tony Blair or even [the Conservative leader] William Hague. I just shrug it off.'[20] He was also frustrated that his status in the Scottish Parliament was not akin to that of Hague at Westminster. 'He wanted a car,' recalled the then Presiding Officer Lord Steel of 'representations' from Salmond. 'He wanted recognition as leader of the opposition.'[21]

Perhaps the only issue that Salmond made any running on during this period was over the Scottish Parliament building fiasco. Although in 1993 he had accepted that in 'an independent nation we would have to be realistic and accept the requirement for a modern, purpose-built parliamentary complex in Scotland's capital',[22] by 1999/2000 circumstances had changed and Salmond sensed Dewar's vulnerability. He referred to the Holyrood site as 'Donald's Dome' and made repeated attempts to link the First Minister with covering up the projected costs of the project. These failed to stick, although the whole affair became damaging not just for Dewar, but the devolution project in general. Salmond was so keen to see Labour get the blame that he blocked SNP MSP George Reid's appointment as chairman of the Holyrood Progress Group lest some of the blame rub off on the SNP too.

Later, Salmond also claimed that the Holyrood building saga had contributed to his decision to quit as SNP leader. 'I didn't think that people would wait 300 years to get a parliament and then concentrate on building a parliament. I just didn't believe that,' he lamented in 2007.

> The vote we took in 1999 [to abandon the Holyrood site] I thought we'd win. I thought we'd turn it over in the first parliament. There were only four votes in it. Donald said, of course, he'd resign. He told his MSPs he'd resign. But I did come up with a good phrase. I said the parliament could meet in a hut and be a parliament if it kept the respect of the people. It could meet in a palace and not be a parliament if it lost the respect of the people.[23]

It was probably the arcane detail of the affair that appealed most to Salmond. When the independent expert John Spencely briefed the four party leaders on the proposed design in 2000, the SNP leader grilled him with typical rigour. 'He was cross-examining me, and I didn't find that an entirely enjoyable experience,' recalled Spencely. 'I didn't take to Mr Salmond, I have to say.'[24]

Beyond this ongoing issue and the weekly First Minister's Questions – memorably dubbed 'hamster wars' by one routinely bored correspondent – Salmond's profile had been uncharacteristically low-key since the previous May. 'He was the face of the party on television, the voice of the party on radio and the only Nationalist really known to the public,' observed the Scottish Daily Mail. 'But since the Scottish parliament elections, many MSPs and activists feel he has almost faded from view.'[25]

Rumours of another leadership challenge began to do the rounds, with Alex Neil, the shadow social security minister, admitting he had been approached to take on Salmond at the September conference. Brian Souter's support for a campaign to prevent the repeal of Section 28 (or Clause 2a as it was known in Scotland), which banned the 'promotion' of homosexuality in schools, also caused the SNP leader problems, particularly as the Stagecoach tycoon had bankrolled the party just a few months previously. Characteristically, Salmond purposefully avoided taking a strong line either way. 'I'm much more concerned with finding a solution and drawing some of the heat out of the debate,' he said obliquely, 'rather than spending my time berating the Labour party or the Clause 28 campaigners.'[26] The active support of some SNP MSPs for retaining Clause 2a, meanwhile, also did not help.

Beyond these little local difficulties, however, Salmond continued to concentrate on the bigger picture. Having re-iterated his target of becoming independent by 2007, Salmond announced that a majority at the polls – either at Westminster or the Scottish Parliament – would no longer mean the SNP had an automatic mandate to negotiate independence. 'Independence must be achieved by a referendum and that should be conducted by the Scottish parliament, not by Westminster,' explained Salmond.[27] This, although it did not seem so at the time, was a hugely significant move, and one that eventually paid considerable dividends: not only did it effectively ring-fence the party's long-standing aim, indicating to voters that they could support the SNP without necessarily getting independence, it established a plebiscite in the public mind as the most logical means of settling the Scottish Question.

At a tense meeting of the SNP's National Council almost three weeks later, Salmond did not manage overwhelming support, but enough (149-112) to win the day. 'It [independence] will be the highest of our priorities,' a relieved Salmond said afterwards. 'Our general election campaign will be a clear clarion call for independence. There is no doubt in anyone's mind that the SNP will evangelise the independence issue.'[28] His words, of course, intended to reassure fundamentalists that the referendum did not represent a watering down of the party's *raison d'être*.

Although there had been criticism from Gordon Wilson ('Referendums are useful things as tactics, but let's not put too much faith in them') and Alex Neil ('No party has gone into a general election campaign saying "vote for us and if we win the election we won't implement the central part of our policy".'), John Swinney, who drafted the new policy, backed the move ('We need to present to the people of Scotland a credible method of winning independence') as did, more usefully, Kenny MacAskill ('Any suggestion this is a dilution of our principles or policy is misguided, wrong and, I have to say, downright insulting').[29] Nevertheless, an initial vote had been close, so much so that according to one of those present, 'even Moira looked worried'.[30] It represented a victory by gradualists on a question, as Gordon Wilson later put it, 'which had vexed the SNP from its formation onwards'.[31]

Ian Blackford, meanwhile, told a closed session of the SNP's next National Council that the party was £400,000 in debt and presented a financial plan that was unanimously endorsed. Although Salmond denied the figure when questioned by reporters after the meeting, his treasurer readily confirmed it. At this point, the party was about to launch a new computer system called 'Broadsword', political intelligence software intended to compete with New Labour's Excalibur database.

Initially established at the SNP's Edinburgh HQ by Stewart Stevenson, a retired IT expert and long-standing friend of Salmond's, it was then due to be extended to the party's offices around Scotland and in the House of Commons. A spokesman said this had been set up at 'minimal cost' (which was surprising given what was involved), while at a press conference unveiling Broadsword even Salmond did not attempt to conceal the fact there had been 'substantial difficulty' with the party's financial situation.[32] Indeed, at around this time he established a new finance committee (chaired by the leader), while in January 2000 a new (but short-lived) entity called 'Independence Merchandising Ltd' was registered.[33] All of this caused considerable tension, not least between Salmond and Blackford.

Then, at a meeting of the SNP's National Executive Committee in June 2000, matters came to a head. Salmond instigated a vote of no confidence in Blackford (who had been unable to attend the meeting), arguing that he was not only an incompetent treasurer but had also become a destabilising influence. Press reports also suggested he blamed Blackford for the election overspend, although others were quite clear the responsibility lay with him and Mike Russell. In any case, the NEC endorsed the vote of no confidence by 18 votes to 3. As Gordon Wilson later observed, it was 'out of character' for Salmond to take such 'a high profile initiative on suspension', though he concluded there 'must have been some calculation since Alex was backed to the hilt by John Swinney'.[34]

Blackford, however, was determined not to take his dismissal lying down. 'It was an act of political cowardice', he told the *Scotsman*, 'to challenge me when I was not there to answer allegations being made against me.' Blackford said Salmond wanted to 'surround himself with yes men who are 100 per cent loyal and reject anyone else with a different opinion. The support I am getting from the party is enormous – Alex Salmond has made a big mistake.'[35]

Blackford's final point was hyperbole, but suggestions the SNP leader took a Stalinist approach to his party were hardly new. 'I am not like Tony Blair, a control freak,' Salmond had remarked a year earlier. 'If you can't win arguments by persuasion, you can't win them by expulsions,'[36] an ironic statement in light of subsequent events. Another Salmond critic, meanwhile, was also targeted. Margo MacDonald stood accused of two serious breaches of party discipline – missing a vote in Parliament without permission and criticising an SNP group decision in a newspaper – and had been ordered to face an internal disciplinary hearing. An emboldened Salmond was trying to lance several boils at once.

One of the boils, however, was not so easily lanced. Having been advised by lawyers that he had 'an open-and-shut case', Blackford decided to sue Salmond for defamation. He explained: 'I have no wish to damage the SNP; this action will be taken against Alex Salmond personally. And while it is ongoing I will remain in position. I have enough support in the party to do so. Salmond has brought this upon the party himself with his control freakery; personally I am happy to work with anybody and everybody in the SNP.'[37]

Salmond responded by invoking emergency rules to suspend Blackford as national treasurer, while John Swinney took care to emphasise that the dispute revolved around a 'breakdown in relationships' rather than 'professional issues' in an attempt to avoid legal action.[38]

What, then, had motivated this untypically brutal purge? 'I'm sure there must be a strategy somewhere,' a senior party figure told one journalist. 'I don't know what it is. But knowing how Alex and John operate, there must be some purpose in it.'[39] The consensus was that Salmond was trying to make the party safe for gradualism, and therefore safe for John Swinney, who was considered his likely successor. The Scottish media, however, was always inclined to see any internal SNP splits as a feature of the great fundamentalist/gradualist divide, when in truth it was an inadequate political yardstick. And Salmond was unusually sensitive (for one so battle-hardened) when it came to negative press coverage. Ian Swanson, who regularly (and accurately) reported what critics of his leadership were saying, remembered walking past Salmond's office to hear him ask sarcastically: 'Spreading any more poison today?'[40]

It seems more likely that personalities rather than ideology were at play. Salmond simply did not like Blackford, whose strict spending controls constrained his ambitions for future campaigning. Blackford also could not escape blame. Despite protestations that his concern was more about the party's finances and future direction than Salmond himself, his on-the-record chats with journalists had not only been highly personal but also politically damaging. Salmond, however, went over the top. Accusing someone who worked for a prestigious international bank of financial incompetence had simply not been credible, while it also risked the disastrous prospect of senior SNP figures being compelled to justify such slurs in court.

It also looked set to be a damagingly long-running battle. The NEC was due to review Blackford's suspension on 8 July 2000, while in September there would be an inevitable showdown as he fought to remain in post as treasurer. Although not an ideal scenario for Salmond, in reality he had little to fear. 'Salmond's greatest asset is his tenure at the top,' assessed the journalist Kenny Farquharson. 'Most SNP members are stubbornly loyal to the leadership, regardless of whether the incumbent is to their personal taste. When it comes to a crunch vote, their instincts are usually to back the boss.'[41]

Salmond's week from hell, meanwhile, got even hotter. The defection to the SNP of a former Tory candidate, Tasmina Ahmed-Sheikh, backfired when it emerged she had been strongly critical of the SNP as a member of the Labour Party as well as the Conservatives, while Lloyd Quinan, the former STV weatherman turned MSP, resigned from the SNP's front bench due to 'mounting unhappiness at the direction in which the party is going'. On 8 July the NEC extended its temporary suspension of Blackford, who was unable to put his side of the story due to a family commitment. The hearing was instead due to take place at the next executive meeting on 12 August.

Then everything changed. On Friday 14 July Salmond summoned his deputy, John Swinney, to his office, Room 2.24 in a temporary office block on Edinburgh's Royal Mile, and informed him he would be resigning as SNP leader the following Monday. 'I can't say it was the most surprising piece of news that I'd ever heard,' Swinney told the author nearly three years later, 'because I had got the impression for a little while before that that Alex was thinking in this direction.'[42] On Sunday Salmond told his constituency party the same news ('They were stunned,' he said later. 'I could hear a sob from the audience. It brought a lump to my throat'[43]) and on Monday morning he despatched a letter to every SNP MSP explaining his decision. He strongly denied any connection with the party's financial problems or the ongoing battle with Ian Blackford, arguing that it was simply time to 'pass the torch' to somebody else. Timing, as ever, was key. 'This will knock Gordon Brown's spending review off the front pages,' a gleeful Salmond told journalists as they assembled at a press conference in Aberdeen's Marcliffe Hotel.

With Moira by his side, Salmond alluded to the impact of the leadership on his lifestyle. 'I've made a great effort over the last year to curb the habit of a lifetime in terms of me always being in front of the TV cameras and microphones,' he said. 'Is it not right that someone else gets a chance to show what they can do? There is a wealth of talent in the SNP.' Finally, asked about his legacy to the SNP, Salmond paused only briefly before replying: 'When I became leader we were at 14 per cent in the polls and had three MPs, we are now at 36 per cent and we have 35 MSPs. I think it's fair to say we have made fairly substantial progress.'[44]

Many senior Nationalists were surprised, to say the least. Party president Winnie Ewing said it was 'totally unexpected',[45] while Roseanna Cunningham later recalled that she 'had absolutely no advanced knowledge or warning . . . it was absolutely gobsmacking'.[46] Others, however, were relieved, having lobbied behind the scenes for Salmond to quit having clearly 'run out of steam by 2000'.[47] When Salmond told his mother the news, meanwhile, she said: 'Well you've done your ten years.' 'I remembered his first speech ten years before,' Mary later explained, 'when he said I'll give it ten years and if Scotland isn't independent I'll pass the torch.'

This explanation, however, appears to have owed more to hindsight than reality. There is no reference to a ten-year limit in Salmond's first speech as SNP leader, or in newspaper reports from that period. 'I had always planned on being about 10 years in the job,' insisted Salmond. 'The late Kenny MacIntyre, the BBC Radio Scotland journalist used to ask me, even after one year when I would step down. And I said that I would step down as the SNP leader after 10 years.'[48]

Salmond, meanwhile, quoted his political hero Harold Wilson: 'It's better to go when they're asking why you're going rather than wait until they're asking why you're staying.' The Wilson analogy was apt. He too had taken his party and the country by surprise by resigning as Labour leader and Prime Minister in 1976, and he too claimed it had been long planned.

Despite Salmond's protestations, however, the political rumour factory went into overdrive: he was seriously ill; he had gambling debts; he was about to be pushed, all of which Salmond brushed off with aplomb. Reports also implied that it had not been a spontaneous decision, Salmond having tried to quit twice since the May 1999 elections, once just before the September 1999 conference, and again as recently as March. 'He had to be talked out of it then,' said a source. 'This time he left it so late that there was nothing that could be done by anyone. He had made his mind up,'[49] a recollection later confirmed by John Swinney.[50]

The truth could probably be found in several quarters. Beyond a desire to spend more time with his wife, the Blackford affair had been both stressful and damaging, while Salmond probably did not relish the prospect of a showdown at conference that might have made his position untenable. The primary reason, however, appears to have been Salmond's genuine concern that the SNP was seen, as critics had so often claimed, as a one-man band. Although he had always taken care to nurture younger political talent, the only way to correct that perception of the party was for him to quit. The media had also been a consideration. Despite complaints much later on about press bias against him and the SNP, Salmond had actually had, in his own words, 'a pretty good run' with the Scottish press corps since his election as an MP in 1987. That, of course, had changed in 1999 and thereafter he 'began to wonder how much of that was . . . because of the SNP, and how much was because I said it?'[51]

Whatever the explanation for the resignation, however, it is worth noting that, at the time, very few journalists accepted Salmond's version of events: it was just too sudden, too unexpected and too out of character. As Andy Nicoll of the *Scottish Sun* put it, leading Scotland to independence had been 'his dream since student days and it's astonishing that he's given it up so easily'.[52] Nevertheless, the press response to Salmond's resignation was generally sympathetic, even from normally critical publications (the *Scottish Daily Mail* praised his 'remarkable contribution' to the SNP). The *Scotsman* summed up his legacy well: 'He has single-handedly rescued what was a demoralised, factious party a decade ago and transformed it into an effective official opposition. His unswerving commitment to an inclusive and humane, civic-style nationalism has brought a sense of maturity to the independence debate. Where Alex Salmond has failed in the balance is rather in his inability to offer a more compelling vision of a new Scotland, post independence.'[53]

More sanguine commentators, however, also made the important observation that despite obvious advances, Salmond had failed to significantly increase support for independence, as distinct from support for the SNP. His old bête noire, the Scottish Labour MP Brian Wilson, said Salmond had left 'his party where he found it – sound-bites and protest votes but going nowhere'. Donald Dewar was more generous, describing him as a 'doughty opponent'.[54] Less than a month later, Salmond paid a similar tribute to Dewar following his premature death, saying he would 'miss the debates and miss the arguments'.[55]

Within the pages of the *Scots Independent*, meanwhile, there were some unusually generous tributes. James Halliday, like Salmond a youthful SNP leader in his day, wrote that with him the SNP 'came of age – not by chance, but because his personal qualities proved to be exactly what the times called for'. 'He knew his stuff,' he added, 'and we all knew that he did; and so confidence spread throughout the ranks.' Two of Salmond's closest political colleagues, the MSPs Andrew Wilson and Duncan Hamilton, also penned glowing newspaper columns on his legacy, which they later framed and presented to him over dinner at his favourite restaurant in Linlithgow.

The resignation of Alex Salmond as leader of the SNP – whatever his legacy – marked the end of an era in Scottish politics. That summer, the Plaid Cymru president Dafydd Wigley also stood down after nine years at his party's helm. Like Salmond he was an experienced politician with a solid Westminster reputation and, having led their respective parties into the Scottish Parliament and the National Assembly for Wales, both men had sometimes looked strangely out of place in the new devolutionary world.

John Swinney, as widely expected, announced his candidacy, as did Alex Neil, a friend of Jim Sillars going back to the 1970s, although he was forced to disassociate himself from the usual Sillars onslaught, which came the day after Salmond's resignation ('He was never big enough for the times,' Sillars said of Salmond. 'He was only a spin machine, spinning in a policy vacuum'[56]). And while Salmond declined to back publicly any candidate for leader or deputy, it was generally understood that Swinney was his preferred successor.

Salmond, however, clearly had no intention of retiring, although he was careful to avoid giving the impression that he would, like Margaret Thatcher, become a back-seat driver. He intended to 'remain very much part of the political scene',[57] as an MSP, MP for Banff and Buchan (although it was understood at this point he would relinquish his Commons seat at the next general election), and in further developing and articulating the economic case for independence.

His Inverness conference swansong, however, was overshadowed by another strong attack from Ian Blackford, still hoping to be re-elected national treasurer. He accused a senior party figure (by implication, Salmond) of misusing SNP funds on taxi fares and a trip to Brussels with his wife. 'I have claimed a fraction of the expenses I would be entitled to claim as leader,'[58] protested Salmond, adding that it 'would be incredible if the leader of the SNP was driving himself around Scotland at election times'.[59] He considered Blackford a 'busted flush' as party treasurer (indeed he would be decisively beaten by Jim Mather, a chartered accountant and future MSP).[60]

In Salmond's final keynote address to conference, he tried hard to rise above yet another troubled gathering. 'It has been a privilege to lead you part of the way,' he told delegates. 'I look forward to helping my successor and you complete our journey.'[61] An emotional moment was marred only by a security alert, which resulted in the police asking delegates to evacuate the conference centre as Salmond finished his speech. An ICM poll for the *Scotsman*, meanwhile, illustrated the outgoing leader's mixed legacy. Although an impressive 76 per cent of those questioned believed he had been effective, support for independence had fallen to just 24 per cent, the lowest for several years.

When the leadership result was announced on 23 September, meanwhile, John Swinney won easily. 'In the years of Alex Salmond's leadership we have moved from the fringes of Scottish politics to the centre stage,' he said in his victory speech. 'We have made such progress that I believe I stand here as the first leader in the history of the SNP who has a hard-headed opportunity to lead our party into government and our country on to independence.'[62] 'The media have moved on from Alex Salmond now,' reflected Norman Harper in the *Press and Journal*. 'The man who has been feted these last few days at the SNP conference is not the man of this morning. For the first time in more than a decade, he must take the back seat.'[63]

Chapter 10

# 'THE KING OVER THE WATER'

Mystery surrounded Alex Salmond's resignation as SNP leader for some time, and there was a general, if unspecific, assumption that Salmond would not be gone for long. At the House of Commons in London, which of course he had never actually left, Salmond became, in the eyes of many, the 'King o'er the water', the old political pretender just waiting for the right time, the perfect moment to make his comeback.

Shorn of the burden of leadership Salmond's deameanour lightened. Jim Eadie, who had worked for the SNP at Westminster a decade earlier, remembered having dinner with him during this period and never having 'seen him so relaxed, bantering with everyone around him and making jokes at his own expense'.[1] Similarly, the Labour MP George Foulkes recalled being invited for a drink. 'He let his guard down for once,' he remembered, 'and said dealing with his MSP group had been like "herding cats".'[2]

There were fewer cats to herd in the House of Commons, where Salmond effectively assumed the leadership of five SNP MPs, all of whom were expected to stand down at the next general election having also become MSPs in 1999. It soon emerged, however, that the Member for Banff and Buchan had other plans; in a bold volte-face that dominated the headlines for several weeks, Salmond decided to ditch the Scottish Parliament and instead remain at Westminster. Stewart Stevenson, a friend of Salmond's since the mid-1970s, was poised to inherit his Scottish Parliament seat.

Salmond was initially coy as the news leaked out, probably realising that the optics of him appearing to prefer London to Edinburgh would require careful management. It was no surprise to colleagues, however, that the House of Commons should be his choice. 'He thrives on the confrontation of Westminster,' a colleague told *Scotland on Sunday*. 'When he hears the heckling and the shouting there is a gleam in his eye.

He loves being heckled and heckling back. I just don't think he ever took to Holyrood in the same way.'[3]

Although this U-turn had to be sanctioned by Salmond's local party and the National Executive Committee, there was little prospect of any serious opposition. Stan Tennant, the convenor of the Banff and Buchan SNP, gave what would become the standard explanation, that Salmond was required to 'guide' new but inexperienced SNP MPs at Westminster following the next general election, while there was also speculation that John Swinney had asked his predecessor to stay on at Westminster.

Swinney also put Salmond in charge of the SNP's general election campaign. 'His candidacy and continued presence at Westminster,' explained the new SNP leader, 'will strengthen our General Election campaign.' There were further changes afoot, although of a more domestic nature. Salmond announced that he was to make Strichen his main base, having moved between homes in London, Linlithgow and his constituency for the past 13 years. He was now selling the Linlithgow and Strichen properties in order to buy Mill o' Strichen, a converted property not far from his old cottage. When it came on the market he and Moira had 'decided it was too good a chance to miss', adding: 'I'm sure we will be very happy there.'[4]

When, on Sunday 14 January 2001, Salmond was confirmed as the SNP's Westminster candidate for Banff and Buchan, Labour had a field day. Brian Wilson accused him of 'dipping his toe in Scottish political water and quickly deciding he didn't like it'. He also alluded to Salmond leaving his 'driver behind' in Edinburgh,[5] a reference to Stewart Stevenson, who was to succeed Salmond in the Scottish Parliament, although he had done more for the party than simply driving Alex around during the 1999 election, indeed they had been friends since the late 1970s.

The SNP's general election campaign launch in May 2001, meanwhile, was its slickest ever. 'We need SNP MPs at Westminster to stand for Scotland, protect our schools and hospitals from London Labour cuts,'[6] declared Salmond, who had also been working on cutting his weight, shedding seven pounds in the process. Curiously, the independence message enjoyed greater prominence in this campaign than it had two years previously. 'Our core belief as a party is that we stand for Scotland becoming a normal independent country,' he explained. 'We stand for Scotland putting its wealth to work for the people, and taking its place as an equal partner in the community of nations.'[7]

The campaign also marked a decisive shift in the SNP's economic and constitutional thinking, perhaps the most important since the adoption of 'independence in Europe' more than a decade earlier. The seeds had been sown the previous year by party treasurer Jim Mather, who had urged SNP MSPs to stop focusing on the deficit issue and instead engage with economic growth. This had won over Andrew Wilson, an MSP since 1999 and the SNP's economics spokesman, and by 2001 he was convinced the SNP ought to be promoting full fiscal autonomy, in other words the devolution to Scotland of everything except defence and foreign affairs. Not only would it give the party another goal short of independence (in keeping with its constitution's commitment to the 'furtherance of all Scottish interests'), it also had the potential to attract cross-party support, certain Labour and Scottish Tory figures having toyed with the concept since the late 1980s.

To that end, Wilson not only convinced Salmond to throw his weight behind the change – although he was careful to do so in a way that did not upset John Swinney – he managed, against extraordinary odds, to get 12 prominent Scottish academics and financial experts to sign a letter endorsing fiscal autonomy in the *Scotsman*. Led by Professor Andrew Hughes-Hallett of Strathclyde University, they claimed Scotland had been subsidising the rest of the UK and that devolving control of taxation and revenue was the only way of 'delivering accountability and responsibility'[8] to the Scottish Parliament. The SNP, meanwhile, presented it as a solution to the so-called 'Barnett squeeze', the phenomenon by which Scotland's share of UK public spending was gradually being reduced.

This intervention enlivened an otherwise dull election campaign, put Labour on the backfoot and, although the issue of fiscal autonomy did not initially figure prominently, introduced an important new dimension to the constitutional debate, one that would become more significant by the time the SNP entered government six years later.

Despite this abundance of ideas, the 2001 election turned out to be yet another disappointment for the SNP. Its share of the vote was down slightly on 1997 while it won just five seats, losing Dumfries and Galloway to the Conservatives. In Banff and Buchan, meanwhile, Salmond's vote held up with an impressive majority of 10,503.

Back at Westminster, Salmond did not waste time in finding things to do, aided by an ever-expanding 24-hour news market ('There's a lot more opportunities,' he chirped, 'I'm sort of resident on Sky'[9]). As the SNP's 'international ambassador', he also embarked upon a whistle-stop lecture tour of the United States shortly after standing down as leader, during which he met the newly elected president, George W. Bush, and his wife Laura. Salmond was impressed by Bush's handling of an incident involving a US spy plane that had crashed in China, while the president regaled him with tales of his booze-fuelled visits to Scotland. 'We've all been misled about Bush,' Salmond later told the Labour MP Chris Mullin. 'He's calm in a crisis, self-deprecating, humorous,' adding hastily: 'Of course that doesn't make him right about Iraq.'[10]

'Some people sneer at his folksy speaking style, complain[ing] that he doesn't have the panache of a Clinton,' Salmond later wrote. 'But the world right now does not need a showman or an orator – but a steady hand at the tiller.'[11] And far from rushing to drop bombs, 'the indications are that Bush is prioritising the necessary but inevitably lower profile tasks of evidence gathering, closing off terrorist finance and alliance building, and eschewing the temptations of a quick hit and easy headlines.'[12] All of that, of course, would change.

There was also praise, of a sort, for Henry McLeish, Donald Dewar's embattled successor as First Minister. Indeed, so embattled was he by late 2001 that it is difficult to believe that Salmond had no regrets about his self-imposed Westminster exile. Consumed by complex questions about equally complex financial arrangements for his Westminster constituency office, Salmond came to his rescue on an edition of the BBC's *Question Time* in early November, gently suggested that McLeish publish his details in full and that no one thought he was dishonest. Despite protests of a 'muddle not a fiddle', however, McLeish resigned a few days later, having been felled by a lack of confidence, media hostility and unsupportive Labour colleagues. 'Whatever our differences, I have seldom doubted that he had Scotland's interests at heart,' wrote Salmond in a generous yet sincere tribute. 'I happen to think that, within political limits, Henry was trying to do the right things in policy terms by distinguishing his programme from that of Westminster. It is a pity that he didn't get the chance to better develop that work.'[13]

None of this, however, made life much easier for John Swinney, who barely had a honeymoon period as SNP leader before getting a rough ride from both the press and his party. Salmond's absence from Edinburgh had been intended to make things easier for his successor, but when the Scottish Parliament decamped to Aberdeen for a week in May 2002, not only was Salmond present in the gallery when Swinney endured a particularly bad First Minister's Questions, but he also led a team of petitioners protesting at the closure of Peterhead prison in his constituency. Given that prison policy was devolved to the Scottish Parliament, some believed – unfairly in retrospect – that Salmond had overstepped the mark. He chided Brian Taylor for the 'tone' of a report

that implied his presence had significance beyond prisons. 'More generally,' recorded Taylor, 'he also ridicules the notion that he envisages a
comeback as leader.'[14]

The suspicion that Salmond was plotting a comeback was further
fuelled when, in an interview with the *Scotsman* on 10 May 2002, he
revealed that he planned to resume his career as an MSP via the north-east
Scotland list in 2007. The SNP had a tendency to overreact to otherwise
innocuous announcements, and this was no exception. Salmond was
accused of deliberately destabilising Swinney's leadership, although the
criticism came mainly from the usual suspects. Salmond protested that he
was 'a strong supporter of John Swinney and a strong supporter of John
Swinney's leadership'.[15]

Salmond's successor as SNP leader, meanwhile, had problems. He
warned his critics to 'put up or shut up' as a row over SNP list rank-
ings rumbled on, giving notice that he intended to change a system
he believed had created a 'cauldron of tension'.[16] George Reid, Mike
Russell and Andrew Wilson, were soon to be put to the boil, receiving
such a low ranking as to make re-election in 2003 apparently impossible, all of which made Swinney all the more determined to introduce
one-member-one-vote for candidate selections. Perhaps Swinney's error,
Gordon Wilson later reflected, 'was to try to emulate the macho style of
his predecessor'.[17]

Swinney's 2002 conference speech also marked a little-noticed
departure from the Salmond years. He wanted to move from repeatedly
stressing what could not be done under devolution, to emphasising what
could be done via independence, summed up in the slogan 'Release Our
Potential'.[18] Swinney, however, found himself wasting valuable political
energy on further rumours about Salmond's comeback plans. 'Alex and
I have been close political associates for many, many years,' he said in
February 2003. 'Alex has made it perfectly clear that he would view it as
ludicrous to come back into the SNP leadership.'[19]

It seems unlikely that Salmond deliberately sought to undermine his
successor. Instead, he stuck to his post-resignation commitment and spent
most of 2003 re-examining the economic case for independence, which
he had been exploring ever since joining the SNP in 1973. Two things
helped in this task: his appointment as visiting professor of economics
at Strathclyde University and the recruitment of the American Jennifer
Erickson, previously an intern, as 'senior economic adviser' to the party.
In February and March 2003, he also delivered the grandly titled 'Alex
Salmond Lectures'.

These mainly raked over old ground, although the second lecture explored what Scotland, 'having won financial independence', might do in policy terms. Unsurprisingly, Salmond concentrated on economic growth and advocated 'substantially' lowering Corporation Tax which, he argued, would not only draw businesses to Scotland but actually 'increase overall corporation tax revenues', his rationale being that government would end up collecting *less* tax but from *more* companies. 'Art Laffer's famous curve is alive and well,' added Salmond.[20] This conversion to neo-liberal economics, of course, was not new, but during his semi-retirement, it became significantly more pronounced.

The third (and final) lecture emphasised Scotland's relative lack of fiscal autonomy. 'The state of Mississippi raises 65 per cent of its revenue directly,' said Salmond. 'The state of Nevada raises 76 per cent. In Scotland, by contrast, less than 15 per cent of the revenue base is controlled by the Scottish Parliament.' He concluded, meanwhile, with a quote from Keynes: 'The difficulty lies not in the new ideas, but in escaping the old ones.'[21]

There were, however, few new ideas in the Alex Salmond Lectures, which was disappointing given the rationale behind his return to Westminster. Indeed, far from re-examining the economic case for independence, Salmond had simply reiterated several old arguments chiefly revolving around the Irish model. The emphasis, however, had been more ostentatiously business-friendly, while it built upon the fiscal autonomy line pushed by the SNP during the 2001 election campaign.

The lectures were published later that year in a volume edited by Jennifer Erickson entitled *The Economics of Independence*. A dedication read: 'For my late mother, Mary Salmond, who attended every lecture.'[22] She had died, aged 81, while out walking with the Linlithgow Ramblers (of which she was honorary president) near Glenmore. A significant figure in Salmond's childhood, not to mention throughout his life, Salmond paid tribute to 'a remarkable woman'.[23] Later he remembered, and regretted, rushing to go canvassing the last time he had seen Mary alive. 'For every boy,' he said in 2011, 'the mother is the most important person.'[24]

Just a few days before the death of Mary Salmond, voters had gone to the polls to elect the second Scottish Parliament. Although John Swinney had endured a reasonable campaign, his party secured just 23.8 per cent of the constituency vote, a fall of nearly 5 per cent, and just 20.9 per cent on the regional ballot, a fall of more than 6 per cent. This resulted in the loss of ten list MSPs, including Mike Russell and Andrew Wilson, both key Salmond allies (Margo MacDonald, meanwhile, survived only by standing on the Lothians list as an independent). The SNP had seriously underestimated the threat from the political fringe as the Scottish Socialist Party and Scottish Green Party won six and seven seats respectively, mostly at the expense of Nationalists.

The result considerably weakened Swinney's leadership, as did the revival of a row over the party's commitment to a pre-legislative referendum on independence. The party's fundamentalist wing, for once, actually did something rather than sniping from the sidelines and fielded Bill Wilson as a stalking horse in a leadership contest, prompting a spirited response from Salmond:

> If the SNP were the largest parliamentary party in Holyrood, party critics of existing policy believe that there should be no independence referendum, and by implication that we should stand aside from the responsibility of governing Scotland. Now that would really impress the people of Scotland: "Vote for us and we'll do nothing except stay in permanent opposition." Ah, but the critics say, we could start "negotiations" with Westminster, either from a minority of votes and seats in Holyrood, or a minority of votes in a Westminster election. You don't need a crystal ball to know what the response of Westminster would be.[25]

Salmond had a point, and one that the fundamentalists found hard to contradict. 'The job of a political leader is not just to paint a vision of a better future, but also the practical means of getting there,' added Salmond. 'Thus, John Swinney is right to highlight the referendum policy – just as he is the right person to lead the SNP.'

Salmond's intervention provoked rebuttals from the SNP MSP Campbell Martin, who would later be suspended and then expelled from the party, and from Jim Sillars, with whom Salmond exchanged several less than gentlemanly letters in the *Scotsman*. 'No one in recent Scottish politics has had more God-given talent,' remarked Salmond more in sorrow than anger, 'and sadly he has wasted it.'[26]

John Swinney, meanwhile, survived Bill Wilson's leadership challenge by 577 votes to 111 (the last time an SNP leader would be elected by conference delegates), while the Scottish press pack soon shifted their attention to an inquiry into the Holyrood building project chaired by the former Conservative minister Lord Fraser. Among those called upon to give evidence were Salmond, and he did not disappoint. There had been, he alleged, 'a deliberate attempt to conceal key costs'.[27]

It was, at least from the media's point of view, 'a stunning return to Scottish political life', underlined by Salmond's confirmation that he would be standing for Holyrood in 2007. 'At a time when the parliament is under assault, then hopefully it's encouraging that somebody wants to be part of it again,' he joked to the *Sunday Herald*. 'I am not standing as SNP leader again. I did 10 years, I loved it,' he declared, pre-empting an inevitable question. 'I had a whale of a time, but . . . that's not my wish or intention.'[28]

The June 2004 European Parliament elections, however, effectively ended Swinney's leadership of the SNP. Although the party retained two Scottish MEPs despite a reduction in Scottish seats, there was a further decline in vote share, something Salmond later described as 'a pretty ropey result'.[29] After another spate of fundamentalist and media attacks – including a dire warning from Mike Russell that 'men in grey kilts' might call upon the SNP leader – Swinney resigned on 22 June 2004. Shortly afterwards, Salmond declared that nothing would persuade him to enter the contest: 'If nominated, I would decline. If drafted, I will defer and, if elected, I will resign.'

The leadership race soon took shape, with Nicola Sturgeon competing against Roseanna Cunningham and Mike Russell, the last of whom was not even an MP or MSP. Then, on 15 July 2004, Salmond took one of the biggest gambles of his political life, declaring his intention to run despite vehement statements to the contrary. In an impressive scoop for the *Herald* newspaper, it emerged that Sturgeon was to step aside and stand as his running mate. 'Champany Inn in Linlithgow will now be etched in the annals of SNP history,' observed the *Herald*, 'as the place where Alex Salmond persuaded Nicola Sturgeon to step aside and let the king return from across the water.'[30]

With perfect timing, his announcement came just before nominations closed; Moira's being the first name on his papers. As Salmond later explained, his wife had had 'an effective veto' over his decision to stand. 'If Moira had said no, that would have been that,' he said. 'Luckily for me, and possibly the party, she said yes.'[31] Salmond was being perfectly genuine. 'In 2004 he was out, he was clear, and from her point of view there was great celebration that he was free from the constant media coverage,' recalled a former aide. 'To deliberately choose to go back to all that was a big call for both of them.'[32] John Swinney later recalled being 'stunned' when Salmond told him he was thinking of making a leadership comeback. 'My first reaction was to say have you gone daft?' he remembered. 'Have you thought this through? Of course with Alex he'd thought everything through.'[33]

Salmond formally announced his comeback at his favourite hotel, the Marcliffe of Pitfodels, the same venue he had used to reveal his resignation almost exactly four years before. 'I announced that I was standing down as SNP leader,' he said. 'I did not expect to ever be doing that job again. But I didn't anticipate that, after waiting 300 years for a Parliament, it would allow itself to sink into something approaching disrepute.' As well as presenting himself as the saviour of devolution, Salmond also quoted General MacArthur to explain his volte-face: 'I shall return.'

'I'm a professor of politics at Strathclyde University [*sic*],' Salmond told the journalist Fraser Nelson afterwards. 'And I'm a member of Inverallochy golf course . . . I have a greenhouse, I have eight Muscovy ducks [an expensive South American breed], a river, two bridges and other stuff.' So why was he giving all that up? 'How can I tell you,' he replied, 'without sounding mawkish? When old-age pensioners write to you and describe how much they've done for the party over their lifetime and how much of their savings they have put to the party, and say "we really do think that it's quite disappointing that things haven't advanced more". It makes you think that you have to do that extra help.'[34]

It was not just old ladies imploring Salmond to return, but also senior figures in the party. Annabelle Ewing, daughter of Winnie, urged him to reconsider in a phone call, while Andrew Wilson and Angus Robertson reinforced Salmond's own inclination to stand during several meals at the Top Curry Centre in Pimlico. 'By that stage it was pretty obvious where the lay of the land was,' recalled someone close to these events. 'It was obvious we needed to get some momentum back into things. We wanted it to be the right change and I think that was pretty obvious to him, albeit privately.'[35]

There was an assumption that Salmond only agreed to stand because it appeared that Roseanna Cunningham (despite a fumbling performance on a recent edition of *Question Time*) would beat Sturgeon, an outcome he believed to be undesirable. 'What was he thinking in 2004? That Nicola wasn't going to win, Mike Russell wasn't in a great place and I think Alex was genuinely reluctant,' recalled a source. 'The party's finances were also in disarray. He was genuinely worried about what might happen, that the party might implode.'[36] One colleague referred to it as the 'ABR strategy – Anyone But Roseanna'.[37]

Later Salmond would present his comeback as part of a grand electoral strategy, although those close to him say he did not, at that point, expect to win the 2007 Holyrood elections. So when he told journalists at the Marcliffe that he was 'not just launching a campaign to be SNP leader' but his 'candidacy to be First Minister of Scotland', he was taking a stab in the dark, adding mischievously that if he 'could nearly beat Donald Dewar' in 1999, he could 'certainly beat Jack McConnell'[38] in 2007. For Gordon Wilson, it demonstrated that his successor as leader was 'never short of bravery, even to the point of recklessness'.[39]

Salmond's other commitments quickly began to suffer. 'Racing columnist Alex Salmond is a non-runner in today's paper after his late entry for the three-horse race to become the new leader of the Scottish National Party,' joked the *Scotsman*. 'The odds-on favourite to succeed John Swinney will be back with his column next week.'[40] Elsewhere in the same newspaper, Jim Sillars blamed the SNP's current predicament on Salmond, although Kenny MacAskill, who had been in the running as deputy leader, bowed out with his belief that 'the Salmond/Sturgeon team is the best to unite the party and take the SNP forward'.[41] Mike Russell, however, vowed to fight on. 'There is no such thing as a coronation in the SNP,' he declared. 'I am not afraid of a policy debate with Alex – not least because I used to write the lines for him.'[42]

'If Nicola and I win then we are both agreed that everyone in the Scottish National Party starts from day one,' Salmond told *Scotland on Sunday*. 'There's no grudges, grievances, no prior record. Everybody starts with a clean slate and we will use all the talents available.' Surprisingly, Salmond was actually the youngest of the three leadership candidates at 49 (Russell and Cunningham were 50 and 52 respectively). 'I just hope they don't try to use my youth and inexperience against me,'[43] he joked. They did not, although both repeatedly stressed the impracticality of having a party leader operating from London. 'Let us not forget the distance between Westminster and the Scottish Parliament,' warned Cunningham in a televised leadership debate from which Salmond was absent.[44]

Such attacks did Salmond's campaign little harm, particularly as he and Sturgeon were engaged in a policy blitz. An education convention, public involvement in choosing Holyrood debates, a bullet train between Edinburgh and Glasgow and the dualling of the A9 between Perth and Inverness were all unveiled in the joint Salmond/Sturgeon manifesto. There was just one gaffe, when Salmond appeared to criticise John Swinney in an interview with the Press Association, saying he had not been 'strong' as a media performer.[45]

Asked by journalist Catherine Deveney about his reputation for arrogance, meanwhile, Salmond said that in his first decade as leader he had been 'cocky' although it had been 'quite deliberate'. 'And provocative, and that was also deliberate,' he added. 'But you're leading a party with

four members, and the first priority is to get yourself noticed.'[46] Indeed,
Salmond repeatedly stressed to journalists how much he had changed:

> You learn lessons as life goes on. I was a young man in a hurry 14 years
> ago, and now I'm a middle-aged man in a hurry . . . I don't know if my
> skin's thicker, but my sense of proportion is greater . . . My style will be
> much more collective, because I have more people to be collective with.
> Even in 1999, with 35 MSPs elected, only six had parliamentary experi-
> ence. Most were learning their trade. A lot of them have.[47]

When the leadership result was announced at the 2004 SNP conference,
Salmond had attracted 75.8 per cent of the 4,952 votes cast, more than 60
per cent of the party membership. Nicola Sturgeon, meanwhile, took 53
per cent of the vote in the deputy leadership contest, a more convincing
victory than many had expected. 'It's good to be back,'[48] Salmond told
cheering supporters. The gamble had been won, however bad the odds,
and won decisively.

## Chapter 11

# SALMOND REDUX

'We intend to lead with the head, the heart, and touch the soul of Scotland,' declared Alex Salmond as he embarked upon his second term as leader of the SNP. The Swinney years, meanwhile, were swiftly buried with a policy review, and Salmond set a target of raising £250,000 to fight the next general election campaign and recruit 1,000 new members over the next few weeks. 'I will be leading it [the SNP] from around Scotland – every nook and cranny, every village and town and city,' he said, 'as we rouse this nation to make progress next year, and secure victory in 2007, and then on to Scottish independence.'[1]

In another series of speeches, Salmond also fleshed out his 'social democratic' vision:

In Scotland today we pay social democratic rates of taxation, we have social democratic levels of spending but we do not have social democratic standards of service. The challenge for those who are concerned with the Common Weal of Scotland is to propose public service reform in Scotland which rejects both the neo-Thatcherite changes South of the Border but also the total inactivity of the Scottish Lib/Lab Executive. We need to find a way – the Scottish Way – to avoid being sucked in to the Blair agenda South of the Border but to ensure first class standards of delivery and service.

His reference to Scots paying social democratic 'rates of taxation' was curious given it was in fact well below that in comparable Scandinavian countries, but as usual, Ireland was Salmond's chosen model, particularly its 'transformation' of education. 'That was achieved by Convention, by consensus and by a social contract between government and people,' he enthused. 'It wasn't brought about by the top down imposition of the latest wheeze from some Downing Street policy geek.'[2]

Increasingly, however, Salmond appeared to face in several ideological directions at once. 'His acceptance speech in Edinburgh was slick, centrist and controlled,' observed Paul Hutcheon in the *Sunday Herald*. 'Later on in Dundee, his pep talk at the adoption meeting was populist, left-wing and folksy.' The 'Penny for Scotland' was dumped, while Salmond agreed with his deputy Nicola Sturgeon that SNP policy had become too 'centrist' (an interesting admission in light of his later record in government), something they planned to rectify by directly electing health boards and other public bodies.

Most SNP activists, meanwhile, were glad to have him back. When Salmond appeared at Stewart Hosie's adoption meeting in Dundee East on the evening of his leadership victory, 'all hell broke loose. Folk laughed, old women cheered and the room lit up. It was as if a celebrity had entered the building.'[3] Elsewhere, there was inevitable criticism from Labour, which delighted in reminding Salmond of Mike Russell's remark about him being an 'absentee laird'. 'It is good to see him leading from London,' joked Scottish Secretary Alistair Darling at the first Scottish Questions following Salmond's comeback, 'and we look forward to his doing that for many months.' ('I am full-time and elected,' retorted Salmond, 'as opposed to part-time and appointed, like him.')[4]

The 2004 SNP conference gave Salmond his first outing as leader since 2000, and the keynote speech was one of his best, 'displaying the pace and extreme self-confidence activists have come to expect'. 'He combined his disparate themes of Iraq, devolution and renewable energy with skill,' judged the *Scotsman*, 'while the passages of serious politics were interlaced with well-delivered humour and quips at the expense of his political opponents.'

Salmond also sought to distance his party from the perceived failures of the Scottish Parliament:

> There are basically two explanations why devolution has been one big let-down. Either there is something wrong with Scotland, or there is something wrong with the leadership that Scotland has been getting. To put it simply, either Scotland's rubbish or Labour's rubbish. I prefer to think that it is New Labour who are the problem, and new leadership is the answer. We campaigned, shoulder to shoulder, for home-rule because we believe in Scotland. We celebrated devolution because it promised to usher in a new era of politics.[5]

It was a neat way of making it clear his leadership would offer something new. Salmond's conference speech also highlighted the plight of

Kenneth Bigley, a Liverpudlian engineer who was being held hostage in Iraq. Indeed, since the war he had made it perfectly clear he wished to see Tony Blair 'politically dead'.[6]

Salmond believed academic research clearly demonstrated that 'on many occasions before, during and after the war, the Prime Minster clearly lied about the information he had received'. And given that Blair would not resign voluntarily, 'the only option left is to support a motion of impeachment', a procedure 'clearly set out in parliamentary rules' but unused since the 19th century.[7] On 24 November 2004, 23 MPs – including Salmond – laid a motion before the House of Commons calling for a select committee to examine the case for impeaching Blair, although of course it did not go anywhere beyond its media impact. Interestingly, in other contexts the SNP leader was always careful not to present himself as a pacifist. 'I think what Tony Blair did over the war with Iraq was appalling, not because there wasn't an argument for taking part in an invasion, but because he misled people as to the reasons for the invasion,' he said during the 2005 general election campaign. 'The argument is not an argument against war, the argument is one in abiding by the rule of international law and the will of the United Nations.'[8]

Salmond launched the SNP's campaign for that election in January 2005, although he refused to set even a modest target in terms of seats. It was not, in the eyes of many journalists, a very stimulating campaign, the *Scotsman*'s Peter MacMahon sensing something amiss, that 'the Salmond of old – the combative, sometimes aggressive performer, the passionate advocate for his cause of independence – seemed to be absent without leave'.[9]

It was an indication that more than a year after his comeback, Salmond redux was not yet up to par. In one election interview he appeared to concede that a majority of Scots did not 'necessarily' support independence,[10] while opinion polls showed Labour enjoying a significant lead over the SNP. 'We have to work harder,' responded Salmond defiantly, 'to get our message across.'[11] The SNP's manifesto was also light on bold new thinking, including a proposal to create two new public holidays in Scotland and cut corporation tax from 30 to 20 per cent (not, in any case, a new policy).

As one former aide recalled, the 2005 general election campaign was 'very badly run':

Alex was also unwell; he had a lingering cold. He just wasn't right and a really inexperienced team was running the show. Moira was quite unhappy about it and Alex was unhappy about it. If you compare the '05 and '07 campaigns there's quite a difference. At the first he spent very long periods away from home and we were sending him all over the country; in '07 he was never away from home for more than two nights.[12]

The SNP was not yet the formidable campaigning machine it would later become, and the result in 2005, just 17.7 per cent of the vote (a fall of 2.4 per cent since 2001), was far removed from the electoral triumphs that would follow. Even so (and considering the number of Scottish constituencies had been cut from 72 to 59 as a delayed consequence of devolution), the party managed to take two seats from Labour, giving them a total of six, one more than in 2001.

The Liberal Democrats, however, beat the SNP into third place in terms of seats and vote share, which given the symbolic merit Salmond had always placed in being Scotland's second party, was certainly a setback. In Banff and Buchan, meanwhile, Salmond's majority held up at 11,837. 'We start the campaign today [for Holyrood in 2007] from an excellent position,' he declared optimistically, 'better than any other party in Scotland.'[13] Indeed, Salmond was genuinely pleased as he was driven from Strichen to SNP HQ (listening to Dougie MacLean sing 'Caledonia') as he explained to an aide that the result was good enough to give him a real shot at becoming First Minister two years later.

There was more electoral woe shortly after the 2005 conference (at which Salmond urged his party to add 'economic efficiency' to its social democratic 'heart'[14]) when the SNP failed to make any headway in two by-elections, one caused by the death of Labour MP Robin Cook (Livingston) and another by the imprisonment of Labour MSP Mike Watson (Glasgow Cathcart) for fire-raising at an Edinburgh hotel.

The results proved too much for Bruce McFee, an SNP MSP for the West of Scotland since 2003. He announced his intention to leave Holyrood at the next election, saying he could not 'in all honesty put myself forward to fight on a policy and a direction I don't believe in' while casting doubt on Salmond's target of winning an additional 20 constituency seats in 2007. 'We have become a party', he said, 'that simply rallies the troops and shouts about independence at the conference.'[15] Although McFee, as later events demonstrated, was being unduly gloomy, his remarks nevertheless represented a genuine strand of opinion in the SNP at that point.

Continuing to shout about independence was Salmond, who unveiled a 28-page document called 'Raising the Standard' towards the end of 2005, which he said constituted the most comprehensive explanation of the process of independence (including a little-noticed decision to retain sterling) ever published. By issuing this 18 months before the Holyrood elections, Salmond was cleverly pre-empting likely Labour accusations of independence being put on the backburner.

Nevertheless, Salmond's leadership of the SNP was not under any serious threat, indeed if anything one-member-one-vote gave him greater legitimacy than ever before, while John Swinney's reforms also meant it was harder for an incumbent leader to be challenged. Thus, as an academic study of the SNP later put it, 'he had both formal institutional protection . . . and his own personal authority',[16] the latter derived from his previous decade-long period as national convener. At the same time, the Salmond who 'came back' in 2004, as one SNP MSP put it, 'was very different from the Alex who'd left in 2000',[17] more collegiate and personally more relaxed.

Thus equipped, Salmond then prepared for another gamble. Rather than standing on the north-east Scotland regional list in 2007, as he had indicated in 2004, he announced he would contest the Gordon constituency, not exactly an easy target for the SNP. On the swing required (7.75 per cent), Gordon ranked 18th on the SNP's target list, but by standing there, instead of virtually guaranteeing election via the regional list, Salmond was demonstrating that his target of winning an additional 20 constituency seats was not just talk. 'I have never lost a constituency election in my life and I don't intend to start now,' he said. 'I'm not just running for a constituency – I'm running to be the first minister of Scotland.'[18]

When the SNP suffered another bad result in the Dunfermline and West Fife Westminster by-election – beaten into third place by the Liberal Democrats – it appeared that Salmond's gamble might have been a foolish one. Then, in April 2006, his luck began to change. Not only did the SNP retain (decisively) the Moray seat in a Holyrood by-election (caused by the death of Salmond's 1990 leadership opponent, Margaret Ewing), but a YouGov poll commissioned by the party found that 56 per cent of those polled agreed with the statement: 'The Labour Party has been in power too long in Scotland, it is time for a change.' 'This is a watershed result,' proclaimed Salmond. 'It shows the public mood is that it's time for a change.'[19] That sentiment, and more specifically the phrase 'it's time', would later form the basis of the SNP's 2007 Scottish Parliament election campaign.

Salmond then tried to maintain what he saw as valuable political momentum by using the summer of 2006 for a series of policy announcements, including the slashing of small business rates and £100 million to abolish student fees and debt. This created the impression of a dynamic party preparing for government, although there remained tensions over the SNP's ideological direction. When, for example, Mike Russell, out of frontline politics since his quixotic bid to become leader in 2004, published a policy manifesto (co-written with Dennis MacLeod, whose home had provided the backdrop for Salmond's Kosovo broadcast) called *Grasping the Thistle*, it later emerged that Salmond, having been given advance sight of its often centre-right contents, had sent Russell five pages of notes with the code 'VD' ('very dangerous'), 'D' (dangerous) and 'RH' ('relatively harmless') next to certain passages.

One section, deemed 'VD' for obvious reasons, read as follows: 'A leader brilliantly suited to guerrilla opposition but much less well attuned to the disciplines and demands of any new politics was followed by a technocratic party manager who was unable to invigorate the national debate and take it in new directions.' It was removed from the published version of *Grasping the Thistle*, and while Russell claimed nothing in the book was an 'indirect or implied'[20] criticism of the SNP, the 'leader' in question was clearly Salmond.

But this incident, which most likely destroyed what little had been left of a once strong friendship, did Salmond and the SNP little harm. Another YouGov poll in August had placed the SNP four points ahead of Labour and, significantly, Salmond as the favoured candidate to become the next First Minister. The party now appeared to have the momentum necessary for electoral victory the following year, something further aided by a £100,000 donation from Kwik-Fit founder Sir Tom Farmer.

Salmond did not disappoint in his final conference speech before the Holyrood battle commenced. 'We can determine the future of Scotland in the next six months, Scotland is there for us to take,' he declared. 'But whether we do so or not depends on what we do; it is in our hands.'[21] Salmond also indicated his intention to run a presidential campaign when he told the *Herald* that Jack McConnell did not 'carry the authority that perhaps a First Minister should'.[22]

With the September 2006 conference speech, Salmond's press coverage also changed for the better. 'I haven't seen Alex Salmond in this kind of form for years,' wrote Andy Nicoll in the *Sun*. 'This is the old-time, "come on if you think you're hard enough" Alex Salmond.'[23] A panicked Labour Party, wrong footed by positive polls and a positive

SNP message, responded by co-coordinating a wave of attacks north and south of the border. 'He didn't fight for the parliament, he didn't build the parliament, he didn't struggle to have it established and he did not even stay with the parliament,' said John Reid in a highly personal attack. 'He would like to run the parliament now that it suits him. I tell you, Alex – dream on.'

In turn, Salmond sought to depict Labour in Scotland as 'incapable of running their own campaign without remote control from their London masters',[24] while capitalising upon a perception that Labour had been in office, in London and Edinburgh, for too long. He also gave the Iraq War a Nationalist twist, arguing that Scotland had been 'dragged into enough foolish, costly and illegal wars'.[25]

Indeed, Jack McConnell believed that Salmond's momentum largely derived from a sustained period of political 'good luck', a combination of the war in Iraq, the resignation of Charles Kennedy as Liberal Democrat leader (which shifted anti-Iraq opposition to the SNP) and the ongoing battle between Blair and Brown. 'The Labour Party in Scotland was actually in better shape than it had been for a while,' reflected McConnell. 'But that battle plagued the Scottish campaign for months. We started to feel as if we were swimming against a tide, we were on the backfoot. For the first time since devolution he [Salmond] was at the centre of it [at Westminster] and I wasn't. During the campaign itself they [the SNP] picked up on the fact that Scots wanted to hear positive stuff so they ran with a very positive campaign and we ended up on the other side of that, sounding negative. They picked up the ball and ran with it.'[26]

Indeed, an unintended consequence of Salmond redux had been his ability to take a perceived weakness – his presence at Westminster – and turn it into a strength. Events south of the border, in other words, had conspired to put the SNP and its leader at the eye of the political storm.

SNP strategists, meanwhile, hit upon the inspired idea of marketing its leader as a brand identity, using the term 'Alex Salmond for First Minister' rather than 'Scottish National Party' on ballot papers for the regional list vote. Not only would this ensure that it came first on alphabetical ballot papers, but it would capitalise upon Salmond's high approval ratings, although Jim Sillars later described this approach as 'Scotland's first ever experience of the cult of personality'.[27]

'It does seem,' remarked Salmond in a mystical frame of mind, 'that circumstances like stars in the heavens are conjoining to create an event which gives us a fantastic opportunity.'[28] Sir George Mathewson, the respected former chairman of the Royal Bank of Scotland, proved to be such a star. 'The reality is I have been somewhat disappointed for some time with work of the Scottish Parliament,' he told the *Scotsman* in March 2007. 'Alex Salmond and the SNP offer the best choice.'[29]

It was a major coup for a delighted Salmond, who had learned of Sir George's support the previous month, but shrewdly convinced him to delay the announcement in order to coincide with a visit to Edinburgh by Tony Blair. It had the desired effect, particularly when the Prime Minister carelessly dismissed Mathewson as 'self-indulgent'.[30] Also happy to indulge himself was the Stagecoach founder Brian Souter, who donated £500,000 to the SNP's campaign. 'The time has come for Alex Salmond to deliver a dynamic government in Scotland which will respect our past,' said Souter, 'respond to our present problems and reflect the future aspirations of the Scottish people.' Salmond, meanwhile, published an American-style plan of action for his first 100 days in office, while talking up his UK credentials. 'I want a more mature relationship with the government of the UK,' he said at the Glasgow Science Centre, 'a relationship of equals.'[31] Warming to his theme, Salmond also referred to the 'manifest unfairness' in the way England had been governed post-devolution. 'Scotland and England would both be far better off with a new 21st century relationship,' he wrote in the *Daily Telegraph*, 'a real partnership based upon equality of status.'[32]

The First Minister-in-waiting also embarked on yet another campaign diet. 'I'm not about to win Slimmer of the Year and I have a long way to go, but my wife is happy about it,' he joked, pledging to cut down on curries, swap much-loved Lucozade for smoothies, while eating porridge for breakfast. 'This isn't for health reasons – although it is probably doing me some good – it's a television thing,' adding that he had never been 'vain' or 'sizeist'.[33] It was clear, however, that Salmond's weight bothered him. He took little or no exercise and was driven everywhere (he claimed he could no longer travel by train because of back trouble), with the result that his 52-year-old frame bore no resemblance to that of the lean (not to mention more left-wing) Alex Salmond of the 1970s.

And although Salmond possessed no self-consciousness about his combative style, party strategists insisted upon media training to make him appear less confrontational during interviews. The SNP MSP Brian Adam later inadvertently revealed that Salmond had found changing his behaviour a 'major challenge'. 'He is not known as Smart Alec for no reason,' he told a group of American students. 'He is a very very able politician . . . but he had to change the way, not only [how] he presented himself, but the way he behaved.' Salmond, concluded Adam, was a charismatic but divisive figure. 'People either love him or they hate him.'[34]

Another of those present at this coaching session, however, recalls Salmond 'getting it from the start'.[35] Run by Claire Howell from a company called Redco, the point was 'knowing where you want to go and being able to get there'.[36] Winning the 2007 election, the argument ran, came down to positive thinking. Salmond was certainly in a positive frame of mind as he hit the campaign trail during April, exploiting an emerging cash-for-peerages scandal to accuse Tony Blair of 'stuffing' the House of Lords with cronies instead of modernising it as he had promised to do in 1997.[37]

This provided further momentum as Salmond launched the SNP's 2007 manifesto, which promised protection for local hospital services, smaller class sizes, more police, help for first-time buyers, a local income tax and a referendum on independence in 2010. 'This is more than a manifesto,' he declared, 'it is a programme for government, with a real opportunity to be implemented in government.'[38]

Once more Salmond emphasised his new, more ecumenical style, promising 'not just to talk to the folk who agree with me', but 'to reach out to people who don't'.[39] Kevin Pringle, a long-standing adviser who had returned to the SNP fold in January 2007, was acknowledged as the brains behind the new Alex. 'The reason for the success of the partnership is perhaps in the contrast of personalities,' observed the *Scotsman*. 'Where Salmond hogs the limelight, the modest Pringle shuns it.'[40]

And when it came to independence, Salmond was also keen to appear flexible 'on content, on timing, on approach, and even on the question formulation that might be asked',[41] a clear attempt to reassure the Liberal Democrats, still considered the most likely coalition partner were the SNP to emerge as the largest party. At a debate in Glasgow, Salmond also pledged that a 'no' vote in an independence referendum would put the issue on hold for around 20 years. 'In my view', he explained, 'it's a once in a generation thing.'[42]

This was all part of a wider strategy to separate support for the SNP from support for independence, two phenomena polls had always suggested did not necessarily overlap. Voters were being urged to give the SNP a chance while Salmond reassured them that if they did, then it did not necessarily mean independence would follow. He even suggested in one interview that independence was 'not a one-way street', and Scotland could vote, 'if it so chooses to become un-independent'.[43]

Jack McConnell, meanwhile, stepped up his attacks on Salmond by claiming he would 'not be a fit person'[44] to be First Minister of Scotland. There were, however, several high-profile Scots who disagreed, for example the Respect MP George Galloway, the comedienne Elaine C. Smith, Archbishop Keith O'Brien and, more unusually, the historian and former Tory candidate Michael Fry. The press also turned in the SNP's favour, the *Scotsman*, *Sunday Herald*, *Sunday Times* and *Scotland on Sunday* all concluding that an SNP role in government, or an SNP-led coalition, would be the best outcome.

On the 300th anniversary of the Act of Union, meanwhile, Tony Blair said it was not the moment 'to shatter [the Union] and go back to the petty rivalries of the past', to which Salmond retorted that Labour had 'no divine right to rule Scotland'.[45] Just a few days later Scotland's long-dominant political party would discover the painful truth of that remark. After a long, dramatic night, the SNP emerged as the largest party, while in Gordon Salmond overcame significant odds to take the constituency from the Liberal Democrats with a majority of just over 2,000.

Eloquently, Salmond invoked Harold Macmillan. 'There is a wind of change blowing through Scottish politics,'[46] he declared, before promising an inquiry (should he become First Minister) into the night's ballot paper chaos that had disenfranchised around 100,000 Scots. That afternoon the SNP leader flew to Edinburgh by helicopter, and effectively claimed victory even before the final results were declared. 'Scotland has chosen a new path,' declared Salmond at his most eloquent, 'one which echoes the hopes and aspirations of a new culture of politics.' He added: 'We will lead with verve and imagination but always mindful that we serve the people – all the people – of this proud and ancient nation. The Scottish writer Alasdair Gray put it well when he wrote – "Work as though you lived in the early days of a better nation". My commitment to Scotland is this – we will work, and these are the early days of a better nation.'[47]

It all hinged on the Highland regional count, but after some initial confusion the SNP emerged with two MSPs, meaning it was ahead of Labour nationally by just a single seat. The SNP MP Angus Robertson then drove Salmond and his wife Moira to The Hub, an arts venue at the top of the Royal Mile near Edinburgh Castle. The atmosphere inside was electric. 'I heard a rumour,' the SNP leader informed his rapturous supporters. 'I think we won the election.' To form a majority Scottish Executive, however, Salmond needed not only the Liberal Democrats (with 16 seats) but also the Greens (with two seats), a prospect he had called a 'progressive coalition . . . to move Scotland forward'.[48]

But when they met in Edinburgh, most of the 16 Liberal Democrat MSPs were not inclined to coalesce with the SNP, although they agreed to negotiate if Salmond was willing to drop his pledge to hold an independence referendum. Salmond and Nicol Stephen, the Scottish Liberal Democrat leader, eventually spoke at around 7 p.m. on the Saturday but failed to reach a compromise. Following further conversations, in which the SNP leader stressed the possibility of a 'creative' solution to the referendum impasse, Stephen called Salmond for the last time on Sunday evening, saying his group's position remained unchanged.

'In these circumstances,' said Stephen in a statement, 'it seems likely there will be a minority SNP government.' That, responded Salmond in a radio interview, was 'not an entirely bad thing'.[49] The following day, the Scottish Greens opted to support the SNP only on an informal basis, at which point it became Salmond's 'working assumption' that the SNP would form a minority administration.[50]

On 9 May Salmond was the first MSP to take the oath at the start of the new session of the Scottish Parliament and, a week later, once it had become clear the Liberal Democrats were not prepared to change their minds, Salmond was elected First Minister at 11.11 a.m., by 49 votes to 46. The new First Minister then shook hands with those around him, hugged Nicola Sturgeon, soon to be his deputy, and embraced Bashir Ahmed, Scotland's first Asian MSP.

Salmond then rose and, in a well-judged acceptance speech, declared that he and every other MSP had 'a responsibility to conduct ourselves in a way that respects the parliament the people have chosen to elect'.

That will take patience, maturity and leadership. My pledge today is that any Scottish government led by me will respect and include this parliament in the governance of Scotland over the next four years. In this century, there are limits to what governments can achieve. But one thing any government I lead will never lack is ambition for Scotland. Today, I commit myself to leadership wholly and exclusively in the Scottish national interest. We will appeal for support policy by policy across this chamber.[51]

There was, noted the *Herald*, 'applause in the chamber – muted on the Labour benches, raucous among his MSPs and thunderous in the public gallery'.[52] Among those watching from above had been Moira, as well Salmond's father Robert. 'My father has never seen me in the chamber because he always refused to set foot in the Palace of Westminster,'

Salmond had remarked in his speech. 'Some people say I should have heeded his advice.'[53]

Once formal proceedings were over, Salmond walked from the Chamber to the Garden Lobby, clutching Moira's hand tightly as he descended the stairs. 'You think you can imagine what it's going to be like,' a clearly emotional First Minister told supporters, 'but, when you imagine, it's never quite the reality. It's a wonderful day.'[54] More than a year later, he described it more concisely as 'a hell of a moment'.[55]

# Chapter 12

# 'IT'S TIME'

Having secured Holyrood's nomination as First Minister, Alex Salmond drove to St Andrew's House to meet Sir John Elvidge, permanent secretary to a newly slimmed down and reorganised Scottish Executive. He then took a congratulatory call from Scottish Secretary Douglas Alexander, although not the outgoing Prime Minister Tony Blair.

Salmond's first acts as First Minister were populist and consensual. Potentially dangerous ship-to-ship oil transfers in the Firth of Forth were halted, accident-and-emergency units at hospitals in Ayr and Monklands reprieved, while in his first formal policy speech to the Scottish Parliament he placed economic growth at the heart of the Scottish Executive's programme for the next four years. 'Scotland's new politics starts now,' he told MSPs, insisting he wanted a 'new style of government' that would be neither 'dogmatic nor intransigent'.[1]

To that end Salmond's adviser Jennifer Erickson established a US-style Council of Economic Advisers, while other ministers cut rates for small businesses, championed renewable energy and ceded control of Scotland's 12 Local Enterprise Companies to local authorities. In June the First Minister spoke of a 'watershed' for the SNP. 'Today we can say something we have always wanted to say,' he told a National Council meeting proudly. 'The Scottish National Party is now a party of government.'[2]

Labour, meanwhile, displayed signs of finding the election result a little hard to digest. In the House of Commons the Labour MP Anne Moffat compared Salmond's election (as a result of PR) with that of Adolf Hitler in 1933, while Tony Blair was less offensive but almost as rude. As the First Minister put it during Holyrood questions: 'He never phones, he never writes.'[3] Perhaps Blair was depressed. 'I knew once Alex Salmond got his feet under the table,' he wrote presciently in his memoirs, 'he could play off against the Westminster government and embed himself. It would be far harder to remove him than to stop him in the first place.'[4]

Relations between Blair and Salmond also plummeted when details emerged of a 'memorandum of understanding' between the UK and Libyan governments regarding prisoner exchange. Although the Prime Minister insisted it did not cover the convicted Lockerbie bomber, Abdelbaset Ali Mohmed al-Megrahi, Salmond demanded clarification. Reminding MSPs that the conviction was under review by the Scottish Criminal Cases Review Commission, he condemned the UK government's lack of consultation with Holyrood as 'clearly unacceptable'.[5]

'The effect of the last six weeks has been devastating,' judged the journalist Iain Macwhirter, who quickly became one of the First Minister's biggest media cheerleaders. 'The SNP hasn't so much hit the ground running as lapped the political field on an almost daily basis. Opposition MSPs have been blown away at what has been happening.'[6] The *Edinburgh Evening News* agreed that Salmond had 'eased into his new role . . . as if he's been in the job for years'.[7] This was partly because, as one adviser later reflected, the opposition parties had 'lowered expectations' by predicting the 'sky would fall in', thus a moderately energetic administration had 'ended up looking amazing'.[8] Similarly, looking back from the vantage point of late 2014, John Swinney (who Salmond had made his Finance Secretary) viewed 2007 as 'the seminal moment' in the SNP's rise.[9]

Winning the election had also cemented Salmond's authority – hitherto never complete – within the SNP, indeed contemporaries later spoke of him blocking 'out the sun' when it came to the SNP's internal politics.[10] Success, as his predecessor Gordon Wilson observed, had produced 'a self-denying ordinance to toe the line, mute criticism and give unswerving support to SNP Ministers'. The party's National Executive Committee, added Wilson, 'had long been neutered', National Council made deferential to ministerial policy and even the annual conference shorn of controversy.[11] But party management was just one aspect of Salmond's success, another was his recognition, as Sir John Elvidge later recalled, that 'a successful minority government' required 'both agility and coherence', with ministers sharing 'a high level of mutual trust'.

Sir John added a third factor, Salmond's personal style. The First Minister, he judged, was a 'dominating political figure' who chaired Cabinet meetings 'forcefully'.[12] His private office understood this better than most, a Civil Service briefing paper released under Freedom of Information later revealing something of Salmond's 'ministerial preferences'. He preferred to work with 'concise facts rather than opinion' (preferably on a single page of A4), 'retains and uses numbers well', worked better with an 'outline narrative' of a speech rather than a full text, and was keen on dispatching letters of thanks or congratulation as promptly as possible.

'The First Minister views the role of the Scottish Government', added the internal briefing, 'as being to enable things to happen.'[13] Salmond also liked to make things happen at the weekly First Minister's Questions (FMQs), although his performance in that context could be erratic. 'I do bite my tongue just occasionally,' admitted Salmond, in order to avoid saying something that 'might cause needless offence'. 'I've always enjoyed political debate,' he added in his defence. 'FMQs could have been made for me.'

Despite the SNP's honeymoon, Salmond soon faced challenges. On 27 June his government was defeated for the first time over an amendment to keep Edinburgh's trams project on track, while three days later a jeep loaded with gas canisters was driven into the main terminal building at Glasgow Airport. Shortly after Salmond spoke to Gordon Brown, only three days into the job as Prime Minister, to co-ordinate Scottish Executive involvement, while he opened the Scottish Executive Emergency Room (SEER) to co-ordinate the purely Scottish response. 'Life in Scotland will continue,' he said at a press conference that evening, 'the people of Scotland will be satisfied and secure that their Government is taking the appropriate level of precaution.'[14]

As a result of the incident, Salmond had missed a special performance of the Gregory Burke play *Black Watch* at the Pleasance in Edinburgh, which he had been supposed to attend with Sir Sean Connery and Moira. His wife had kept a typically low profile since May's election, only emerging from the shadows when Salmond joked privately that Bute House was 'minging' and that Moira had been 'on her hands and knees'[15] scrubbing the floors in the Charlotte Square townhouse. The Georgian townhouse also aggravated the asthma from which Salmond had suffered since childhood, triggering mild attacks and causing him to wake in the middle of the night.

Newspapers, meanwhile, tried in vain to produce some original copy on Moira Salmond, but so fiercely did Salmond protect her privacy that all they could find were bland off-the-record quotes to the effect that she was 'chic and witty'[16]. Some anecdotes also scraped the barrel of absurdity. At 'the Edinburgh branch of Slater Menswear,' reported the *Scottish Daily Mail*, 'an emphatic Mrs Salmond was overheard telling her husband quite simply: "You will not be getting those trousers." '[17] Salmond opened up a little more when interviewed in early 2009 by the *Guardian*'s Ian Jack, who observed that he had 'flourished in politics without the conventional prerequisites of a public family life'. Moira, Salmond told him, 'does stuff . . . events, races, dinners, all the things that a political spouse does', adding: 'It's a lot of trouble for absolutely no reward whatsoever, but she does it gracefully and willingly.'[18]

Moira was present, albeit not publicly, when Salmond visited Europe for the first time since becoming First Minister, telling a Brussels audience that it was 'time for Scotland to assume' its 'obligations and responsibilities and to help mould the world around us'.[19] That summer, meanwhile, there was a run on the English mortgage bank Northern Rock, the first since the traumatic failure of the City of Glasgow bank back in 1878. Salmond was aware of the historical analogy from his time at the Royal Bank of Scotland, although the repercussions of Northern Rock's collapse, and subsequent nationalisation, were yet to sink in.

'Since the heady days of the election,' wrote Salmond after the 2007 summer recess, 'I believe that we have governed responsibly and imaginatively . . . with an early record and pace of delivery that has left the opposition gasping to keep up.'[20] Indeed, it became increasingly clear that the Liberal Democrats had miscalculated in not having coalesced with the SNP after the election. 'We thought minority government would be so difficult,' reflected a senior Liberal Democrat, 'that they [the SNP] would come running to us by October.'[21]

On the contrary, Salmond had quickly come to view minority government as a help rather than a hindrance. 'My dad used to . . . say play the ball as it lies,' he remarked, 'and the ball as it lies is with minority government.'[22] It did not lie, however, with independence, on which the First Minister tread carefully, refusing to set out a clear timetable for actually holding a referendum ('Rome wasn't built in a day,' he joked, 'not even 100 days'), while calling upon his opponents to take part in an 'open, robust and dignified' debate on Scotland's constitutional future.

This was to be the so-called 'National Conversation' with the people of Scotland, and Salmond indicated that might include, ultimately, a third referendum question on additional powers for Holyrood, so-called 'devo-max'. Ten years earlier this would have caused ructions within the SNP and possibly threatened Salmond's leadership, but now only Pete Wishart, the SNP MP for Perth and North Perthshire, urged caution, saying the SNP had to be 'careful that this key choice [independence] does not become obscured in a plethora of other options'.[23]

Salmond, meanwhile, cleverly pursued independence by stealth in rebranding the Scottish Executive the 'Scottish Government', something Henry McLeish had attempted during his tenure as First Minister but abandoned amid internal Labour hostility. 'Scottish Government surely is something which expresses what we are,' Salmond explained shortly after. 'Scottish Executive sounds like a briefcase or something, it's a ridiculous description, a sort of bureaucratic nothingness.'[24]

The new nomenclature first appeared on Salmond's maiden legislative programme, which he unveiled on 4 September, setting out 11 largely unremarkable bills covering predictable administrative reforms. The reality of minority government had kicked in, and while certain manifesto pledges were swiftly met (abolition of bridge tolls and the graduate endowment), others were conspicuous by their absence (eradicating student debt). Opinion polls, however, continued to show considerable support for the SNP, however loudly the opposition spoke of 'broken promises'.

The First Minister was also aided by the failures of his political opponents. Although Annabel Goldie, the leader of the Scottish Conservatives, had forged a constructive relationship with the SNP since the election, the Liberal Democrats – led by former Deputy First Minister Nicol Stephen – had often appeared listless, while Wendy Alexander, Jack McConnell's successor as Labour leader, had quickly been consumed by a row over donations to her leadership campaign. Alexander managed to recover some momentum with her proposal for a 'grand, if informal, Unionist coalition'[25] (later to become the Calman Commission) to agree further powers for the Scottish Parliament, although even that indicated the extent to which Salmond controlled the terms of debate.

There was of course controversy. In December 2007 Aberdeenshire Council's strategic planning body rejected Donald Trump's plan for a £500 million luxury golf resort in the north east of Scotland. Salmond, who had backed the project before becoming First Minister, decided to 'call in' the application after meeting with one of Trump's representatives at a hotel near Aberdeen. In an intervention at First Minister's Questions, however, Nicol Stephen said Salmond's involvement 'smells of sleaze'.[26]

'I hardly know Alex Salmond, but what I know is that he's an amazing man,' gushed Trump. 'He's a person who believes strongly in Scotland and he wants economic development in Scotland.' Holyrood's Local Government Committee, meanwhile, twice questioned the First Minister over his handling of the affair. He acquitted himself well, or rather the committee failed to land any blows, and when it reported in May 2008 Salmond was charged with having taken a 'cavalier' approach to his involvement, displaying, 'at best, exceptionally poor judgement and a worrying lack of awareness about the consequence of his actions'.[27] Later Trump and Salmond would trade insults rather than compliments, the former having taken against the SNP leader's renewables vision.

Salmond played a defter hand as negotiations over his first budget continued into early February 2008, telling Kevin Pringle, perhaps his most influential adviser, to slip into his post-Cabinet briefing a warning that the First Minister would resign and force an election if the budget was defeated. 'I'll quit, warns Salmond' was the message on many front pages the following day, and that afternoon the budget passed with Conservative support, no mean achievement for a minority government. A key component of the budget was a so-called 'historic concordat' with Scotland's 32 local authorities to freeze the council tax. Although criticised for disproportionally benefiting the well-off and therefore directly contradicting, as Professor David Bell argued, the SNP's 'cherished aim of reducing inequality',[28] it was, not surprisingly, hugely popular.

In May 2008 the Scottish Labour leader Wendy Alexander urged the Scottish Government to 'bring it on'[29] (meaning an independence referendum) a brave and imaginative move that in different circumstances might have caused serious problems for Salmond. But Gordon Brown pointedly refused to endorse Alexander's plan in the House of Commons, enabling the SNP leader to fend off her attack. On 28 June, meanwhile, Alexander resigned as a consequence of an ongoing row about donations to her leadership campaign the previous year, effectively killing her referendum ploy, while a few days later Nicol Stephen also announced his departure as Liberal Democrat leader.

The SNP, by contrast, continued to ride high, particularly when John Mason spectacularly won the Glasgow East Westminster by-election on 24 July. The First Minister had predicted a 'political earthquake', and although it proved to be more of a tremor (Mason's majority was 365), the political aftershocks were felt for several weeks. Not only was Labour's candidate, the popular MSP Margaret Curran, humiliated (although she would take the seat two years later), but a beleaguered Gordon Brown had to endure yet more negative headlines and leadership speculation.

The result, meanwhile, made the SNP and its leader appear unstoppable. Following the 2008 summer recess Salmond now faced two new opponents – Iain Gray (Labour) and Tavish Scott (Liberal Democrat) – as he entered his 18th year in front-line politics. 'I suppose', Salmond told the blogger Iain Dale in a September 2008 interview, 'I have tried to bring the SNP into the mainstream of Scotland.'

> We have a very competitive economic agenda. Many business people have warmed towards the SNP. We need a competitive edge, a competitive advantage – get on with it, get things done, speed up decision making, reduce bureaucracy. The SNP has a strong social conscience, which is very Scottish in itself. One of the reasons Scotland didn't take to Lady Thatcher was because of that. We didn't mind the economic side so much. But we didn't like the social side at all.[30]

That final sentence caused a media storm. Under heavy fire from Labour politicians and, as usual, Jim Sillars, for daring to claim that Mrs Thatcher's economic reforms had been necessary, the First Minister took the extraordinary step of phoning the BBC to explain (live on air) that he had not meant to imply that Scots had 'liked [Mrs Thatcher's] economic policies, just that we liked her lack of concern for social consequences even less'.[31] Salmond, of course, had said precisely the opposite, but contradicting himself with such self-assurance was fast becoming a hallmark of his First Ministerial style.

Salmond was fond of referring to Scotland joining what he called an 'arc of prosperity of small, highly successful independent countries',[32] but when the Edinburgh-based bank HBOS was compelled to merge with Lloyds TSB following a share price plunge, the resulting crisis made that appear a distant prospect. The First Minister condemned the merger as a 'shotgun marriage' driven by 'a bunch of short-selling spivs and speculators in the financial markets', [33] a version of events not only open to question, but embarrassing given it later emerged that the chairman of Salmond's Council of Economic Advisers, Sir George Mathewson, was himself an unrepentant practitioner of short-selling.

Trouble at the Royal Bank of Scotland (RBS), meanwhile, posed even greater problems for Salmond. Not only did he feel its pain as a former employee, but his political connections with the Edinburgh-based banking group – Mathewson and Andrew Wilson, who had returned to an RBS career having lost his Holyrood seat in 2003 – almost seemed to put it beyond criticism. 'It is in Scottish interests for RBS to be successful,' Salmond had written to its chief executive Sir Fred Goodwin shortly after becoming First Minister, 'and I would like to offer any assistance my office can provide. Good luck with the bid.'[34] This was for the Dutch bank ABN Amro, a purchase that precipitated RBS's problems.

When RBS subsequently announced the second-largest loss in banking history, Salmond said he was certain the bank would 'overcome current challenges to become both highly profitable and highly successful once again'.[35] Asked about Sir Fred's position, meanwhile, the First Minister demonstrated his loyalty by saying that he should stay in post, shortly before Goodwin was removed as a condition of the UK government's part-nationalisation of RBS. Confronted with his comments on *Newsnight Scotland* that evening, Salmond appeared untypically lost for words, while thereafter he resisted persistent invitations to criticise RBS in particular and bankers in general.

Indeed, the whole financial crisis put Salmond in a difficult position, with historic claims that 'Scottish banks are among the most stable financial institutions in the world' (February 2008),[36] 'with the right strategy, there are no limits to success in the modern global economy' (Harvard, also 2008), not to forget his April 2007 pledge to introduce a 'light-touch regulation suitable to a Scottish financial sector with its outstanding reputation for probity',[37] coming back to haunt him, statements that made the First Minister's subsequent attempts to depict the crash as 'London's boom and bust'[38] all the more unconvincing.

Indeed, Salmond confidently argued that recent events had actually 'strengthened the case for Scotland to be given more control of its economy to protect jobs, investment and stability', adding that the International Monetary Fund had predicted that the economies of Norway, Denmark, Finland and Sweden ('all smaller European nations') would keep on growing over the next two years. He also argued that Ireland, whatever its present difficulties, remained a good model for an independent Scotland, having been 'able to act quickly and decisively to bring stability to its banking sector by guaranteeing all deposits . . . a clear demonstration of just how effective smaller independent nations can be when the going gets tough'.[39]

As a former professional economist Salmond had long been content to present himself as an ally of the Scottish financial sector, relying on its reputation to shore up the economic case for independence. Only several months later was he willing to venture even mild criticism of bankers, telling the General Assembly of the Church of Scotland in May 2009 that 'the rewards to some individuals [were] completely divorced from basic ideas of fairness, or service'.[40] And while the Scottish Government agitated for a public expenditure-led response to the economic crisis (it brought forward £100 million in capital expenditure), beyond that neither Salmond nor John Swinney made any public statement about the lessons to be drawn beyond, as the veteran SNP thinker Stephen Maxwell put it, 'vague murmurings that it must be consistent with reform of the international system'.[41] The Scottish Government, observed the former SNP leader Gordon Wilson, 'gave a convincing impression of a rabbit in the middle of a road facing the headlights of an oncoming vehicle – and largely said nothing'.[42]

Despite much talk of 'social justice', meanwhile, there were compromises in other respects. In August 2008 the SNP bowed to pressure from the Catholic Church in Scotland over an annual vaccination programme for 30,000 Scottish schoolgirls to protect them from cervical cancer, omitting advice on safe sex as a result. And in May 2009 the Scottish Government minister Fiona Hyslop even lobbied Whitehall seeking an opt-out from equality legislation allowing gay couples to adopt children, again under pressure from the Catholic Church and despite a 2006 Holyrood law to the contrary. The clear aim was to keep on board a powerful element of the expanding SNP 'tent', even if it meant adopting illiberal policies. As the journalist Kenny Farquharson later observed, during his first term Salmond 'was not a man who readily stood up against vested interests'. 'Teachers, trade unions, banks,' he added, 'show him a vested interest and his instinct was to pander to it.'[43]

After nearly 18 months in office, Salmond was also tired. The *Guardian* journalist Ian Jack thought he looked 'a lot less chipper . . . puffy and grey complexioned and suddenly slower on his feet'.[44] Despite frequent attempts at dieting, the First Minister's weight had also increased noticeably since May 2007. In time, however, Salmond would bounce back – as he usually did – for example when the SNP 'won' the June 2009 European elections in Scotland with more than 29 per cent of the vote, a result Salmond hailed as 'historic'.[45]

In December 2008, meanwhile, the Calman Commission had published its interim report, recommending that Holyrood ought to set its own 'Scottish rate' of income tax, although Salmond said it was not 'anything remotely matching the substantial new powers Scotland needs'.[46] Given the 'pressure on family budgets', he later reflected, it would not have 'been sensible or reasonable to look for an increase in that bit of direct taxation that we controlled'.[47] Instead the First Minister argued for borrowing powers, something he believed would allow Scotland to better 'respond to the global economic challenges and protect the interests of our people'.[48]

Salmond had recently suffered his first defeat in a Holyrood division since the Edinburgh trams vote in his first few weeks as First Minister.

Having failed to appease two Green MSPs over a home insulation scheme, the Scottish Government's second budget had fallen on 28 January 2009. The Finance Secretary promised a revised budget as soon as possible, although the Labour MSP group, which had voted against, threatened to table a motion of no confidence in the First Minister should that meet a similar fate. Salmond, in response, repeated his resignation threat from 2008, adding that he was 'putting the SNP on an election footing'.[49]

That, of course, did not prove necessary, and when the budget was re-introduced it passed with near unanimous support from all but the two Green MSPs who had scuppered it in the first place. Not long after this close shave, the Scottish Government also announced its plan to jettison its Local Income Tax policy, citing lack of Parliamentary support. Iain Gray, who tore up a copy of the 2007 SNP manifesto at First Minister's Questions in order to highlight 'broken promises', said Salmond had been 'caught red-handed selling short Scottish voters' and ought to apologise. On the contrary, replied the First Minister, apologies were 'required from the council tax cabal of Labour and the Tories, who have voted to uphold the council tax in Scotland'.[50]

That same week, Salmond reshuffled his Cabinet for the first time since taking power, replacing three junior ministers in the process. Mike Russell, now almost rehabilitated following the 2004 leadership race, replaced Linda Fabiani as culture minister (his environment portfolio was taken by Roseanna Cunningham), while Keith Brown took over from Maureen Watt as schools minister and Alex Neil succeeded Stewart Maxwell at housing and communities. Salmond behaved sensitively, stressing that there had 'been no failures in the ministerial team', but wanted to give other 'colleagues an opportunity to show what they can contribute'.[51]

The appointment of Cunningham and Neil took many by surprise, not least the new ministers. Yet their appointments demonstrated several aspects of Salmond's character: an inability to hold long-standing grudges against those he believed had been disloyal, and also a genuine desire to build as capable a ministerial team as possible, thereby defying his reputation as a 'one-man band'. 'The timing was very important,' observed someone close to the First Minister. 'He was waiting to see what they would do, whether they would become fundies [fundamentalists].'[52] Interestingly, Cunningham's appointment also meant four veterans of the 79 Group now served as ministers, including Salmond, Justice Secretary Kenny MacAskill and transport minister Stewart Stevenson.

Perhaps the biggest focus of the reshuffled Scottish Government was to be the development of Scotland's renewable energy capacity. Salmond had been interested in this since his undergraduate days and remained just as engaged three decades later. 'Energy is one of the things that enthuses him the most, perhaps even more so than the constitution,' said a source, 'it's not just token. He really gets into the detail of that and thinks we're on the cusp of a big turning point.'[53]

Indeed, Salmond saw it being as significant as the discovery of North Sea oil three decades before. Renewables, he said in March 2009, was 'a new energy revolution'. 'With firm resolve, shared purpose, and wise decision-making,' he added, 'we can ensure that the promise of renewable energy matches that of North Sea oil and gas.'[54] To mark his second anniversary as First Minister, Salmond boasted that his administration had approved 'no less than 20 major renewable projects', mainly wind farms, while the 'Saltire Prize' had been designed to 'spur innovation around the world' in terms of marine projects, not least in the Pentland Firth. But the old hostility towards nuclear power ('unreliable and unwanted in Scotland'[55]) being part of Scotland's energy mix remained.

Salmond took a similar message to the Copenhagen summit on climate change in mid-December, arguing that his ambitious target for cutting carbon emissions should allow him to take part in the main negotiations. Although this was not granted ('I'm not a head of state, I'm not leading a delegation,' he conceded. 'Scotland is not an independent country.'), the First Minister flew to Denmark anyway, and ended up signing an agreement to help the Maldives become the world's first 'carbon-neutral country'.[56] Salmond was certainly energetic, even persuading Scottish and Southern Energy to team up with the Japanese engineering giant Mitsubishi to co-operate on a range of projects, from developing electric cars to a new generation of offshore wind farms. Even the normally hostile *Daily Record* praised him for 'championing the country's green future', something it acknowledged 'could prove his greatest legacy to Scotland'.[57]

Other sectors of the Scottish economy, meanwhile, were struggling. In July 2009 the drinks giant Diageo announced controversial proposals that threatened 900 jobs at the Johnnie Walker packaging plant in Kilmarnock and the Port Dundas grain distillery in Glasgow. Salmond's reaction did not show him at his best. After a hastily arranged meeting with Paul Walsh, Diageo's chief executive, the First Minister cancelled at 15 minutes' notice so he could appear on the BBC2 programme *The Daily Politics*. Given that Salmond had earlier referred to the possible job losses as 'cataclysmic', it was a curious way to behave.

Salmond was also accused of 'grandstanding' when he personally led a march through Kilmarnock protesting at the job losses, while Iain McMillan, director of CBI Scotland, said Diageo had been the target of 'unusually aggressive behaviour' from ministers. A Scottish Government rescue package was then rejected, although Salmond bluntly rejected criticisms that his negotiating technique had not made a compromise possible, saying simply 'we gave it our best shot'.[58]

Almost two months later Salmond was accused of trying to 'bully' another drinks firm, the French company Pernod Ricard, into supporting his plans for a minimum alcohol price. 'Salmond went over there [Paris] and was quite aggressive,' said one industry insider. 'The people at Pernod were shocked by his behaviour.' Salmond's office strongly denied these reports, claiming the meeting had in fact been 'very positive'.[59] Whatever had happened at that Paris meeting, Salmond could certainly be abrasive, and occasionally patronising. During an exchange of views on the cancellation of the Glasgow Airport Rail Link, for example, he told the respected leader of Glasgow City Council, Steven Purcell, to 'behave like a grown-up'.[60]

Salmond also faced scrutiny over his Commons finances as the Westminster expenses row dominated headlines throughout May and June 2009. The *Sunday Herald* reported that as well as claiming rent on a flat in the prestigious Dolphin Square, Salmond had claimed almost £1,100 for staying in London hotels while on government business and £1,751 for food despite rarely being in the UK capital. Salmond claimed he had done nothing wrong (indeed an external audit by Sir Thomas Legg exonerated him), and in spite of it all the First Minister retained a Teflon coating three years after his historic election win.

Although Justice Secretary Kenny MacAskill's announcement that the convicted Lockerbie bomber Abdelbaset Ali al-Megrahi, who had been diagnosed with terminal cancer, was to be released on 'compassionate' grounds had been widely trailed, the actual confirmation in late August 2009 still generated political shockwaves. As criticism of the decision grew both nationally and internationally – not helped by television footage of jubilant crowds waving Scottish saltires as al-Megrahi arrived home in Tripoli – Salmond told the BBC 'it was the right thing to do in terms of the Scottish justice system'.[61]

MacAskill consistently argued that he had, in his quasi-judicial capacity as Justice Secretary, considered al-Megrahi's application for release on purely medical advice, although he refused to disclose that advice in full. As for the question of al-Megrahi's guilt, Salmond made no public comment but had little time for conspiracy theories. Indeed, on becoming First Minister he had reviewed all the relevant Lockerbie papers and believed al-Megrahi's conviction to be sound.

There were also wider considerations. Although the decision attracted international condemnation, it also drew attention to Scotland's distinct identity, both legally and morally. US news networks carried MacAskill's statement – with its invocation of the Scots as 'a compassionate people' – live, while President Obama's condemnation was balanced out by Nelson Mandela's praise. That, it might be said, had done more for Scotland's profile, not to mention that of the SNP, than innumerable marketing campaigns.

Later, Salmond ably batted aside a US Senate inquiry and also allegations that certain oil companies had leaned on the Scottish Government prior to its decision. Even when *Vanity Fair* alleged that Salmond had offered Jack Straw (the then Foreign Secretary) a *quid pro quo* (helping end a raft of law suits in relation to 'slopping out' in Scottish prisons) in return for dropping his objections to al-Megrahi's release, almost everyone accepted the First Minister's swift rebuttal that it was 'Balderdash'.[62] Whitehall's own review, he claimed, demonstrated that Tony Blair's government had been 'complicit in the greatest orchestrated political hypocrisy in Scottish . . . history',[63] while in 2015 he claimed that 'BP lobbied' to protect oil contracts in the region 'and the UK government jumped' to include al-Megrahi in the prisoner transfer agreement as a result.[64]

Although opinion polls suggested a majority of Scots believed the release to have been a mistake, as with so many other things it did not damage the First Minister's standing. Even when a clearly ailing al-Megrahi became a political football in the final moments of the Libyan regime, Salmond defended himself with ease. 'What has been proven in every enquiry,' he said in August 2011, 'is that the Scottish Government – almost alone among people acting in this – always acted in good faith and according to the due process of law.'[65] Al-Megrahi, meanwhile, died in May 2012, nearly three years after his release.

'There's a vast, overwhelming majority of people in Scotland, regardless of political preference, who rather like the idea of the Westminster parliament being hung by a Scottish rope,' Salmond told the *Daily Telegraph* ahead of the 2009 SNP conference. 'I don't think a Tory majority is a shoo-in by any means. I think a hung parliament or a balanced parliament of some kind is still more than an arithmetic possibility.'[66]

Opinion polls, however, told a different story, with the SNP continuing to slide behind Labour in terms of Westminster voting intentions. The Glasgow North East by-election on 12 November 2009 had been a case in point, with Labour's Willie Bain winning a decisive 59 per cent of the vote ('Some hills,' reflected Salmond, 'are higher to climb than others'[67]), while support for independence languished at around 30 per cent. Undeterred, Salmond unveiled yet another white paper on St Andrew's Day, this time setting out four possible options: the status quo, more devolved powers as recommended by the Calman Commission, 'devo-max' or the SNP's preferred option of full independence. 'The debate in Scottish politics is no longer between change or no change,' Salmond said at the launch, 'It's about the kind of change we seek and the right of the people to choose their future in a free and fair referendum.'[68]

Salmond, ever the realist, realised he needed to get at least one opposition party on board – most likely the Liberal Democrats – if the referendum bill was to stand any chance of getting through Parliament. Not only was he no longer 'wedded' to the idea of a vote taking place on St Andrew's Day 2010, but he also indicated that Holyrood would be free to frame the wording of any third question. And if MSPs chose not to pass the bill, then Salmond predicted the constitution would become 'a huge, perhaps dominating, question in the 2011 Scottish elections'.[69]

Meanwhile the First Minister assumed direct responsibility for the constitution (which was, after all, reserved) following a limited reshuffle in which Education Secretary Fiona Hyslop was demoted in order to draw a line under a long-running row over the SNP's election pledge to reduce class sizes. Despite these little local difficulties, some observers believed all was not lost. 'History shows you should expect the unexpected with the SNP,' wrote Murray Ritchie, the *Herald*'s former political correspondent. 'If the high road via a referendum next year is closed,' he added, 'then it is only sensible to take the low.'[70]

In early 2010 the three Unionist parties vowed to kill off any referendum bill (the high road) and Salmond responded by announcing yet another consultation (the low road) prior to publication of a draft referendum bill towards the end of February. This confirmed Salmond's earlier backing for three separate questions, albeit in a slightly different form. Firstly, voters were to be asked to vote 'yes' or 'no' on whether they supported the Scottish Parliament being given new devolved powers, and secondly whether the 'parliament's powers should also be extended to enable independence to be achieved'. 'The people want our parliament to be able to do more, so the debate is now about how much more,' declared Salmond. 'And it is time the people had their say.'[71]

Distracting from this further constitutional repositioning had been two 'sleaze' rows that at points threatened to engulf Salmond and his deputy, the able and popular Health Secretary Nicola Sturgeon. The first involved the auctioning of private lunches at Holyrood for SNP donors, apparently in breach of Parliamentary rules, a row that escalated when the *Sunday Herald* obtained video footage of the auction itself, in which Salmond could clearly be seen handling a cheque for £500, while the auctioneer Humza Yousaf, who worked for Salmond and Sturgeon at Holyrood, repeatedly emphasised Salmond's status as First Minister, rather than as leader of the SNP. Whether Salmond had actually breached any rules was a moot point, but it did not look good.

To make matters worse, Salmond was then forced to defend Sturgeon when it emerged that she had lobbied a sheriff court on behalf of a constituent who also happened to be a convicted fraudster. Salmond told MSPs she had his '110 per cent' support but then went further, arguing that MSPs had an 'absolute obligation' to represent constituents 'without fear or favour'.[72] This was, at the very least, an overstatement; as Mike Dailly of the Govan Law Centre observed, Salmond had a 'horrible propensity to invent these concepts on the hoof'.[73]

This demonstrated Salmond at his best, his instinctive loyalty towards Sturgeon, and also his worst, using poorly chosen language and pushing things a little too far. Both rows eventually died down, the first after a Parliamentary investigation cleared Salmond and Sturgeon of any wrongdoing, and the second following a well-handled apology from the Health Secretary. Indeed, with that contrite Holyrood performance, Sturgeon convinced many she was ready to succeed Salmond should a vacancy arise. Although there was occasionally tension, the relationship between Sturgeon and Salmond ('she has the ability to bite her tongue,' explained an aide[74]) was perhaps the most important within the Scottish Government.

Salmond attempted to recover ground ahead of the 2010 UK general election by warning that any move by the UK government to cut public spending in Scotland would be 'neither understood nor forgiven' by Scots. Nevertheless, a series of polls appeared to show declining SNP support, while Gordon Brown's approval ratings surpassed those of Salmond. This, together with an ongoing row over televised leadership debates from which the SNP was to be excluded, enabled the SNP to present itself as the underdog ahead of polling day. 'The more SNP MPs elected the stronger Scotland's position will be,' declared Salmond at his party's campaign launch. 'Because at this election the message is simple: More Nats Means Less Cuts.'[75]

Beyond such dodgy grammar, the SNP's broader election campaign lacked imagination, simply reviving Salmond's 'balanced Parliament' strategy as deployed at almost every UK general election since 1987. 'I have more experience than anyone in these islands', had become a regular quip, 'on how to deal with a hung Parliament.'[76] The election also marked his reluctant departure from the House of Commons after 23 years as the Member for Banff and Buchan. 'I have met and clashed with a number of formidable debaters and speakers from both sides of the House,' he told MPs in a valedictory speech, adding that his Commons career had also served to strengthen his 'absolute conviction that the case for our having full determination over Scotland's finances and resources has never been more urgent and has never required to be better made than it is now'.[77]

On polling day the SNP managed to hold its six MPs and around 20 per cent of the vote, compared with a relatively impressive result for Labour, which polled 42 per cent, up almost 3 per cent compared with 2005. Typically, Salmond (who had set a target of 20 seats) made the best of a disappointing result, pointing to his party's exclusion from the televised debates and attempting to seize the initiative by ruling out a formal coalition with either the Conservatives or Labour (a 'balanced Parliament' having come to pass). Salmond, however, went a little far in also claiming to be in direct contact with the Labour Party, something the former Scotland Office minister David Cairns promptly dismissed as 'fantasy'.[78]

Finally, Salmond called upon the Liberal Democrats to join a 'progressive alliance' comprising Labour, the SNP and Plaid Cymru, presciently predicting that the alternative, what he called a Liberal Democrat 'stitch up' with the Conservatives, could lead to 'the complete collapse of Lib Dem support in Scotland'.[79] A few days after the election, meanwhile, the new Prime Minister (David Cameron), made a point of visiting Salmond in Edinburgh to underline what he called the 'respect agenda'. The First Minister urged him to 'spring a political surprise' and implement 'devo-max', although this, as he later revealed, got 'short shrift' from the new coalition government.[80]

'The centre of gravity in Scottish politics currently is clearly not independence,' Salmond told *The Times* in June 2010, pointing instead to 'fiscal responsibility' as a more achievable aim.[81] When this led to follow-up coverage in other newspapers the First Minister, perhaps wary of reviving his party's long-buried fundamentalist/gradualist tensions, said he had in fact said 'exactly the opposite . . . that the centre of gravity in Scottish politics is shifting towards independence, not away from it.'[82]

This not only demonstrated breathtaking chutzpah, but a tendency to rewrite history (Salmond went on to claim the SNP had campaigned for devolution and the Calman settlement, which was only half true), although it concealed a serious point: the SNP had long pursued a twin aim, independence and, as the party's constitution clearly stated, 'the furtherance of all Scottish interests', a rather vague goal the First Minister now reinterpreted as support for full fiscal responsibility.

'Fiscal responsibility is a good cause,' judged *The Economist*, 'but Mr Salmond may find it just as hard to sell as independence.'[83] Indeed, within days of his *Times* interview the Scottish Government confirmed it would not be tabling its long-awaited referendum bill before the Holyrood summer recess, meaning it would be almost impossible to hold the ballot, as planned, on St Andrew's Day 2010. Then came a further retreat: a bill would not be forthcoming at all.

Explaining his decision the following day, Salmond predicted that the independence referendum would be a 'transcending issue' of the forthcoming election campaign,[84] and when the decision was discussed (or rather rubber-stamped) by a Scottish Cabinet meeting in Kilmarnock on 7 September 2010, not a single SNP MSP or MP criticised the move. Speaking at Holyrood, Salmond declared the 'first age of devolution' to be 'over' while implying, ironically, that his Unionist opponents were scared of a referendum. As the Liberal Democrat leader Tavish Scott said, it was 'a classic high-wire, total risk, all or nothing Salmond gamble. It is independence or opposition'.[85]

At the SNP conference the following month Salmond gave a speech at times defiant ('as you know, I fight and I do not give up'), at points curiously valedictory, and also very bold: 'I am the First Minister of Scotland, and I intend to continue to be.' 'The independence I seek is the independence to create jobs,' Salmond told delegates, keen to emphasise the tangible benefits of the SNP's core aim. 'This is not an arcane question removed from the people – it is the people, you and me, and how we protect our society, and grow our economy.'[86]

And with the 2011 Holyrood election now just months away, SNP advisers made a conscious effort to 'humanise' the First Minister. He recorded an edition of the popular BBC Radio 4 series *Desert Island Discs*, talking about his late mother and wife Moira, and also engaged with the influential online 'Mumsnet' forum, both of which garnered extensive follow-up coverage. 'No one had ever doubted his credentials as a politician,' explained one senior Nationalist, 'but what they had doubted was him as a person. We needed to sell him as a good guy. To his credit, he agreed to that, considering he's a very private person.'[87] Indeed, as Michael Portillo noted in his BBC profile of the SNP leader, there remained 'a shiver of discomfort' at any mention of his 'private life'.[88]

Towards the end of 2010 Salmond and the Scottish Government came under attack on a number of fronts, over its handling of the 'Homecoming' clan gathering, the lapsed 'Scottish Variable Rate' (Holyrood's power to vary the basic rate of income tax) and, latterly, its response to extreme winter weather, which ended the ministerial career of Salmond's old friend Stewart Stevenson. Yet the First Minister retained an uncanny ability to rise above the fray. 'Our team is better than their team,' he declared in early 2011, touching upon what would become one of the election campaign's key themes. 'The people believe that as well.'[89]

At around the same time Salmond attended a key strategy meeting in Aberdeen, which included a series of team-building sessions led by the 'life coach' Claire Howell, with whom the First Minister had struck up a good working relationship. Out of this session emerged the rhetorical trio of 'team, record, vision', while a subsequent pre-election conference found the SNP leader on almost messianic form:

> This movement, this nation, has been patronized, talked down, told it wasn't good enough. And yet this party has risen from a few MPs and a land without a Parliament, to a Scotland with a Parliament, and an SNP government. We never lost the strength of hope – and we fought on to triumph. But we, in our mix of the national and the international, of the personal and the political, we fought not to govern over people, but for the people to govern over themselves. It is for that reason and that reason above all that we are the Friends of the People of Scotland and for that reason we shall prevail.[90]

Indeed, Salmond remained utterly confident the election could be won, even though public opinion polls had yet to move into line with private data showing the SNP to be ahead of Labour. Then, on 3 April 2011, a *Sunday Times* poll indicated a lead for the first time and, when two further polls turned this into a trend, an initially lacklustre campaign moved up a level.

At a slick manifesto launch at the Royal Scottish Academy of Music and Drama in Glasgow, a giant screen screamed 'RE-ELECT', a message repeated on the manifesto's cover and therefore featured in most newspapers the following day. Beyond these attention-grabbing optics, however, even Christopher Harvie, an outgoing SNP MSP, called his party's manifesto another exercise in 'safety first', the commentator Gerry Hassan having observed earlier that year that in spite of the rhetoric, the first SNP administration had 'not been a transformational government', but rather 'one of caution and timidity'.[91]

Salmond went straight from the manifesto launch to record an edition of the BBC's popular current affairs debate programme *Question Time* in Liverpool. Initially, the audience was lukewarm, but by the end he had them eating out of his hand, particularly his warning not to let English politicians destroy 'their' NHS. Also adding to the SNP's sense of momentum was the backing of the *Scottish Sun*, a coup given its hostility four years before. Salmond had spent years carefully cultivating the tabloid, while during the campaign itself the paper produced two memorable front pages, 'Play it again, Salm'[92] announcing the newspaper's support and, on polling day, 'Keep Salm and Carry On'.[93]

The SNP's referendum policy, meanwhile, did not enjoy the prominence Salmond had predicted, rather the proposed date seemed to get further away as the campaign progressed. Initially, he refused to set out a timescale (unlike in 2007), later indicated that a referendum would not occur until the second half of the new Parliamentary term and finally let it be known that it would actually take place 'well into the second half of the five-year term', signalling that Salmond's constitutional priority upon re-election would be giving the Scotland Bill 'economic teeth'.[94]

The contrast between Salmond and Scottish Labour leader Iain Gray was also played out in three televised leaders' debates. Although these did not dominate in the manner of the 2010 general election, SNP advisers felt they were useful in reminding voters of Salmond's 'competence' and confidence. There were a few discordant notes ('all of Scotland', he hubristically claimed towards the end of April, 'is backing the SNP now'[95]), but they were generally drowned out by the sheer vigour of Salmond's overall performance. On polling day the First Minister voted in his constituency and then based himself at the Holiday Inn near the Aberdeen Exhibition & Conference Centre where, shortly before 4 a.m., he arrived at the count amid a scrum of cameras. Minutes later he was re-elected with a majority of 15,295 in the new Holyrood constituency of Aberdeenshire East.

In his victory speech Salmond said Scotland had 'outgrown negative campaigning' while the SNP could 'finally claim' it had 'lived up to that [old] accolade as the National Party of Scotland'. He then linked his overwhelming mandate to extending Holyrood's powers: 'Which is why in this term of the Parliament we will bring forward a referendum, and trust the people with Scotland's own constitutional future.'[96] Later, when asked about Labour's election losses, Salmond departed from his generally positive script. 'This idea that Labour had ownership over parts of Scotland, well that's gone forever hasn't it,' he said. 'I suppose it's a bit like the American bison, I mean I dare say we'll still see one or two dotted about here and there but the great herds of Labour have gone forever.'[97]

At this point Salmond did not realise the SNP was on course for something deemed impossible by psephologists – an overall majority. Indeed, when the party's chief executive Peter Murrell informed his leader of this likelihood at around 6.30 a.m., Salmond simply murmured, 'that's not possible'. But when all the results were in, it became clear the SNP had seized a remarkable 45.4 per cent of the constituency vote (to Labour's 31.7 per cent), and 44 per cent on the regional list (to Labour's 26.3 per cent). This translated into 69 SNP MSPs (to Labour's 37), thus Salmond's long campaign to displace Labour as Scotland's dominant centre-left party had finally come to pass.

After a few hours' sleep, Salmond, Moira and his adviser Geoff Aberdein boarded 'Saltire One' for the short flight to the Scottish capital, during which he went over the final draft of a speech to be delivered outside Prestonfield House Hotel. Descriptions of Salmond's mood at this point ranged from 'energised' and 'obviously ecstatic' to 'elated, about as high as the helicopter he'd just come down in'.[98] As Aberdein later recalled: 'I think he was overwhelmed by it: we were going to have a referendum. That was the stage at which it dawned.'[99]

In 2007, Salmond had urged Scots 'to work as if you live in the early days of a better nation', and almost exactly four years later little had changed as he positioned himself in front of a Saltire and behind a yellow lectern, this time emblazoned with the call to 'be part of better'. Otherwise he struck a statesmanlike tone, confident enough to speak for the country as a whole but also careful to appear conciliatory, for 'although the SNP has a majority of the seats, we don't have a monopoly of wisdom'.

I believe the SNP won this election because Scotland wants to travel in hope and to aim high. Scotland has chosen to believe in itself and our shared capacity to build a fair society. The nation can be better, it wants to be better, and I will do all I can as First Minister to make it better. We have given ourselves the permission to be bold and we will govern fairly and wisely, with an eye to the future but a heart to forgive.[100]

The last line was a quote from the Corries song 'Scotland Will Flourish' and had been Salmond's own idea. With that, he retreated back to the hotel to have tea with Moira and watch continuing television news coverage of the election.

Everything was still sinking in as the First Minister made a brief stop at Bute House before heading to the Jam House on Queen Street for the SNP's victory party. 'I've heard another rumour,' he told those present, referencing his speech to the same gathering four years earlier, 'we won another election.' Then, in his catch-all Scottish accent, he added: 'A' was thinking that a' the seats a' flew over in ma helicopter were yellow.'[101]

Alex Salmond, who had gone into politics with no realistic expectation of savouring such a moment, could be forgiven a moment of triumphalism. Winning an overall majority under an electoral system designed to prevent precisely that had been a remarkable feat. But Salmond did not stay long at the celebrations, instead moving on to one of his favourite restaurants to have dinner with Moira, whom he had married on 6 May 1981. It was their 30th anniversary, although neither of them could have anticipated such a memorable present.

# Chapter 13

# 'A CHANGE IS COMING'

The SNP's astonishing 2011 election victory was, in the context of the party's recent history, ironic. Until the year 2000 it had considered winning a majority of Scottish seats at either Westminster or in a devolved Scottish Parliament a 'mandate' for opening independence negotiations. But now having achieved that, Nationalists found themselves faced with a referendum rather than crunch talks in Whitehall.

But then Alex Salmond realised that his party had not won a landslide victory on the basis of *independence*, rather it had been the electorate's perception of its 'competence' (and indeed the perceived *incompetence* of the alternatives) that had attracted voters in their droves. Salmond had run an attractive, upbeat campaign on the basis of 'team, record, vision', and had been rewarded handsomely. A post-election study, meanwhile, revealed the 'vision' part of that vote-winning triumvirate was actually the least popular. It put support for independence at just 24 per cent, with the status quo and 'more powers' tied on 38 per cent.[1]

Forty-five per cent of Scots (on a turnout of just 50 per cent) might have backed the SNP to run a second devolved government, but strategists were acutely aware those voters (many of whom were middle class) were not an independence-friendly coalition. Salmond, therefore, was not in a hurry, and having bought time during the election campaign by repeatedly pushing back the potential date of a referendum, he instead claimed his immediate priorities were jobs and the economy, as well as beefing up the UK government's Scotland Bill, shortly to be debated at Westminster.

The result had caught even the SNP unawares, so much so that the so-called 'Salmond Six', a demand for more powers over broadcasting, excise duty, greater borrowing powers, corporation tax, revenue from the Crown Estate and increased representation for Scottish ministers at EU level, did not constitute a strategy but rather the product of a brainstorming session with the First Minister and his advisers shortly after the election. Nevertheless, just days after the election Salmond asserted that 'the destination of independence' was 'more or less inevitable',[2] while SNP strategists floated the concept of 'independence-lite', whereby Scotland would assume full economic sovereignty but 'pool' areas such as defence and foreign affairs with the UK. This 'thinking on independence', claimed a spokesman, was 'modern and forward looking', unlike 'old-fashioned and backward looking' Unionism.[3]

Shortly after the election, Salmond admitted the SNP had been presenting its case for independence 'in a way which reflects the realities of modern world'. 'The resumption of independence is the resumption of political and economic sovereignty,' he explained. 'How you then choose to exercise that sovereignty reflects the inter-relationships with principally the other countries in these islands.'[4] This provided some sort of intellectual justification for compromises both old (Europe and the monarchy) and new (currency and energy), indeed Salmond went to extraordinary lengths to expunge a 1997 SNP conference resolution to hold 'a referendum in the term of office of the first independent Parliament of Scotland on whether to retain the monarch' (see Chapter 8).

The First Minister simply claimed the policy had changed (although no one could pinpoint exactly when), and such was his authority there was no internal dissent, not even from known republicans such as Environment Minister Roseanna Cunningham, who had proposed the 1997 resolution. Salmond's monarchism, meanwhile, became ever more ostentatious. He had attended the wedding of Prince William and Kate Middleton during the election campaign ('I should have had this entire city [Edinburgh] covered in royal standards' he told an interviewer regretfully), and regularly gushed about the selfless devotion of the present 'Queen of Scots'. 'There is a better case for an English republic than a Scottish one,' he said at one point. 'I'm not saying Scotland is a classless society, but I still think inequalities in Scotland are not generally linked to the monarchy.'[5]

More broadly, since an internal review by Sir Neil MacCormick a decade earlier, little serious thinking had been done by the SNP on the constitution.[6] Ewan Crawford, who would shortly rejoin the Scottish Government as an adviser, said it was 'one area where work needs to be done',[7] while the former MSP Duncan Hamilton said the 'SNP will, and must, define and explain independence'.[8] Salmond, meanwhile, took to depicting independence as the 'logical next step' on Scotland's 'home rule' journey[9] (language intended to attract Liberal Democrat support) and indeed he was the key driver. Herbert Morrison once said socialism was whatever the Labour Party did, and after 2011 'independence' became whatever the SNP – or more accurately what its leader – said it was.

Partly this was simply an acknowledgement of reality – 'independence' no longer meant what it had in the 19th century or even in the 1970s – and partly it reflected Salmond's big-tent approach to campaigning. Indeed the 2011 election win had hinged upon, as journalist Euan McColm put it, 'the First Minister's brilliant salesmanship of the idea that a vote for them is not necessarily a vote for the break-up of the United Kingdom'.[10] It was simply a continuation of his long-standing 'gradualist' efforts to make independence appear less threatening.

'A change is coming, and the people are ready,' Salmond told MSPs in his first speech after the May landslide, deploying similarly open-ended language: 'Whatever changes take place in our constitution, we will remain close to our neighbours. We will continue to share a landmass, a language and a wealth of experience and history with the other peoples of these islands. My dearest wish is to see the countries of Scotland and England stand together as equals.'

'There is a difference between partnership and subordination,' he added with uncharacteristic touchiness. 'The first encourages mutual respect. The second breeds resentment.'[11]

Partnership, of course, need not mean full independence, indeed the recent SNP manifesto had promised a ballot on 'full economic powers' rather than independence (without any mention of it being in the second half of that parliamentary term).[12] And in the summer of 2011, once the euphoria of the election had died down, Salmond and his senior advisers gathered at the Apex Hotel on Dundee's waterfront, primarily to decide whether Scots would be asked to endorse independence or 'devo-max' (loosely defined, the devolution of everything bar foreign affairs and defence) in a referendum, with the First Minister strongly inclined towards the latter option.

'Alex came in and said it's an each-way bet,' recalled one former adviser, 'we either go for independence or devo-max.'[13] Salmond's reasoning was reasonably straightforward. Instinct told him a binary referendum on independence could not be won whereas one on devo-max, certainly judging by most opinion polls, could. 'His view was that devo-max would be independence in all but name,' remembered another former adviser, 'then there would be a divergence on foreign affairs and defence, such as a war, which would finish the job.'[14]

Others present even believed Salmond 'only wanted devo-max',[15] and indeed at this point strategists had not ruled out the prospect of Westminster making a constitutional offer so radical that a referendum would not actually be necessary. Following the 2010 general election the UK Government had seemed open to this, and renewed overtures followed the 2011 election. Salmond even met the Chancellor George Osborne and the Treasury permanent secretary Sir Nicholas Macpherson, and although their encounter lasted two hours rather than the scheduled 45 minutes, he emerged empty-handed. 'Osborne is clever,' he later remarked. 'You wouldn't want to go into the jungle with him.'[16] Macpherson, meanwhile, 'radiated hostility',[17] for which Salmond would get his revenge several years later.

None of this was made public, for if it had become known the widely respected and popular leader of the National Movement was prepared to ditch independence for a lesser option, the SNP, in the words of former adviser, would have gone 'ballistic'.[18] Instead Salmond said the Scottish Government was 'willing' or 'hoping' to include a second question, but put the onus on the three Unionist parties to 'come forward and give us the detail'.[19] The prospect of an informal (rather than Westminster-backed) referendum on devo-max or independence also explained the SNP leader's aggressive approach towards the UK Supreme Court that summer, a pre-emptive strike lest it challenge such a move as *ultra vires*, constitutional matters being reserved to Westminster.

There was also the question of timing. At the same meeting in Dundee the strategist Stephen Noon suggested holding the referendum on the same day as local government elections due in May 2012. Initially dismissed by Salmond, he then warmed to the idea of exploiting an obvious tide of support favouring the SNP (if not independence), although the result of that election (in which Nationalist momentum appeared to wane) would later vindicate the First Minister's first instinct. Besides, he had promised it would occur late in the 2011–16 Holyrood term, not a year in.

It was agreed the SNP would pursue a twin-track referendum strategy, with policy chief Alex Bell tasked with fleshing out the devo-max option (as defined by a 2009 'National Conversation' paper), and the independence strand, if anything, being allowed to drift. At the 2011 SNP conference Salmond even said in his keynote speech that 'fiscal responsibility, financial freedom, real economic powers' was 'a legitimate proposal',[20] although the response from some delegates – which ranged from bemusement to outright opposition – indicated what a hard sell it might be; journalists were not used to finding activists willing to criticise the party's position.

At that conference Salmond was on evangelical form, invoking Scotland's 'divine legacy' and predicting that independence was 'closer than ever before'. 'The SNP has the momentum, all of the momentum,' he argued, 'as we move towards the independence referendum', while speaking of younger Scots as 'the independence generation'. And, added Salmond, one thing was certain: 'The days of Westminster politicians telling Scotland what to do or what to think are over.'[21]

Beyond spirited rhetoric, however, Salmond's second term lacked the dynamism of his first '100 days' back in 2007. The First Minister's assault on the UK Supreme Court had shown him at his worst, including personal attacks on Lord Hope (although he gave as good as he got) and the respected human rights lawyer Tony Kelly (who hinted at legal action). An incident at First Minister's Questions (FMQs), meanwhile, revealed the hidden wiring of the Salmond-led machine when he tried to defuse Professor Matt Qvortrup's critique of a two-question referendum by claiming the academic had since written to *The Times* to say the SNP's plans were 'fair, reasonable and clear'.[22] Only he had not, the words being those of the First Minister's official spokesman, Kevin Pringle. Salmond swiftly apologised, but later used FMQs to attack the economist Professor John McLaren (a regular critic of SNP policy) on the basis that he had once worked for former First Minister Henry McLeish, applying similarly tribal logic to Dave Scott, a former researcher for a Labour MSP and head of the anti-bigotry organisation Nil by Mouth.

Nil by Mouth had voiced concerns over the Scottish Government's Offensive Behaviour at Football Bill, as had the Roman Catholic Church in Scotland. Yet the legislation was railroaded through Holyrood despite sustained opposition, apparently undermining Salmond's claim following the 2011 election that he did not enjoy a 'monopoly' of wisdom. Economically, meanwhile, the First Minister pushed hard for 'Plan McB' (Keynes rather than austerity) but got flak for increasing business rates and introducing a 'Tesco tax'. And when *The Economist* depicted Scotland as 'Skintland' on its cover, Salmond warned it would 'rue the day'. 'This is Unionism boiled down to its essence,' he thundered melodramatically, 'and stuck on a front page for every community in Scotland to see their sneering condescension.'[23]

Even Nationalists found themselves dismayed at Salmond's behaviour, which lacked the grace and ecumenicalism of 2007–11. For all the First Minister's 'undoubted prowess', blogged Andrew Tickell, 'his much-vaunted mystique can all too readily imperil our balanced judgement of his judgement'. For him, post-election, the SNP had 'presided over a political period which has been by turns despairing, girning, partisan, vacuous and dreary. What a squandering of possibilities; what a waste; what folly.'[24]

A lot of these problems sprang from Salmond's tendency to concern himself with a myriad of different areas. Like Tony Blair in 1997, the election result had theoretically equipped the First Minister with the luxury of not having to fight, negotiate and cajole his way through every vote in the Holyrood chamber, as between 2007 and 2011. Budgets would look after themselves, while Salmond could look forward to devoting his time and energy to the bigger picture, not least the referendum. In practice, however, it did not work out that way. 'In the second term his plan had been to try and take a step back,' recalled a former adviser, 'set out a vision given the majority. But he ended up getting involved in day-to-day stuff.'[25]

The criticism from Salmond's political opponents was more predictable but also deliberately fierce and sustained, with Unionists conscious the SNP leader appeared to possess, as the *Financial Times* put it, 'unstoppable political momentum'.[26] In September 2011 the Liberal Democrat leader and Deputy Prime Minister Nick Clegg charged that the First Minister's 'sole obsession' was to 'yank' Scotland out of the UK; Scottish Secretary Michael Moore said he was using 'conflict and grievance' to duck awkward questions about independence;[27] outgoing Scottish Conservative leader Annabel Goldie asserted that 'the face of Salmond is not the face of Scotland';[28] Scottish Liberal Democrat leader Willie Rennie alleged 'creeping, political control' of the Civil Service in Scotland,[29] while the outgoing Scottish Labour leader Iain Gray went even further, attacking the 'ugly' side of Nationalism and accusing Salmond's SNP of bringing 'vile poison' into politics.[30] By comparison, David Cameron branding Salmond 'a big feartie' over his referendum dithering appeared rather mild.[31]

There was little sense, however, that any of these attacks had any impact, nor that the First Minister cared. His approval ratings remained high – well into the 60s – which explained why he appeared subject to different rules from other politicians, reinforcing a long-standing Teflon quality. As an academic study of the 2011 election later concluded, despite polarizing public opinion, the 'Salmond effect' was now more important than it had been in 2007, indeed he had 'become such a prominent and dominant figure within his party that the two are almost seen as interchangeable or equivalent in voters' minds'.[32] 'Mr Salmond will decide,' Ian Bell had observed in May 2011. 'That has become the singular, overarching fact of Scottish politics. His authority is as near absolute now as it could be. He has no rivals in sight, in any party.'[33]

But a feeling of invincibility in a politician had obvious drawbacks, not least a tendency towards hubris. Following the landslide election win Salmond, recalled one adviser, 'was incredibly buoyed up',[34] while there were reports he had initiated the refurbishment of the old Governor's House, a grand, 200-year-old castellated residence adjacent to St Andrew's House. He certainly revelled (despite protestations to the contrary) in both the trappings and status of power. 'Emperor or viceroy?' inquired *The Times* in September 2011, to which Salmond replied, obviously in jest: 'The Chinese Consul-General always called me Your High Excellency. For modesty, I'll settle for that.'[35]

Indeed China formed the centrepiece of Salmond's second term, building on his role as Scotland's global salesman. In November he embarked upon his third trade mission, just as the giant pandas Tian Tian and Yang Guang left for their new home in Scotland, a loan, said the First Minister, which symbolised 'the great and growing friendship between Scotland and China'.[36] But although such trips had obvious benefits in terms of trade and international profile, they also exposed tensions in the SNP's stance on foreign affairs. Obviously, China was not a democracy (nor were Qatar or the UAE, to which Salmond had travelled the previous month), while its record on human rights presented a dilemma for any visiting politician. The First Minister rejected charges of kow-towing to the Chinese government, saying he had raised concerns in a 'friendly' way rather than 'jumping up and down from a distance and having no effect whatsoever'.[37]

In the summer of 2012, meanwhile, Salmond declined to meet the Dalai Lama during a visit by the Tibetan spiritual leader to Scotland. The First Minister refused to say if the matter had been raised when he had met China's UK ambassador Liu Xiaoming (it had), and when asked if such a meeting might have threatened Chinese investment in Scotland, Salmond replied blandly: 'We do what is appropriate for the benefit of the Scottish people.' For a centre-left party that championed the self-determination of small nations, it was clearly an uncomfortable situation for the SNP leader. He had no qualms, on the other hand, when it came to delivering a speech on climate change to the party school of the Central Committee of the Communist Party in Beijing.

On his return from China, meanwhile, Salmond attempted to take advantage of the fallout from the Prime Minister's 'veto' of a European Union treaty change following a Brussels summit. David Cameron, he stormed, was guilty of 'isolationism' and 'irresponsible posturing' (a more valid criticism had been his failure to consult with the devolved Scottish Government), although when challenged as to what a hypothetically independent Scotland might have done in the circumstances, Salmond resorted to posturing of his own, arguing unconvincingly that it 'would have been possible to produce a situation where agreement could have been produced on the Treaty',[38] even though the change to which Cameron had objected (financial regulation) was shared by the SNP.

Again, none of this did Salmond any harm for, as most observers realised, he appeared to 'put Scotland first' or 'stand up for Scotland', particularly on the world stage, and as long as the First Minister did so a majority of Scots were willing to forgive him the occasional lapse. Salmond himself acknowledged that 'if people think your heart's in the right place . . . they'll forgive you a great deal. If they believe your heart's in the wrong place . . . they won't forgive you anything'.[39] Thus by demonising Salmond, Unionists risked appearing to put party before country and 'talk Scotland down', as the SNP frequently accused them of doing. He was also lucky, lucky in terms of external events and lucky when it came to his opponents, who for most of the period after the May 2011 election were leaderless and without a discernable strategy.

Which was not to say the SNP's second term was policy heavy. The September 2011 legislative programme had been, as one adviser recalled, 'pretty bland', while the referendum process began to highlight just how weak the party was in non-devolved areas. Salmond still advocated a cut in Corporation Tax (although a few of his advisers believed it was counterproductive and 'hackneyed'), but when it came to welfare and macroeconomics there was seldom little beyond debating points. Even in devolved areas there was scant appetite for creative policy-making, a reluctance that came from the top. 'Alex saw everything in tactical terms,' recalled one former adviser with obvious frustration. 'There was a profound resistance to actually using the powers of the Parliament to do stuff.'[40]

And while social justice was rhetorically central to modern Scottish Nationalism, the commentator Kenny Farquharson reckoned the First Minister avoided straying into such territory 'because social and moral issues by their very nature divide opinion',[41] hence Salmond's don't-rock-the-boat approach to anything (such as gay marriage) that might upset Scotland's Catholic hierarchy. And while he had established the Christie Commission on the Future Delivery of Public Services in November 2010, its thoughtful recommendations (published in late June 2011) were more or less ignored. External advisers also suggested the Scottish Government establish a 'fairness' commission (an idea gleaned from a couple of local authorities in London), but word came back that Salmond did not consider it a priority.[42]

Curiously, the First Minister's reputation at Westminster continued to grow, not least because of his apparent ability to make 'progressive' left-wing politics electorally popular, whatever the obvious contradictions. The *Guardian* lauded Salmond as a 'political wizard, weaving the national destiny',[43] while the political philosopher John Gray called him the 'most consistently able operator in British politics'.[44] There was also a concerted strategy to 'sell' Salmond in England through lectures and television appearances including the BBC's *One Show* and ITV's *This Morning*. The First Minister had always enjoyed performing on as large a political stage as possible, and happily obliged, collecting several other plaudits on the way: in 2011 the *Spectator* and *Herald* named him politician of the year, while *The Times* even anointed him 'Briton of the Year', although given Salmond's increasing willingness to embrace a 'British' element to his identity that was not as inappropriate as it at first appeared.

But while Salmond was undoubtedly riding high as a momentous year drew to a close, the point remained that he was not (yet) in full control of the process that would deliver a legitimate referendum on independence, for despite his summer onslaught against the UK Supreme Court, it became increasingly clear the Scottish Government could not act unilaterally in holding a referendum and, in any case, in early 2012 the Prime Minister forced the SNP's hand by declaring his intention to (temporarily) equip Holyrood with the powers to hold a 'fair, legal and decisive' plebiscite in order to 'clear up the legal situation' and bring the Scottish Question 'to a conclusion'.[45]

By coincidence, senior Nationalists were in the middle of a strategy meeting in Aberdeen as Cameron uttered those words. Privately, the response was one of relief rather than surprise, for although Salmond had been ready to launch his own referendum consultation the previous October, he had held back, realising it would spark a prolonged legal row. Officials had produced a form of words – which talked about transferring more powers to the Scottish Parliament rather than independence – they believed could get round the legal barrier, but it was so contrived that it was likely to fall foul of any Electoral Commission scrutiny, which was why the Scottish Government had proposed using its own *ad hoc* referendum commission to oversee the process. None of this, however, resembled a sustainable position.

Initially, as was his habit, the First Minister went to ground, refusing to give interviews from his Aberdeenshire East constituency, but when Salmond did surface, he came out fighting. A Section 30 Order (the mechanism proposed by the Prime Minister), he said, was nothing more than a 'smokescreen' for Westminster 'trying to pull the strings' of the referendum (although, confusingly, he also said he had 'no objection' to its possible use); the UK government were 'control freaks', while David Cameron ought to 'keep his nose out of Scottish business'.[46]

Then, on the evening of Tuesday 10 January 2012, Salmond dropped his own bombshell, informing Sky News as he left a Scottish Cabinet meeting that the referendum would be held in the 'autumn' of 2014 which, he argued, would allow 'the Scottish people to hear all the arguments' as well as giving enough time for all the 'necessary legislation' to be passed. 'This has to be a referendum which is built in Scotland,' he added, 'which is made in Scotland and goes through the Scottish Parliament.' By announcing the date as Scottish Secretary Michael Moore outlined the UK government's referendum consultation in the House of Commons, Salmond had reclaimed the initiative from Westminster.

Salmond's typically shrewd move not only effectively bounced the UK government into accepting his timescale (Cameron had spoken of a ballot sooner rather than later) but also ensured any Westminster-initiated referendum was effectively dead in the water. By the time the First Minister launched his consultation at Edinburgh Castle on 25 January 2012 (Burns Night), meanwhile, he appeared to concede the need for a Section 30 Order (or 'an adjustment of legislative competence') would be necessary for the Scottish Government to pose its preferred question: 'Do you agree Scotland should be an independent country?'[47] Indeed, Salmond was particularly keen that the phrase 'United Kingdom' not feature (as desired by some Unionists), explaining to Andrew Marr that as the 1603 Union of the Crowns 'would be maintained after Scottish political independence',[48] it was not relevant. He also made it clear Scotland was 'not oppressed' and had 'no need to be liberated'.[49]

On 16 February the Prime Minister travelled to Edinburgh to set out his case for a 'No' vote in the referendum, a speech spiced up with the promise of more powers should a majority of Scots follow his advice. Salmond was predictably dismissive, harking back to a similar pledge from another Old Etonian Tory, Lord Home, who had promised a 'better' scheme of devolution if Scots rejected devolution in the 1979 referendum. 'The shadow of Sir Alec Douglas-Home I think is cast very large over this,' he said. 'What's the old saying: "fool me once, shame on you, fool me twice shame on me"? Scotland, I don't believe, will be fooled twice.'[50]

Salmond was doing his best to make sure the Prime Minister's vague offer of 'more powers' did not gain significant traction, and his subtle delegitimisation did not end there. Increasingly, the BBC became a target of First Ministerial broadsides; in February 2012 he referred to some BBC staff as 'Gauleiters' (a term used to describe Nazi officials in occupied France) after being barred from commentating on a Scotland–England rugby match on grounds of impartiality. Salmond also raised concerns with BBC Chairman Lord Patten over the use of words 'separation' and 'separatist' in its reportage. 'My deeper concern is that these incidents stem from an editorial approach', he added in a letter, 'which falls short in explaining the current constitutional context objectively and in the round.'[51]

Accusations of BBC 'bias' would become a common Salmond refrain over the next few years, while at the 2012 Edinburgh Television Festival he reiterated plans to replace the Corporation with a new public sector broadcaster, potentially part-funded by advertising. Significantly, however, while condemning the BBC, the SNP leader actively courted Rupert Murdoch and News International (NI) as part of a long-standing strategy to win the *Scottish Sun*'s backing, not only for the SNP (as in 2011) but for independence.

It was all the more significant because as most other politicians distanced themselves from the Murdoch empire, if anything Salmond moved closer, referring to its patriarch as 'the most substantial figure in British journalism'[52] and maintaining the charm offensive (in a string of often fawning letters) even after the Milly Dowler hacking scandal prompted Murdoch to close down the *News of the World*. The 'questions the probe is looking at relate to the industry,' he wrote of the subsequent Leveson Inquiry in a friendly op-ed piece, 'not one newspaper or company'.[53] And when the new *Scottish Sun on Sunday* claimed to know the date of the referendum (18 October 2014), it prompted accusations of an inappropriate relationship between the First Minister and NI. 'A possible date can't be leaked,' was Salmond's curious defence, although it certainly had been. 'The view was,' recalled an aide, 'that we had to give the Sun [on Sunday] something',[54] and indeed October 2014 remained the working assumption for the referendum until at least the middle of 2012.

The Salmond/Murdoch relationship was later subject to prolonged scrutiny when the Leveson Inquiry published emails that appeared to show Salmond's willingness ('striking' was Lord Leveson's adjective) to lobby the UK government in support of Murdoch's bid for a takeover of BSkyB. The implication was that this had been a *quid pro quo* for having secured the *Scottish Sun*'s support prior to the 2011 Holyrood election. The First Minister vehemently denied any such deal, maintaining his sole aim had been protecting 'jobs and investment' in Scotland, a line he reiterated during his own low-key appearance at Leveson on 13 June 2012. On neither occasion, however, did he produce firm evidence that either was under any immediate threat. 'Often we were discussing Scotland and his Scottish ancestry,' Salmond said of his few meetings with Murdoch.[55] And asked if he liked him in 2014, the First Minister simply replied: 'I think he is a remarkable guy.'[56]

There was a curious coda to all of this, Salmond's belated interest in press regulation that, perhaps unintentionally, had been devolved to Scotland under the 1998 Scotland Act (broadcasting, however, had been specifically reserved). Initially, the Scottish Government appeared unaware it had control, then the First Minister proposed a separate Scottish regime based on the Irish Press Council and a specifically Scottish inquiry headed up by Lord McCluskey. Ultimately, however, he backtracked and instead ended up seeking to influence a UK-wide regulatory regime, an odd approach for the leading proponent of independence.

With the option of a straight yes/no vote on 'devo-max' off the table, meanwhile, Salmond shifted his focus to the possibility of a 'second' question on additional powers as negotiations began between the UK and Scottish Governments, thus reviving the idea of a multi-option referendum he had been exploring for more than two decades. Always a gradualist on constitutional matters, he was virtually the only senior minister of this view, and despite pressure from Nicola Sturgeon and others to go all out for independence he held firm, an equivocal stance that meant the inter-governmental talks progressed much more slowly.

As someone involved in the negotiations recalled: 'Alex pushed a second question all the way. He required the possibility always be kept open in our discussions. In discussions with Bruce [Crawford, the responsible Scottish minister] we couldn't make an assumption about the number of questions. They will claim they never formally asked for a second question, but nor did they allow discussion to proceed on the basis of there only being one.'[57]

And while Bruce Crawford and Scotland Office minister David Mundell were able to sort out most of the non-contentious issues surrounding the referendum, it was clear at Westminster that Crawford 'didn't have the authority to seal the deal'. The key shift, therefore, came in September 2012, when a Scottish Government reshuffle saw the former Health Secretary Nicola Sturgeon replace Crawford as minister for the referendum. Suddenly, as a UK government official recalled, things 'unblocked . . . there was a huge shift in attitude once Sturgeon was in post'.[58]

A key ministerial meeting had finally cleared the way a few weeks before. 'When it was put to Cabinet they were very gung ho about going for the main goal [of independence],' recalled a former adviser, 'and the same was true among the Spads [special advisers].'[59] Realising he was in a minority of one, Salmond bowed to the inevitable, acutely aware all the 'second question' kites he had flown since the previous May had floated away, not least the 'Future of Scotland' coalition drawn from civic Scotland. 'After I heard them out around the Cabinet table,' he recalled in his referendum diary, 'I sprang a surprise by saying: "Fine, let's do that. YES/NO it is then."'[60] The SNP leader also suspected his party would reject a second question if consulted at conference. 'So we began to think', recalled an aide, 'that their red line was actually okay.'[61]

Indeed, by stringing UK government ministers along on this front, Salmond believed he had kept their eyes off how the question would actually be worded. This, however, was in the hands of the Electoral Commission rather than ministers in London. Although for a long time Salmond would claim he had not asked for a second question (which was half true), he later admitted his 'support for [putting] devo max on the ballot paper was not initially a negotiating posture, but when it eventually became one it was highly successful'.[62] As one long-serving aide put it, Salmond had always been 'a master at riding two horses at once'.[63]

Although Salmond's presence had loomed over the referendum negotiations since the beginning of 2012, he only became publicly involved as the talks drew to a close. With the Prime Minister he had a curious relationship, simultaneously antagonistic ('so what drove the Camerons out of Scotland?' the First Minister once asked him nonchalantly, a barbed reference to Cameron's Scottish ancestry[64]) and respectful of his status. Similarly, Cameron found the SNP leader intriguing (as did George Osborne), recognising a fellow political animal who revelled in tactics rather than policy detail. Salmond even confessed to Alastair Campbell that he had been impressed at Cameron's ability to establish 'Prime Ministerial authority' in 'tricky' circumstances, i.e. in the year that followed the 2010 general election.[65]

But on 15 October the two leaders, separated by age, political outlook and class, met at St Andrew's House in Edinburgh to sign what became known as the 'Edinburgh Agreement' in the First Minister's rather unre-markable office. Mischievously, Salmond had made sure a predominantly yellow electoral map of Scotland was clearly visible behind them, a reminder of the landslide that had led to this moment. After more than a year of political shadow boxing they had agreed that Scots would vote on independence in a referendum to be held by the end of 2014, with the Scottish Parliament deciding the precise date and franchise, while the Electoral Commission would have oversight of the wording and campaign financing.

Symbolically and politically the Agreement was a significant achieve-ment for Salmond. Not only had a UK Prime Minister travelled to Edinburgh to meet with the First Minister in *his* office, but he had signed off on a referendum he did not want and on a question which – if answered positively – would consign Cameron to the history books as the last Prime Minister of the UK. The Agreement, Salmond told reporters, paved the way 'for the most important decision our country of Scotland has made in several hundred years'. 'We're in the business of developing a new relationship between the peoples of these islands,' he remarked at a press conference. 'I think a more beneficial, independent and equal relationship.'[66]

'My passion has never been to cross some imaginary constitutional finishing line and think the race is won,' wrote Salmond (a little disin-genuously) in the *Guardian* a few days later. 'My aim now, as it always has been, is to deliver a better and fairer society for the people of Scotland. It happens that independence is the way to do this.' Key to this 'better and fairer society' was what the First Minister called Scotland's 'social contract', 'which has delivered universal benefits such as free university education and personal care for our elderly'; a contract he claimed was 'now threatened by both Labour and the Tories'. Only a 'yes' vote, therefore, could 'properly protect these gains'.[67]

Despite the absence of any groundswell in support for independence, the First Minister's sheer force of personality and his recent electoral success had created the sense that anything was possible. But while he maintained his usual relentless optimism, Salmond was not absolutely certain independence could be won, thus his prevarication over the number of questions until the last possible moment. Nevertheless he believed, as he told the BBC in October 2012, that 'a lot of folk in Scotland' had passed a 'psychological tipping point' and were no longer prepared to accept certain arguments against independence.

Therefore, whatever the opinion polls showed, there was a momentum 'leading in a certain direction'.[68] And throughout his eventful career the SNP leader had been acutely aware of the need to harness and maintain that momentum; like Lyndon Johnson, Salmond did not believe it was 'a mysterious mistress' but a 'controllable fact of political life',[69] while realising, like one of Johnson's successors as president, Ronald Reagan, that a successful politician had to 'own' optimism about the future, although that in itself was no guarantee of success. 'I can't claim to know what the timetable is, even now,' observed the First Minister revealingly, 'but I'm pretty certain the destination is set.'[70]

Chapter 14

# 'THE DREAM SHALL NEVER DIE'

The launch of 'Yes Scotland', the formal pro-independence campaign, at an Edinburgh cinema on 25 May 2012 was a curious affair. Given the SNP's reputation for slick organisation it appeared amateurish, while the 'Independence Declaration' unveiled by Alex Salmond seemed an odd device upon which to focus campaigning activity.

In his speech, meanwhile, the First Minister said the next two years were necessary to give 'form and substance' to the desire for independence. He continued:

> We're at the start of something very, very special: the beginning of a campaign to restore nationhood to the nation of Scotland. Our opponents are rich and they're powerful and therefore to win and to win well, we're going to have to galvanise the whole community of the realm of Scotland . . . by the time we enter the referendum campaign in autumn 2014, our intention is to have one million Scots who have signed the independence for Scotland declaration. Friends, if we achieve that, then we shall win an independent Scotland.[1]

It would take time for Yes Scotland to find a campaigning groove (two weeks after its launch Scottish Green co-leader Patrick Harvie criticised it as 'entirely an SNP vehicle'[2]) and while Salmond would only become fully engaged with it two years later, from the beginning he was central to its perceived success or failure. By instinct a micro-manager, he had never been entirely comfortable about relinquishing control to an ostensibly 'independent' organisation, although he realised that doing so was politically necessary. Its public face, meanwhile, was the former television executive Blair Jenkins, who had chaired Salmond's Scottish Broadcasting Commission back in 2007–08.

Given Salmond's reference to 'rich' and 'powerful' opponents (the cross-party 'Better Together' campaign launched exactly a month after Yes Scotland), fund-raising was key. Indeed when, in July 2011, he saw news of Ayrshire couple Colin and Christine Weir winning £161 million in the EuroMillions lottery, he at once spotted an opportunity. 'When I . . . heard the fantastic news that a Scot had landed the Euro lottery jackpot,' wrote a chirpy Salmond to the Weirs. 'I did wonder if this was the same Colin Weir who helped produce SNP party political broadcasts for a young party publicity vice-convener all these years ago.'[3]

In addition to £918,000 bequeathed to the SNP by the poet Edwin Morgan in June 2011, the Weirs donated £1m to the party four days after being treated to tea by Salmond at his official residence in Edinburgh. The following year the couple donated the same sum again to fund the first seven months of Yes Scotland, and by May 2014 had given a total of £5.5m to the SNP and pro-independence campaign. A chance lottery win combined with the Salmond charm had ensured that, at the very least, Better Together would not be able to significantly outspend Yes Scotland over the next two years.

Yet despite these flashes of inspiration, the period between 2012 and 2014, which ought to have found Salmond at his best, often found him at his most ill-disciplined, lapses that provided his Unionist opponents with plentiful lines of attack. He, his party and its policies were under much greater scrutiny than ever before, and there were several weaknesses, a good example of which was Europe, or specifically the likely status of an independent Scotland in the European Union. In March 2012 the BBC's Andrew Neil had asked the First Minister if he had 'sought advice' on this question from his law officers, to which Salmond replied 'yes, in terms of the [debate],'[4] an imprecise answer which would later come back to haunt him.

In July the Scottish Government decided to challenge legally a ruling from the Scottish Freedom of Information Commissioner to publicly state whether or not such advice existed (at a cost of £20,000), and while Salmond cited 'authoritative' sources in support of his claim that Scotland would 'automatically' remain in the EU as a successor state, as the Labour MEP David Martin pointed out, most of them were dead and their 'advice' more than two decades out of date, an indication that little serious thought had been given to the issue since the late 1980s. As one aide admitted, many in the SNP were conscious of the need to 'sort out the Europe issue', but the First Minister did not share their sense of urgency.[5]

A paper in the name of Fiona Hyslop (minister for 'External Affairs'),

'Scotland's Membership of the European Union', did come before the Scottish Cabinet in early May 2012, although its observations did not please the First Minister. Its working premise was that although an independent Scotland *would* continue as a member of the EU, it would not be, as Salmond maintained, an 'automatic' process. Rather it would have to launch a 'new' application and thus be subject to 'a political decision requiring unanimity amongst EU Member States'. The paper also warned that the establishment of 'appropriate administrative and regulatory structures' would most likely 'be expensive and lengthy', requiring not only temporary derogations but support from the UK government; the exact 'point' of independence, meanwhile, would be key.

Hyslop also considered 'timing . . . one of the biggest risks to Scotland's continued membership of the EU', observing that at best (as in the case of Austria, Sweden and Finland) it might take as little as two years, and at worst (as in the case of Croatia, the EU's newest member) more than five years. She warned that an independent Scotland would 'encounter particular challenges' when it came to retention of a share of the UK's rebate and opt-outs from the single currency and Schengen. But the key point was that, as the paper concluded, 'we are at present unable to determine what process Scotland would follow in order to continue its membership of the EU', i.e. it would not be 'automatic' and therefore not as straightforward as the First Minister regularly argued it would be.

None of this, of course, became public, with speculation instead focusing on the legal dimension, even though Hyslop's paper had concluded that an independent Scotland's membership of the EU would 'be decided on a political basis' rather than on that 'of any legal arguments'.[6] Nevertheless, in October 2012 Nicola Sturgeon dropped a bombshell by informing the Scottish Parliament that contrary to Salmond's March interview, no advice from the Scottish law officers existed (but had now been commissioned). Although the First Minister insisted his comments had been taken out of context, the result was his worst barrage of newspaper headlines since taking office in 2007; 'EU LIAR' screamed the front page of the hitherto friendly *Scottish Sun*.

For Better Together, which made sure a clip of Salmond's original comments were widely circulated, it was viewed as a 'turning point'. 'Up till then we hadn't been able to lay a glove on him,' recalled one strategist, 'but this was an important trust issue.'[7] The SNP MEP Alyn Smith later called the incident 'an unforgiveable own goal',[8] while a former adviser was rather more frank. 'It was a stupid way of phrasing things by him [Salmond] and by us [the SNP],' he said of the 'automatic' EU membership claim, 'we should have handled it better; fortunately, it was miles before the referendum.'[9]

Time was also on Salmond's side when it came to an independent Scotland's membership of the North Atlantic Treaty Organisation (NATO), an issue that was much better handled from a personal and party point of view. The question of membership had been hanging over the SNP for some time, although Salmond had been reluctant to pick a fight with the left of his party, which regarded opposition to NATO as part and parcel of its anti-nuclear stance. So at first he moved slowly, telling the US magazine *Time* that an independent Scotland might consider an 'alliance' with NATO, while two weeks before the 2012 SNP conference he also tried to reassure critics by advocating an 'explicit ban' on nuclear weapons ('or indeed any weapons of mass destruction') as part of a written constitution.[10]

Unusually, Salmond had agreed for the proposed policy change to be openly debated at conference, a significant departure from his long-standing determination to keep proceedings as bland as possible. The debate itself was memorable, and at points the speakers opposed to any change were so vehement (and so enthusiastically applauded) that it looked as if the SNP leader would make a personal appeal. Instead Salmond sat it out (on the main conference stage), watching as the main motion passed narrowly. His personal authority had helped sway many unhappy delegates, although revealingly there had been no attempt to argue that membership of NATO was a good thing in itself, rather that it was a tactical requirement ahead of the referendum; a clear attempt to close down a particular line of opposition attack.

Nevertheless, the conference vote – which split the party right down the middle – had repercussions, with two Highlands and Islands MSPs, John Finnie and Jean Urquhart, later resigning the SNP whip in protest. For a party that had prided itself on unity and discipline since 2007, this was quite a blow. Indeed, Urquhart got the full works in an attempt to prevent her departure: a phone call from party chairman Derek Mackay, followed by John Swinney, then Salmond and finally his wife Moira, who tearfully told Urquhart she could not resign because it would 'damage the party'.[11] Urquhart held firm, later joining a new grouping of independent and Green MSPs in the Scottish Parliament.

NATO aside, foreign affairs had never been particularly strong territory for Salmond, who all too often resorted to platitudes. He told Sir David Frost, for example, that the Scots were 'determined to be good world citizens',[12] and when it became clear that Better Together would use the UK's international 'clout' as an argument against independence, the First Minister downgraded previous SNP statements about Scotland taking its place at the world's top tables by dismissing what he called 'baubles of prestige', meaning little to Scots lacking jobs or benefits.[13]

For Salmond, the Iraq War ('illegal, disastrous, all-consuming in human life') continued to be emblematic of UK foreign policy arrogance, although he believed the 2011 Allied action in Libya had been 'justified, proportionate and successful'.[14] On other fronts he contradicted his own arguments over Iraq; when, for example, the House of Commons dramatically defied David Cameron and opposed military intervention in Syria, Salmond appeared unhappy it had chosen to reject an 'illegal' war (i.e. one without a United Nations mandate) and said an independent Scotland would *not* have ruled out military action. He also distanced himself from fraternal independence movements, depriving Quebec premier Pauline Marois of her desired 'summit' during a visit in February 2013 and also offending Catalans – gearing up for their own informal referendum in 2014 – by stressing that it was a 'different' case.

On 7 November 2012, meanwhile, Salmond became Scotland's longest-serving First Minister, surpassing the record of his predecessor Jack McConnell. For the past five years he had dominated Scottish politics and increasingly intruded upon the UK stage, although when it came to the referendum there was a feeling of drift as that year drew to a close. Nor was Yes Scotland dazzling in campaigning terms, and Salmond was not alone in being mystified at what exactly large amounts of money – including donations from the Weirs – were being spent on.

Several strategists had spoken to the SNP leader regarding their 'concerns', and matters came to a head when the campaign's inner circle gathered at the Park Inn Hotel in Aberdeen in early 2013. At this meeting Blair Jenkins, the solid but uninspiring chief executive of Yes Scotland, made a presentation detailing progress to date, including the introduction of a new voter data system and the creation of various Yes 'shop fronts' around the country. After this, according to those present, Salmond 'went for' Jenkins or, in another account, 'eviscerated' him. The SNP leader was well known for such onslaughts, but this one was so intense that Jenkins had to be 'saved' by the mild-mannered SNP chief executive Peter Murrell, who had been on the receiving end himself.[15]

It would take until the summer of 2013 for major changes to take effect at Yes Scotland HQ, and in the meantime Salmond finally announced (in March) that the referendum would take place on 18 September 2014 rather than the following month as indicated to the *Scottish Sun on Sunday*. 'It's worth reflecting, just for a moment,' he told the Scottish Parliament, 'on the privilege this nation and this generation will have: nothing less than choosing the future course of our country.'[16] Speaking to the *New Statesman* in June, however, Salmond frankly admitted the referendum campaign to date had been 'the phoney war'. 'This is not the campaign,' he added. 'I went into an election in 2011, 20 points behind in the polls and ended up 15 in front. The real game hasn't even started. We are just clearing the ground.'[17]

Salmond meant in terms of closing down potentially troublesome issues such as NATO and Europe (which, despite his gaffe, had been brought under control by Nicola Sturgeon), although the SNP was also clearing the ground to seize more direct control of the ostensibly cross-party Yes campaign. During another meeting of the inner circle in Aberdeen that summer, Blair Jenkins 'basically relinquished control' to Mark Shaw, a North-east businessman and SNP fixer who conducted a review of the campaign organisation that resulted in the departure of several senior directors. He also got Yes Scotland back onto a firmer financial footing while Jenkins was retained as chief executive in name only. 'We had an extremely good campaigning machine in the SNP,' reflected a Scottish Government adviser, 'and a lot of people were asking – why don't we use it?'[18] That included Salmond, who feared a loss of momentum so close to referendum day.

At the same time, Yes Scotland was attempting to distance itself not only from the SNP (ironically given recent developments) and also from the First Minister. Although his approval ratings remained remarkably high, advisers realised the party had 'maxed out' on Salmond's appeal, in other words there were not any more pro-independence votes to be gained by pushing the panda-faced SNP leader down voters' throats. In August 2013 the independence campaigner and actress Elaine C. Smith even urged the growing Yes movement to 'reclaim' the debate from the First Minister, declaring: 'This is not about Alex Salmond.'[19]

Although in a Survation opinion poll 36 per cent of Scots claimed the thought of Salmond running an independent Scotland was pushing them towards a No vote, this was most likely an exaggeration. The SNP leader had long been a Marmite politician, a love-him-or-loathe-him figure, which explained why Nicola Sturgeon enjoyed such prominence during the campaign (other ministers, such as John Swinney and Mike Russell, were conspicuous by their absence). At Wimbledon, for example, the First Minister 'photo-bombed' David Cameron (who was spectating in front of him) by unfurling a large saltire to celebrate Andy Murray's win. Although criticised by many as crass, in fact Salmond had cleverly (if cynically) ensured the resulting media coverage of a 'British' sporting triumph included a clear Scottish dimension.

As usual the SNP leader had embarked upon an election (or rather referendum) diet, following George Osborne's lead in adopting the '5:2' regime, which involved fasting two days each week. Although he found it 'harder and harder to sustain'[20] as the campaign wore on, Salmond lost two stone but had to bat aside rumours that his weight loss had been the result of a heart scare ('absolutely nothing to do with it'[21]).

The First Minister also continued to reinterpret independence, and increasingly stressed his inner Unionism. The 'political union', he said during a speech in Nigg, was 'only one of six unions that govern our lives today in Scotland', adding that independence would 'still leave five other unions intact'. Thus the First Minister presented himself as a reforming Unionist, hoping to 'change' those five unions and 'improve them', but at the same time 'basically' maintaining them.[22] As the commentator Alf Young pointed out, by his own admission the SNP leader was 'five-sixths a unionist'.[23]

Salmond had not included energy on his list, but after the SNP made it clear it intended to preserve a a UK-wide energy market even in the event of independence, it looked as if the approaching referendum was fuel-ling further Nationalist triangulation. Brian Wilson, a former UK energy minister, also praised the First Minister's renewables vision as 'profoundly Unionist in character',[24] so dependent was it upon Westminster subsidies. That, however, demonstrated another Salmond strength: formidable networking.

Firms such as Areva, Gamesa and Samsung noticed Salmond's zeal for 'clean' energy, not least his pledge to generate 100 per cent of Scotland's electricity needs from renewable sources by 2020, and lined up to invest. At the same time the First Minister had a habit of overstating the poten-tial benefits: in late 2012, for example, he had to apologise to MSPs after erroneously claiming the sector had created 18,000 jobs in Scotland when in fact the figure was closer to 11,000. And despite Salmond boasting of Scotland becoming the 'Silicon Valley' of marine energy on a trade mission to California, there was little tangible progress in that sector.[25]

Salmond was 'incredibly keen', as one former aide recalled, on his ministers and advisers 'working their networks',[26] and the First Minister practised what he preached. Another former staffer observed that his 'key skill' – not least during the referendum – was investing 'time and energy' in certain relationships and then 'exploiting those networks in times of need'.[27] When it came to industrial disputes, for example, the First Minister took (in his own words) 'a highly interventionist stance';[28] in October 2013, when Ineos threatened to close the Grangemouth petrochemical plant with the loss of 800 jobs, Salmond scoured the globe for a potential buyer, and, when that proved unnecessary, highlighted the Scottish Government's role in securing a reprieve.

And in August 2014, when Scotland's last commercial shipbuilder, Ferguson's on the Clyde, went into receivership with the potential loss of 70 jobs, Jim McColl of Clyde Blowers – one of Salmond's key business contacts – stepped in to give it a new lease of life. 'Alex was involved in every SDI [Scottish Development International] decision,' recalled a former adviser, 'hounding companies to get them to invest in Scotland; he was ruthless at it, playing golf with them, flying out to see them.'[29] The pharmaceutical giant GlaxoSmithKline's investment in Montrose was but one product of Salmond's hounding.

Salmond took a similar approach to purely political matters, although with more uneven results. Despite attempts during the referendum to get US congressman Mike McIntyre to table a 'favourable motion' concerning Scottish independence, and to get support from former Labour First Minister Henry McLeish, both initiatives went nowhere.[30] One person's 'networking', meanwhile, looked to others like bullying. When, for example, the principal of St Andrews University, Louise Richardson, voiced concerns about the research funding implications of independence, the First Minister telephoned her and, in a 'loud and heated' conversation, suggested she issue a statement more amenable to the Scottish Government.[31]

But throughout the referendum, indeed throughout his tenure as First Minister, Salmond could never have been accused of laziness. In the midst of the Commonwealth Games he grabbed a few days' holiday at Castle Stuart, his last 'serious' break having been in 2010.[32] 'Alex works hard, stupid hard, ridiculously hard,' recalled one former adviser, and he expected those around him to do the same. 'Alex has no sense of entitlement,' reflected another former aide, 'He works every day with the same level of attention and energy.' And like many workaholics, he was rarely off duty, appearing, in the words of another, 'to be just as acute at 9 a.m. as he is at 9 p.m'.

This graft set the general tenor of government, with Spads and ministers realising they would get a 'hounding' from Salmond if they appeared not to be on top of their respective briefs. 'Ministers prepared like buggery

for Cabinet meetings,' explained a former aide, 'because they didn't want
to be the minister who got picked on by the First Minister.'[33] Salmond
also prepared intensively for the weekly First Minister's Question Times,
devoting most of Wednesday evening and Thursday morning to gaming
likely scenarios. Aides encouraged him to appear statesmanlike in the
Chamber but he was inconsistent, fluctuating between what Scottish
Labour leader Johann Lamont called Salmond's 'wee quiet voice' and
pugilistic tribalism.[34] Many descriptions evoke Margaret Thatcher, the
First Minister having had a similar motivating – and occasionally terrifying – impact on his team. As one former aide put it: 'You never ever
go to Alex only with a problem – you go with a solution.'[35]

But with the exception of energy, Salmond was not quite as diligent
when it came to policy development. Along with the additional pressure
on the First Minister, the long referendum campaign highlighted how
weak the SNP was in many reserved areas. On welfare, for example,
beyond opposition to Conservative reforms at Westminster the party's
policy, as one former adviser put it, was 'non-existent', and so an Expert
Working Group was established in early 2013 in an attempt to put
that right, although it ended up describing the status quo rather than
prescribing change.

In his January 2013 Jimmy Reid Lecture Salmond pointed out that
– under its existing powers – all the Scottish Government could do in
terms of welfare amounted to 'mitigation – nothing more'. But he could
manage little more than vague generalisations when asked what might
take its place under independence, chiefly 'a welfare system which makes
work pay without reducing people to penury and despair'. Similarly, the
First Minister was confident that once Scots had 'decided to become an
independent nation', then they would also 'choose to become a fairer
nation, as well as a more prosperous one'.[36]

And when it came to 'prosperity', or rather the economics of independence, a lot of the old Salmond refrains sounded increasingly tired.
Corporation Tax remained central to his strategy, although a Scottish
Government paper on the proposed 3p cut, as well as another on broader
'economic strategy', struck many as embarrassingly thin. In spring 2013,
meanwhile, Salmond attempted to explain his economic and political
philosophy during a speech at Princeton University. The nub of his
argument was that Adam Smith's seminal work *The Wealth of Nations*
ought not to be considered in isolation, but rather alongside the Scottish
Enlightenment writer's earlier – and in Salmond's opinion – 'equally

significant' work, *The Theory of Moral Sentiments*. 'Taken together,' he said, 'the moral philosophy of the first and the science of economics of the second provide the balanced outlook that the world needs to confront the major challenges of today.'[37]

That hardly amounted to a general theory, or one that stood out as ideologically distinct (Margaret Thatcher had made a similar point as Leader of the Opposition in the 1970s). Asked about income tax, for example, the former advocate of a 'Penny for Scotland' now believed an independent Scotland would likely 'align' its income tax rates with those 'across these islands'.[38] At various points in 2013, meanwhile, he floated the idea of tax breaks for film makers, targeted VAT reductions for Scotland's restaurauteurs and 'a reduction, or indeed even an elimination' of air passenger duty, which Salmond told the *Wall Street Journal* would 'more than pay for itself',[39] an indication that he remained a devotee of Laffer Curve economics.

When it came to the 2007–08 economic crisis, meanwhile, Salmond belatedly acquired a narrative, arguing that an independent Scotland would only have been liable for around five per cent of the RBS and HBOS bailouts, although pressed as to whether he had any regrets about his (and others') pre-crash hubris, all Salmond could muster was: 'If everybody had the benefit of hindsight we'd all act differently.'[40] His introduction to a Scottish Government paper on *Sustainable, Responsible Banking* referred obliquely to addressing the 'issues of the past' and building a 'new relationship' with customers, 'firmly based on traditional Scottish banking values'.[41]

In terms of North Sea oil, meanwhile, Salmond both downgraded the energy resource, arguing it was a 'bonus' rather than the basis of an independent Scotland's wealth (although the Scottish Government's own statistics suggested otherwise), while also exaggerating its worth by conveniently skirting over the sheer extent of foreign ownership, memorably claiming it would amount to '£300,000 for every man, woman and child in Scotland'.[42] Salmond also rolled back from an earlier promise to invest £1 billion a year in an oil fund,[43] adding the important caveat 'when fiscal circumstances allow'.[44]

This tendency to rely on old arguments and debating points – many of which dated from the 1990s – was fine for a television interview but increasingly inadequate under the referendum microscope. At a policy level, recalled one former adviser, the Scottish Government after 2012 was 'quite dysfunctional'. Scoping papers on various policy areas were produced for Cabinet in spring that year, but were deliberately bland (a notable exception being one in the name of John Swinney, later leaked to the delight of Better Together), while in autumn 2012 there was another attempt to stimulate policy ideas, albeit without much success.

There were two competing views within the SNP, that of policy chief Alex Bell, who believed the referendum could only be one on the basis of a 'big offer' (later set out in his 2014 book *The people we could be*), and the other being Stephen Noon's, that the best hope lay in a re-run of the 2011 election campaign, i.e. fighting on a few carefully chosen (devolved) policy fronts. In the event, the Noon analysis won out and Bell relinquished his post. At the same time there were uncharacteristic slips on the part of certain ministers, Education Secretary Mike Russell's handling of the further education sector (which, unlike its higher equivalent, experienced cuts), and Justice Secretary Kenny MacAskill's missteps in attempting to abolish corroboration. A reputation for competence had been key to the SNP's success in 2011, and was seen as equally important in delivering independence.

In truth, Salmond was uncomfortable with both policy and ideology, viewing politics largely in tactical and strategic terms. In his Hugo Young Memorial Lecture in early 2012 the First Minister had spoken of an independent Scotland becoming 'a beacon for progressive opinion south of the border and further afield',[45] although by that point 'progressive' had become a much misused word in the Scottish and British political lexicon.

The First Minister's definition rested upon policies like free university tuition, free prescriptions and a council tax freeze, none of which were particularly 'progressive', but then Salmond had long abandoned Marxism for a sort of catch-all, all-things-to-all-men political philosophy that he chose to call 'social democracy', i.e. 'believing in a competitive economy' but also 'a just distribution of resources'.[46] Commentators had long highlighted the contradictions in advocating Scandinavian-style social services paid for by US levels of tax, but in the context of the referendum the tensions implicit in Salmond's economic case for independence came under fresh attack.

The First Minister did not much care, making it clear in November 2012 (in response to a gathering of the ostentatiously left-wing Radical Independence Campaign) that he welcomed 'voices to the left of the SNP's social democratic position speaking up in favour of independence', just as he welcomed support 'from the entrepreneurial and more free-market perspective'. After all, he added, 'post-independence the people of Scotland will have the opportunity to choose from a range of political perspectives and parties'.[47]

As even the normally friendly journalist Jamie Maxwell observed, the Labour leader Ed Miliband had 'displayed a willingness to confront "vested interests" generally lacking in the Scottish First Minister',[48] while the veteran left-winger Tariq Ali expressed his support for independence but believed Salmond to be 'too caught up in the stale politics of neoliberalism'.[49]

This ideological incongruity culminated with the publication of the Scottish Government's White Paper on independence – *Scotland's Future* – in November 2013, a document Salmond had hyperbolically predicted would 'resonate down through the ages', even encouraging speculation the writer William McIlvanney might pen an inspirational précis.[50]

The White Paper, however, was not only considerably longer (at 670 pages) than the Declaration of Arbroath (to which the First Minister also alluded) but took a lot longer to prepare. Even a week before it was due to be printed and bound it lacked, as one adviser put it, a 'coherent narrative', while whole chapters had to be rewritten in great haste. And while Nicola Sturgeon had been more directly involved, the end product, as one former adviser reflected, was 'a very Salmond White Paper, full of didactic arguments about money and oil'.[51]

It contained no 'big idea' to justify independence, rather its headline commitment was a commitment to increasing childcare provision, although even that later unravelled under scrutiny. On devolved policy such as health and education the White Paper was relatively strong, while the sections covering reserved areas were much thinner, although both reflected the First Minister's curious blend of 1980s left-wing rhetoric and 1990s free-market orthodoxy. And while Yes Scotland would later argue that the referendum was not about the proposals set out in *Scotland's Future*, Salmond was quite clear the vote was 'on the White Paper',[52] which was, all in all, a pretty conservative vision of independence.

By this point the broader Yes movement had grown beyond all recognition, a plethora of local groups and 'sectoral' organisations having flooded Scotland with pro-independence activity. Although many of these groups represented quantity rather than quality, they were important in disassociating independence from the SNP and its leader. Revealingly, Salmond took a closer interest in some groups than others. He welcomed, for example, the left-wing 'Common Weal' umbrella of academics while distancing himself from its more radical proposals and even struggling to remember its name at private gatherings.[53] By contrast, meanwhile, he enthused about 'Wealthy Nation', launched in late 2013 by the historian (and late convert to independence) Michael Fry and the Dutch financier Peter de Vink, both long-standing members of the Salmond network. Having once lambasted his former treasurer (Ian Blackford) for addressing the Tory-leaning Tuesday Club, the First Minister was its guest (twice) during 2013 and also became a fixture at the establishment New Club on Edinburgh's Princes Street. He and Fry went back to Salmond's RBS days, but Wealthy Nation betrayed the First Minister's schizophrenic approach to the broader independence 'movement': when, for example, Fry suggested 'floating' a separate Scottish currency, word came back from Bute House that it was not viewed as helpful.[54]

Advisers recall Salmond only becoming more fully engaged with Yes Scotland at the beginning of 2014. 'When he got more involved it kind of glued a bit more,' recalled one former aide,[55] although there was also concern that 'peak Salmond', i.e. saturation coverage of him at such a sensitive stage in the campaign, might prove counterproductive. Things not only 'glued', but there was a remarkable turnaround in confidence within the Yes camp, almost as if Salmond's relentless optimism had finally rubbed off, and although his private polling target of 40 per cent (supporting independence) by the end of 2013 had not been met (post-White Paper surveys showed Yes at between 27 and 36 per cent), Salmond genuinely believed it could be achieved against the odds.

Former advisers, meanwhile, returned to the fold. Andrew Wilson, who Salmond had invited to deliver the 'Donaldson Lecture' at the 2013 SNP conference, began attending informal Tuesday night meetings at Bute House or the Scottish Parliament, where they would chew over recent developments and future strategy, while Duncan Hamilton, like Wilson a former SNP MSP, reprised his old speech-writing job. Salmond relaxed in the company of Wilson and Hamilton, lightening the atmosphere and making life easier for aides on less intimate terms with 'the Boss'. Advice for improving his performance, i.e. not laughing at his own jokes and appearing less arrogant, were often delivered via Claire Howell (a key figure in 2007 and 2011), who enjoyed a particularly good relationship with the First Minister.

Together this team of advisers helped Salmond rebut increasingly strident attacks on the Scottish Government's independence prospectus, the centrepiece of which had been a prolonged assault on the SNP's proposed 'currency union'. This policy of retaining sterling after independence had actually been adopted amid little fanfare back in 2005,[56] a pragmatic stance very much in keeping with Salmond's 'gradualist' approach, albeit one let down over the past decade by statements to the effect that sterling was 'sinking like a stone' (2009), or represented a 'millstone round Scotland's neck' (1999).

Since 2011 the First Minister had also consistently played down the importance of monetary policy, telling *Time* magazine it was not 'a *sine qua non* of independence', while the following year he said people 'often exaggerate the importance of monetary policy; fiscal policy has primacy in the modern world'. The 'essence' of economic independence, he added in April 2013, was the ability to control tax rates, which, under 'independence in Europe' meant Scotland would control 100 per cent of its taxation base, rather than 8 per cent under the status quo. And while Salmond accepted the need for a 'sustainability arrangement' with the Bank of England, he denied this would give it 'oversight' of an independent Scotland's budget.[57]

Salmond also raised the stakes in another respect. 'If the Westminster government's position is that we should not be entitled to our own currency and other shared assets,' he argued, 'then the only logical extension of that argument is that an independent Scotland will not inherit any share of the UK's debts.'[58] On this he had a point, for if the UK insisted on being the sole successor state then international precedents suggested only it would be liable in terms of debt, a threat the First Minister wielded again in February 2014 when George Osborne travelled to Edinburgh to state unequivocally – armed with formal Treasury advice – that the UK government would not sanction a currency union, a stance later supported by Labour and the Liberal Democrats. In response, Salmond launched into full outrage mode, accusing the three Unionist parties of 'bluff, bluster and bullying', while warning them the move would 'backfire spectacularly'.[59] Nevertheless the pan-Unionist front represented a major challenge to a central element of the independence proposition, and one closely associated with Salmond. It had always smacked of compromise, the best of a bad bunch of monetary options, and defending it gave rise to all sorts of intellectual contortions; for when it came to sterling, the First Minister appeared to be arguing that Scotland and rUK were, to borrow a phrase, better together.

Over the weekend that followed the Chancellor's intervention there was an obvious wobble on the part of SNP and Yes Scotland strategists, although when Salmond responded formally in a speech to Business for Scotland on the Monday, it included no substantial response beyond personal attacks on George Osborne, the plan being to associate the veto in voters' minds with an unpopular Tory Cabinet minister. Thereafter the First Minister widened the options, adding that in addition to his mooted currency union there existed 'Plans B, C, D, E and F' (although significantly his own 'Fiscal Commission' had warned against one of them, so-called 'sterlingisation'). At Holyrood, meanwhile, he declared: 'It's our pound and we're keeping it.'[60]

And, for once, there were indications of internal discontent, with the *Daily Record* splashing on a quote from a 'senior' SNP source who said:

> It shouldn't exactly have been a surprise that Osborne would make this announcement. It was more a matter of when rather than if. We should have made sure that we had a stronger alternative to offer, just saying they are 'bluffing' isn't persuasive to the voters we need to win round. It's great for the converted but it's not going to bring don't knows on board. Alex's line won't hold for seven months. We should have sorted an alternative proposal months ago. Even if his line that Westminster is bullying Scotland gets any traction, that's not going make people gamble with their mortgage rates or their pensions.[61]

But this quote, which many in the party believed emanated from Moray MP Angus Robertson (whose star had waned since 2011), only turned out to be half true: although economic uncertainty – including over the currency – turned many undecided voters towards the No camp, not only did Salmond's 'bluffing' line hold until referendum day, but polling eventually showed that forced to choose between trusting him and George Osborne a majority chose the former.

And when, a few weeks later, the *Guardian* splashed with comments from a 'senior' UK government saying 'of course there will be a currency union'[62] (with the *quid pro quo* that Trident would remain in Scotland), it not only strengthened Salmond's resolve but also appeared to vindicate his argument about the 'veto' being little more than a bluff. He also worked hard on Mark Carney, the Governor of the Bank of England, a Canadian whom he considered a 'thoroughly decent sort'.[63] The First Minister repeatedly presented him as an ally, even though a major speech by the Governor flagged up the difficulties inherent in any currency union. Nevertheless, Salmond tried to persuade Carney to make a statement on contingency plans.

At the SNP's April spring conference in Aberdeen, meanwhile, many of those present felt winning a Yes vote was achievable for the first time, while in his speech the First Minister made a further pitch for the female vote by promoting two junior ministers – Shona Robison and Angela

Constance – to Cabinet rank (he had also been urging several prestigious golf clubs to lift their bans on female members).

Salmond prided himself (unlike Nicola Sturgeon) on refusing to countenance a No vote, although in June 2014 he told the *Daily Record* he intended to 'stand again in 2016, whatever the political circumstances'.[64] Although that was to an extent true ('at that stage Alex hadn't ruled out running in 2016' recalled an adviser[65]), on 18 July Salmond privately informed Sturgeon he would be 'minded to resign' if there was a No vote, although his decision would 'depend on the exact circumstances at the time'.[66] Elsewhere he also held firm to his belief that constitutional referendums were 'a once-in-a-generation opportunity',[67] pointing to the 18-year gap between Scotland's two devolution ballots as an illustration.

Elections to the European Parliament on 22 May 2014, however, indicated that momentum was not necessarily with the SNP just four months out from the referendum. Its campaign switched halfway through from depicting UKIP as an irrelevance to arguing that the battle over a third seat was between the SNP and Nigel Farage's merry band of Little Englanders. Nationalists had also underestimated the degree of Euroscepticism in Scotland (polls suggested around a third of Scots wanted out) and it was only in the last week that, as Gordon Wilson recorded, 'mild Euro-sceptic noises were heard', albeit 'too late to correct a view that the SNP was too slavishly European'.[68] In the event, UKIP won one of Scotland's five European seats, prompting Salmond to blame the BBC for having 'beamed' UKIP 'into Scotland', which in turn prompted Better Together chief Alistair Darling to accuse the SNP leader of behaving like former North Korean leader Kim Jong-il.[69] It had been – as with local government elections in May 2012 – a failure of expectation management.

Salmond's dig at the BBC also typified his increasingly aggressive approach to the broadcaster, as well as the media in general. He had been irritated by Freedom of Information requests from certain newspapers, including one concerning a trip to Chicago during the 2012 Ryder Cup during which the First Minister and his wife had accumulated a £3,000 bill at the five-start Peninsula Hotel. This Salmond dismissed as 'ridiculous frippery',[70] although typically he went to extraordinary lengths to prevent such information reaching the public domain.

Indeed, Salmond's obsession with the print media was almost John Major-like. He believed the *Scotsman*, as he wrote in his referendum diary, was 'on a suicide mission', *The Times* regularly displayed 'anti-Scottish bias' (and pointing this out to its editor gave him 'considerable pleasure'), while he was incredulous when the *Sunday Post* splashed on another hotel expenses story ('it would be possible to meet company CEOs or international dignitaries at the local Holiday Inn, but I'm not sure how well that would work for Scotland's benefit'), and recorded for posterity his attempt to offer a young *Telegraph* journalist 'a packet of liquorice allsorts for good attendance at every press event'. When, inexplicably in Salmond's eyes, Ben Riley-Smith took 'exception' to such a condescending gesture, Salmond put his 'tetchiness' down to low morale at the *Telegraph*, which was, after all, 'a subdivision of the NO campaign'.[71] At the same time he tried to play down the Fourth Estate's importance in political terms. 'If having the bulk of press on side was a determination of success in elections,' Salmond had remarked in July 2013, 'then I wouldn't be First Minister,' a comment that conveniently ignored the support he had enjoyed in 2007 and particularly 2011.[72]

Salmond, meanwhile, rarely missed an opportunity to take aim at the British Broadcasting Corporation (without ever actually boycotting it). One story – perhaps apocryphal but certainly believable – had it that he told one meeting of BBC Scotland management 'that if the BBC was on fire' he 'wouldn't piss on it'.[73] Asked directly if its reporting was biased, the First Minister replied: 'Yes, absolutely, of course it is . . . but they don't realise they're biased. It's the unconscious bias, which is the most extraordinary thing of all.'[74] And when the BBC was not being 'biased' it was, in his view, guilty of 'incompetence', with Salmond repeatedly calling its director-general Tony Hall to complain of its 'near-colonial attitude' or it being 'a disgrace to public service broadcasting', with it being 'difficult to tell where the network BBC stops and the NO campaign begins'. In his referendum diary Salmond acknowledged this would not achieve anything, but recorded 'really enjoyed saying it'.[75]

Part of Salmond's aim was to neutralise what critics began calling the 'mainstream media' (or MSM) ahead of the referendum, having concluded back in 1999 that if it could not be beaten then it was best to delegitimise it, while bypassing its outlets via social media and grassroots campaigning. Indeed, while at this stage Better Together was clearly winning the 'air war', the traditional political game of claim and counter-claim, the pro-independence campaign was winning the 'ground war', one-on-one, door-to-door engagement. As one former adviser put it: 'There was a strategy going back years on this – we knew it had to be won on a community level, but we didn't anticipate how successful that could be; it had always been an aspiration.'[76]

Boiled down, the Yes strategy had three stages: could, should and must, convincing voters that independence was possible, then desirable, and finally necessary in order to avoid the Unionist alternative. Key in the latter respect was the NHS, which a month before referendum day Salmond said had emerged as the 'single key issue',[77] chiefly a rather convoluted claim that a No vote would compel the Scottish Government to privatise the health service in Scotland, protection against which was even to form part of an already overcrowded constitution of an independent Scotland.

Nevertheless, as Salmond recorded in his referendum diary, in late June the 'atmosphere' remained 'downbeat', something he found 'pretty infuriating' given that in his 'best estimation we are doing pretty well'. Thus he decided to 'take a much stronger hand in the direction of the campaign', not least because Yes Scotland had, in his words, 'found it difficult, even with great goodwill, to provide a coherent strategic direction'. Salmond's solution was to 'mimic' the 2011 Holyrood election campaign and deploy many of his long-standing 'battle-hardened' advisers to that end.[78]

Thereafter came a long-anticipated summer of fun, including the Homecoming, Bannockburn anniversary and Commonwealth Games, all of which Salmond believed would form a helpful backdrop to the referendum campaign's final phase. On 30 June the First Minister described Bannockburn as 'the birthplace' of modern Scotland, demonstrating a primordial nationalism that made some of his advisers 'uncomfortable' ('your soul', he retorted, 'would have to be dead to not be inspired by that'[79]), while the following month Salmond's 'self-denying ordinance', a pledge to keep politics out of the Commonwealth Games, was quickly undermined, for example when he predicted the host city of Glasgow would vote Yes (he called it 'Freedom City').[80]

Better Together and the UK government, meanwhile, continued to bombard the pro-independence campaign with heavy political artillery; even a significant intervention from President Obama could not throw Salmond off his stride ('an independent Scotland will mean that America has two great friends and allies here rather than one'), although he seemed more rattled by subsequent remarks from presidential hopeful Hillary Clinton ('Scots don't like being told what to do'). In late July Salmond continued to believe the polls would soon 'tighten' (as they would) and detected 'a real change in the air', though in mid-August he considered the lack of movement 'perplexing' given what he was feeling 'on the ground'.[81]

The First Minister's tendency to be his own worst enemy also appeared undiminished even at such a sensitive stage in the campaign. His *GQ* interview with Tony Blair's former spin doctor Alastair Campbell, for example, was a gift that kept on giving, with allusions to Scotland as 'a nation of drunks' and, more significantly, an admission he admired 'certain aspects' of Russian president Vladimir Putin, including his having 'restored a substantial part of Russian pride'. Although this was heavily caveated (Salmond later claimed Campbell had 'trapped' him into saying it, which seemed unlikely given his media nous), the resulting furore rumbled on for weeks, made even worse by the First Minister's refusal to apologise and his initial mishandling of a meeting with Scotland's Ukrainian community.

In the same interview, Salmond had referred to UKIP leader Nigel Farage as possessing a 'certain bonhomie', while confessing 'a sneaking regard for anyone who takes on powerful establishments'.[82] And the feeling was mutual, Farage praising the SNP leader as 'brilliant', adding that they both led 'anti-Establishment insurgent parties'. But when left-wing independence supporters disrupted the UKIP leader's visit to Edinburgh, Farage depicted 'some parts of Scottish Nationalism' as being 'akin to fascism'. 'A student demonstration', retorted Salmond when asked to condemn what had happened, 'ain't the Dreyfus trial.'[83]

Indeed, in the final stages of the referendum campaign Salmond was often guilty of dog-whistle politics. While many at Yes Scotland were appalled at protests staged outside BBC Scotland's Glasgow HQ, the First Minister hailed one gathering as 'peaceful and joyous',[84] while he even refused to dismiss stories circulating about a supposedly 'secret' oil field under the Clair Ridge ('Oh yes, it's credible . . . '). During the last full week of campaigning, meanwhile, Salmond said people queuing to register to vote in Dundee was 'almost reminiscent of scenes in South Africa . . . when people queued up to vote in the first free elections';[85] several 'metropolitan' television reporters were likened to Alistair Darling if they dared question his proposed currency union, and when the BBC's political editor Nick Robinson clashed with the First Minister at an international press conference populated with Yes campaigners, it transformed him into a hate figure for those protesting outside Pacific Quay.

The major feature of the last '100 days' were two televised debates with Alistair Darling, which Salmond and his advisers realised were largely about expectation management. The First Minister therefore consented to a 'two-debate strategy' in which he would initially keep his powder dry before coming back with all guns blazing (heavily influencing this approach was Claire Howell). The consensus was that an aggressive start from Salmond might have produced a 'win' within the political bubble but risk turning off women voters, who remained relatively unconvinced about independence.

Everyone on Salmond's preparation team read Darling's book on the financial crisis, *Back from the Brink*, and also reached the conclusion that if the former Chancellor was going to come across as 'feisty and punchy' then he could do so only once. Even so, when the STV-hosted debate took place on 5 August, Salmond was not only low-key but often appeared to flounder, particularly under scrutiny from Darling over his plans for sterling. A snap poll gave the former Chancellor the edge, with 56 per cent of viewers deeming him the winner.[86] 'Alex Salmond said it would be Bannockburn,' spun Better Together, paraphrasing an earlier tweet from the SNP MP Pete Wishart. 'It turned out to be his Waterloo.'[87]

'I lost,' recorded Salmond in his diary, which he found frustrating having, in his view, 'won every single' televised debate since 1992. During preparation he had expressed reservations about the 'ring readiness' of his debate team and their 'unanimous advice to tone down' his debating style.[88] 'There were words in the green room afterwards I didn't know existed,'[89] recalled one of those involved in preparing Salmond for the first debate. Later the First Minister would blame having been 'persuaded to act out of character',[90] although he also acknowledged having fluffed the exchanges on currency. He had actually rehearsed producing a £5 or £10 note from his pocket, waving it at Darling and saying 'you tell the people of Scotland they can't use this',[91] but for whatever reason it had not made it to the final cut.

Preparation for the second debate on 25 August (this time hosted by the BBC), meanwhile, deliberately involved Nicola Sturgeon, which many of those involved considered key to a stronger performance by Salmond, who completely steamrollered his often-fumbling opponent. 'It was the old Alex,' observed one of the First Minister's advisers, 'but it worked!'[92] A snap poll found that a decisive 71 per cent of Scots considered Salmond the winner and, post hoc, Yes strategists cleverly spun it as all part of a typically Salmondite grand plan, to bounce back from adversity.

One of the most stinging remarks the SNP leader had thrown at Darling was that he was 'in bed with the Tories', an indication the Yes campaign fully understood the potency of guilt-by-association attacks on Labour for sharing a No umbrella with the ever-toxic Conservatives. The second TV debate also consolidated Salmond's belief that the currency question had been settled once and for all. When the BBC's Nick Robinson asked him about it on 2 September, for example, he observed that it was almost 'as if the debate with Alistair Darling had never even taken place'.[93] Indeed, Salmond considered most critiques of his currency union policy to be 'low-grade and empty nonsense'.[94]

Meanwhile the appropriately named 'NationBuilder', the US software that was to the referendum campaign what 'Activate' had been to the 2011 Holyrood election, was moving towards a Yes vote, indeed several strategists remember that it 'turned' following Salmond's perceived 'win' in the BBC debate. 'No one, however,' recalled one aide, 'wanted to believe it.'[95] Then, late on the evening of Saturday 6 September, details emerged of a YouGov poll that put Yes ahead for the first time, news that reached Salmond in Inverness during one of the three golf 'escapes' he had promised himself during the referendum.[96] Initially he misunderstood, believing No to be one point ahead, and only when he got to the clubhouse was that clarified. But although elated at such a breakthrough, the First Minister and his advisers realised it had come too early. Not only did it wake up the financial markets, but the poll compelled Better Together to ratchet up its offer on 'more powers', while Labour's 'big beast' Gordon Brown also roared into life, a figure Salmond privately feared would resonate with undecided voters.

The No campaign's heavy economic artillery soon started pounding the airwaves: supermarkets and mobile-phone operators claimed prices would go up; banks threatened to move their registered headquarters (including Salmond's old employer RBS); and energy firms also issued warnings, all designed to target the Yes campaign's key weakness: the economy. Better Together called it 'Alex Salmond's Black Wednesday'.[97]

Although the First Minister hit back by demanding an inquiry into a Treasury leak of RBS's decision before it had been officially signed off, it was nevertheless embarrassing given his professional provenance. The First Minister had been particularly keen to maintain banking neutrality during the referendum, concluding at a meeting on 28 July they were under 'no risk' from a Yes vote, and that even if registered offices were to leave Scotland it would have 'limited or no impact on real banking operations'.[98] That might have been true but if, as the BBC's Nick Robinson observed in his diary, 'it doesn't matter a damn where companies are based it's curious that Salmond himself has tried so hard to persuade firms to move their headquarters north of the border'.[99] Indeed, such a goal had been central to Salmond's 'economic case' for more than two decades.

There was also the so-called 'Vow', a joint statement from the Prime

Minister, Labour leader Ed Miliband and Liberal Democrat leader (and Deputy Prime Minister) Nick Clegg promising greater powers for Holyrood in the event of the No vote. Although it said little that was new, Salmond admired it as 'technically a very good job' (the statement had been presented by the *Daily Record* as a mock-medieval parchment) and feared that if 'offered a slightly easier option where change is inevitable', then undecided voters would opt for that.[100]

Meanwhile Salmond and the SNP had ditched specific fact-based arguments and switched to abstract reasoning in support of independence, emphasising the referendum as a 'once in a lifetime opportunity' (although he would subsequently caveat that as 'a personal view') and 'our only chance'. The First Minister even suggested he would 'retire from politics tomorrow' if it meant securing a Yes vote,[101] while in early September he marked his tenth year as SNP leader amid an adulatory mob in Glasgow. Salmond even buried the hatchet with Jim Sillars, whose wife Margo MacDonald had passed away earlier that year, although his old deputy soon caused problems by predicting 'a day of reckoning' for major Scottish employers opposed to independence. This led to a 'difficult conversation' between the once-close pair, although after Sillars claimed he had just been trying to get media attention, Salmond called to thank him 'for getting things back onto an even keel'.[102]

At an eve-of-poll rally at Perth Concert Hall Salmond looked tired as he spoke of writing 'a new chapter in the history of this ancient nation',[103] and indeed his departure from the agreed script led to 'a huge bust up' with his speechwriter Duncan Hamilton.[104] Despite fraying tempers, most senior Nationalists believed they were on the cusp of an historic victory, a feeling fuelled by two Canadian number crunchers who, based on an anticipated 80 per cent turnout, had predicted a Yes vote. Although this was supposed to be private, Rupert Murdoch tweeted that Salmond's private 'pollsters' [*sic*] were predicting 54 per cent in favour of independence. Canvassing data, however, was 'much tighter',[105] while Murdoch's social media activity belied his decision to adopt a position of 'benign neutrality' in the *Scottish Sun*.[106] The First Minister had called him on 7 September in a last-ditch attempt to secure a commitment to independence, but the News International chief replied, 'as he always does, that "it is up to my editors" '.[107]

Nevertheless Salmond remained confident of success in the final week of campaigning, which included a visit to his childhood home at Preston Road in Linlithgow. 'He was upbeat and cheerful,' recalled someone who saw a lot of him in the last few weeks. 'He genuinely thought we were in with a great chance of winning: in the closing weeks of the campaign everything about [his demeanour] said that.'[108] No one could ever accuse the SNP leader, an eternal optimist, of lacking confidence, only on this occasion it had interfered with his political judgement. One Yes Scotland strategist later said it was 'emphatically' the view from the First Minister down that a Yes vote was within sight. Indeed, so emphatic that some journalists were even informed at 10 p.m. where and when Salmond would make his victory speech.

On the day itself Salmond was in his East Aberdeenshire constituency, posing for photographers at a local polling station, something he found 'a strange experience'. 'I've waited for this day all of my life,' he explained in his referendum diary. 'And it finally dawns, just like any other day. What had I expected? A heavenly host trumpeting in the sky?'[109] The First Minister also spent part of the day ensuring all the Scottish Government's plans were in order:

> Statements have been prepared, including a joint statement with the UK government, a financial statement from the Scottish government, the announcement of the Monetary Authority, and the taking forward of the European discussions. The key personnel have all accepted their positions. All is ready. All is in place. I learned in 2007 that, in the aftermath of a close-run thing, the man with the plan has a huge advantage. I make the calls because I think they will be necessary.

The respected economist John Kay had agreed to head up a Scottish Monetary Authority (he had been suggested by former Bank of England Governor Mervyn King), although the reference to a 'joint state-ment' with the UK government was misleading: Salmond might have prepared such a document, but it had been without co-operation from Westminster.

Before the polls closed the First Minister went for a meal at one of his favourite haunts, Eat on the Green, where his entourage had set up camp for the night. Two exchanges between Mr and Mrs Salmond, meanwhile, captured the highs and lows of that day. 'Have we won?' asked Moira at one stage. 'I think so,' replied Salmond, but later, following the first declaration in Clackmannanshire, Moira asked: 'How bad is that?' 'It's only the first result and it's pretty close,' replied her husband diplomati-cally, before retiring to work on his concession speech.[110] 'When the first result came in I knew we had lost,' he later admitted. 'If Yes were going to win, we should have won Clackmannanshire.'[111]

Contrary to reports on the night, however, the First Minister was never scheduled to attend his local count, thus his no-show had nothing to do with the turn of events. At around 3 a.m. Salmond was driven to Dyce to board a private flight to Turnhouse, during which a photographer captured him looking tired and disappointed in the back seat of a car, although in reality he had been gazing at the latest results on his iPad, the glare from which had lent him a pallid demeanour, while contemplating his next move. The wide distribution of that image would still anger him several weeks later.

After a quick stop at his Bute House residence the First Minister arrived at the back entrance of Edinburgh's Dynamic Earth, where Duncan Hamilton had prepared two speeches, although of course it was the one marked 'No' that the First Minister delivered at around 6.30 a.m. 'Scotland has, by a majority, decided not, *at this stage*, to become an independent country,' he said (author's italics), already backtracking on his assurance that the referendum would be a 'once-in-a-generation' event.[112]

Rumours, meanwhile, began to swirl of resignation. In keeping with the First Minister's optimistic outlook, there had been almost no discussion of this in advance of referendum day. The morning after the night before, however, everything looked very different. Although, typically, Salmond was calm and collected as he considered his future, others were visibly emotional, even in tears, upset not just about the result but now the prospect of losing the most successful leader the National Movement had ever had; most of the First Minister's key staff had not slept in more than two days.

By 10 a.m. Salmond was set on his decision. 'You do what your instinct tells you,' Moira had told him. 'Your instinct is always right.'[113] The First Minister then met his deputy, Nicola Sturgeon, at Bute House. 'I tried to persuade him not to do it,' she later recalled, although of course she had known since July what he might do. 'I tried to persuade him at the very least not to do it that day, to take more time to think it through, to let the dust settle, to let the emotion of it all subside, but as I was doing that I knew that I wasn't going to succeed.'[114]

By lunchtime it was clear to most of the First Minister's staff that he would soon announce his resignation. His statement, largely written himself, showed the veteran SNP leader at his best: graceful and eloquent, although his belief that the Prime Minister's refusal to commit to a second reading on a new Scotland Bill by 27 March represented some sort of 'betrayal' was mistaken (the pre-referendum pledge had been 'immediately' following the 2015 general election). Then came the key passage:

> But today the point is this. The real guardians of progress are not the politicians at Westminster, or even at Holyrood, but the energised activism of tens of thousands of people who I predict will refuse meekly to go back into the political shadows. For me right now, therefore there is a decision as to who is best placed to lead this process forward politically. I believe that in this new exciting situation, redolent with possibility, Party, Parliament and country would benefit from new leadership. Therefore I have told the National Secretary of the SNP that I will not accept nomination to be a candidate for leader at the Annual Conference in Perth.[115]

Salmond concluded with an ad-libbed remark absent from his prepared text: 'For me as leader my time is nearly over. But for Scotland, the campaign continues and the dream shall never die.'[116] Those last five words, 'the dream shall never die', would later become the title of his published account of the referendum.

The First Minister felt 'suddenly unencumbered' according to someone who was at Bute House that afternoon. 'You could tell he was feeling "well, I've done my bit",' recalled the aide, 'he was clearly feeling demob happy.'[117] That evening Salmond was driven to Prestonfield House Hotel – the elegant setting for his 2007 and 2011 victories – and then taken by helicopter back to Aberdeenshire. Ever the pro, he made sure someone tweeted an image of him and Moira smiling before take off, also indulging in a memorable exchange with his Twitter alter ego 'Angry Salmond'. 'For the record, I never lost,' wrote the outgoing First Minister. 'I simply repositioned the location of victory.'[118]

# Chapter 15

## 'THE QUICKEST POLITICAL COMEBACK IN HISTORY'

Alex Salmond had always been acutely aware that in politics, timing was everything. By resigning immediately after the referendum, not only had he taken almost everyone by surprise, but he cleverly cleared the way for his successor and maintained media focus on the SNP rather than Better Together's narrower-than-expected victory. In other words, Salmond took ownership of defeat, thus giving him control of a post-referendum narrative he believed was 'redolent' with opportunity.

Back on solid ground after helicoptering back to his political base in the north east of Scotland, meanwhile, Salmond and his wife headed to his favourite Aberdeenshire hotel, the Marcliffe, for dinner. There, a message reached them from their gardener, warning that a media scrum had formed outside the Salmonds' Strichen home. Understandably reluctant to face a barrage of cameras after more than two days without sleep, the First Minister and his wife instead headed to the nearby Meldrum House for the night.

Back in Strichen the next day, as Salmond later recalled, he 'sat on the wall outside the house and did an impromptu press conference'.[1] On Sunday, meanwhile, he missed a service of reconciliation at Edinburgh's St Giles' Cathedral and instead gave several television interviews. And, having handled the difficult part of a No vote with considerable style (his resignation), it seemed the outgoing First Minister was determined to execute what should have been the easy bit (his departure) as gracelessly as possible.

Although in the early hours of Friday morning Salmond had pledged to accept the outcome of the referendum, he now gave the impression of having changed his mind, telling presenter Andrew Neil that certain voters had been 'misled', 'gulled' and effectively 'tricked' into voting No by the promise of more powers. And while by that point a cross-party commission (chaired by Lord Smith of Kelvin) had already begun discussions on that very pledge, Salmond also said it was clear the Unionist parties were 'cavilling and reneging' on their pre-referendum 'Vow'. As the journalist Kenneth Roy later observed: 'He will be remembered as the leader who accepted the democratic will of the people, but only for a few hours.'[2]

But when Neil reminded Salmond of his own 'vow' that the referendum would be a 'once-in-a-generation' event the First Minister – who had a habit of holding his opponents to higher standards of consistency than himself – said it had been a 'personal view' and that 'circumstances' might change, such as the UK leaving the European Union, or a failure to honour the promise of 'extensive new powers'.[3]

Next Salmond told Sky News' Dermot Murnaghan that in spite of the result independence was 'inevitable', blamed elderly voters for impeding 'progress for the next generation' and observed that while a referendum remained the 'best route' to independence there were other means by which it could be achieved, hinting at a Rhodesian-style UDI.[4] So having promised to help 'bring Scotland together' following the referendum, Salmond was instead aligning himself with the self-styled 'forty-five'.

This curious behaviour continued over the next few weeks. Salmond took the unusual step of attacking this author in the letters pages of the *Herald* (following a critical column concerning his legacy), while also phoning the BBC's *Morning Call* programme and getting into an on-air argument with local councillor Jim Gifford about local authorities pursuing old Poll Tax debts.[5] To admirers it was 'vintage' Salmond, although to others it sounded like hectoring populism; opening a Lidl store in Rutherglen a few weeks later he even took a pop at their rival Asda for having raised concerns about food prices during the referendum.

Opponents naturally had fun teasing the outgoing First Minister. 'You lost the argument,' Alistair Darling told him 'you lost the referendum, you've lost office, and now you've lost the plot',[6] while Deputy Prime Minister Nick Clegg said Salmond reminded him 'of a Japanese soldier found in the jungle 20 years after the war had finished, still ducking at every shadow, thinking the war was still on'.[7] As one UK government minister observed: 'He'd dropped any façade of being in any way constructive or non-political, which just demeaned him.'[8]

In his first statement to the Scottish Parliament a few days after the result, Salmond adopted a more conciliatory tone, thanking 'every single campaigner and voter, whatever your view or whatever your vote' for taking part in the 'greatest democratic experience in Scotland's history'. The First Minister also said there existed an 'unanswerable case' for giving 16- and 17-year-olds a vote in all UK elections, as well as a 'responsibility to hold Westminster's feet to the fire' to ensure pre-referendum pledges on more powers were met.[9]

The following day Nicola Sturgeon, as expected, announced her candidacy for the SNP leadership and, therefore, also for First Minister, and with that process due to conclude in mid-November, it meant Salmond could enjoy a swansong lasting almost two months. Tributes flowed. The Archbishop of Glasgow, Philip Tartaglia, referred to his 'outstanding career in politics' and to his having been 'a wonderful ambassador and champion for Scotland at home and abroad',[10] while, controversially, Heriot Watt University carved in stone his oft-stated promise that the 'rocks would melt in the sun' before he countenanced tuition fees, and invited the outgoing First Minister along to its unveiling.

Indeed, the response to that demonstrated that Salmond remained a divisive figure even as he approached the end of his ministerial career – and not just in Scotland. On 5 November, the town of Lewes on the south coast of England planned to burn a Salmond effigy as part of its Guy Fawkes' commemorations, while at the *Spectator*'s parliamentarian of the year awards Iain Martin observed that the SNP leader's 'wrongheaded notion that he is always absolutely hilarious' was, if anything, 'getting worse' now he was standing down as First Minister.[11] There were indeed flashes of hubris. Salmond, for example, claimed that had he stayed at RBS instead of becoming a politician then he 'might have been able to save' it from the international banking crisis,[12] an odd argument given his encouragement of the the ABN Amro bid that had helped take it to the brink.

In other respects Salmond made efforts to temper previous remarks relating to the referendum, disingenuously claiming that his 'once-in-a-generation' remark referred only to the gap between the two devolution referendums of 1979 and 1997 – the *Guardian* cartoonist Steve Bell depicted the SNP leader ('I've been betrayed!') as the 'Loch Yes Monster' and the legend: 'That was a quick generation!'[13] – while back-peddling on his apparent flirtation with alternative routes to independence. 'I think a referendum is the right route to independence,' he told Andrew Marr in early November. 'I've always held . . . that having a referendum is the correct route.'[14]

Although Salmond's lack of discipline occasionally frustrated his colleagues and advisers, it sprang in part from his considerable energy even as he approached his 60th birthday. 'I'm not recognising it,' he told one interviewer. 'I don't even consider myself middle-aged yet.' And apart from activating what he called his 'quiet time policy', not leaving his Strichen home for five days after the referendum ('the first time I've ever done that'),[15] it seemed highly unlikely he would go gently into that good night.

A group of Salmond's advisers – past and present – bade farewell to 'the Boss' at Contini's restaurant in Edinburgh. His former economic adviser Jennifer Erickson even flew in from the United States, and during the evening he paid emotional tributes to those who had worked for him over the past 25 years, only finding himself lost for words on getting to Kevin Pringle, who had been among the longest serving, most dedicated and – some might have said – longest suffering.

As the MSP Stewart Stevenson put it in his Holyrood tribute, Salmond was 'the toughest boss I have ever worked for or with, and the fairest', but however tough he might have been on his colleagues, 'he has always been tougher on himself'.[16] Always diligent with his correspondence, he spent his last two weeks as First Minister working his way through 14 different files of letters – one a night – letters from both home and abroad, responding to each one individually. 'He guards it all,' reflected a long-standing adviser, 'but underneath it all he really gives a shit about the working man – and they like him back.'[17]

Indeed, Salmond even suffered physically as a consequence of his popularity, months of shaking hands having left him with repetitive strain injury in his right arm for which he had to wear a black elasticated support. He earned praise for auctioning his personal effects to raise money for charity (and also donating his First Ministerial pension), while it emerged that the SNP was preparing to provide him with a driver, Salmond having been a stranger to public transport for much of the last decade. Meanwhile the party was swelling beyond all recognition, doubling its membership to more than 50,000 in the wake of the referendum, not a bad legacy given how small the SNP had been when Salmond had first been elected leader back in 1990.

On 18 November MSPs gathered at Holyrood to hear Salmond bid a final farewell, Nicola Sturgeon having been declared his successor (unopposed) at the annual SNP conference in Perth. 'I wish every single member of this Parliament well,' he said humbly, 'and say goodbye and good luck.'[18] The following day Sturgeon was nominated by the Scottish Parliament as Scotland's fifth First Minister, and the first female to hold that position. The Salmond era – spanning almost a quarter of a century – was at an end, or so it appeared.

On the morning Salmond formally relinquished office the BBC Radio Scotland presenter Gary Robertson asked him if he had made any mistakes during the referendum. 'Not every interview was perfect,'[19] was the former First Minister's grudging response, but there was little evidence he or his party had seriously reflected – privately or publicly – on their referendum defeat.

Eventually Salmond admitted there were 'certain differences' he would have made in the 'presentation of certain aspects, for example the currency argument', although he did not go into specifics,[20] while also conceding the Yes campaign should have focused on domestic policy issues like the NHS much 'earlier' in the campaign instead of trying to 'answer every iota' of the 'nonsense' emanating from Better Together.[21]

Instead the former First Minister allocated blame: older voters had been his initial target (but not, to his credit, non-Scottish voters), the media (i.e. its coverage of Unionist 'scaremongering') and chiefly the last-minute 'Vow', even though early academic analysis concluded this offer of 'more powers' had had minimal impact on final voting intentions. Salmond, however, had 'no doubt' it had been 'extremely successful' in giving undecided voters 'an easy option, or at least an apparently easy option, a less rocky road'.[22] He reckoned upwards of 10 per cent of the Scottish electorate had been swayed by that offer, again an observation without much supporting evidence.

Salmond (who carried on wearing a 'Yes' lapel badge for several weeks after 18 September) went even further, asserting that many No voters had subsequently regretted their decision. 'After the referendum, people told me two things,' he told the Newsweek journalist Alex Perry. 'Thanks and sorry. Sorry that they were not able to find a way to vote YES.'[23] Thus he believed around 60 per cent of the Scottish electorate were persuadable in the event of another referendum, something the former First Minister clearly believed was inevitable. 'I think the pendulum has swung,' was a common observation, 'It didn't swing as far as I wanted it to [but] I think we're beyond tipping point; I think we're now basically arguing about timescale and method as opposed to destination.'[24] As he characterised it elsewhere, it was 'possible to win a battle and lose a war, just as it is possible to lose a referendum and still win the end game'.[25]

Significantly, however, Salmond rarely acknowledged much personal responsibility (beyond matters of 'presentation') for losing that refer-endum war, even as it became clear the economic arguments for inde-pendence (as well as, to a degree, hostility towards him personally) had been more significant factors than the eleventh-hour 'Vow'. After all, Salmond's personality and debating points, not least over currency, had been front and centre. 'The mistakes (and there were a few)', he wrote in his referendum diary, 'were my responsibility and mine alone',[26] but he did not actually describe any beyond his handling of the first televised debate.

His predecessor Gordon Wilson, for example, believed the impact of the Vow had been 'zilch', arguing that it had been used as a 'political instrument' to justify defeat and distract attention from problematic positions on currency, pensions and an 'over-egging' of North Sea oil revenue.[27] Even some of those closer to Salmond rejected his implication that voters had somehow 'bottled it' on polling day, pointing instead to higher than anticipated turnout, which had made it harder for Yes to get past 50 per cent of the vote.[28] Others, meanwhile, suspected inexperienced canvassers and problems with NationBuilder had led to over-confidence in the Yes camp.[29]

Nevertheless, Salmond was correct in believing that one of the 'big gains' of the referendum had been firmly establishing the 'route by which Scotland can become independent', precedence being 'everything in these islands'.[30] He was also clear-sighted in framing the terms of political debate in the days and months following 18 September 2014. He argued, for example, that 'a huge gap' had emerged between the Vow and the UK government's command paper detailing further devolution for Scotland. Key in this respect had been the Prime Minister's speech on 19 September, in which he had indicated that more powers for Scotland would proceed 'in tandem' with English Votes for English Laws (EVEL). This, as Salmond later wrote in his referendum diary, had 'opened' a 'door' through which the SNP had to quickly 'drive'.[31]

On this, Salmond's position was politically shrewd but logically contrived, for even once it became clear the two processes would not have the same timescale, he stuck to his line that Westminster was betraying its 'solemn commitment'.[32] But not only had the Vow *not* promised, as he kept claiming, 'near federalism', 'devo to the max' (a phrase used only by Salmond) or 'Home Rule' – rather it had referred vaguely to 'extensive new powers' – but on EVEL the former First Minister shame-lessly exploited a proposed reform that he had hitherto supported, indeed SNP MPs (with notable exceptions) had long refrained from voting in the House of Commons on purely English matters. By December 2014 Salmond had suggested the SNP would ditch this self-denying ordinance, a U-turn confirmed by Sturgeon early the following year.

When it came to the Labour Party, meanwhile, Salmond worked hard to remind its supporters – a sizeable minority of whom had voted Yes in the referendum – that its leaders had stood 'shoulder to shoulder, hand in glove, side by side with the Conservatives' during the campaign, the sight of them 'linking arms' and 'high fiving each other' having proved a 'supreme turn off' for traditional Labour voters.[33] Although Salmond had correctly identified the political damage that guilt-by-association could cause Labour, he was again guilty of inconsistency and exaggeration. Not only had the SNP governed 'hand in glove' with the Scottish Conservatives between 2007-11, he would also have struggled to provide examples of Labour politicians 'linking arms' with or 'high fiving' Conservative colleagues, largely because they did not exist.

Meanwhile, and having long campaigned on two distinct constitutional paths – independence and 'fiscal autonomy' – Salmond made clear attempts to shift the debate onto the latter following the No vote. In early 2015 he told the *Courier* (for which he was now writing a weekly column, also published in the *Press & Journal*) that a clear general election aim was 'Home Rule', that is 'control of all domestic affairs and taxation'. 'There is massive evidence that's what Scotland wants,'[34] he explained, while implying that the Vow had pledged 'full fiscal autonomy', which of course it had not.

Not only were such statements perceived as interference (it ought to have been Sturgeon setting out election goals rather than her predecessor) but it would later lead to considerable fire-fighting by the SNP, not least because it re-opened referendum-era debates about the likely financial consequences of severing all fiscal ties with Westminster. Salmond repeated this argument in his referendum diary, *The Dream Shall Never Die*, a book that finally appeared in March 2015 having first been announced the weekend after the referendum. Given his long-standing relationship with, and admiration for, Rupert Murdoch, Salmond chose as his publisher William Collins (an imprint historically based in Glasgow) and granted serialisation rights to the *Scottish Sun*, an editor from which had helped knocked the book into shape.

Reports suggested Salmond had been paid a six-figure advance for his first book, although he later declared £91,800 for sales, royalties and payments, paid to an outfit called 'The Chronicles of Deer', which he established to manage his outside income and thus potentially reduce his tax liabilities. The book itself – subtitled '100 Days that Changed Scotland Forever' – was disappointing. Only two long-standing associates of the author, the journalist Alan Taylor and the academic James Mitchell, found much to praise, the latter concluding that the diaries were 'more interesting and revealing than most expected or will admit',[35] only what it revealed was often narcissistic, petty and verbose.

Instead of producing a big, important analysis of an historic event (which Salmond was more than capable of writing), he had instead written a small, transient tome that gave little away. There were, however, flashes of self-awareness. In the book's epilogue, for example, Salmond noted that his advisers and private office had not always seen 'the sunniest side' of his 'nature', and indeed at other points in the book he positively relished his ability to put powerful individuals in their place. He adopted 'a tone of controlled menace' in speaking to the chief executive of FirstGroup, noting that the 'tone of total contrition' he got in response helped 'greatly'.[36] Salmond also launched a highly personal attack on the Treasury permanent secretary Sir Nicholas Macpherson, whom he had first encountered in 2011. Later, he revealed that Sir Nicholas had threatened both the *Sun* and HarperCollins with legal action 'in a last-ditch and futile attempt' to get certain references removed.[37]

The Treasury chief was not, however, blameless, and when he later admitted in a speech that his department had operated politically during the referendum campaign, Salmond called on him to resign. *The Dream Shall Never Die* was at least a relative commercial success, topping the *Sunday Times* best-seller list and shifting more than 12,000 hardback copies by the summer of 2015. An extended book tour in Scotland and London also revealed that its author remained hugely popular. In Aberdeen, for example, a huge queue of people waited for signatures and photographs with the former First Minister, and at every event Salmond, accompanied by three aides and a bodyguard, would not leave until he had obliged every one of them.

By this point, Salmond had confirmed his intention to contest the Westminster constituency of Gordon at the UK general election due on 7 May 2015, in what one former adviser dubbed 'the quickest political comeback in history'.[38] In a career full of surprise departures and returns, not to forget his obvious affection for the House of Commons, it had quickly become obvious that he found the prospect of returning to the green benches irresistible, not least so he could help hold, as he was fond of saying, Westminster's 'feet to the fire'.

Although this was also ironic – for such a strong critic of the Westminster 'system' or 'elite' Salmond seemed remarkably keen to rejoin it – it was a no-brainer: not only was the image of such a big beast contenting himself with life as a Holyrood backbencher an unconvincing one, but it made sense for Nicola Sturgeon to harness her predecessor's obvious popularity and talent as part of what looked likely to be a considerably enhanced team of MPs in London.

But Salmond's comeback also created challenges for his party, not least the former First Minister's habit, as one former aide put it, of going 'off piste'.[39] Indeed, in the course of promoting his referendum diary he often gave the impression that he remained in charge of the party's post-election strategy, while as the 'only politician in the UK to have led a minority government' (Salmond seemed unaware of several Welsh examples) he clearly relished the prospect of another 'hung' or 'balanced' Parliament – the crux of many an SNP general election strategy since the 1980s. On one occasion Salmond even strayed from his party's anti-Tory script, telling the journalist Kevin McKenna that he did not rule out squeezing concessions from a minority Conservative government on an issue-by-issue basis. 'I know, from difficult experience,' he said, 'how to make the pips squeak.'[40] As he put it to Andrew Marr: 'If you hold the balance, you hold the power.'[41]

Such observations (fuelled by a newfound love of pink champagne) tended to dominate the front pages and thus clearly undermine the authority of Salmond's successor. He was also inconsistent, quickly reversing his position on deals with the Conservatives and instead referring to confidence-and-supply as a 'possible' arrangement but an issue-by-issue arrangement with a minority Labour government as more 'probable'.[42] But having made it clear (as had Sturgeon) that his aim was to 'lock' David Cameron out of Downing Street come what may, it meant the SNP's potential influence over a Labour Prime Minister, which Salmond appeared to indicate his party would never bring down, was in reality quite minimal.

Even after Nicola Sturgeon had clearly asked Salmond to keep a lower profile, the former First Minister found himself an unlikely star of the UK Conservative campaign, his benign countenance gazing at a miniature Ed Miliband (situated in his top pocket) on election posters all over England. The Tories later released a cartoon showing Salmond playing a whistle while Ed Miliband danced to his tune, while another billboard poster even depicted Salmond as a burglar attempting to steal cash from England's back pocket. But Lynton Crosby, David Cameron's election strategist, knew exactly what he was doing: not only was Salmond mark-edly less popular in England (unlike Sturgeon) but the prospect of the SNP dragging a minority Labour government to the left proved to be a powerful recruiting sergeant for floating voters in Middle England; Scotland and Salmond had been 'weaponised' by CCHQ.

For most of the campaign, however, an unusually quiet Salmond confined himself to the fight in Gordon, where polling had indicated he would easily take the hitherto Liberal Democrat-held seat. As he had observed late the previous year, every 'single political organisation that has ever gone into an alliance, agreement or cohabitation with the Conservative party has ended up destroyed' (although of course he did not mean to include the SNP between 2007 and 2011).[43] But even Salmond's local campaign was not free of controversy, with one of his leaflets claiming his party had 'led the way' in providing free personal care and bus passes for pensioners, when in fact both policies had been introduced by a Labour/Liberal Democrat Scottish Executive *after* Salmond stood down as an MSP in 2001, and *before* he became First Minister in 2007.

In terms of the national campaign Salmond had become, as the *Daily Mail*'s Quentin Letts observed at the SNP manifesto launch in Edinburgh, 'an unperson, not required on journey, as inconvenient to the roseate horizon as a toppled Politburo member in Soviet Moscow'.[44] Before 7 May he only resurfaced during brief détentes, for example to attack the Institute of Fiscal Studies' critical analysis of his party's proposed alterna-tive to 'austerity' (by this stage he appeared to have shed any regard for economic facts and figures), while on election night, when Salmond's comeback was secured with a 8,687 majority over his Liberal Democrat opponent, he declared that the 'Scottish lion' had 'roared'.[45] But instead of the widely-anticipated 'balanced' Parliament (on which Salmond had said he 'would lay odds'[46]), there had emerged a clear Conservative majority.

The result, in which the SNP secured a remarkable 56 out of a possible 59 Scottish constituencies, had been due in no small part to Salmond's skilful framing of the post-referendum terrain and also the popularity of his successor Nicola Sturgeon, who had emerged as the star of the general election campaign, not just in Scotland but across the rest of the UK. She was well aware that her predecessor would require careful handling, and, amidst regular visits to London, it eventually became clear he would not lead the Westminster group (as he had between 2001-04) but rather fulfil a 'floating midfielder' role as foreign affairs spokesman. 'He is Nicola Sturgeon's Ambassador to London television studios', judged the *Spectator* blogger Alex Massie, 'and his brief is to stir up trouble wherever he can.'[47]

Salmond had held a dual mandate before, 1999-2001 and again 2007-10, indeed he had only stood down as an MP in 2010, although he quickly made it clear he would relinquish his Holyrood berth in 2016.[48] And back in the Commons with 55 colleagues instead of two (as in 1987), the former First Minister was clearly in his element, once again drawing inspiration from Charles Stewart Parnell, who had advanced the cause of Irish Home Rule in the late 19th century.[49] A bust of the Irish Nationalist leader had even been situated in the new SNP whips' office, while Salmond made sure every SNP MP possessed a copy of the House of Commons rulebook, dubbing them the 'feisty fifty-six' rather than the 'feeble fifty',[50] the latter being the pejorative term he had coined for the Scottish Labour group of MPs nearly 30 years before. He identified four 'battleground areas': Europe, austerity, autonomy and Trident, which Salmond called 'EATT'; 'we will be eating them for breakfast, lunch and dinner'.[51]

Although Salmond would demonstrate his undiminished talent for Commons guerilla warfare over David Cameron's EU Referendum Bill (during which he sought to depict the SNP as the 'real' opposition), almost immediately his mere presence at Westminster (and the media profile it provided) created tensions between the former and current First Ministers. Back in September 2014 he had instinctively realised the need 'to get out of the road' and clear the way for his successor, thus making him – in his own words – 'John the Baptist to Nicola Sturgeon'.[52] But if that were true, it would take more than baptism to forgive John's sins, not least a continuing lack of discipline the more cautious Sturgeon must have found infuriating.

She had wondered aloud to the French ambassador as to 'what kind of mischief' Salmond would get up to at Westminster,[53] and he did not disappoint. On his first day back in the Commons, for example, the former First Minister was widely assumed to be the source of a story (that inconveniently appeared the very morning Sturgeon met with David Cameron) to the effect that another, informal, referendum could be won with between 50-60 per cent of the vote. He also broke the SNP's no-Tory rule by indicating he would share a platform with Conservatives like George Osborne during the EU referendum (Sturgeon said she would not), while even his political style – pugilistic interviews and self-indulgent, niggling speeches in the Commons – repeatedly contrasted with Sturgeon's more constructive, conciliatory approach.

And given that the new First Minister had made a point of majoring on her feminism and gender inequality, her predecessor's old-fashioned language also caused problems. Asked, for example, about his successor's attitude to cutting Corporation Tax, Salmond alluded to 'the women' having 'excised' his long-standing 'little heresy'.[54] Worse was his 'behave yourself, woman' instruction to the Tory MP and minister Anna Soubry (with whom Salmond had clashed during the election campaign) in the House of Commons debate, which the First Minister found herself defending during a high-profile trip to the United States. She knew no man, protested Sturgeon, 'who is less sexist'.[55] Typically, he dug himself deeper by defending his comments as an example of the 'Scottish idiom', protesting that he had frequently said 'behave yourself, man' in the Scottish Parliament (although according to its Official Report he had not).

It did not seem to matter for, as the historian Lord Hennessy observed, Salmond appeared to be surrounded by a political 'force field',[56] apparently subject to different rules than most of his contemporaries. Nevertheless every Sturgeon success served to highlight Salmond's weaknesses. The *Newsnight* presenter Evan Davis even showed him a clip of his successor's appearance on Jon Stewart's *Daily Show*, observing that her leadership seemed 'less divisive' than his. 'Different strokes for different folks,' responded Salmond. 'People have different styles, and perhaps we're from different eras . . . quite rightly she's developing her own style as First Minster – and isn't she doing it very well?'[57]

'Alex', claimed Nicola, 'will never undermine me,' while Salmond wondered why on earth he would 'possibly resent' Sturgeon's success when everything seemed 'to be working out quite well'.[58] All of that was true, for Salmond certainly had no intention of *deliberately* undermining his successor, and more to the point neither, as the journalist Ian Bell observed, 'would break the bond by describing the bond'.[59] They had been a formidably successful political duo for more than a decade; indeed Nicola Sturgeon's success as First Minister was arguably one aspect of her predecessor's substantial, yet complicated, political legacy.

## Chapter 16

# 'TO WIN OR LOSE IT ALL'

> He either fears his fate too much,
> Or his deserts are small,
> That puts it not unto the touch
> To win or lose it all.

Those words are from a poem by James Graham, the 1st Marquess of Montrose, a Scottish nobleman and soldier who initially joined the Covenanters in the Wars of the Three Kingdoms but subsequently supported King Charles I in the English Civil War. Despite that troubled provenance, Alex Salmond liked to quote these four lines at key moments in his career.

A favourite of his father's, the poem 'My Dear and Only Love' first surfaces in the summer of 1990 when Salmond was campaigning to become leader of the SNP. It was certainly a gamble; Margaret Ewing was considered the favourite and her young rival was only 35. 'What happened to Montrose?' asked one former SNP MP at the time. 'He was hanged for his trouble.'[1] Salmond's opponents expected the same fate to befall him.

Yet Salmond put it to 'the touch' and won the election, not least because he had meticulously planned his campaign as if he were a latter-day Montrose. He quoted the lines again in the late 1990s as he persuaded his party to embrace devolution, and again before the 2007 elections that saw him emerge as First Minister of Scotland. In 1999 he had tempted fate and lost, quitting as leader shortly thereafter; in 2007 Salmond won the top job and the main prize of independence appeared closer than ever before.

On referendum day, meanwhile, Salmond could not get the lines out of his head, although on that occasion he failed to persuade a majority of voters that independence was worth the risk. Nevertheless, Salmond had never shrunk from putting matters to the touch, generally approving of those 'prepared to take individual risks in order to assert our national rights'.[2]

As the academic James Mitchell concluded: 'Often portrayed as a gambler, this is a man who has the courage of his convictions but has never doubted the scale of the challenge.'[3] The term 'gambler', however, did not quite capture what Salmond was about, for although he could occasionally be reckless, he was just as capable of tactical retreats, as in 2000 and 2014. 'Alec is at his best when the chips are down,' reflected Geoff Aberdein, a long-standing aide, 'the more the pressure the better he performs.'[4]

During Richard Nixon's visit to Beijing in 1972, the Chinese premier Zhou Enlai was asked about the impact of the French Revolution, to which he was said to have replied that it was 'too early to say'. The same might be said of Salmond's legacy, with its true impact only likely to become evident in decades to come, although certain aspects are already clear less than a year after his resignation as First Minister and SNP leader.

Strikingly, Salmond altered the terms of debate, something very few politicians can lay claim to. On first becoming leader of the SNP back in 1990, and even when he returned in 2004, the Scottish Question certainly loomed large, but not to the extent it did, increasingly, 2006-12, and most prominently during and after the referendum campaign of 2012-14. Just as Margaret Thatcher changed the terms of economic debate in the 1980s, and Tony Blair its social equivalent the following decade, Salmond succeeded in re-orientating Scottish (and to an extent UK) politics along constitutional rather than traditional left/right lines. Certainly after 2007 one could often witness Unionist opponents dancing to his tune, constantly reviewing Scotland's devolution settlement in the hope of swapping it for something with a slower tempo.

Salmond's 'gradualist' constitutional strategy, meanwhile, was fully vindicated by events. A supporter of a Scottish Assembly as a 'stepping stone' to independence in the 1970s, throughout the 1980s and his first period as leader 1990-2000 he faced considerable opposition within the SNP as he slowly persuaded them to stop worrying and learn to if not love devolution, then at least appreciate its strategic importance. And although it initially looked as if the Scottish Parliament had killed Nationalism, as Labour's George Robertson hoped, 'stone dead', in fact it proved crucial to the reinvention of the SNP as a potential party of government, a reality Salmond grasped and ultimately exploited.

Hugely significant in this respect was the party's decision in 1997 to campaign *for* a Scottish Parliament, and in 2000 to adopt a referendum as the means by which independence would be achieved, both stances engineered by Salmond over the past decade. In doing so he both neutralised independence and provided space for it to be advanced separately from (but heavily influenced by) the SNP. Meanwhile, he continued to interpret inventively his party's constitution, promoting not only independence but also the 'furtherance of all Scottish interests', which he generally took to mean the idea of 'fiscal autonomy'.

For a quarter of a century the SNP 'notionally abided by both aims', as his predecessor Gordon Wilson put it, although 'from time to time one could be in the ascendant over the other'.[5] Salmond considered the resumption of sovereignty to be key, and thereafter it was 'a question of choice' as to how one exercised it.[6] Some of those choices – which he took care to articulate in advance – were not always popular with other Nationalists, but Salmond considered them essential to building support for the SNP's *raison d'être*. Embracing Europe, the monarchy, sterling and, latterly, NATO, all involved ceding or pooling that sovereignty but, as Salmond put it in 1998, more than anything else his 'leadership project' was about fashioning an 'independence movement that threatens no one in Scotland'.[7]

Salmond frequently demonstrated how at ease he was with aspects of Unionism and, more strikingly, Britishness, but then another key part of his legacy was in shifting Scottish Nationalism away from kilts and bagpipes onto more utilitarian, civic territory. And impressively, he was always prepared to play the long game, not least when it came to building support for the SNP, without which independence would have remained a quixotic dream. Always a formidable networker, Salmond spent decades constructing what some called a 'big tent', under which he gathered an incredible range of individuals, beliefs and interests; as First Minister, meanwhile, he skilfully seized control of the decades-old 'Scottish Lobby' and set about making it his own.

All of which enabled Salmond to detoxify independence in sections of Scottish society hitherto hostile to the concept, gradually building the 'economic case' for independence (although ironically by embracing the orthodox British view that the path to economic success lay via a competitive tax regime) and therefore its broader credibility. Under his leadership, 'independence' moved from the fringe to the mainstream; from being supported by around a third of voters to 45 per cent; it became the new normal.

'I've always believed, and I would be astonished if I were proved wrong,' Salmond had reflected in 2008, 'that a success of the SNP and the government will translate into increased confidence in Scotland, increased confidence in the Scottish Government, and increased confidence in the case for independence.'[8] Although it took a long time to manifest itself, 'confidence' was indeed key, not least among Scotland's Catholic and Asian communities – both of which were assiduously cultivated by Salmond over two decades. This played to Salmond's 'Civic Nationalism', stressing shared values rather than ethnicity. As far as he was concerned, everyone regardless of provenance, nationality and outlook was a potential convert to the independence cause; he zealously cultivated his own networks and encouraged his colleagues and advisers to do the same; newspaper editors and reporters were cajoled into positive coverage, and robustly persuaded to spike that which was negative or unhelpful.

This was interesting, for Salmond's Nationalism was, at root, primordial. He repeatedly stressed Scotland's 'ancient' nature and drew an unbroken line between the Declaration of Arbroath and Battle of Bannockburn to contemporary political fights. 'I think the fundamental reason for believing in independence,' he once commented, 'is that nations are better when they govern themselves.'[9] And writing after the referendum, he observed that everything he had 'been taught or experienced, from the science of economics to the art of politics' was 'overlaid' on 'the belief that Scotland is a singular place and that the people of Scotland are capable of great things'.[10] Yet he was an existential Nationalist who deployed utilitarian rhetoric, claiming in late 2010 that he governed 'not for the SNP, but for Scotland', the 'welfare of the nation' and its five million people being what 'guides my actions'.[11]

And like the generation of politicians and strategists who would create New Labour, Salmond realised that professionalism was key, thus another of his legacies was the transformation of the SNP from an ill-disciplined, fringe political party into a formidable campaigning machine capable of winning near-majority support. He established a Shadow Cabinet, recruited a chief executive, sharpened up its media operation and created a command-and-control leadership structure that that mirrored his often-volatile personality. Paradoxically, Salmond was not much interested in the party itself, indeed the most significant reforms (from which he would later benefit) would actually be implemented by John Swinney.

And from the beginning Salmond took great care to build a leadership team, not only to dispel notions of the SNP as a 'one-man band' (which had never really been true) but also to prepare the ground for future success, not least in government. Nicola Sturgeon, Andrew Wilson, Duncan Hamilton and many others were identified and encouraged, helping forge the close 'team' that would prove crucial to the success of his administrations between 2007 and 2014, and also during the referendum campaign. No other mainstream Scottish or UK political party could point to a similar record.

'My administration has been grounded on loyalty to colleagues,' Salmond reflected in June 2014. 'Even when they make silly mistakes. Leaders who fling people overboard can't lead.'[12] Indeed, throughout his leadership of the SNP he rarely removed ministers, and if it proved necessary he did so sensitively, while also making a point of giving even sworn enemies a second chance. This loyalty tended to be repaid: after 2007 public dissent was rare, while the presence of two capable lieutenants, leaders past (John Swinney) and future (Nicola Sturgeon), was crucial in terms of compensating for his weaknesses. He was more collegiate in his second leadership phase, happier to share power as one third of that triumvirate. 'Like Alexander I will reign, And I will reign alone,' in the words of Montrose, although unlike Graham Salmond did not always disdain a rival on his throne.

But although often impressive as First Minister – many in 2007 noticed how naturally he assumed the role – Salmond was perhaps best understood as an opposition politician and the SNP as an oppositionist party, more comfortable defining themselves in terms of what they were *against* rather than what they stood *for*. In that sense the late 1980s, during which the 'young Robespierre' cut his teeth as the MP for Banff and Buchan, left an indelible mark on his political style. Then, getting noticed required shameless opportunism and a vivid phrase contrived to grab a sub-editor's attention, but even two decades later (after several years in government) he behaved in much the same way, often opposing rather than persuading, campaigning rather than governing.

Salmond could also be deeply tribal, finding it difficult to acknowledge that any party other than the SNP could possibly 'stand up for Scotland' or advance its best interests. He often told a childhood story of a Labour canvasser who had insulted the SNP and thus converted his father Robert (a golfing friend of whom was a member of the party) to the Nationalist cause. Reflecting on his second televised debate with Alistair Darling during the referendum campaign, meanwhile, Salmond likened the former Chancellor to 'that Labour canvasser at my father's door all of these years ago, all about what Scotland couldn't do'. Similarly, he reckoned the former Labour First Minister Henry McLeish, whom he was trying to persuade to back a Yes vote, was 'clearly torn between loyalty to party and country'.[13]

Indeed, Salmond became increasingly Manichean with age while clearly possessing an elevated opinion of his own status in the Nationalist pantheon. There were certainly people, he reflected in November 2011, who had 'made their entire careers out of confining the possibilities of their country', and while he rejected the label 'Quislings', he certainly considered them 'yes-men':

> Are they people who put their personal futures before the concept of a national future? Definitely. Are they therefore to be less well regarded than people who did the reverse, people who sacrificed their personal futures to pursue an aim? Most of us believe that people who do that are more worthy of admiration.[14]

Salmond undoubtedly saw himself as someone who had sacrificed his 'personal future' – perhaps a lucrative career in banking – to pursue a bigger political goal, a belief that helped explain his hostility towards other Scots, including contemporaries like the Conservative Michael Forsyth, who had pursued alternative, Unionist paths.

But under Salmond's leadership of the SNP there was also a profound shift in how that goal of independence was to be achieved, a deliberate move away from abstract concepts to concrete goals, and a related shift away from policy-making to fighting (and preferably winning) elections. As he reflected shortly before the referendum:

> I spent a lot of time losing elections . . . and I was convinced by a strong lady [Claire Howell] who was giving us some instruction in psychology and winning that, in order to change that, I had to do a couple of things. One was to get out of an oppositionist mode . . . you are no longer just trying to get a headline . . . and she convinced me (and I know I was prepared to be convinced) I had to start thinking entirely differently if you are going to win elections . . . You have to believe you're going to win and therefore 2007, 2011, 2014.[15]

But significantly Salmond did not view detailed policy or a coherent ideological agenda as necessarily important in achieving this electoral success, thus his legacy in intellectual terms is considerably weaker. Even as an undergraduate, contemporaries did not detect much interest in policy, ideology or abstract reasoning, something he later dismissed as 'namby-pamby theory'.[16] Rather, he was concerned with tactics and strategy (though some doubted the latter), fashioning a media-friendly 'line' and positioning his party on prime political terrain; politics to him was a contact sport rather than an academic seminar.

'He doesn't burn with anger and rage about poverty in Scotland,' commented Kenny MacAskill in 1997. 'It would be wrong to say he's not genuinely committed, but he's got no fire within him,'[17] while a few years later Jim Sillars dismissed Salmond as merely 'a spin machine, spinning in a policy vacuum'.[18] As Duncan Hamilton observed more approvingly, it 'couldn't be any other way – politics is what makes Alex tick, it is what excites him and defines him'.[19] Salmond's book, *The Dream Shall Never Die*, is a case in point, containing next to nothing about policy or inequality but lengthy accounts of tactics and strategy.

In more reflective moments Salmond conceded he was 'reasonably adept at defending virtually any position', putting 'a gloss on statistics or any economic figure' in order to build a political case.[20] Or, as he revealingly put it elsewhere: 'The art of politics is actually not to lie.'[21] While of course this was true of most politicians, in Salmond's case it was a question of degree, and too often it looked as if politics to him was little more than a game and the 'truth' whatever happened to work in the moment. And given his obsession with consistency, it meant he spent a lot of time squaring circles and dancing on the head of a pin. As the journalist Harry Reid put it, 'Salmond's high ability in the political arts' was also his 'biggest weakness', inevitably tempting him 'to busk, to rely on his immense native wit rather than always attend to the tiresome detail'.[22]

Therefore the strength of Salmond's 'big tent' in electoral terms was also its weakness intellectually, for it inevitably compelled him to become all things to all men. At St Andrews University he had paid lip service to Marxism, later declaring himself a 'socialist' and, latterly, a 'social democrat'. Of course others had embarked upon a similar journey, although few of his contemporaries managed to present themselves in so many guises: left-wing radical, centre-right economist, monarchist, anti-establishmentarian; whatever he judged a particular context required, the most important change of clothes having been that in the mid-1980s, when Salmond shifted his political base from the urban central belt to rural north east.

An added irony was that as Salmond spent the 1980s and 1990s deriding (New) Labour for moving onto centre-right territory he was busy taking the SNP on a very similar ideological journey, embracing free-market economics and attempting to woo big business with his own prawn cocktail offensive. Indeed, his political analysis was not far removed from that of Blair, a belief in a 'Third Way' between capitalism and socialism, i.e. skimming off the proceeds of growth to pay for more generous social policies. And like most other politicians, the closer to power Salmond moved the more pragmatic he became.

Initially determined to give the SNP a much clearer political identity, it was ironic that Salmond actually ended up leading his party some way from an unequivocally centre-left position and instead established himself as an arch triangulater, determined to appeal to the right as well as the left. Meanwhile his grasp of economics, from which he derived so much authority and credibility early in his career, increasingly became in thrall to what Keynes once called 'some defunct economist'. In Salmond's case it was Art Laffer, whose thinking about the potential of tax cuts to boost revenue he embraced during his leadership sabbatical and never quite relinquished, even in 2015 he described the Laffer Curve as 'one of the holy grails of public finance'.[23] On the financial crash of 2007-08 Salmond had little of substance to say, but so strong was his quixotic belief in a high spend/low tax Scotland that even under new leadership post-2014, the SNP found it impossible to move beyond its ideological contradictions.

It spoke to the fact that Salmond never appeared to have given much thought to what sort of country an independent Scotland might be, rather he aligned himself with widely-accepted but problematic concepts of Scotland as communitarian and enterprising, a land forever defined by the Welfare State and a more contemporary hatred of the Conservatives. Often, therefore, he presented independence as an essentially conservative force (as had many with devolution in the 1980s and 1990s), designed to preserve all that he deemed good about Scotland in the late 20th century, which might have made it less frightening to some voters, but also less worthwhile. And while his arguments for independence became synonymous with the pursuit of social justice and economic growth, he did little to give those twin (and perhaps contradictory) goals a substantive form beyond glib debating points.

Even as First Minister between 2007 and 2014, the journalist John Lloyd's 2006 assessment of Salmond as 'brilliantly opportunist' but 'politically shallow' still applied,[24] for although he proved adept at exploiting events both foreign (Iraq) and domestic (internal Labour strife) for electoral gain, success bred complacency, fuelling Salmond's instinctive belief that a few retail 'offers' and a slick campaign was worth a thousand coherent policies. In opposition, Salmond's simplistic arguments had rarely been scrutinised to any degree, but in government his weaknesses became much more obvious, and for the first time it had a material impact, not only at St Andrew's House, but also in local government; with power came responsibility and, at least in theory, accountability.

In office, meanwhile, Salmond continued to divert policy-making to strategic ends. Chiefly, this involved winning over what he had identified back in 1996 as 'the middle-class psyche', i.e. pursuing 'a tiger economy with a social concern on health, on education and a personal tax structure which is fair, not penal, and a business tax structure which is very competitive'. Initially, this strategy involved middle-class Scots paying 'a bit more' in tax,[25] although stung by the perceived failure of his 'Penny for Scotland' policy in 1999, thereafter Salmond determined not to go into another election pledging tax increases.

Salmond, therefore, was able to appeal to Middle Scotland on a 'progressive' basis while reassuring them there would be no related hit in terms of tax, thus playing brilliantly (if cynically) to how many Scots liked to see themselves (if not how they actually were), and creating new vested interests, not least in terms of 'free' education and endlessly frozen council tax, that would prove difficult to reverse. But Salmond's assertions about Scots' inherent progressiveness did not have to be true, for it formed the centrepiece of what even Tony Blair's former spin doctor Alastair Campbell acknowledged as 'a clever soundtrack to . . . an upbeat, devolved Scotland',[26] a significant departure from the more negative, reactionary strategy associated with the first phase of Salmond's leadership.

He had always understood the power of political narrative, the need to tell a good story about Scotland and its future, and importantly Salmond gradually co-opted the Labour 'story' of Scotland formerly mobilised in order to establish a devolved Scottish Parliament. Central to this was what he misleadingly called Scotland's 'centuries-old tradition of free education',[27] something he held up as his proudest achievement. This was revealing, for although undoubtedly popular with Middle Scotland, the policy of 'free' university tuition was ineffective when it came to widening access while, strikingly, during his seven years as First Minister almost all those poor enough to receive a bursary ended up net losers, losing more from his cuts to grants than they gained from his government's abolition of the graduate endowment (a related 2007 pledge to 'eradicate' student debt was quietly dropped). In many ways it was a fitting monument to a politician with great presentational flair but little obvious interest in affecting genuine social change. The main thing, as far as Salmond was concerned, was that it made life difficult for the Labour Party.

Elsewhere Salmond pointed to renewable energy as another significant legacy, although here his record was more substantial. Although there was a lot of hyperbole – he promised to 'reindustrialise' Scotland in 2011 (and again in 2014) but never developed a proper industrial strategy, and had a tendency to exaggerate the impact of 'clean' energy in terms of investment (many of the wave and tidal initiatives backed by Salmond failed), manufacturing (most turbines were built on the Continent) and jobs (modest given the scale of government subsidy) – by the time he left Bute House his target of generating 100 per cent (equivalent) of electrical consumption from renewable sources by 2020 was well on track. This amounted to an inexorable shift in Scotland's energy system, and one that had been personally driven by Salmond, making good (at least in part) on a personal vision first articulated as an undergraduate.

As First Minister Salmond marshalled the machinery of government towards renewables in particular and economic development in general, making effective use of what Theodore Roosevelt called a 'bully pulpit', in his case the White House and in Salmond's the Georgian splendour of Bute House. And while he often pushed this too far, sailing close to the wind in the case of Donald Trump and a golf course application early in his first government, or when accused of 'politicising' the Civil Service during the referendum campaign, it was undoubtedly effective, not least in transforming how Scots perceived the 'Scottish Executive', less a quasi-regional devolved administration and more the seat of a national 'Scottish Government', or at least that of an independent nation-in-waiting. As Gordon Wilson observed, Salmond managed to achieve UK and international prominence in a way his counterparts in Wales and Northern Ireland could only dream of. 'For some watching from abroad,' wrote Wilson, 'he seemed to be Prime Minister of an independent country.'[28]

This would prove a crucial element in the growth of SNP hegemony during Salmond's time as First Minister, although it was very much government in his own image, primarily concerned with politics rather than governance. Indeed as someone said of the SNP in office, they 'don't believe they're a government. They are a campaign',[29] and that mindset came right from the top. This also manifested itself in a centralist instinct unusual for a party that had long prided itself on a decentralist agenda: hitherto regional police and fire services were reconstituted along 'national' lines, colleges consolidated and councils robbed even of the autonomy to set local taxation.

Driving it all was Salmond's obsession with keeping on top of the media agenda, another habit he found difficult to shed from his long years as an opposition politician. As the former Justice Secretary Kenny MacAskill later revealed, even his government's stance on whether or not to grant prisoners the right to vote in the referendum was contrived to avoid negative headlines in the *Daily Mail* rather than on any legal, ethical or principled basis, while the Scottish Government's record on numerous fronts might have been 'competent' (the main reason he won in 2011), but nowhere near as transformative as Salmond liked to claim.[30] Overall he emerged as a Scottish version of Bill Clinton, considered by himself and others as a 'progressive' force but without the record to match; popular and populist, and blessed with a Teflon coating that disguised his policy triangulation and more divisive qualities.

And Salmond could certainly be divisive. Expelled from the SNP in the early 1980s, even several years into his first term as leader it took many colleagues and activists a long time to regard him with affection as well as respect. Only after 2004, judged James Mitchell, would the party 'put its trust' in his leadership 'to an extent it had never done during his first term as party leader'.[31] As many would conclude later on, Salmond could either win people over to his cause or repel them.

Part of the problem was a personality that was central to his political style. The biographer Philip Short identified a characteristic of 'uncommon leaders everywhere' as being a natural authority rooted in an 'inner solitude', and like Francois Mitterrand there was a part of Salmond's being that was forever 'locked, inaccessible to others'.[32] Beyond his wife Moira (seventeen years his senior) he had colleagues rather than friends, a court rather than an intimate circle. To the journalist Chris Deerin Salmond was 'an extraordinary, gifted and charismatic man', although he sometimes gave 'the impression that an alien is wearing his skin as a suit'.[33]

From his time at St Andrews University Salmond had channelled most of his considerable energy into frenetic political activity, planning and campaigning rather than philosophising and considered thought, and he cajoled others into doing the same. As First Minister he expected his staff's hours and productivity to match his, so much so that ministers and aides were known to complain privately that lacking other priorities (i.e. children), his expectations often did not reflect the reality of modern life.

But it was a very specific sort of work; Salmond's authoritarian, micro-managing leadership style did not, for example, encourage creative policy thinking. 'Having become such a totemic figure,' posited one former adviser after his resignation in 2014, 'he'd almost withdrawn other people's ability to do things for themselves.'[34] Rather Salmond expected diligent implementation of *his* agenda, a dynamic that certainly produced some very close working relationships. Certain advisers, such as Kevin Pringle and Geoff Aberdein, became almost like surrogate sons, and they remained in his employ – in Pringle's case over the course of two decades – despite gruelling schedules and frequent rows, for the worst kept secret at Holyrood was the First Minster's volcanic temper. Former aides flinched at the memory of particular dressings down, and as a result very few were brave enough to tell him things they knew he did not want to hear. 'He will blaze at you for two minutes if you have done something wrong,' observed Stephen Noon in 1999, 'but then it's forgotten.'[35]

At the same time Salmond could be charming, indulging in random acts of generosity and displaying great sensitivity to the personal difficulties of those who worked so hard for him, a sort of one-man good cop/bad cop routine that induced extreme loyalty among his circle of advisers. Privately, aides would admit to frustrations about the First Minster's tardiness (he was habitually late), cancelling appointments at the last minute and often damaging habit of straying off the script. Efforts to keep his worst traits in check – chuckling, for example, at his own jokes – sometimes worked, and sometimes did not.

Salmond tended to admire larger-than-life characters, dominant personalities who made the political weather, thus his qualified praise for Vladimir Putin and UKIP leader Nigel Farage. Salmond also loved depicting himself as somehow an anti-establishment politician, which given he had spent seven years living in Bute House stretched credulity. He revelled in a somewhat contrived 'man of the people' persona while staying at luxury hotels and travelling around the country in helicopters, private jets and chauffeur-driven cars.

Often he contradicted himself, but then Salmond contained multitudes, both confident ('to do what I'm trying to do', he observed in 1992, 'you need a good conceit of yourself'[36]) and also oddly insecure (he would spend a lot of time in 2014-15 reminding interviewers how popular he had been as First Minister); he both craved media attention and resented its assessments. Salmond's political persona mixed pugnaciousness with jocularity, combining, as the journalist Andrew Marr put it, 'challenging eye contact with a faintly mocking smile',[37] or what the Liberal politician Charles Kennedy described in 1990 as 'that piercing stare which always seems about to go one of two ways – towards coldness or laughter'.[38]

'Like all populists with a passionate cause,' was Matthew Parris's perceptive assessment, 'he combines an open countenance with an instinct for the low blow.'[39] It was a persona that many party activists and voters clearly found attractive. By 2007 he had established extraordinary authority over the SNP, an almost demagogic ability to convince activists that he knew what was best, while an increasing proportion of the electorate seemed convinced that Salmond was *on their side*, apparently determined to improve their lot in the face of Labour and Conservative governments led by people who could never match him in terms of Scottishness or down-to-earth punter appeal. It was more, remarked one adviser, 'than knowing what people want to hear', Salmond had 'an instinct for knowing what people want him to be, how they want him to fit in'.[40] Voters sensed – rightly or wrongly – that he was 'standing up' for them as well as well as for Scotland.

'What he likes to stress,' observed the journalist Ian Jack, 'is his kinship with ordinary Scotland – a kind of Scottish everyman, affable, plain-speaking, dry-witted, dipping naturally into the idiom of lowland Scotland, "wiz" for "was", "fir" for "for", whenever it suits.'[41] And once voters had decided to give Salmond the benefit of the doubt, they seemed prepared to tolerate inconsistencies and personal foibles that they found intolerable in others. Indeed, there was a demonstrable change in Salmond's behaviour following the 2011 Holyrood election at which, against the odds, the SNP won an overall majority. Frequently it was lack of discipline (ironic considering his call for 'self-discipline throughout the party and particularly among our prominent members'[42] on first becoming leader), saying and doing things that embarrassed his party, providing his opponents with lines of attack and journalists with 'good' (in other words bad) copy. And despite lofty rhetoric about campaigning positively, divide-and-rule increasingly became a hallmark of Salmond in his second term: anyone not perceived as a threat was treated with charm and thoughtfulness, but for those who fell outside that category condescension, pettiness and downright rudeness was often the order of the day.

Some called Salmond a bully, and he certainly demonstrated such tendencies towards certain opponents and the media, although Nicola Sturgeon rejected that as 'complete and utter nonsense'. 'Yes, he's a hard taskmaster but somebody in his position should be: anybody who works for the First Minister of Scotland shouldn't expect an easy ride.'[43] Salmond himself reflected that there was 'no purpose in politics in offending someone, at least unnecessarily',[44] although between 2011 and 2014 he seemed to find it increasingly necessary. The contrast with his four years at the head of a minority government – during which he was more ecumenical through sheer necessity – was obvious, although many of his weaknesses only became clear in light of Nicola Sturgeon's subsequent success. While he had often tried to bulldoze his way to independence, his successor attempted to kill Unionism with charm, and initial indications suggested hers was the more effective approach.

'One thing about Alex', observed a close colleague, 'is he always needs an enemy to fight.'[45] And emboldened by his historic win in 2011, Salmond picked a fight with the UK Supreme Court, the UK government (more than usual), think tanks, economists and, latterly, the 'metropolitan' media, chiefly the BBC in London. Although most of these battles were fuelled by phony outrage at both perceived misdeamours and real, his broader aim was to neutralise opposition by subtly conflating the SNP (or independence movement) with Scotland, framing the debate as 'Team Scotland' versus the 'Westminster system', thus meaning criticism of the former could also be presented as an attack on the latter. Although Salmond had lobbied for a 'second' referendum question, in fact the binary nature of a yes/no plebiscite suited him down to the ground.

The experience of the 1999 Scottish Parliament election had been key: then Salmond had watched helplessly as his battle cries were filtered via the 'mainstream media', thus in 2014 he sought to delegitimise both Unionist attacks ('scaremongering') and the media outlets likely to take them seriously ('bias'). What he had tried to do with the *Scotland's Voice* 'newspaper' during the 1999 campaign now took flight thanks to social media and grassroots campaigning, acutely aware that the influence of what he would later call the 'old media' had been in decline for some time.

But Salmond's 'hope versus fear' referendum strategy also led the National Movement away from the 'big tent', consensus-building approach he had long championed. It suited his post-2011 temperament, gliding confidently over detail and inducing in many of his supporters a revivalist spirit that trumped inconvenient truths, but intimidated others and failed to engage – let alone convince – a majority of the practical and economic utility of independence. To an extent, however, Salmond had little choice but to appeal to the heart rather than the head because so many of his arguments simply did not stack up; thus playing the man rather than the ball typified his public interventions, accompanied by a cavalier attitude to facts or consistency, all faults echoed online, his forthright style having sent a signal to others – particularly on Twitter – that such an approach to public discourse was acceptable. For several years Salmond sanctioned strategy, tactics and timing that only appeared credible by virtue of a weak No campaign.

And while several positive aspects of Salmond's legacy gelled during the referendum (not least a formidable campaign and the rise of Nicola Sturgeon as a political star in her own right) so too did the more negative elements. For having undeniably created a political machine that could (and did) dominate the electoral scene in Edinburgh and London, when that machine was challenged as to what it stood for it was often found wanting, not least in intellectual terms. The *Scotland's Future* White Paper published in late 2013 neatly encapsulated Salmondism: a triumph of style over substance, debating points over detailed policy.

What made this even more puzzling was that Salmond had lacked neither time nor, after 2007, public funds to reflect more deeply on emerging political realities. His four-year sabbatical between 2000 and 2004 had been a case in point, billed as a period in which he would ruminate on the economics of independence, all he had to show for it were four lectures at Strathclyde University that effectively embraced the neoliberal orthodoxy of never-ending growth sustained by tax cuts. Similarly, between 2007 and 2014 his administrations were cautious and conservative, actively shunning a debate everyone knew had to he had about the nature of the state in the early 21st century. Finally, between 2012 and 2014 Salmond fought a referendum that combined the economic analysis of Joseph Stiglitz and Art Laffer, simultaneously embracing a left-wing analysis and an arguably outdated right-wing response.

In the process Salmond helped make the SNP into what he claimed to despise, a political party that – much like Tony Blair's New Labour – found itself guided more by political expediency and public opinion than points of principle or a radical policy agenda. And like Blair, Salmond modernised 'social democracy' beyond recognition, unconsciously emulating the 'Labourism' identified by the political theorist Tom Nairn, what the historian Ben Jackson characterised as 'a gradual pursuit of social reform bound by the conventional proprieties of parliamentarism', but without any acknowledgement that 'a Scottish Labourism in one country would have to reckon with the same headwinds now faced by Labour at a British level'.[46] Salmond (whose political hero, it is worth remembering, was Harold Wilson) was certainly conscious of what David Marquand called the 'progressive dilemma', the difficulty of mobilising the electorate behind a genuinely progressive policy agenda, but persistently deployed mythology and clever retail politics in order to evade difficult issues, prepared only to commission inquiries rather than recalibrate modern Scotland, and particularly resistant to altering its precarious balance of tax and spend.

So while Salmond's greatest legacy lay in redrawing the rules of the game in his own image, implicit in that achievement was a profound shift in Scottish political discourse. Although of course there did not exist a golden age of enlightened public debate, by the time he resigned as First Minister and SNP leader in November 2014 it was overwhelmingly characterised by displacement, externalised blame and the politics of assertion; an environment in which slick debating points trumped objective fact and self-interest could masquerade as 'progressive' altruism.

While endlessly extolling the virtues of the 'new politics', more ecumenical, more prepared to accept criticisms than the old, in fact Salmond gave a new lease of life to uncompromising tribalism, an alpha male mantra of 'never explain, never apologise'. The SNP simultaneously constructed a big tent while shunning alternative analyses and anyone intent on pursuing a different path. Only if other visions of Scotland (on the left or right) conceded the necessity of independence were they taken seriously, thus the Marmite politician bequeathed a Marmite nation.

In doing so, paradoxically, Salmond actually helped increase political engagement (perhaps the referendum did that, but then without him there would have been no referendum). No matter how great the intellectual contortions, something about him induced increasing numbers of Scots to give him the benefit of the doubt, attracted by his opposition to austerity, Thatcherism and Euroscepticism and willing to believe he would come up with something better, what James Mitchell called a 'debilitating oppositional grievance culture masquerading as radicalism'.[47] And while frequently revealing himself to be every bit as cynical and opportunist as those he demonised, Salmond managed to convince voters that somehow he was *different*, that he would deliver where lesser mortals invariably failed.

In what was widely accepted as the age of apathy, that was no mean feat. Nevertheless, when it came to Salmond, Enoch Powell's aphorism certainly held: 'All political lives, unless they are cut off in midstream at a happy juncture, end in failure, because that is the nature of politics and of human affairs.'[48] For having spent a political lifetime building support for himself, the SNP and, eventually, independence, arguably Salmond ended up squandering the remarkable opportunity he had worked so hard to create. Analysis showed that the majority No vote had little to do with 'the Vow' (as he chose to believe) and rather more to do with economics, thus the Yes proposition foundering upon a 'currency union', the risk of capital flight and broader economic uncertainty represented a weakness inseparable from Salmond himself. Thus Salmond was both the *sine qua non* of the independence referendum, but also its Achilles heel.

In the second edition of this biography I quoted the French historian Albert Sorel's division of politicians into two groups, those 'who seek to change the world to suit their ideas' and those 'who seek to modify their actions to suit the world'.[49] In late 2011 it seemed to me that Salmond belonged in the latter category, but on reflection (and as outlined above) he actually straddled both. Throughout his career he had rarely flinched from political fate and, having put independence to the touch on 18 September 2014, appropriately enough the veteran poet–warrior appeared to have it both ways, defeated in battle but his army poised for future victory; to paraphrase Montrose, winning *and* losing it all.

# Notes

PREFACE TO THE THIRD EDITION

1   Crick, *George Orwell*, 31.
2   Campbell, *Edward Heath*, xi.


CHAPTER 1 'A REAL BLACK BITCH'

1   *Herald*, 29 December 1994.
2   *Scotland on Sunday*, 15 August 2004.
3   The minister responsible was the Rev Dr David Steel, who served at St Michael's 1957–76. His son, also David, later became leader of the Liberal Party.
4   *Independent on Sunday*, 8 February 1992.
5   *Linlithgowshire Journal and Gazette*, 26 May 1972.
6   Christopher Harvie, *Broonland*, 38.
7   Interview with Peter Brunskill, 1 February 2010.
8   *Scottish Sunday Express*, 20 November 2011.
9   This was later corrected to Robert Fyfe Findlay Salmond, the two middle names coming from the minister who christened him.
10  http://www.scotland.gov.uk/News/This-Week/Speeches/First-Minister/genassembly09
11  John MacLeod to the author, 19 October 2009.
12  William Barclay (1907–78) was a minister, author and television presenter.
13  *Life and Work*, June 2008.
14  *Sunday Times*, 25 July 2009.
15  Tom Devine, *Being Scottish*, 243.
16  *The Salmond Years* (STV), 18 February 2001.
17  Devine, 243–44.
18  *Scottish Daily Mail*, 31 May 2008.
19  *Herald*, 6 September 1995.
20  *Scottish Daily Mail*, 31 May 2008.

21  *Scotland on Sunday*, 28 February 1999.
22  *Scotsman*, 30 October 1996.
23  *Edinburgh Evening News*, 17 July 2000.
24  Perry, *Scotland the Brave*.
25  *Times Educational Supplement Scotland*, 25 February 2011.
26  Perry, *Scotland the Brave*.
27  *Linlithgowshire Journal and Gazette*, 5 July 1929.
28  *Linlithgowshire Journal and Gazette* 4 April 1941.
29  'Brother' William Milne was a past master of Lodge Ancient Brazen No 17, Linlithgow.
30  *Linlithgowshire Journal and Gazette*, 8 November 1935.
31  *West Lothian Courier*, 4 April 1941.
32  *Linlithgowshire Journal and Gazette*, 4 April 1941.
33  The author is indebted to Tom Gordon for providing these hitherto unpublished quotes, obtained for the *Sunday Times* in the summer of 2008.
34  Private information.
35  *Sunday Times (Scotland)*, 10 October 2010.
36  Robert Salmond, Alex's brother, was active in the SNP while at Aberdeen University in the late 1980s.
37  *Scottish Sunday Express*, 30 April 2011.
38  *Guardian*, 31 January 2009.
39  *Sunday Post*, 4 November 1990.
40  *The Salmond Years* (STV), 18 February 2001.
41  *Scottish Daily Mail*, 31 May 2008.
42  *Herald*, 3 June 1993.
43  *Scotsman*, 8 February 2003.
44  *Racing Post*, 30 July 2000.
45  *Scotland on Sunday*, 25 April 1999.
46  Interview with Mary Salmond, 2 February 2001 (STV B66161).
47  Peter Brunskill to the author, 7 June 2010.
48  Interview with Alex Salmond MSP, February 2008 (courtesy of Katherine Haddon).
49  *Independent*, 10 August 2008.
50  *Sunday Post*, 4 November 1990.
51  *Herald*, 21 July 1994.
52  Peter Lynch, *SNP*, 103–04.
53  Private information.
54  Interview with Mary Salmond.
55  *Sunday Times*, 29 March 2009.
56  Interview with Mary Salmond.
57  *Linlithgowshire Journal and Gazette*, 8 December 1967.
58  *Sunday Times*, 29 March 2009.
59  *Planet* 204, November 2011.
60  Interview with Gordon Currie, 8 February 2010.

61   *The One Show* (BBC1), August 2010.
62   *Scotsman*, 5 April 2003.
63   *Edinburgh Evening News*, 10 April 1997.

CHAPTER 2 'ACT OF REBELLION'

1    Douglas Young, *Scotland*, 262–63.
2    *The Student*, 13 January 2009.
3    Interview with Pam Chesters, 5 March 2010.
4    *Daily Record*, 16 October 2006.
5    *Racing Post*, 30 July 2000.
6    Quintin Oliver to the author, 17 June 2015.
7    *Guardian*, 31 January 2009.
8    Peter Jones to the author, 22 September 2009.
9    Interview with Charlie Woods, 17 November 2009.
10   Paul Henderson Scott, *A Twentieth Century Life*, 288.
11   Brian Taylor, *The Scottish Parliament*, 163.
12   *Aien*, 1 December 1976.
13   Despite several attempts by journalists (and this biographer) to locate
     Debbie Horton, it is not clear what happened to her after graduating from
     St Andrews.
14   *Sunday Herald*, 4 February 2007.
15   *Scottish Daily Mail*, 31 May 2008.
16   Interview with Peter Brunskill, 1 February 2010.
17   Christina Dykes to the author, 5 June 2015.
18   *Edinburgh Evening News*, 31 May 2007.
19   Interview with Peter Brunskill.
20   Christina Dykes to the author, 5 June 2015.
21   Interview with Peter Brunskill.
22   Interview with Robert Salmond, 2 February 2001 (STV B66161).
23   http://www.snp.org/node/16799
24   Quintin Oliver to the author.
25   *St Andrews Citizen*, 10 May 1975.
26   Interview with Mark Lazarowicz, 23 September 2009.
27   *Linlithgowshire Journal and Gazette*, 27 August 1976.
28   Interview with Peter Brunskill.
29   *Planet* 204, November 2011.
30   Interview with Peter Brunskill.
31   Roth, *Parliamentary Profiles S-Z*, 1906.
32   Webb, *The Growth of Nationalism in Scotland*, 109.
33   Interview with Mark Lazarowicz.
34   *Holyrood*, 28 September 2009.
35   *Guardian*, 20 August 1990.
36   *Daily Record*, 28 April 1997.

37   *Herald*, 13 December 1995.
38   Interview with Peter Brunskill.
39   When students voted in November 1977, however, St Andrews opted to remain neutral, affiliating to neither the NUS nor the Scottish Union of Students.
40   Interview with Stewart Stevenson MSP, 29 June 2010.
41   *Free Student Press*, autumn 1975.
42   *Free Student Press*, summer 1976.
43   *St Andrews Citizen*, 24 September 1977.
44   *Free Student Press*, winter 1977.
45   Interview with Peter Brunskill.
46   Interview with Jamie Stone MSP, 12 January 2010.
47   Alistair Hicks to the author, 13 January 2010.
48   Interview with Cllr Tim McKay, 5 January 2010.
49   *Daily Record*, 10 February 2001.
50   Interview with Cllr Tim McKay.
51   Interview with Dave Smith, 26 January 2010.
52   Des Swayne to the author, 21 October 2009.
53   Interview with Peter Brunskill.
54   Interview with Cllr Tim McKay.
55   *Scotsman*, 19 August 2010.
56   *Aien*, 9 February 1977.
57   *The Student* 13 January 2009.
58   Interview with Cllr Tim McKay.
59   *Aien*, 15 February 1978.
60   Flyer courtesy of Cllr Tim McKay.
61   *Aien*, 1 March 1978. Bainbridge received 517 votes, Salmond 506 and Hogg 288.
62   *University of Aberdeen Magazine*, December 2008.
63   Peter Bainbridge to the author, 8 March 2010.
64   Peter Bainbridge to the author, 9 March 2010.
65   *Sunday Mail*, 1 May 2011.
66   Interview with Peter Brunskill.
67   Peter Bainbridge to the author, 9 March 2010.
68   *Aien*, 15 February 1978.
69   http://www.nls.uk/events/donald_dewar_lectures/2008_salmond/transcript.html
70   *St Andrews Citizen*, 18 February 1978.
71   http://www.st-andrews.ac.uk/news/archive/2007/Title,17906,en.html

CHAPTER 3 'WEST LOTHIAN LEFT'

1    Interview with Brian Taylor, 22 September 2009.
2    Interview with Peter Brunskill, 1 February 2010.

3  *Linlithgowshire Journal and Gazette*, 10 November 1978.
4  *Herald*, 30 July 1997.
5  Interview with David Dalgetty, 25 September 2009.
6  *Linlithgowshire Gazette*, 19 June 1981.
7  Private information.
8  *Scots Independent*, November 1978.
9  *Linlithgowshire Gazette*, 27 October 1978.
10  *Linlithgowshire Gazette*, 10 November 1978.
11  *Guardian*, 25 September 1978.
12  *Linlithgowshire Gazette*, 27 October 1978.
13  *Linlithgowshire Gazette*, 26 January 1979.
14  Ascherson, *Stone Voices*, 103. The SLP was Jim Sillars' short-lived Scottish Labour Party.
15  *The Week In Politics* (Grampian TV), 5 September 2002.
16  *Linlithgowshire Journal and Gazette*, 6 April 1979.
17  Interview with Tam Dalyell, 2 July 2010.
18  *Linlithgowshire Gazette*, 6 April 1979.
19  *Linlithgowshire Gazette*, 29 June 1979.
20  Interview with Stewart Stevenson MSP, 29 June 2010.
21  *Herald*, 20 March 1996.
22  *Scotland on Sunday*, 3 September 2000.
23  *Herald*, 19 August 1993.
24  Sir Robert McIntyre Papers Acc 10090/170.
25  *Cencrastus*, summer 1985.
26  Gavin Kennedy Papers Acc 11565/23.
27  *Scotsman*, 24 June 1982.
28  *The Salmond Years* (STV), 18 February 2001.
29  Interview with Rob Gibson MSP, 3 February 2009.
30  Gavin Kennedy Papers Acc 11565/23.
31  *Linlithgowshire Gazette*, 9 May 1980.
32  *Linlithgowshire Gazette*, 6 June 1980.
33  *Linlithgowshire Gazette*, 31 October 1980.
34  *Linlithgowshire Gazette* 21 December 1979.
35  Maxwell, *The Case for Left-Wing Nationalism*, 22.
36  *Glasgow Herald*, 27 January 1982.
37  Salmond, *The Scottish Industrial Resistance*, 2-4.
38  *The Salmond Years* (STV).
39  *Linlithgowshire Gazette*, 6 June 1980.
40  *The Salmond Years* (STV).
41  STV North tape L0042.
42  Salmond, 2.
43  Gordon Wilson Papers Acc 13099/36.
44  *Linlithgowshire Gazette*, 28 November 1980.
45  Gordon Wilson Papers Acc 13099/9.

46   *Linlithgowshire Gazette*, 19 June 1981.
47   Interview with Iain More, 23 April 2010.
48   Gordon Wilson Papers Acc 13099/23.
49   *Sunday Standard*, 8 August 1982.
50   Gavin Kennedy Papers Acc 11565/23.
51   *Independent on Sunday*, 8 February 1992.
52   *Linlithgowshire Gazette*, 30 October 1981.
53   Gavin Kennedy Papers Acc 11565/23.
54   SNP Papers Acc 11987/43.
55   *Scotsman*, 4 June 1982.
56   Kemp, *The Hollow Drum*, 169.
57   Salmond, 3.
58   *Scotsman*, 5 June 1982.
59   *79 Group News*, August 1982.
60   *The Salmond Years* (STV).
61   *Scotsman*, 24 June 1982.
62   *Scotsman*, 30 June 1982.
63   Gordon Wilson Papers Acc 13099/27.
64   *Scotsman*, 27 September 1982.
65   *Total Politics*, September 2008.
66   *Scotsman*, 16 September 1990.
67   *The Salmond Years* (STV).
68   *The Cause* (BBC Radio Scotland), 15 October 2012.
69   Interview with Stephen Maxwell, 2 March 2010.

CHAPTER 4 'THE PRAGMATIC LEFT'

1    *The Salmond Years* (STV), 18 February 2001.
2    Marr, *The Battle for Scotland*, 191.
3    Interview with Stephen Maxwell, 2 March 2010.
4    *Radical Scotland*, June/July 1983.
5    Interview with Stewart Stevenson MSP, 29 June 2010.
6    *Scotland on Sunday*, 17 September 2000.
7    Interview with Jonathan Mitchell, QC, 3 November 2009.
8    Gordon Wilson Papers Acc 13099/10.
9    Wilson, *SNP: The Turbulent Years*, 215-16.
10   Interview with Gordon Wilson, 16 July 2010.
11   *The Cause* (BBC Radio Scotland), 15 October 2012.
12   Lynch, *SNP*, 174.
13   Stephen Maxwell Papers.
14   *Herald*, 15 May 1996.
15   http://www.scotland.gov.uk/News/This-Week/Speeches/First-Minister/
     Edinburghlecture
16   Salmond, *The Royal Bank in Glasgow*, 11.

17  Interview with Michael Fry, 18 March 2010.
18  *Glasgow Herald*, 21 September 1987.
19  *New Left Review*, May/June 1968.
20  Interview with Michael Fry.
21  Interview with Peter Clarke, 9 February 2010.
22  *Newsline*, April 1984.
23  Interview with Grant Baird, 22 January 2010.
24  *Newsline*, April 1984.
25  Interview with Glynne Baird, 22 January 2010.
26  Interview with Peter Brunskill, 1 February 2010.
27  This was a 'third format' that had been introduced to the European market in 1979. Although considered technically superior to its Betamax and VHS rivals, it was obsolete by 1985.
28  *The Times*, 21 September 1982.
29  Wilson, 223.
30  SNP Papers Acc 11987/79.
31  Wilson, 226.
32  *Political Quarterly* 59 4 (1988).
33  SNP Papers Acc 11987/46.
34  *Scotsman*, 21 August 1984.
35  *Toronto Star*, 31 August 1986.
36  Sillars, *The Case for Optimism*, 145–50.
37  *Guardian*, 25 February 1985.
38  *Glasgow Herald*, 22 February 1985.
39  Interview with Isobel Lindsay, 23 February 2010.
40  Wilson, 227.
41  *Scots Independent*, June 1985.
42  *Radical Scotland*, April/May 1986.
43  *Scots Independent*, June 1985.
44  SNP Papers Acc 11987/47.
45  Wilson, 180.
46  SNP Papers Acc 11987/47.
47  Gordon Wilson Papers Acc 13099/12.
48  *Glasgow Herald*, 22 August 1986.
49  SNP Papers Acc 11987/48.
50  *Scots Independent*, September 1986.
51  *Scots Independent*, November 1986.
52  SNP Papers Acc 11987/49.
53  *Scotsman*, 8 March 1987.
54  *Scotsman*, 20 May 1987.
55  *The Salmond Years* (STV).
56  *Press and Journal*, 23 January 1985.
57  *Press and Journal*, 30 January 1985.
58  *Glasgow Herald*, 22 February 1985.

59  *Scotland on Sunday*, 3 September 2000.
60  *Glasgow Herald*, 21 September 1987.
61  *Scotland on Sunday*, 3 September 2000.
62  *Scotsman*, 18 May 1987.
63  *Scotsman*, 4 June 1987.
64  John MacLeod to the author, 23 October 2009.
65  *Glasgow Herald*, 30 May 1987.
66  Interview with Robert and Mary Salmond, 2 February 2001 (STV B66161).
67  *Scotland on Sunday*, 3 September 2000.
68  SNP Papers Acc 11987/49.
69  *Alex Salmond – A Rebel's Journey* (BBC Scotland), 19 November 2014.


CHAPTER 5 'THE INFANT ROBESPIERRE'

1   *Scotland on Sunday*, 10 September 2000.
2   Hansard 129 c1008.
3   *Glasgow Herald*, 16 March 1988.
4   *Banffshire Journal*, 23 March 2010.
5   *Scotland on Sunday*, 10 September 2000.
6   *Glasgow Herald & Scotsman*, 16 March 1988.
7   *Independent*, 20 September 1998.
8   *Banffshire Journal*, 23 March 2010.
9   *Scotland on Sunday*, 10 September 2000.
10  Lawson, *The View From No. 11*, 816.
11  *Glasgow Herald*, 16 March 1988.
12  *Scotsman*, 16 March 1988.
13  *Independent on Sunday*, 8 February 1992.
14  *Scotsman*, 17 March 1988.
15  *Scots Independent*, April 1988.
16  *Scotsman*, 23 March 1988.
17  *Alex Salmond – A Rebel's Journey* (BBC Scotland), 19 November 2014.
18  Alex Salmond to Bernard Ponsonby, January 2001 (author's collection).
19  *Scotland on Sunday*, 10 September 2000.
20  *Herald*, 7 April 1994.
21  Mitchell, *Strategies for Self-Government*, 222.
22  Hansard *118 cc321-25*.
23  Gordon Wilson Papers Acc 13099/76.
24  *Glasgow Herald*, 21 September 1987.
25  *Scotsman*, 16 November 1987.
26  Wilson, *SNP: The Turbulent Years*, 235.
27  *Glasgow Herald*, 25 September 1987.
28  *Glasgow Herald* 24 September 1987.
29  Interview with Mike Russell MSP, 15 January 2001 (STV B111940).
30  *Scotsman*, 25 September 1987.

31   *Scotsman*, 2 September 1987.
32   Mitchell, 185.
33   Sillars, *The Case for Optimism*, 186-190.
34   Hansard 136 c1112.
35   *Radical Scotland*, August/September 1988.
36   *Scotsman*, 13 June 1989.
37   SNP Papers Acc 11987/50.
38   *Scotsman*, 22 April 1988.
39   *Scotsman*, 29 April 1988.
40   *The Salmond Years* (STV), 18 February 2001.
41   Brown, *Scottish Government Yearbook 1991*, 125.
42   Hansard 125 c159.
43   Hansard 136 cc1087-94.
44   Gordon Wilson Papers Acc 13099/40.
45   *Scotsman*, 12 November 1988.
46   *Scotsman* 15 November 1988.
47   SNP Papers Acc 11987/50.
48   *Observer*, 24 September 1989.
49   *Scotsman*, 30 January 1989.
50   Kemp, *The Hollow Drum*, 162.
51   SNP Papers Acc 11987/49.
52   Kemp, 162.
53   Taylor, *The Scottish Parliament*, 41.
54   Gordon Wilson Papers Acc 13099/57.
55   *The Salmond Years* (STV).
56   Kemp, 162.
57   *Observer*, 5 February 1989.
58   *Glasgow Herald*, 6 March 1989.
59   Brown, *Scottish Government Yearbook 1990*, 29.
60   *The Salmond Years* (STV).
61   Interview with Isobel Lindsay, 23 February 2010.
62   *Scotsman*, 6 March 1989.
63   *Scotsman*, 17 March 1989.
64   *Scotsman*, 23 September 1989.
65   *Observer*, 18 June 1989.
66   SNP Papers Acc 11987/50.
67   Gordon Wilson Papers Acc 13099/51.
68   *Scotsman*, 25 February 1989.
69   *Observer*, 28 May 1989.
70   *Scotsman*, 20 May 1989.
71   *Scots Independent*, October 1989.
72   *Scotsman*, 27 July 1989.
73   Gordon Wilson Papers Acc 13099/14.
74   Lynch, *SNP*, 192-93

75   Wilson, 246.
76   Interview with Jim Sillars, 17 September 2009.
77   Private information.
78   Interview with Margo MacDonald MSP, 28 June 2010.
79   *The Salmond Years* (STV).
80   Wilson, 246.
81   *Scotland on Sunday*, 23 September 1990.
82   *Observer*, 20 May 1990.
83   *Scotland on Sunday*, 23 September 1990.
84   Lynch, 193.
85   *Observer*, 10 June 1990.
86   *Scotland on Sunday*, 23 September 1990.
87   *Scotsman*, 16 September 1990.
88   *Guardian*, 12 July 1990.
89   *Scotsman*, 15 August 1990.
90   *Scotland on Sunday*, 23 September 1990.
91   Ewing, *Stop the World*, 244.
92   Two of whom were Peter Murrell, then Salmond's constituency assistant,
     and Stuart Pratt, Salmond's agent and a senior SNP councillor in Banff and
     Buchan.
93   *Scotsman*, 9 August 1990.
94   *Scotsman*, 28 August 1990.
95   *Alex Salmond – A Rebel's Journey* (BBC Scotland).
96   *Scotsman*, 23 September 1990.
97   *Scotsman*, 30 August 1990.
98   *Scotsman*, 7 August 1990.
99   *Radical Scotland*, August/September 1990.
100  *Scotland on Sunday*, 23 September 1990.
101  *Scotsman*, 15 August 1990.
102  *Scotland on Sunday*, 23 September 1990.
103  *Scotsman*, 22 September 1990.
104  *Scotsman*, 19 September 1990.
105  *Scotsman*, 22 September 1990.
106  *Scotsman*, 23 September 1990.
107  *Scotsman*, 24 September 1990.
108  *Scotsman*, 23 September 1990.
109  Churchill, *Second World War I*, 526–27.

Chapter 6 'Free by '93'

1   Mitchell, *Strategies for Self-Government*, 245.
2   *Scotsman*, 23 September 1990.
3   *Sunday Post*, 4 November 1990.
4   *Scotsman*, 23 September 1990.

5   Interview with Chris McLean, 22 March 2010.
6   Private information.
7   Interview with John Swinney MSP, 19 January 2001 (STV B102765).
8   *Scotsman*, 23 September 1990.
9   Gallagher, *Nationalism in the Nineties*, 1 & 28.
10  *The Times*, 22 November 1990.
11  *Scotsman*, 20 May 1989.
12  Henderson Scott, *A Twentieth-Century Life*, 298.
13  *Sunday Post,* 4 November 1990.
14  *Walden Interviews Alex Salmond* (LWT), 15 March 1992. These remarks were made off-air.
15  *Sunday Post*, 4 November 1990.
16  Kenny Farquharson to the author, 15 July 2010.
17  *Sunday Post*, 4 November 1990.
18  *The Times*, 24 September 1990.
19  *Scotsman*, 25 February 1991.
20  Wilson, *The Battle for Independence*, 16.
21  *Scotsman*, 25 February 1991.
22  *Scotsman*, 24 March 1991.
23  Linklater, *Anatomy of Scotland*, 389.
24  *Scotsman*, 12 September 1991.
25  *Sunday Herald*, 14 June 2009.
26  *Scotsman*, 17 September 1991.
27  *Scotsman*, 30 August 1991.
28  *Independent on Sunday*, 8 February 1992.
29  *Scotsman*, 17 September 1991.
30  *Scotsman*, 20 September 1991.
31  *Scotland on Sunday*, 23 July 2000.
32  *Scotsman*, 19 September 1991.
33  *The Salmond Years* (STV), 18 February 2001.
34  *Scotland on Sunday*, 10 September 2000.
35  *The Salmond Years* (STV).
36  *Scotland on Sunday*, 10 September 2000.
37  *Scotsman*, 19 September 1991.
38  *Scotland on Sunday*, 22 September 1991.
39  *Scotsman*, 23 September 1991.
40  *Guardian*, 2 December 1991.
41  *Independent on Sunday*, 8 February 1992.
42  *Guardian*, 2 December 1991.
43  *Scotsman*, 1 August 1991.
44  *Scotland: A Time to Choose* (BBC Scotland), 1992.
45  *Scots Independent*, August 2000.
46  *Scotland on Sunday*, 10 September 2000.
47  *Scottish Sun*, 23 January 1992.

48  *Edinburgh Evening News*, 29 January 1992.
49  *Scotland on Sunday*, 10 September 2000.
50  *Scotland on* Sunday, 1 March 1992.
51  *Edinburgh Evening News*, 6 March 1992.
52  *Walden Interviews Alex Salmond* (LWT).
53  *Reporting Scotland* (BBC Scotland), April 1992.
54  *The Salmond Years* (STV).
55  Macdonald, *Unionist Scotland 1800-1997*, 128.
56  Harvie, *Scotland & Nationalism*, 205.
57  *Scotland on Sunday*, 10 September 2000.


CHAPTER 7 THE FUTURE OF NATIONALISM

1   *Scotland on Sunday*, 10 September 2000.
2   Lynch, *SNP*, 194.
3   *Scotland on Sunday*, 10 September 2000.
4   Interview with Mike Russell MSP, 15 January 2001 (STV B111940).
5   *Scotland on Sunday*, 3 September 2000.
6   *Herald*, 8 June 1992.
7   *Scotsman*, 8 June 1992.
8   Marr, *The Battle for Scotland*, 218.
9   *Scottish Affairs* 1, autumn 1992.
10  Private information.
11  *Scotland on Sunday*, 14 March 1993.
12  Interview with Jim Eadie, 13 February 2010.
13  *Herald*, 19 March 1993.
14  *Edinburgh Evening News*, 7 June 1993.
15  *Scotsman*, 18 August 1993. Author's italics.
16  *Scotland on Sunday*, 15 August 1993.
17  Salmond, *Horizons Without Bars*, 57-62.
18  Interview with Mike Russell MSP.
19  *Scotsman*, 21 September 1993.
20  *Scotland on Sunday*, 19 September 1993.
21  Salmond, *The Dream Shall Never Die*, 24.
22  *Herald*, 23 September 1993.
23  *Herald*, 25 September 1993.
24  *Scotsman*, 25 September 1993.
25  *Scotsman*, 26 September 1993.
26  *Herald*, 3 February 1994.
27  *Scotsman*, 5 February 1994.
28  *Herald*, 7 May 1994.
29  *Scottish Affairs* 8, summer 1994.
30  *Herald*, 27 September 1994.
31  *Herald*, 2 July 1994.

32 *Herald*, 1 July 1994.
33 *Herald*, 2 July 1994.
34 *The Times*, 18 March 2009.
35 *Scottish Affairs* 13, autumn 1995.
36 McGinty, *This Turbulent Priest*, 337-38.
37 *The Times*, 18 March 2009.
38 *Herald*, 6 October 1994.
39 SNP conference (BBC Scotland), October 1993.
40 *Herald*, 14 April 1994.
41 *Scotsman*, 21 September 1994.
42 *Herald*, 24 September 1994.
43 *Guardian*, 24 September 1994.
44 *Herald*, 26 September 1994.
45 Wilson, *The Battle for Independence*, 32.
46 *Herald*, 27 September 1994.
47 *New Statesman*, 10 March 1995.
48 Salmond was paid £127 per column, a modest rate for the mid-1990s.
49 *Scotland on Sunday*, 29 January 1995.
50 BBC Radio Scotland, 31 January 1995.
51 *Scotland on Sunday*, 12 February 1995.
52 Interview with Mike Russell MSP.
53 Ascherson, *Stone Voices*, 122.
54 Wilson, 33.
55 *Herald*, 11 March 1995.
56 *Herald*, 8 March 1995.
57 *Herald*, 17 May 1995.
58 *Herald*, 6 October 1994.
59 Sheridan, *A Time To Rage*, 175.
60 *Herald*, 16 March 1995.
61 *Guardian*, 7 April 1997.
62 *Herald*, 20 March 1996.
63 *Scotsman*, 29 September 1995.
64 *Edinburgh Evening News*, 23 August 1996.
65 Interview with Andrew Wilson, 29 January 2010.
66 Scottish Liberal Democrats, *Alex in Wonderland*, 2.
67 *Scotsman*, 27 June 1996.
68 *Toronto Star*, 8 September 1996.
69 *Herald*, 2 April 1997.
70 *Scotsman*, 28 September 1996.
71 *Scotsman*, 27 January 1997.
72 *Scotland on Sunday*, 12 January 1997.
73 *Herald*, 2 April 1997.
74 *Scotsman*, 3 April 1997.
75 *Herald*, 12 March 1997.

76   *Scotsman*, 16 April 1997.
77   *Independent*, 5 January 1997.
78   *Herald*, 7 April 1994.


CHAPTER 8 'THE SPIRIT OF '97'

1    *Scotland on Sunday*, 3 September 2000.
2    *Scotland on Sunday*, 10 September 2000.
3    *Scotsman*, 9 May 1997.
4    Brian Wilson to the author, 28 July 2010.
5    *The Salmond Years* (STV), 18 February 2001.
6    Hansard 294 c725.
7    Transcript of Alex Salmond's interview with *GQ* (FOI/14/00936).
8    *Daily Record*, 22 August 1997.
9    *Guardian*, 28 July 1997.
10   *Observer,* 3 August 1997.
11   *Independent*, 20 September 1998.
12   *Scotland on Sunday*, 23 July 2000.
13   Anonymous, *Donald Dewar*, 91–92.
14   *Edinburgh Evening* News, 3 September 1997.
15   *Scotland on Sunday*, 3 September 2000.
16   *Scots Independent*, August 2000.
17   *Scotsman*, 8 May 1999.
18   *Scotsman*, 5 November 2003.
19   *Sunday Herald*, 4 February 2007.
20   *Scotsman*, 26 September 1997.
21   *Herald*, 19 February 1998.
22   *Scotsman*, 16 March 1998.
23   *Daily Record*, 7 May 1998.
24   *Scotsman*, 2 May 1998.
25   *Scotsman*, 18 July 1998.
26   *Edinburgh Evening News*, 27 July 1998.
27   *Scotland on Sunday*, 12 April 1998.
28   *Scotsman*, 10 August 1998.
29   *Guardian*, 27 July 1998.
30   *Independent*, 20 September 1998.
31   *Scotsman*, 11 August 1998.
32   *Scotsman*, 21 September 1998.
33   'Poems, Prayers and Profits' for *Platform* (STV), 1997.
34   *Scotsman*, 10 August 1998.
35   *Independent*, 20 September 1998.
36   *Scotsman*, 23 September 1998.
37   *Scotland on Sunday*, 17 September 2000.
38   *Mirror*, 17 December 1998.

39   *Scotland on Sunday*, 22 April 2007.

40   *Mirror*, 4 September 1998.

41   *Independent*, 20 September 1998.

42   *Scotsman*, 24 September 1998.

43   *Scotsman*, 26 September 1998.

44   *Edinburgh Evening News*, 25 November 1998.

45   *Scotsman*, 27 November 1998.

46   *Daily Mail*, 1 December 1998.

47   *Mirror*, 17 December 1998.

48   Campbell, *The Blair Years*, 365.

49   Campbell, *Diaries II*, 687.

50   *Daily Record*, 18 February 1999.

51   Private information.

52   *Sunday Herald*, 21 February 1999.

53   *Daily Mail*, 26 February 1999.

54   Press Association, 26 February 1999.

55   Private information.

56   Interview with Andrew Wilson, 29 January 2010.

57   Private information.

58   *Scotsman*, 29 March 1999.

59   *Scotsman*, 30 March 1999.

60   Campbell, 372.

61   *Edinburgh Evening News,* 31 March 1999.

62   *Scotsman*, 31 March 1999.

63   Taylor, *Scotland's Parliament*, 161.

64   *The Salmond Years.*

65   Ritchie, *Scotland Reclaimed*, 68–70.

66   *Scotland on Sunday*, 17 September 2000.

67   Private information.

68   Wilson, *The Battle for Independence*, 52.

69   Taylor, 171.

70   *The Salmond Years.*

71   Taylor, 165-66.

72   *Scotsman*, 28 April 2007.

73   Ritchie, 89-90.

74   *Scotsman*, 16 April 1999.

75   *Sunday Mirror*, 18 April 1999.

76   *Guardian*, 22 April 1999.

77   Ritchie, 116.

78   *Scotsman*, 23 April 1999.

79   *Guardian*, 23 April 1999.

80   *Scotsman*, 24 April 1999.

81   *The Times*, 24 April 1999.

82   *Sunday Herald*, 25 April 1999.

83   Ritchie, 133–34.
84   The Scottish Conservatives memorably, if not particularly effectively, portrayed Salmond as a Teletubby 'living in Scot-la-la land' (*Scotsman*, 5 May 1999).
85   *Sunday Herald*, 4 February 2007.
86   *Scotsman*, 7 May 1999.
87   *Scotland on Sunday*, 9 May 1999.
88   *Scotsman*, 18 July 2000.
89   *Scotland on Sunday*, 9 May 1999.
90   Rawnsley, *Servants of the People*, 254.

CHAPTER 9 'DYNAMIC OPPOSITION'

1    *Edinburgh Evening News*, 7 May 1999.
2    Interview with Alex Salmond MSP, March 2009 (courtesy of Colin Mackay).
3    Scottish Parliament Official Report, 12 May 1999.
4    Watson, *Year Zero*, 14.
5    Scottish Parliament Official Report, 13 May 1999.
6    *Herald*, 27 May 1999.
7    *Daily Express*, 12 August 1999.
8    *Edinburgh Evening News*, 23 August 1999.
9    *Scotsman*, 2 September 1999.
10   Interview with Alex Salmond MSP, March 2009.
11   *Scotsman*, 20 September 1999.
12   http://news.bbc.co.uk/1/hi/uk_politics/456038.stm
13   *Scotland on Sunday*, 17 October 1999.
14   *Scotsman*, 16 November 1999.
15   Scottish Parliament Official Report, 2 July 1999.
16   McLeish, *Scotland First*, 218.
17   Scottish Parliament Official Report, 11 May 2000.
18   Watson, 34.
19   *Edinburgh Evening News*, 1 February 2000.
20   *Scottish Daily Mail*, 17 February 2000.
21   Interview with Lord Steel, 3 July 2012.
22   *Herald*, 19 August 1993.
23   *Sunday Herald*, 4 February 2007.
24   Bain, *Holyrood: The Inside Story*, 97.
25   *Scottish Daily Mail*, 17 February 2000.
26   *Mirror* 24 January 2000.
27   *Scotsman*, 9 March 2000.
28   *Holyrood* (BBC Scotland), 26 March 2000.
29   *Scotsman*, 27 March 2000.
30   Private information.
31   Wilson, *The Battle for Independence*, 64.

32   *Scotsman*, 14 July 2000.
33   http://companycheck.co.uk/company/SC203193
34   Wilson, 65.
35   *Scotsman*, 12 June 2000.
36   *Scotsman*, 14 June 2000.
37   *Scotsman*, 13 June 2000.
38   *Scotsman*, 14 June 2000.
39   *Edinburgh Evening News*, 15 June 2000.
40   Conversation with Ian Swanson, 23 June 2010.
41   *Sunday Times*, 18 June 2000.
42   *The Week In Politics* (Grampian TV), 9 January 2003.
43   *Scotland on Sunday*, 23 July 2000.
44   *Scotsman*, 18 July 2000.
45   Ewing, *Stop the World*, 305.
46   *The Salmond Years* (STV), 18 February 2001.
47   Private information.
48   *Scotland on Sunday*, 23 July 2000.
49   *Scotsman*, 18 July 2000.
50   *Alex Salmond – A Rebel's Journey* (BBC Scotland), 19 November 2014.
51   Interview with Alex Salmond MSP, March 2009.
52   *Scottish Sun*, 23 September 2000.
53   *Scotsman*, 18 July 2000.
54   *The Times*, 18 July 2000.
55   http://news.bbc.co.uk/1/hi/scotland/967258.stm
56   *Scottish Sun*, 18 July 2000.
57   *Sunday Herald*, 23 July 2000.
58   *Edinburgh Evening News*, 22 September 2000.
59   *Scotsman*, 22 September 2000.
60   *Mirror*, 22 September 2000.
61   *Edinburgh Evening News*, 22 September 2000.
62   *News of the World*, 24 September 2000.
63   *Press & Journal*, 23 September 2000.

CHAPTER 10 'THE KING OVER THE WATER'

1   Interview with Jim Eadie, 13 February 2010.
2   Interview with Lord Foulkes MSP, 4 February 2010.
3   *Scotland on Sunday*, 14 January 2001.
4   *Aberdeen Evening Express*, 15 January 2001.
5   *Scotsman*, 15 January 2001.
6   *Scotland on Sunday*, 20 May 2001.
7   *Scotsman*, 30 May 2001.
8   *Scotsman*, 21 May 2001.
9   *Sunday Herald*, 15 August 2004.

10   Mullin, *A View from the Foothills*, 369.
11   *Scotsman*, 25 September 2001.
12   *Scotsman*, 29 September 2001.
13   *Scotsman*, 9 November 2001.
14   Taylor, *Scotland's Parliament*, 174.
15   *Scotsman*, 21 May 2002.
16   *Scotsman*, 10 June 2002.
17   Wilson, *The Battle for Independence*, 101.
18   *Scotsman*, 26 September 2002.
19   *Scotsman*, 11 February 2003.
20   *Scotsman*, 25 February 2003.
21   *Scotsman*, 3 March 2003.
22   Erickson, *The Economics of Independence*.
23   *Edinburgh Evening News*, 6 May 2003.
24   *Desert Island Discs* (BBC Radio 4), 16 January 2011.
25   *Scotsman*, 16 August 2003.
26   *Scotsman*, 25 September 2003.
27   *Mirror*, 14 November 2003.
28   *Sunday Herald*, 16 November 2003.
29   Interview with Alex Salmond MSP, May 2007 (courtesy of Colin Mackay).
30   *Herald*, 16 July 2004.
31   *Scottish Daily Mail*, 25 August 2007.
32   Anonymous interview.
33   *Alex Salmond – A Rebel's Journey* (BBC Scotland), 19 November 2014.
34   *Scotsman*, 16 July 2004.
35   Private information.
36   Private information.
37   Interview, 13 January 2015.
38   *Scottish Daily Mail*, 19 July 2007.
39   Wilson, 103.
40   *Scotsman*, 17 July 2004.
41   http://news.bbc.co.uk/2/hi/uk_news/scotland/3895575.stm
42   *Scotsman*, 16 July 2004.
43   *Scotland on Sunday*, 18 July 2004.
44   *Scotsman*, 29 July 2004.
45   Press Association, 12 August 2004.
46   *Scotland on Sunday*, 15 August 2004.
47   *Sunday Herald*, 15 August 2004.
48   *Edinburgh Evening News*, 4 September 2004.

CHAPTER 11 SALMOND REDUX

1   *Scotsman*, 4 September 2004.
2   http://www.snp.org/node/10890

3    *Sunday Herald*, 5 September 2004.
4    Hansard 424 c591.
5    *Scotsman*, 25 September 2004.
6    *Sunday Herald*, 16 November 2003.
7    *Scotsman*, 26 August 2004.
8    *Scottish 500* (STV), 14 April 2005.
9    *Scotsman*, 11 March 2005.
10   *Scotsman*, 10 March 2005.
11   *Scotsman*, 2 April 2005.
12   Private information.
13   *Scotsman*, 7 May 2005.
14   *Scotsman*, 24 September 2005.
15   *Scotsman*, 19 November 2005.
16   Mitchell, *Transition to Power*, 46.
17   Interview, 13 January 2015.
18   *Herald*, 17 January 2006.
19   *Scotsman*, 18 April 2006.
20   *Sunday Herald*, 1 October 2006.
21   *Scotsman*, 11 October 2006.
22   *Herald*, 11 October 2006.
23   *Scottish* Sun, 14 October 2006.
24   http://news.bbc.co.uk/1/hi/uk/6182762.stm
25   http://news.bbc.co.uk/1/hi/scotland/6219745.stm
26   Interview with Lord McConnell MSP, 22 April 2010.
27   *Holyrood Magazine*, 29 June 2009.
28   *Sunday Herald*, 4 February 2007.
29   *Scotsman*, 16 March 2007.
30   *Mirror*, 17 March 2007.
31   *Scotsman*, 19 March 2007.
32   *Daily Telegraph*, 20 March 2007.
33   *Scotsman*, 31 March 2007.
34   *Sunday Herald*, 22 November 2009.
35   Private information.
36   http://www.redco.uk.com/coaching.htm
37   Watt, *Inside Out*, 43.
38   *Edinburgh Evening News*, 12 April 2007.
39   *Scotland on Sunday*, 22 April 2007.
40   *Scotsman*, 14 July 2009.
41   *Scotland on Sunday*, 22 April 2007.
42   *Edinburgh Evening News*, 26 April 2007.
43   http://news.bbc.co.uk/1/hi/scotland/6604995.stm
44   *The Times*, 23 April 2007.
45   *Scotsman*, 2 May 2007.
46   *Scotsman*, 4 May 2007.

47   *Daily Express*, 5 May 2007.
48   *Herald*, 5 May 2007.
49   *Edinburgh Evening News*, 7 May 2007.
50   *Scotsman*, 8 May 2007.
51   Scottish Parliament Official Report, 16 May 2007.
52   *Herald*, 17 May 2007.
53   Scottish Parliament Official Report, 16 May 2007.
54   *Scotsman*, 17 May 2007.
55   *Total Politics*, September 2008.

CHAPTER 12 'IT'S TIME'

1   Scottish Parliament Official Report, 23 May 2007.
2   *Sunday Herald*, 23 June 2007.
3   Scottish Parliament Official Report, 31 May 2007.
4   Blair, *A Journey*, 651.
5   Scottish Parliament Official Report, 7 June 2007.
6   *Sunday Herald*, 24 June 2007.
7   *Edinburgh Evening News*, 9 August 2007.
8   Interview, 22 September 2014.
9   *Alex Salmond – A Rebel's Journey* (BBC Scotland), 19 November 2014.
10   Mitchell, *The Transition to Power*, 48.
11   Wilson, *The Battle for Independence*, 125.
12   http://www.instituteforgovernment.org.uk/sites/default/files/publications/Northern%20Exposure.pdf
13   http://www.gov.scot/Resource/0039/00395172.pdf
14   *Salmond's 100 Days* (STV), 21 August 2007.
15   *Edinburgh Evening News* 26 May 2007. This incident also sparked the famous Salmond temper. 'He started ripping into me. He told me never to do anything like that again,' said Angus Blackburn, a press photographer who overheard the remark and decided to publicise it. 'It was not in a balanced manner – he was really, really angry' (*Scotland on Sunday*, 27 May 2007).
16   *Daily Telegraph*, 10 May 2007.
17   *Scottish Daily Mail*, 25 August 2007.
18   *Guardian*, 31 January 2009.
19   *Sunday Herald, 14 July 2007.*
20   *Scotland on Sunday*, 12 August 2007.
21   Private information.
22   *Salmond's 100 Days* (STV).
23   *Sunday Times*, 16 September 2007.
24   *Salmond's 100 Days* (STV).
25   *Herald*, 8 December 2007.
26   Scottish Parliament Official Report, 13 December 2007.
27   http://news.bbc.co.uk/1/hi/scotland/north_east/7294059.stm

28   *Scotsman,* 4 December 2007.
29   *Politics Show* (BBC2), 4 May 2008.
30   *Total Politics,* September 2008.
31   *Good Morning Scotland* (BBC Radio Scotland), 22 August 2008.
32   Interview with Alex Salmond MSP, February 2008.
33   http://news.bbc.co.uk/1/hi/scotland/edinburgh_and_east/7621153.stm
34   *Sunday Herald,* 8 August 2010.
35   *Sunday Herald,* 24 August 2008.
36   http://news.bbc.co.uk/1/hi/scotland/7224987.stm
37   *Scotland on Sunday,* 18 October 2008.
38   *Scotsman,* 20 October 2008.
39   *The Times,* 20 October 2008.
40   http://www.scotland.gov.uk/News/This-Week/Speeches/
     First-Minister/genassembly09
41   Hassan, *The Modern SNP,* 132.
42   Wilson, 136.
43   *Scotland on Sunday,* 16 October 2011.
44   *Guardian,* 31 January 2009.
45   *Guardian,* 9 June 2009.
46   *Scotland on Sunday,* 30 November 2008.
47   https://www.youtube.com/watch?v=jS42dvyJsBA
48   http://www.scotland.gov.uk/News/This-Week/Speeches/First-Minister/
     FMgeorgetown
49   *Guardian,* 29 January 2009.
50   Scottish Parliament Official Report, 12 February 2009.
51   *Herald,* 10 February 2009.
52   Private information.
53   Private information.
54   http://www.scotland.gov.uk/News/This-Week/Speeches/First-Minister/
     scdi3809
55   *Scotsman,* 13 May 2009.
56   http://www.scotland.gov.uk/News/This-Week/Speeches/First-Minister/
     Edinburghlecture
57   *Daily Record,* 17 July 2010.
58   *The Times,* 10 September 2009.
59   *Scottish Daily Mail,* 29 October 2009.
60   *Scotsman,* 25 September 2009.
61   http://news.bbc.co.uk/1/hi/uk/8216589.stm
62   *Scotsman,* 26 January 2011.
63   *Newsnight Scotland* (BBC2), 7 February 2011.
64   Salmond, *The Dream Shall Never Die,* 204.
65   Scottish Government press release, 29 August 2011.
66   *Daily Telegraph,* 10 October 2009.
67   *Holyrood Magazine,* 15 March 2010.

68    *Herald*, 30 November 2009.
69    *Scotsman*, 1 December 2009.
70    http://www.scottishreview.net/MRitchie180.html
71    http://news.bbc.co.uk/1/hi/scotland/8535946.stm
72    Scottish Parliament Official Report, 11 February 2010.
73    *Scotsman*, 12 February 2010.
74    Private information.
75    http://www.snp.org/node/16758
76    *Andrew Marr* (BBC1), 21 March 2010.
77    Hansard 508 c710.
78    http://news.bbc.co.uk/1/hi/uk_politics/election_2010/scotland/
      8668114.stm
79    *Herald*, 10 May 2010.
80    Salmond, 18.
81    *The Times*, 25 June 2010.
82    *Scotsman*, 28 June 2010.
83    *The Economist*, 1 July 2010.
84    *Scotland Live* (BBC Radio Scotland), 6 September 2010.
85    Scottish Parliament Official Report, 8 September 2010.
86    http://www.bbc.co.uk/news/mobile/uk-scotland-11560698
87    Private information.
88    *Portillo on Salmond* (BBC Scotland), 15 May 2011.
89    *Sunday Herald*, 9 January 2011.
90    SNP press release, 12 March 2011.
91    *Scotsman*, 14 January 2011.
92    *Scottish Sun*, 19 April 2011.
93    *Scottish Sun*, 5 May 2011.
94    *Sunday Times*, 1 May 2011.
95    *Daily Telegraph*, 27 April 2011.
96    *Guardian*, 6 May 2011.
97    http://www.guardian.co.uk/politics/2011/may/06/scottish-elections-
      salmond-historic-victory-snp
98    Private information.
99    *Alex Salmond – A Rebel's Journey* (BBC Scotland).
100   http://legacy.holyrood.com/2011/05on-the-record
101   *Sunday Herald*, 8 May 2011.

CHAPTER 13 'A CHANGE IS COMING'

1    http://www.scottishelectionstudy.org.uk/data.htm
2    *Scotsman*, 9 May 2011.
3    *Daily Record*, 14 May 2011.
4    *Scotsman*, 16 May 2011.
5    *Prospect*, June 2011.

6    See Wilson, *The Battle for Independence*, 83–86.

7    *Scotsman*, 7 May 2011.

8    *Scotland on Sunday*, 14 August 2011.

9    Alex Salmond, *Your Scotland, Your Future*, October 2011.

10   *Scotland on Sunday*, 31 July 2011.

11   Scottish Parliament Official Report, 18 May 2011.

12   http://votesnp.com/campaigns/SNP_Manifesto_2011_lowRes.pdf

13   Interview, 23 September 2014.

14   Interview, 22 September 2014.

15   Interview, 21 October 2014.

16   http://www.newsweek.com/2014/11/21/interview-alex-salmond-plots-his-next-moves-against-british-state-283751.html

17   Salmond, *The Dream Shall Never Die*, 20.

18   Interview, 22 September 2014.

19   *Scotsman*, 25 October 2011 & 14 December 2011.

20   http://www.snp.org/blog/post/2011/oct/alex-salmond-delivers-keynote-speech

21   SNP press release, 22 October 2011.

22   *Scotsman*, 28 October 2011.

23   *Scotland on Sunday*, 15 April 2012.

24   http://lallandspeatworrier.blogspot.com/2011/11/no-parliament-for-all-seasons.html

25   Interview, 22 September 2014.

26   *Financial Times*, 29 October 2011.

27   *Guardian*, 20 September 2011.

28   Scottish Conservative press release, 3 October 2011.

29   *Sunday Herald*, 9 October 2011.

30   *Scotland on Sunday*, 30 October 2011.

31   *Herald*, 4 October 2011.

32   Carman, *More Scottish Than British*, 72.

33   *Herald*, 7 May 2011.

34   Interview, 23 September 2014.

35   *The Times*, 17 September 2011.

36   *Herald*, 29 November 2011.

37   *Good Morning Scotland* (BBC Radio Scotland), 7 December 2011.

38   *Today Programme* (BBC Radio 4), 14 December 2011.

39   *The Cause* (BBC Radio Scotland), 22 October 2012.

40   Interview, 23 September 2014.

41   *Scotland on Sunday*, 14 August 2011.

42   Private information.

43   *Guardian*, 14 May 2011.

44   *Guardian*, 16 July 2011.

45   *Andrew Marr* (BBC1), 7 January 2012.

46   http://www.bbc.co.uk/news/uk-scotland-16478121

47   http://www.scotland.gov.uk/Resource/0038/00386122.pdf
48   http://news.bbc.co.uk/1/hi/programmes/andrew_marr_show/9689183.stm
49   http://www.gov.scot/Publications/2012/01/1006/1
50   *Herald*, 17 February 2012.
51   Torrance, *The Battle for Britain*, 214.
52   *Today Programme* (BBC Radio 4), 28 April 2012.
53   *Scottish Sun on Sunday*, 26 February 2012.
54   Interview, 23 September 2014.
55   http://webarchive.nationalarchives.gov.uk/20140122145147/http:/www.
     levesoninquiry.org.uk/wp-content/uploads/2012/06/Witness-Statement-
     of-Alex-Salmond.pdf
56   Transcript of interview with *GQ*.
57   Interview, 17 October 2012.
58   Correspondence, 8 July 2013.
59   Interview, 23 September 2014.
60   Salmond, 24.
61   Interview, 23 March 2013.
62   Salmond, 25.
63   Interview, 16 September 2014.
64   Torrance, 2.
65   Transcript of Alex Salmond's interview with *GQ* (FOI/14/00936).
66   Torrance, 6.
67   http://www.theguardian.com/commentisfree/2012/oct/16/voting-yes-
     create-new-scotland
68   *The Cause* (BBC Radio Scotland).
69   Caro, *The Passage of Power*, 601.
70   *The Cause* (BBC Radio Scotland).

## Chapter 14 'The dream shall never die'

1   http://www.theguardian.com/politics/2012/may/25/alex-salmond-yes-
    scotland-independence
2   http://www.theguardian.com/politics/2012/jun/10/scottish-greens-snp-
    independence-campaign
3   *Daily Record*, 21 August 2011. Weir had also contested Ayr for the SNP at
    the 1987 general election, coming fourth.
4   https://www.youtube.com/watch?v=p1pt-zOnU9c
5   Interview, 23 March 2013.
6   'Scotland's Membership of the European Union', SC(12)50.
7   Interview, 28 February 2014.
8   *Sunday Herald*, 16 December 2012.
9   Interview, 6 July 2013.
10  *Sunday Herald*, 14 October 2012.
11  Torrance, *The Battle for Britain*, 147.

12  http://www.scotland.gov.uk/News/Releases/2012/02/international
    18022012

13  Scottish Parliament Official Report, 9 May 2013.

14  http://articles.latimes.com/2012/sep/22/world/la-fg-britain-salmond-
    qa-20120923

15  Interviews, 12 & 9 October 2014.

16  http://www.bbc.com/news/uk-scotland-scotland-politics-21828424

17  http://www.newstatesman.com/2013/06/phoney-war-not-campaign

18  Interview, 7 October 2014.

19  *Scotsman*, 13 August 2013.

20  Salmond, *The Dream Shall Never Die*, 103.

21  Interview with Alex Salmond, 11 September 2014 (courtesy of Tom
    Gordon).

22  http://news.scotland.gov.uk/News/Democracy-at-heart-of-independence-
    case-for-fundamental-change-to-political-and-economic-union-266.aspx

23  *Scotsman*, 27 July 2013.

24  *Scotsman*, 12 July 2011.

25  http://www.bbc.co.uk/news/uk-scotland-scotland-politics-18517306

26  Interview, 22 September 2014.

27  Interview, 12 October 2014.

28  Salmond, 162.

29  Interview, 12 October 2014.

30  Salmond, 126.

31  *Daily Telegraph*, 17 September 2014.

32  Salmond, 126.

33  Interviews, 23 September 2014.

34  http://www.bbc.com/news/uk-scotland-21621169

35  Interview, 22 September 2014.

36  http://www.scotland.gov.uk/News/Speeches/jimmy-reid-lecture-29012013

37  http://www.snp.org/blog/post/2013/apr/empathy-needed-now-more-
    ever-fm

38  Author's notes, Institute of Directors conference, London, 25 April 2012.

39  http://www.wsj.com/articles/SB10001424127887324474004578446632367
    7535680

40  Raymond Buchanan to the author, 1 February 2012.

41  http://www.scotland.gov.uk/Resource/0042/00422011.pdf

42  *Good Morning Scotland* (BBC Radio Scotland), 23 July 2013.

43  http://www.scotland.gov.uk/Resource/Doc/280368/0084457.pdf

44  http://www.scotland.gov.uk/News/Speeches/scotlandandunion

45  http://www.snp.org/blog/post/2012/jan/hugo-young-lecture-scotlands-
    place-world

46  *Scotland Tonight* (STV), 30 January 2012.

47  http://www.snp.org/media-centre/news/2012/nov/alex-salmond-welcomes-
    radical-indy-conference

48 http://www.newstatesman.com/politics/2014/03/why-ed-miliband-alex-salmonds-biggest-foe-fight-scottish-independence

49 *Sunday Mail*, 9 March 2014.

50 http://www.theguardian.com/politics/2013/jul/13/alex-salmond-white-paper-william-mcilvanney

51 Interview, 23 September 2014.

52 *Good Morning Scotland* (BBC Radio Scotland), 18 August 2014.

53 Private information.

54 Private information.

55 Interview, 12 October 2014.

56 The SNP paper 'Raise the Standard' stated: 'The currency shall continue to be sterling until such time as Parliament decides to change that position.'

57 Torrance, 97.

58 *Mail on Sunday*, 5 May 2013.

59 http://newsnet.scot/2014/02/salmond-osborne-bully-boy-tactics-over-pound-will-backfire/

60 Scottish Parliament Official Report, 7 August 2014.

61 http://www.dailyrecord.co.uk/news/politics/senior-snp-figures-stick-knife-4015023

62 *Guardian*, 29 March 2014.

63 Salmond, 119.

64 *Daily Record*, 10 June 2014.

65 Interview, 12 October 2014.

66 Salmond, 105.

67 Author's notes, SPJA lunch with Alex Salmond, 26 February 2014.

68 Wilson, *The Battle for Independence*, 156-57.

69 http://www.newstatesman.com/politics/2014/06/alistair-darling-interview-salmond-behaving-kim-jong-il

70 *Daily Telegraph*, 24 January 2014.

71 Salmond, 189.

72 *The Times*, 13 July 2013.

73 http://www.conservativehome.com/thecolumnists/2014/05/iain-dale-the-idiocy-of-lord-oakeshott.html

74 *Sunday Herald*, 14 September 2014.

75 Salmond, 223.

76 Interview, 22 September 2014.

77 *Scotland Tonight* (STV), 18 August 2014.

78 Salmond, 72.

79 http://www.buzzfeed.com/jamieross/alex-salmond-wont-give-an-insch#.ty1oVKyzMv

80 *Evening Times*, 23 June 2014.

81 Salmond, 122 & 155.

82 http://www.gq-magazine.co.uk/comment/articles/2014-05/28/alastair-campbell-alex-salmond-interview/viewall

83  *Financial Times*, 18 May 2013.

84  http://www.dailyrecord.co.uk/news/politics/independence-referendum-
protest-outside-bbc-4263938

85  http://www.dailymail.co.uk/news/article-2750002/Anger-Salmond-plays-
apartheid-card-He-likens-Scots-clamour-vote-South-Africa-s-election.
html#ixzz3cgeifyju

86  Helping prep Darling was Quintin Oliver, a Northern Irish referendum
expert who had been a direct contemporary of Salmond's at St Andrews
University.

87  http://www.bbc.co.uk/news/uk-scotland-28649354

88  Salmond, 132.

89  Interview, 21 October 2014.

90  Salmond, 138.

91  Interview, 21 October 2014.

92  Interview, 12 October 2014.

93  Salmond, 185.

94  Salmond, 149.

95  Interview, 23 September 2014.

96  Salmond, 66.

97  *Daily Mail*, 11 September 2014.

98  Salmond, 129.

99  Robinson, *Election Notebook*, 113.

100  *Alex Salmond – A Rebel's Journey* (BBC Scotland).

101  *Scotsman*, 19 August 2014.

102  Salmond, 217.

103  Author's notes, Perth Concert Hall, 17 September 2014.

104  Interview, 23 September 2014.

105  Salmond, 219.

106  Salmond, 225.

107  Salmond, 198.

108  Interview, 15 October 2014.

109  Salmond, 229.

110  Salmond, 232-33.

111  *Courier*, 10 January 2015.

112  https://www.youtube.com/watch?v=OAkZW7ofMks

113  *Courier*, 10 January 2015.

114  *Alex Salmond – A Rebel's Journey* (BBC Scotland).

115  http://www.snp.org/media-centre/news/2014/sep/statement-first-minister-
alex-salmond

116  http://www.bbc.com/news/uk-scotland-29284169

117  Interview, 9 October 2014.

118  http://www.buzzfeed.com/jamieross/angry-salmond-interview

CHAPTER 15 'THE QUICKEST POLITICAL COMEBACK IN HISTORY'

1   *Courier*, 9 January 2015.
2   http://www.scottishreview.net/KennethRoy176.shtml?utm_source=
    Sign-Up.to&utm_medium=email&utm_campaign=8427-326595-Who+is
    +the+real+first+minister%3F
3   *Sunday Politics* (BBC1), 21 September 2014.
4   *Murnaghan* (Sky News), 21 September 2014.
5   http://www.bbc.co.uk/programmes/p027v2p8
6   http://www.bbc.co.uk/news/uk-scotland-scotland-politics-29303968
7   *Daily Telegraph*, 21 October 2014.
8   Interview, 18 October 2014.
9   Scottish Parliament Official Report, 23 September 2014.
10  http://www.thetablet.co.uk/blogs/1/625/the-close-relationship-between-
    scottish-bishops-and-the-snp
11  http://www.telegraph.co.uk/news/uknews/scotland/11289633/Can-
    someone-please-tell-Alex-Salmond-hes-making-a-fool-of-himself.html
12  *Daily Telegraph*, 18 November 2014.
13  *Guardian*, 15 October 2015.
14  *Andrew Marr* (BBC1), 2 November 2014.
15  *Courier*, 11 January 2015.
16  Scottish Parliament Official Report, 18 November 2014.
17  Interview, 23 September 2014.
18  Scottish Parliament Official Report, 18 November 2014.
19  *Good Morning Scotland* (BBC Radio Scotland), 19 November 2014.
20  https://www.youtube.com/watch?feature=youtu.be&v=Ej8A59jBkBg&app=
    desktop
21  Author's notes of Alex Salmond's appearance at Waterstones, London, 23
    March 2015.
22  *Holyrood*, 10 November 2014.
23  Perry, *Scotland the Brave*.
24  *Scotland 2014* (BBC2), 23 September 2014.
25  Salmond, *The Dream Shall Never Die*, 34.
26  Salmond, 37.
27  *Daily Telegraph*, 11 March 2015.
28  Interview, 13 October 2014.
29  Interview, 15 October 2014.
30  Author's notes, Alex Salmond at Waterstones, Piccadilly, London, 23
    March 2015.
31  Salmond, 3.
32  *Today Programme* (BBC Radio 4), 14 October 2014.
33  http://www.thecourier.co.uk/news/politics/the-alex-salmond-interviews-
    day-1-home-rule-is-my-goal-1.776652
34  *Courier*, 8 January 2015.

35  http://theconversation.com/what-alex-salmonds-diaries-reveal-about-the-man-who-led-the-referendum-39201

36  Salmond, 127.

37  *The National*, 6 April 2015.

38  Correspondence, 17 October 2014.

39  Interview, 23 September 2014.

40  *Observer*, 7 December 2014.

41  *Andrew Marr* (BBC1), 22 March 2015.

42  http://blogs.spectator.co.uk/fraser-nelson/2015/03/alex-salmond-misery/

43  http://www.newsweek.com/2014/11/21/interview-alex-salmond-plots-his-next-moves-against-british-state-283751.html

44  http://www.dailymail.co.uk/news/article-3047983/I-ll-charge-said-La-Sturgeon-Poor-Ed-QUENTIN-LETTS-sees-SNP-faithful-worship-leader.html#ixzz3XzC4uiPP

45  http://www.theguardian.com/politics/video/2015/may/08/alex-salmond-general-election-gordon-snp-video

46  *Independent*, 19 December 2014.

47  http://blogs.spectator.co.uk/coffeehouse/2015/03/could-the-tories-do-a-deal-with-the-snp-yes-they-could/

48  http://www.buzzfeed.com/jamieross/the-salmond-is-back-in-town#.yi24Wdq9QE

49  *Independent*, 19 December 2014.

50  http://www.buzzfeed.com/jamieross/the-salmond-is-back-in-town#.yi24Wdq9QE

51  *The Times*, 27 June 2015.

52  *The Times*, 13 June 2015.

53  *Daily Telegraph*, 4 April 2015.

54  Alex Salmond at Waterstones.

55  http://www.huffingtonpost.co.uk/2015/06/09/nicola-sturgeon-defends-alex-salmond-sexist-comments_n_7548840.html

56  Hennessy, *The Kingdom to Come*, 78.

57  *Newsnight* (BBC2), 9 June 2015.

58  *Panorama: The Most Dangerous Woman in Britain?* (BBC1), 1 June 2015.

59  https://twitter.com/ianbell1916/status/592324651457617920

Chapter 16 'To win or lose it all'

1  *Scotland on Sunday*, 23 September 1990.

2  Hamilton, *Stone of Destiny*, vii.

3  http://theconversation.com/what-alex-salmonds-diaries-reveal-about-the-man-who-led-the-referendum-39201

4  *Alex Salmond – A Rebel's Journey* (BBC Scotland), 19 November 2014.

5  Wilson, *The Battle for Independence*, 95-96.

6   http://www.nytimes.com/2014/04/19/world/europe/alex-salmond-scottish-independence.html

7   *Independent*, 20 September 1998.

8   Interview with Alex Salmond MSP, February 2008 (courtesy of Katherine Haddon).

9   *Face to Face* (STV), 19 April 2007.

10  Salmond, 8.

11  *Metro*, 30 November 2010.

12  Salmond, *The Dream Shall Never Die*, 51.

13  Salmond, 169 & 186.

14  *Planet* 204, November 2011.

15  Transcript of Salmond's interview with *GQ*.

16  *Planet* 204, November 2011.

17  *Scotland on Sunday*, 27 January 1997.

18  *Scottish Sun,* 18 July 2000.

19  *Glasgow Evening Times*, 18 July 2000.

20  Perry, *Scotland the Brave.*

21  *This Week* (BBC1), 28 May 2015.

22  *Scottish Review of Books*, Vol 8, Number 2, 2012.

23  Salmond, 249.

24  http://www.guardian.co.uk/commentisfree/2006/nov/30/scotsbarbsand englishcommen

25  *Scotsman*, 23 September 1996.

26  *Scotland on Sunday*, 21 November 2010.

27  http://www.snp.org/blog/post/2012/dec/first-ministers-new-year-message

28  Wilson, 160-61.

29  *Scotland on Sunday*, 1 February 2009.

30  http://www.prospectmagazine.co.uk/blogs/prospector-blog/why-the-snp-has-been-bad-for-scotland

31  Mitchell, *The Scottish Question*, 434.

32  Short, *Mitterrand*, 11.

33  *Scottish Daily Mail*, 9 August 2014.

34  Interview, 23 September 2014.

35  *Independent*, 20 January 1999.

36  *Independent on Sunday*, 8 February 1992.

37  Roth, *Parliamentary Profiles S-Z*, 1906.

38  *Scotsman*, 23 September 1990.

39  *The Times*, 22 April 1998.

40  http://www.independent.co.uk/news/people/profiles/alex-salmond-profile-scottish-independence-campaign-gives-us-a-braveheart-forthe-21st-century-9730499.html

41  *Guardian*, 31 January 2009.

42  *Scotsman*, 30 August 1991.

43  *Good Morning Scotland* (BBC Radio Scotland), 18 November 2014.

44   Salmond, 41.
45   Interview, 21 October 2014.
46   http://www.academia.edu/5997045/The_Political_Thought_of_Scottish_
     Nationalism
47   Mitchell, 453.
48   Powell, *Joseph Chamberlain*, 151.
49   Sorel, *L'Europe et la Revolution Francaise*, 474.

# BIBLIOGRAPHY

## Archives

Sir Robert McIntyre Papers (National Library of Scotland)
Gavin Kennedy Papers (National Library of Scotland)
Gordon Wilson Papers (National Library of Scotland)
Scottish National Party Papers (National Library of Scotland)
Stephen Maxwell Papers (private collection)

## Bibliography

Anonymous, *Donald Dewar 1937-2000: A Book of Tribute* (Norwich 2000)
Ascherson, Neal, *Stone Voices* (London 2002)
Bain, Susan, *Holyrood: The Inside Story* (Edinburgh 2005)
Bell, Alex, *The People We Could Be* (Edinburgh 2014)
Blair, Tony, *A Journey* (London 2010)
Campbell, Alastair, *The Blair Years: Extracts from The Alastair Campbell Diaries* (London 2007)
—, *The Alastair Campbell Diaries Volume Two: Power and the People 1997-1999* (London 2011)
Campbell, John, *Edward Heath: A Biography* (London 1993)
Caro, Robert A., *The Years of Lyndon Johnson: The Passage of Power* (New York 2012)
Christopher Carman, Robert Johns and James Mitchell, *More Scottish than British: The 2011 Scottish Parliament Election* (Comparative Territorial Politics) (Basingstoke 2014)
Churchill, Sir Winston, *Second World War I: The Gathering Storm* (London 1964)
Crick, Bernard, *George Orwell: A Life* (London 1982)
Devine, Tom, and Logue, Paddy, eds., *Being Scottish: Personal Reflections on Scottish Identity Today* (Edinburgh 2002)
Erickson, Jennifer, ed., *The Economics of Independence: Alex Salmond MP* (Glasgow 2003)

Ewing, Winnie, *Stop the World: The Autobiography of Winnie Ewing* (Edinburgh 2004)

Gallagher, Tom, ed., *Nationalism in the Nineties* (Edinburgh 1991)

Hamilton, Ian, *Stone of Destiny: The True Story* (Edinburgh 2008)

Harvie, Christopher, *Broonland: The Last Days of Gordon Brown* (London 2010)

—, *Scotland and Nationalism: Scottish Society and Politics, 1707-1994* (London 1994)

Hassan, Gerry, ed., *The Modern SNP: From Protest to Power* (Edinburgh 2009)

Henderson Scott, Paul, *A Twentieth Century Life* (Argyll 2002)

Hennessy, Peter, *The Kingdom to Come: Thoughts on the Union before and after the Scottish referendum* (London 2015)

Kemp, Arnold, *The Hollow Drum? Scotland Since the War* (Edinburgh 1993)

Lawson, Nigel, *The View From No. 11: Memoirs of a Tory Radical* (London 1992)

Linklater, Magnus, and Denniston, Robin, eds., *Anatomy of Scotland: how Scotland works* (Edinburgh 1992)

Lynch, Peter, *SNP: The History of the Scottish National Party* (Cardiff 2002)

Macdonald, Catriona, ed., *Unionist Scotland 1800-1997* (Edinburgh 1998)

McGinty, Stephen, *The Life of Cardinal Winning: This Turbulent Priest* (London 2003)

McLeish, Henry, *Scotland First: Truth and Consequences* (Edinburgh 2004)

Marr, Andrew, *The Battle for Scotland* (London 1992)

Maxwell, Stephen, *The Case for Left-Wing Nationalism* (Aberdeen 1981)

Mitchell, James, *The Scottish Question* (Oxford 2014, iBooks edition)

—, *Strategies for Self-Government: The Campaigns for a Scottish Parliament* (Edinburgh 1996)

Mitchell, James, Bennie, Lynn, and Johns, Rob, *The Scottish National Party: Transition to Power* (Oxford 2012)

Mullin, Chris, *A View from the Foothills: The Diaries of Chris Mullin* (London 2009)

Alex Perry, *Scotland the Brave: The unstoppable faith of Alex Salmond*, Newsweek Insights (London 2015)

Powell, Enoch, *Joseph Chamberlain* (London, 1977)

Rawnsley, Andrew, *Servants of the People: The Inside Story of New Labour* (London 2000)

Ritchie, Murray, *Scotland Reclaimed: The Inside Story of Scotland's First Democratic Parliamentary Election* (Edinburgh 2000)

Robinson, Nick, *Election Notebook: The inside story of the battle over Britain's future and my personal battle to report it* (London 2015)

Roth, Andrew, and Criddle, Byron, *Parliamentary Profiles, 1997-2002: S-Z* (London 2000)

Salmond, Alex, ed., *The Dream Shall Never Die* (London 2015)

—, *"Horizons Without Bars": The Future of Scotland – A series of speeches by Alex Salmond MP* (1993)

—, *The Royal Bank in Glasgow 1783-1983* (Edinburgh 1983)

—, *The Scottish Industrial Resistance* (Aberdeen 1982)

Sheridan, Tommy, *A Time To Rage* (Edinburgh 1994)

Short, Philip, *Mitterrand: A Study in Ambiguity* (London 2013)

Sillars, Jim, *The Case for Optimism* (Edinburgh 1986)

Sorel, Albert, *L'Europe et la Revolution Francaise* (Paris 1908)

Taylor, Brian, *Scotland's Parliament* (Edinburgh 2003)

—, *The Scottish Parliament* (Edinburgh 2000)

Torrance, David, *The Battle for Britain: Scotland and the Independence Referendum* (London 2013)

Watson, Mike, *Year Zero: An Inside View of the Scottish Parliament* (Edinburgh 2001)

Watt, Peter, *Inside Out: My Story of Betrayal and Cowardice at the Heart of New Labour* (London 2010)

Webb, Keith, *The Growth of Nationalism in Scotland* (London 1978)

Wilson, Gordon, *Scotland – The Battle for Independence: A History of the Scottish National Party 1990-2014* (2014)

—, *SNP: The Turbulent Years 1960-1990* (2009)

Young, Douglas, *St Andrews: Town and Gown Royal and Ancient* (London 1969)

## Broadcast sources

*Alex Salmond – A Rebel's Journey* (BBC Scotland, 2014)

*The Cause* (BBC Radio Scotland, 2012)

*Desert Island Discs* (BBC Radio 4, 2011)

*Panorama: The Most Dangerous Woman in Britain?* (BBC1, 2015)

*Portillo on Salmond* (BBC Scotland, 2011)

*The Salmond Years* (STV, 2000)

*Salmond's 100 Days* (STV, 2007)

*The Scotsman Debate – Scotland: A Time to Choose* (BBC Scotland, 1992)

*Walden Interviews Alex Salmond* (London Weekend Television, 1992)

# INDEX